PRINCIPLES OF PSYCHOANALYSIS

PRINCIPLES OF PSYCHOANALYSIS

Their Application to the Neuroses

By HERMAN NUNBERG, M.D.

Foreword by SIGMUND FREUD

Translated by MADLYN KAHR AND SIDNEY KAHR, M.D.

INTERNATIONAL UNIVERSITIES PRESS, INC.
New York   New York

CONTENTS

PREFACE

This book was first published in German in 1932 by Hans Huber Verlag, Berne, Switzerland, under the title, *Allgemeine Neurosenlehre auf psychoanalytischer Grundlage*. The task I had undertaken was to present the principles of psychoanalysis as exemplified in the neuroses.

Although almost a quarter of a century has elapsed since the publication of this book, I believe that the principles set forth in it are as valid today as they were then. Much valuable work has been done since, contributing greatly to a better understanding of specific problems, but the basic concepts of psychoanalysis have not changed. To cite all of these publications has not been possible. However, I have made emendations in the light of Freud's contributions published after 1932, added two new chapters, rewritten another, and made changes wherever it seemed necessary.

H.N.

New York, April, 1955

FOREWORD BY SIGMUND FREUD

In this book Nunberg gives the most complete and accurate presentation we have at this time of a psychoanalytic theory of neurotic processes. Those who seek a simplification and a glossing over of the problems with which it deals will be disappointed in this book. Those, however, who prefer scientific thinking, who appreciate theoretical formulations which never abandon their ties to experience, those who can savor the rich diversity of psychic events—those persons will value and eagerly study this work.

INTRODUCTION

Freud laid down the foundations for the study of the neuroses in his many papers and presented them succinctly in *Allgemeine Neuro-senlehre,* Part III of his *Introductory Lectures.* Since then, however, there have come from his pen new and important contributions which complete or modify some of the views expressed in those earlier works. Because of the complexity of the psychoanalytic viewpoint, these supplementary contributions have given rise to misunderstandings even among trained analysts; it is, then, easy to understand that the novice and student may be confused. Accordingly my first task has been to show that the "new," having developed organically on the basis of the "old," now forms an integral part of the entire psychoanalytic system and can perfectly well be brought into harmony with the "earlier" views. In my courses, I sought in a unified way to present the state of our present-day psychoanalytic knowledge and to apply it to the neuroses.

For this purpose, many well-known facts had to be reviewed and fused with new, less familiar observations. On this account, and because I had to assume differences in the background and stage of preparation of the students, a certain unevenness in the lectures has resulted; sometimes they seemed very easy to understand; at others, they appeared too difficult. Still another difficulty arose from my concern to impart only knowledge that was certain. I may add that where I have attempted my own explanations, I believe I have filled in only such gaps as seemed too great for my own requirements as to causality. In this connection, I wish to stress my own responsibility, especially for the role which I have assigned to the synthetic function of the ego, and for the conceptions of adaptation to reality, and of the feeling of guilt.

It is very difficult to acquire an understanding of psychoanalysis from lectures and reading alone. An analysis of one's self is of paramount importance. There are cogent reasons in support of the requirement that a person be psychoanalyzed himself before engaging in professional practice as an analyst. In the first place, he should personally experience what he will later undertake with the patients who entrust themselves to him; he must learn psychoanalysis by seeing it from within. By understanding himself he will gain a better understanding of others. Secondly, through his own analysis he is freed from certain emotional attitudes which otherwise would disturb him in his professional work. Anyone who wishes to practice psychoanalysis must be able to approach psychic phenomena free from prejudice and rigidity. Unanalyzed, his view might be obscured by unconscious motives, so that he would see what he wishes to see, or have a blind spot for what is to be seen.

Psychoanalysis is an empirical science. Through observations, chiefly of sick adults and of children, certain previously unnoticed or misunderstood facts were ascertained, correlated with the whole of psychic life, and formulated into an organized, if still somewhat imperfect theory of the dynamics of psychic processes, of the structure of the psychic apparatus, and of the functioning of the mind. Psychoanalysis has come to be an independent science. It is, however, noteworthy that in this science, exploring and doing research coincide with treating and curing the sick human being. We shall not deal with the psychoanalytic method itself, or with general psychoanalytic concepts, except to draw on them when necessary for a better understanding of our subject. The subject matter we are concerned with comprises the insights gained through treating sick people by the psychoanalytic method—in other words, *a psychopathology of neuroses along Freudian lines.*

Although the starting point of psychoanalytic endeavors was interest in the suffering human being, the study of neuroses is important for others besides the physician who is planning to practice psychoanalysis. Indeed, the insights obtained through the treatment of sick people was soon carried over and applied to other spheres of human life, such as child education, the study of religion, the social sciences, and so on.

Every phenomenon in nature has many aspects. If it is fully to be understood, it must be considered from many angles. Therefore, we shall at one point discuss the neuroses as manifestations of the instinctual life, at another time as manifestations of the unconscious psychic life, and from still another viewpoint as ego manifestations. The etiology of neurosis will be treated in a separate chapter. Some difficulty may at first be encountered in comprehending the material, since this method of presentation leads to apparent contradictions which are resolved only later. Moreover, we can here merely present on one plane what actually

takes place on many levels and in many dimensions. Because of the inter-
weaving of psychic processes, repetition cannot be avoided.

The starting point of our theoretical considerations is always, as far as
possible, material from patients. No detailed case histories are included,
however, for a single complete case record would extend beyond the com-
pass of this presentation. We shall be limited at first to short, simple
examples, which will be more instructive for the student than complicated, long analyses. Later in the work, however, a few more extensive
examples will be necessary.

PRINCIPLES OF PSYCHOANALYSIS

Chapter I

THE UNCONSCIOUS IN THE NEUROSIS

Some years ago I was called to see a young girl who was suffering from severe vomiting. I examined the patient but found no abnormal physical changes. Since her psychic state aroused my interest, I asked her whether something unusual had happened to upset her, but received a negative reply. Upon pressing this question further, however, I learned that a few hours earlier she had taken a walk through the woods with an elderly man whom I happened to know. Because I was acquainted with her companion, I immediately had an idea as to what might have occurred in the woods, and I communicated my surmise to the patient. She was greatly astonished and asked how I could possibly have known "that." Finally she admitted that she had had a sexual experience. She spoke to me freely about it, whereupon her nausea and vomiting disappeared. Suddenly she felt quite well again, got up and went to lunch.

The above can by no means be considered a psychoanalysis, but merely an exploration dictated by my psychoanalytic approach. My conjecture called forth the recollection of a sexual attack which the girl had suffered. Up to this point she had not been aware of the connection between this experience and her vomiting. It became conscious to her only after I had confronted her with the connection.

Here we come face to face with the most important point in psychoanalysis: *Something psychic which is producing illness is, for the time being, unconscious.*

Let us try at first to understand what role the *unconscious* plays in the neurosis. Continuing with our example, it is noteworthy that the experience which had a strong emotional tone and which was intensely unpleasant to the patient, was for the moment forgotten, but a symptom—vomiting—took its place. *The symptom is thus a substitute for an important experience which has become unconscious.*[1] There is a gap in memory

[1] The forgetting of a recent experience as such does not, of course, produce a neurotic symptom; for a recent experience to become pathogenic, other factors must be involved.

3

at the point where something important has happened in the patient's life. We meet with similar gaps in memory in every neurotic patient. They are called *amnesias* and extend deep into earliest childhood. On the other hand, the same patients may have strange, disjointed memories which emerge here and there. At first we do not know why these disconnected, apparently meaningless memories escape being forgotten. In analysis, however, we discover that important unconscious experiences are concealed behind them. For this reason, Freud gave them the name of *screen memories*. We can best understand their significance by an example:

In the beginning of her analysis, a patient told me of a strange game which she used to play between her fifth and sixth year. About that time, a sister was born. When the patient felt that no one was watching her, she would drag the baby forward in its carriage until the little head could be seen in front of the curtains (which in those days hung from the hood of the carriage to shield the infant from the sun); the next moment she would let the baby fall back into the carriage. She repeated this play persistently without tiring of it. For many months this memory could not be dealt with in the analysis; it remained unintelligible. Slowly, however, other memories emerged which belonged to the same constellation. First the patient remembered the day of the sister's birth. An uncle had informed her of this event. When she asked him about the details of the birth, he explained briefly that the stork had brought the baby. She could not believe this and questioned him further as to how the stork had been able to enter the room. Her uncle replied: through the window. Her objection that the window had been closed remained unanswered. The child then sought to solve the puzzle in her own way: the stork had come into the room while the window had been open, stayed in hiding behind the curtains and, when the mother was alone, had jumped out from there. For her to pull her baby sister forward in the carriage until the baby's head became visible in front of the curtains was thus a dramatic enactment of the five-year-old girl's notions about the birth of her sister.

But what was the meaning of the second part of the game—making the little sister disappear again in the depths of the baby carriage? The birth of a younger sibling often has a traumatic effect. Usually the child tries to overcome the trauma with the aid of fantasies. Such was the case with this patient. However, she represented not only birth in her play. We know that the birth of a younger sibling likewise arouses jealousy and hatred. As the trauma of the birth is overcome through fantasies, so, too, the hate and death wishes toward the new sibling are discharged through fantasies. The birth of the little sister was most unwelcome to the patient; she wished the newcomer out of the way again. Once before, at the age of two and a half, she had had the unpleasant experience of a new sibling, a brother. At that time she was so angry at the intruder that she had attacked him with a stick. Her mother and the nurse had had to guard the infant to protect him from her rage. (Even now, at the age of thirty-five, she has not overcome her hatred for her two younger siblings.) Making the little sister disappear behind the curtains of the baby carriage represented her wish to get this baby out of the way, just as earlier she had wished to kill her brother.

Now we are in a position to understand the whole play: it represents the birth and death of the little sister. Behind the game is also concealed the still deeper hatred of the brother. Only through the analysis of this memory were we enabled to understand the patient's attitude toward her brother. Her actual *conscious* attitude toward him reflected her *unconscious* hatred and jealousy which stemmed from early childhood.

Screen memories thus represent fragments of memories; to a certain degree they fill in deficiencies in memories. They may be compared with the ruins of a past civilization, with clues which indicate to the archaeologist the direction his work of excavation should take.

In certain cases, gaps in memories are filled in by screen memories. In others, however, the amnesias are so complete that they can be cleared up only in a thorough analysis. But amnesias, on the whole, are not characteristic only of neurotics. Most individuals have forgotten their early childhood up to approximately the fourth or fifth year of life. We can perhaps understand why we forget the experiences of just these first five years when we realize that infantile sexuality reaches its fullest development in this period, and that its normal fate is to be repressed, that is, forgotten. The consequences of the infantile repression are so enduring that even as a mature person one refuses to remember anything about his infantile period of sexuality.

Complete amnesias are most frequently encountered in hysteria; they are characteristic of this illness. In compulsion neurosis, as well as in schizophrenia, where compulsive remembering sometimes occurs, patients *do* recall individual experiences from early childhood, but the connection between memories is lacking, so that they remain isolated from their contexts.

A young girl with various compulsions suffered from insomnia. The insomnia was brought on by a cumbersome ritual. The patient had to take a certain fixed position in bed, lying on her back with her legs pressed together and bent at the knees. Only her neck, knees, and toes were permitted to touch the covers; the rest of her body, especially the abdomen, was not permitted to come into contact with the covers.

At the beginning of treatment, the patient had no suspicion as to what the meaning of this ritual could be. Only much later did she report the apparently unrelated fact that up to her sixteenth year she had slept in a bedroom adjoining that of her parents, with the door ajar, and had often been able to overhear her parents' sexual intercourse. This excited her sexually and kept her awake. At another time she reported that while listening to her parents, she had had fantasies of how the father lay on top of the mother and how their abdomens touched. At this point she would become disgusted and break off the fantasy. At still another time she recalled how she used to struggle against masturbation by avoiding touching her genitals. Although she felt a strong impulse to touch her abdomen and genitals, she succeeded in restraining herself. She had never forgotten any of these memories; they had always been conscious. What she did not know was the fact that they belonged together, and that only when they were connected did they have a meaning, namely that she wanted to undo in her mind the sexual intercourse between her parents while at the same time struggling against her own masturbation. The impressions and experiences which led to her symptom had remained conscious, but the connection between these impressions and experiences, which gave them a meaning, was unconscious.

Memory of the experiences linked with the illness may thus be preserved and conscious, while the connection of these experiences with the symptom, and therefore also its meaning, remain unconscious. The cause of illness then is frequently conscious, but its *motive*, the "what for," is always unconscious. The state of unconsciousness of the contents of a psychic process is not necessarily involved when a symptom develops, but it is a precondition of symptom development that the *connections and motives of this psychic process* are unconscious. These motives contain the meaning of the symptom.

What is to be understood by the "meaning" of a symptom? In our example, the symptom had its point of origin in the patient's overhearing of her parents' intercourse and in her struggle against masturbation. In her sleeping ritual the patient tried to undo her parents' intercourse and to ward off her impulse to masturbate. The "meaning" of the symptom then, its purpose or motive, is, generally speaking, the repetition of important repressed experiences and impulses: the simultaneous satisfaction of an instinct and the denial of its gratification, in a way which is not accessible to consciousness.

Since every neurotic symptom betrays a part of the unconscious *psychic life,* we must endeavor to give a brief account of what is to be understood by the term "unconscious."

This is no easy task, for we do not possess direct evidence of the existence of the unconscious. We deduce it from indirect evidence—from the study of dreams, fantasies, parapraxes, and particularly from the developmental history of neurotic symptoms, as well as from behavior. The indirect evidence is so manifold and so convincing that it leaves no doubt as to the existence of unconscious psychic phenomena.

Psychoanalysis is not alone in assuming an unconscious psychic life. There are philosophies and psychologies which recognize the existence of an unconscious. Our conception of the unconscious, however, differs in principle from that of the philosophers. They recognize an unconscious only in a negative sense, and designate as unconscious *everything* which is not conscious. Psychoanalysis conceives of the unconscious as something psychologically positive; that is, we distinguish it from the conscious by certain characteristics which pertain only to the unconscious psychic life. Dreams, neurotic symptoms, certain involuntary actions, parapraxes, fantasies, religious systems clearly display the distinguishing marks of the unconscious.

Like the philosophers, we also speak of the unconscious in a *descriptive* sense. But it is clear to us not only that the unconscious is revealed through its contents, such as experiences, thoughts, ideas, wishes, and emotions, but that these contents are endowed with psychic energy. Our conception therefore requires investigation of the dynamics of the unconscious. Hence we also speak of the unconscious in a *dynamic sense*.

While the term "unconscious" simply identifies a fact, the dynamic concept gives an idea of the *interaction of unconscious forces* which govern our psychic life when we are healthy as well as when we are ill. For the unconscious forces have an effect on all psychic life and always participate in the shaping of our conscious experiences.

Chapter II

THE DREAM

For a better understanding of the problem of the unconscious and hence of psychoanalysis, we must first consider the structure and the function of the dream, even though we can do so only in a very incomplete way.

It is imperative to understand the dream if one wishes to gain insight into man's mental life. Neurotic symptoms, as an example, are formed to a great extent after the pattern of the dream. The interpretation of dreams, therefore, aids in the understanding of the conflicts underlying symptom formation. Freud said that in difficult situations, dream interpretation proved a reliable guide to him; at times when he had to struggle with perplexing problems, a dream correctly interpreted would restore his self-confidence.

Perhaps no other psychic phenomenon has kindled man's imagination as much as has the dream. Whether he is literate or illiterate, enlightened or superstitious, man is always interested in his dreams. There are dreams so striking that one never forgets them and continues to be haunted by them, as by something uncanny, throughout one's life. It is easy to understand that mankind in all ages has been concerned with dreams, and has tried to comprehend them. The understanding of dreams always corresponds to the cultural stage of man's development. Thus, primitive peoples see dreams as the manifestations of the returning spirits of their ancestors or as the work of demons; they believe that through dreams they communicate with another, supernatural world. Peoples with developed theistic religions see dreams as divine communications. Since very early times, peoples of many different cultures have concerned themselves with the meaning of dreams, and have tried to unravel the predictions which they believed to be hidden in them. Thus the ancient Chaldeans and Egyptians as well as the Hebrews developed a special art of interpreting dreams in order to predict the future from them. But what was formerly religious belief has been degraded to the level of superstition in the unenlightened strata of contemporary mankind.

In the animistic stage of his development, it was not always easy for man to distinguish between his inner life and that which occurred in the external world. He confounded his inner processes, thoughts, ideas, wishes, and strivings with the phenomena of the external world, and thus believed his mental life to be external reality, and vice versa. Moreover, primitive man experiences the world as well as himself as magic; he believes himself to be endowed with supernatural powers which, at the same time, he attributes to the external world. Thus, his mental life is mirrored in his external world. The vague demarcation of the ego of the primitive from the outside world explains his conception of the dream as a phenomenon outside his ego, endowed with magical powers. In certain psychotic states, the boundary between the internal and the external world is likewise vague; here, too, they merge together. Hence the deranged person takes his own mental life for external reality, much as do small children who, in reporting a dream, do not say "I dreamed this or that," but "I saw this or that or did this or that during the night." To the psychotic, the dream appears as reality, and it occurs frequently that such a patient wishes to live according to this dream reality. Sometimes a psychosis starts with a dream, and when such a patient awakens from the dream, he continues to hallucinate and to have delusions as in the dream. In a normal individual, the "psychotic" state of dreaming ends with the end of sleep.

In the course of development, mankind very gradually changed its concept of the dream. When man learned to distinguish clearly between mental processes and those which occur in the external world, as he grew able to tell himself that this process is a mental one and that a real one, he gradually had to give up his conviction that what he was thinking or wishing was objective reality. Since, with this development, the understanding of reality progressed, the idea of the supernatural origin of dreams could no longer be maintained.

In the course of time there evolved numerous dream theories, none of which could survive scientific criticism. Freud was the first to succeed in unraveling the psychology of the dream and thus in bringing it closer to our understanding.

Freud induced his patients to say whatever came to mind, without selection or criticism, that is, to associate freely. He thus substituted for the traditional anamnesis, the patient's coordinated, logical report about his illness, a disorderly and occasionally confused one, which is known as the "method of free associations." For this change Freud's experience with hypnosis may have been responsible. The following considerations formed the theoretical basis of the method of free associations: all our thinking is aim-directed, that is, it has a goal. Sometimes we know this goal, sometimes we do not. If we know, consciously or half-consciously (preconsciously), what we wish to express, we use our criticism and logic, we eliminate certain associations and encourage others, we select what we are going to say. We muster our knowledge and experiences in an orderly manner, in order to make our point, which is more or less known to us in advance. However, when the goal of our thinking or wishing is *completely* unknown to us, no conscious effort will succeed in making it known to us, in making it conscious. In this case, we employ the method of free associations which—as all our thinking is aim-directed—will bring the unknown, unconscious goal to the surface. Thus, while the goal of our conscious (or preconscious) thinking is more or less known to us in advance, the goal of our unconscious thinking becomes known to us only at the end of a chain of free associations (and other operations which will be discussed later on).

In the course of their free associations Freud's patients reported fantasies, dreams and daydreams (all of which have a similar structure). He did not dismiss them as unimportant, but treated them as he did other mental creations of his patients: he subjected them to the process of further free associations and interpretation. He found then that all dreams have a meaning. The analysis of dreams enabled him, furthermore, to lay the foundation for the hypothesis about the structure and function of the psychic apparatus.

The preliminary condition for dreaming is sleep. It is true that one may have dreams in the waking state, too, so-called daydreams or fantasies; however, these are markedly influenced by the requirements of conscious thought processes and are therefore more complicated than night dreams. Scholars still argue about the nature of sleep. Their dispute does not alter the fact that in deep sleep, interest is lost in the external as well as in the internal world, that in deep sleep man does not perceive stimuli from his environment or from within (physical excitations or psychic ones); one hears, sees, senses and feels nothing. It is to be assumed that the human being rests from the strain of waking life by shutting off the activity of his sense organs. Not every sleep, however, proceeds so restfully. One may see pictures in sleep, entire scenes; one may hear words; one may talk at length, think, feel joy, sorrow, anxiety and pain—in other words, one may dream. Mental activity, then, has not fully ceased in sleep.

It may be stirred up by excessive stimuli from without or within—predominantly by internal stimuli—and, when it has reached a certain intensity, force itself upon the sleeper's consciousness in the form of a dream and thus disturb profound sleep. But Freud states that the main function of the dream is to be a *guardian of sleep*. Let us see how this apparent contradiction can be resolved.

Man wishes to suspend all mental and physical activity after the strains and stresses of the day, and puts himself to sleep. The wish to sleep can be satisfied through discontinuance of all relations with reality, that is, with the *external world,* and by returning to a developmental state of self-sufficiency, comparable to that in the mother's womb. In fact, Freud maintains that sleep satisfies an unconscious instinctual wish to return to the mother's womb; in a sense, an *instinct to sleep* is born at birth. The dream *seemingly* counteracts the sleeper's wish to forget all the day's worries and strains in sleep. But in sleep, activated unconscious drives and wishes reach the sleeper's specific consciousness in the dream. These would awaken the sleeper if they were not checked. And this control of the unconscious drives and wishes is the task of the dream. If the dream succeeds in fulfilling an unconscious wish, then sleep can continue. *In this sense the dream is a guardian of sleep.*

The aspect of the dream as a wish fulfillment, however, is not obvious. The *manifest* dream, the mental activity that is remembered after awaking, is usually incoherent, meaningless. With the help of free associations, a corresponding *latent* dream emerges which is hidden behind the manifest dream. Only when the former is transformed into the latter is its meaning uncovered, and the fulfillment of the unconscious wish revealed.

In order to transform the manifest dream into the latent one, the dreamer has to associate freely to the whole dream or to its elements. Through the interpretation of the material brought forth by the associations, in other words, *through translation of the dream language into the normal speech of waking life,* we arrive at an understanding of the latent dream thoughts. The activity that distorts the latent dream thoughts and forms the manifest dream is called *dream work*. The work which is aimed at the opposite result, at the conversion of the manifest dream into the latent dream thoughts, is called *dream interpretation* or *dream analysis*.

An example of a dream will illustrate what has just been said:

A patient dreamt that she was bathing a newborn child. She associated to this dream that her best friend had given birth to a child the day preceding the dream. This event reactivated her strong desire for a child of her own, a wish which, for certain reasons, could not be fulfilled. In the dream, she handled a child as if it were her own, as if she herself had a child.

Obviously, the dream fulfilled a wish of long standing for this patient. Indeed, *every dream contains the fulfillment of a frustrated wish*. With some slight modifications, this formula is valid for all dreams.

The contention that every dream represents a wish fulfillment will probably not be received without contradiction. The objection may be raised that dreams with unpleasant contents, such as anxiety dreams, cannot possibly express unfulfilled wishes. Now, firstly, conscious wishes very rarely express themselves in dreams; the wishes that appear are unconscious wishes which stand in opposition to the conscious personality and therefore have had to be suppressed. Since self-control is weaker in sleep than in the waking state, such repressed wishes may on occasion re-emerge in the dream.

The question of how dreams with unpleasant contents could be wish fulfillments might perhaps be answered by a counter-question: is it inconceivable that at times one might wish for something unpleasant and satisfy this desire in the dream? How one came to wish for something disagreeable to happen is another problem. Many factors are involved; as they cannot be discussed here in detail, a few intimations must suffice. Sometimes there may be a wish for a lesser evil in order to escape from a disaster of major proportions; often unpleasant dreams of this kind are sacrificial in character. More frequently unpleasant dreams serve the needs of those who suffer from severe feelings of guilt. These individuals often wish to be punished, to suffer. They grant themselves this desired punishment in the dream.

Anxiety dreams are not wish dreams. Anxiety plays a paramount role in the dream as well as in the neurosis. The problem of anxiety is not a specific dream problem, but it is a problem in itself to which we shall devote much time further on. In the present connection we need only note that anxiety is always an indication of a severe psychic conflict, of a struggle between certain strivings and that part of the personality which, even in sleep, opposes their gratification. From such a dream, the sleeper usually wakes up; anxiety prevents him from fulfilling the desire and interrupts the dream. Thus the anxiety dream is not a wish-fulfillment dream; it is just the opposite.

To return to our dream example, there was an evident connection between the birth of the friend's child and the dream. One of the experiences of the day called forth the dream on the following night. Actually it is a rule that certain experiences of the day, called *day residues,* are factors precipitating the dream. Not only external events, as in our dream, form such day residues, but also internal experiences such as worries, preoccupation with certain ideas, or important memories. Every dream contains fragments of recollections of or allusions to experiences of the preceding day. And yet, not every experience of the day acts as a dream instigator. Only those residues which associate with certain unconscious thoughts, drives, or wishes enter the dream. *In other words, a dream is stimulated only by those events of waking life that find a sounding board in the unconscious.*

Discovering the connection between the day residue and the corresponding unconscious thoughts or drives facilitates the interpretation of the dream and its acceptance by the dreamer. For through this discovery he can see the attraction, like a magnet on steel, that his unconscious exercises on an experience of everyday life; then the interpretation appears not academic to him, but as an immediate experience.

It is, perhaps, not superfluous to point out that the latent dream is not a creation of the dream night itself, but has been formed previously and in the specific night merely turns into the manifest dream under the influence of the day residue. The unconscious material seizes on the day residue, and it appears as though past experiences, thoughts, memories were hiding behind an immediate actual experience.

Our dreamer accepted without difficulty the interpretation of her dream as a wish for a child. This wish was not wholly unknown to her; the fact that it could not be fulfilled had actually caused her much suffering. But when she first reported the dream, she was not aware of her preoccupation with this wish. Only in the course of her associations did she gradually become aware of the fact that she had had this wish for years, although she was not always conscious of it.

We call *preconscious* those experiences, ideas, urges and the like, that are conscious at one time, and not conscious at another, yet that can easily enter consciousness. Our dreamer's wish was, then, preconscious. It has just been shown that a day residue participates in forming a dream only if it associates with an instinctual drive. Now, the patient did not dream that she "gave birth" to a child, but that she "was bathing" a child. This version is a symbolic representation of birth. Indeed very often, though not always, the dream contains symbols. Water (bathing) is related to birth and in symbolic language means giving birth or being born. Thus the patient in a symbolic way fulfilled her wish for a child.

Another patient dreamt that she was riding on a green and blue striped bird and landed in the midst of a magnificent landscape. Althought to all the other elements of the dream she had numerous associations which yielded a multiple, well-determined meaning, she was unable to associate to the bird itself. Since the bird is a well-known symbol for the male sex organ, and riding, in popular language, has the symbolic meaning of sexual intercourse, the dream must mean that the dreamer practices or wishes to practice sexual intercourse like a man, that is, from above. The accuracy of this interpretation is confirmed by the fact that the dreamer's husband was in psychoanalytic treatment for psychic impotence and that his ailment had improved to the extent that he could have intercourse, though only in the female position, where the wife had to play the part of the male. Lately, however, he had again withdrawn from her. Thus this dream is a wish fulfillment expressed in symbolic form.

Symbolism is not confined to dreams; it is a subject worthy of treatment in a wider frame of reference. All languages of all peoples are permeated by symbols. They are encountered in folklore, in jokes and jests; they have their place in superstition, in manners and customs, in fairy tales, myths, and legends. There are typical symbols, established since primeval times (fire = love); yet new symbols are constantly evolving, even in our day and age (the airplane, for instance, and the automobile). Those symbols which are in the process of developing may express a different content in different people. Basically, the typical symbols always have the same meaning, aside from insignificant individual variations which may occasionally occur. They invariably refer to the human body, especially to its sex organs and sex functions.

The dream employs the same symbols that are encountered in other situations. Here, too, they may at one time have an individual meaning, and then again a typical meaning. When dealing with the individual symbols, one has to consider every detail with the utmost accuracy if one wishes to avoid mistakes. But even the typical symbols may not be used automatically. Only when all associations are found wanting, or when the dreamer is unable to associate to an element which is known to us as a typical symbol, may we substitute its meaning. It is true that familiarity with symbols contributes much to the understanding of dreams. But if symbolic interpretation is used carelessly and indiscriminately, dream analysis falls to the level of cryptography.

To avoid any misunderstanding, I should like to emphasize that the dream has taught us nothing new about the origin and meaning of symbols. In symbol interpretation we merely make use of what has been learned from other sources. The study of these sources which have been mentioned above, has taught us that symbol language corresponds to a primitive way of thinking and is an integral part, perhaps the main part, of communication among primitive men. In the normal waking state this type of thinking has almost completely disappeared; in the dream it reappears over and over again. Inasmuch as thoughts are expressed in symbols, the thinking process in the dream returns to a lower stage of development; it becomes archaic. Symbolic language is a truly international language.

The primitiveness of thinking in the dream manifests itself not only in symbolic language but also in other modes of expression. Basically, the dreamer does not think in concepts nor in words. When he pronounces meaningful words or sentences, they have in fact not been formed in the dream but in his waking life prior to the dream. The dreamer uses them in order to hide certain unconscious dream thoughts behind a meaningful façade. These speeches or words are preconscious, whereas the dream thoughts which they help to disguise are unconscious. Exceptions to this rule are words and speeches which were actually heard in childhood; these belong to the unconscious, as is true of auditory hallucinations in schizophrenia and "audible thoughts" in obsessional neurosis. The unconscious thinking of the dream is very different from thinking in the waking state. It does not take the form of ideas, concepts and words, but of pictures. The dreamer experiences pictorial scenes. In the scene where the dreamer was bathing a child, she hallucinated an idea, a wish, and thus *represented dramatically the birth of a child.*

Such a transposition of thoughts into visual experience is likewise not characteristic of the dream alone; picture language is as ancient and primitive as is symbol language and was employed by the early Egyptians and other ancient cultures.

Thus in the dream, abstract thinking is transformed into concrete thinking, that is, ideas are presented as things. Words are changed into animate or inanimate matter and are treated as if they were things. A patient, for example, dreamt about a mad dog. She had the notion that I was "treating her badly," like a "mad dog."

The primitive and archaic elements of psychic life correspond to a precipitate of the historical development of mankind, a precipitate that in waking life has been overcome essentially, but that is restored in the dream. The individual in his development from infancy to maturity goes through similar stages as did mankind, though of course in a condensed form. Just as it is a fact that each developmental era of mankind has left traces which have been overcome in later stages, so it is true of each developmental stage of the individual. These traces form his individual past, which may re-emerge under certain conditions, as for instance in the dream. This past, embracing earliest childhood, finds expression not merely in the revival of archaic forms of thinking but also in the reappearance of ideas and instinctual impulses which belong to the past. Hence the dream is replete with contents and needs from childhood and from the history of mankind. In almost every dream the parents or their substitutes appear in some form or other, and through them the dream gratifies infantile instinctual needs. Moreover, the dream may repeat, in distorted or undistorted form, ideas and fantasies of childhood referring to birth, death, and life, to the difference between the sexes, and many other problems. In short, in its deepest layer, the dream reflects the genuine infantile psyche with all its fancies and wishes. It is thus evident that the dream is not only a primitive but also an infantile configuration. Since, furthermore, the starting point of the dream lies in the present, it belongs to both the past and the present; it represents an infantile wish (of the past) as fulfilled (in the present). Thus the dream reverts to a primitive way of functioning of the psychic apparatus in which wishes or the first beginnings of thoughts are hallucinated.

Returning again to our dream example, we see an apparent contradiction in the fact that the dream contains on the one hand a preconscious wish, and on the other, an unconscious wish as expressed in symbols. This contradiction is immediately resolved when we learn that the unconscious appears in two forms: (1) as the preconscious, which means a psychic process that is only temporarily unconscious and can turn into a conscious one at any time; and (2) as the unconscious proper, which either never was conscious or is repressed and can become conscious again only after certain changes have taken place in the mental apparatus. Our patient's dream is a good example of this. At the time of her dream, she was aware of her wish for a baby; gradually, however, recollections of fantasies and children's games began to emerge that disclosed the existence of a wish in her childhood to have a baby with her father. In the period of her life which preceded the dream, she wished to have a baby by her husband. What she did not know, however, was that in her unconscious he was a substitute for her father and that her wish for a child originated in her childhood. That her husband was a substitute for her father and that the wish for a baby by her father had been active in her childhood, was not conscious at the time of the dream; it was unconscious.

Now, a wish or any other psychic material that is neither conscious nor preconscious, yet exists, according to *circumstantial evidence,* belongs to the *unconscious proper,* as indicated above. Our patient, a mature woman, was totally unaware of any idea even remotely connected with a wish to have a baby with her father. Should such a wish have existed in some corner of her conscious mind, she would have had to inhibit it at all costs, and in fact she did succeed in keeping it entirely away from consciousness. Accordingly it remained unconscious during her waking life. In sleep, however, a state in which the inhibiting or repressing factors of the ego are weakened, her infantile wish could form a dream and enter consciousness. Had this wish not been distorted to such an extent that it could not be recognized by her sleeping ego, her sleep would have been disturbed and she would have awakened. The distortion made it possible for her to remain asleep. Her wish could be fulfilled without offending her conscience, for the manifest dream did not say "I wish to have a baby by my father" but "I am bathing a child."

Thus it is evident that a dream can contain both preconscious and unconscious wishes. However, a preconscious wish is not taken up by the dreamer unless it is fed by the energy of a corresponding unconscious wish. It is thus the fulfillment of an *infantile* wish that ensures sleep.

In our dream example, the original, infantile wish was disguised through a symbolic representation of birth. It is in fact a rule that the manifest dream contains the latent dream thoughts in a *distorted* form. There are numerous forms of distortion with which we shall deal at the proper place. Here I would like to call attention to two forms of distortion of the latent dream thoughts that strike us in our example: firstly, distortion by the *symbolic* method of representation; secondly by *omission*. In the latent dream thoughts, the patient's father played an important part, while in the manifest dream he was not mentioned at all. Indeed, omission is one of the most effective methods of dream distortion. It causes the latent dream material to be expressed in considerably compressed form by the manifest dream. Sometimes the manifest dream may contain only a single word or picture.

The analysis of another dream will show more of the mechanisms of dream *distortion* and dream *disguise.* The dream is the following:

"I took a pistol and shot at the alarm clock. The bullet went right through the figure 3 on the face of the clock. I felt satisfied with my shot because it seemed to me that I had hit exactly the spot I had aimed at. . . ."

Before going to bed, the dreamer had set her alarm clock. When the clock awakened her at the set time, she did not get up, but fell asleep again. The clock went on ringing—a sound to which she obviously reacted with the dream. She remembered that she was angry when she finally woke up. Did her anger arise when the clock had started to ring or had she been angry before? During the last few days preceding the dream, her analysis had been difficult and on the day before the dream she complained about being unsuccessful in life; about being so slow in everything; she expressed fear that she would never reach her goal. Her whole day was spent in thoughts about her alleged incapacities and inferiorities (in point of fact she was a very talented person). In this vexed, hopeless mood she went to bed and fell asleep. She was probably angered by the ringing of the alarm, and went back to sleep after awakening, as if she were saying: "I don't want to know anything of my painful thoughts." The shooting at the alarm clock brought to her mind the phrase "to kill time." To this she associated that the idea of time is symbolized in drawings representing an old man with a long, white beard, carrying a scythe, and called "Father Time." Her favorite song was one called "Father Time," and its words were as follows:

> Father Time is a crafty man,
> And he's set in his ways.
> And we know that we never can
> Make him give back past days.
> So "20" while we are here
> Let's be friends firm and true.
> Let's have a gay time
> While we have a play time
> For we all love to play with you.

The shooting at the clock, then, represents pictorially the reproachful thought that she was wasting time; and actually, when on the preceding day she had complained about her shortcomings, she used the phrase "I kill time." These thoughts went back to joyful reminiscences of childhood when loss of time meant nothing; one was young and could play without worries. The sad and painful meditations of the day were changed in the latent dream thoughts to pleasant memories of wasting time in childhood. In actuality, she was unhappy; in her latent dream thoughts she was happy; thus she reversed her mood. So far, the dream represents a wish fulfillment by which the passing of time is annulled.

The song "Father Time" was connected in her mind with something else, namely with the sentence, "I took a pistol." She always associated a pistol with the fact that her father had committed suicide by shooting himself in the temple with a revolver. He had owned the revolver for many years, and she remembered that she had seen it several times in her childhood. She was "scared to death of it" and would not go near it.

After her father's death she was deeply shaken and reproached herself for being to blame for the tragic event. In the dream she was in possession of the weapon that belonged to her father and that she had not dared to touch during his lifetime. Now she was shooting with it at "cruel time," the old man of the clock, Father Time, the relentless man who never gives back past days. She was shooting as her father had done in reality. In the dream, however, she was not shooting herself as her father had shot himself, but she was shooting at the cruel Father Time who does not bring back past happiness. Her father took her happy childhood away from her by his suicide. After his death, she was numb and sank into sleep as if she wanted to forget what had happened.

It is significant that upon awaking from this dream, she was angry with me. In her opinion, her anger was provoked by my endeavors to elicit from her recollections of her past which she could not and would not produce. She would rather sleep. In shooting at Father Time, she was obviously aiming at me and at her father whom she could not forgive for what he had done to her by his suicide.

In the dream picture of the bullet going right through the figure 3, there were represented in a most condensed form her accusations against her father with her simultaneous feelings of guilt, her self-accusations and inferiority feeling, as well as her love for her father and her disappointment in him. She had the association to that picture that there is a song called "Three O'clock in the Morning." She could not remember the words of the song, but knew that it was an English waltz tune to which she had often danced. It was the only dance her father had ever tried with her when she was a child. He had done this only two or three times because he had not liked the way she danced it; he had said that she did not keep step with him. She was very unhappy about that. Actually, she had not been able to adapt herself readily to her father's style of dancing. He had the reputation of being a very good dancer. She added regretfully that had she known how to be a good follower, she would have gotten along with him much better.

The dancing reminded her of the fact that her father, who had practically given up playing the violin, did occasionally take it down and play for a few minutes, with her as his accompanist. It often happened that when she was playing the piano she would start singing and playing a popular song of that period called "Sing Me to Sleep." This song, like the above-mentioned waltz, is also in ¾ time. When her father was in good humor, he took the violin and played the obligato while she sang and accompanied him on the piano, but he always ended by finding all kinds of fault with her playing. Most particularly he would criticize her for the tempo (Time!). He said she took too many liberties with the tempo; when the music said *Ritardando* she retarded too much, and when it said *Accelerando,* she accelerated too quickly. Her father had been a real musician, she stated, and she recognized much later that her own playing was too sentimental and undisciplined. However, at the time she did not understand this and could not see why her interpretation was wrong. She suffered greatly under the lash of her father's tongue; she felt that his criticism of her was contemptuous. Worse even than his criticism was the fact that after a few attempts, he gave up playing entirely because he was so disgusted with his accompanist. In the same way he had given up dancing because her dancing did not suit him. At least that was her understanding of his ceasing to play the violin as well as to dance. She complained that he never took the trouble to teach her how to do things the way he wanted them; if she did not perform to perfection he would have nothing more to do with her. Thus she became discouraged and thought she was a complete, hopeless failure; she thought she could never become a good dancer or pianist. In colloquial speech, she added, a musician who renders a composition badly is said to "murder" the music. She thought it likely that her father might have told her that she "murdered" the pieces she played.

These associations no longer concern themselves with "killing time," but with "killing" music, dance, and song. Her father's criticism made her desperate, and convinced her that she was no good; she was inferior. However, for her the worst thing was that her father gave up dancing and playing with her. It is interesting to note that at the time of the dream, *she feared that I might give up treating her if she did not work* well in the analysis.

In contrast to the thoughts preceding the dream, she was satisfied with herself in the dream: *she hit exactly the spot she had aimed at.* In this connection she remarked that hitting the figure 3 reminded her of "hitting the bull's eye," the small black spot in the center of a target. In the dream, the figure 3 represented the bull's eye (in addition to the tempo of dance and music), in spite of the fact that it was not at the center of the target (the clock). By hitting the bull's eye, the figure 3 which she was aiming at, she showed perfect marksmanship. Her success in the dream was in contrast to her very bad marksmanship in childhood when she tried painstakingly to hit a target with bow and arrow without ever succeeding, whereas her playmates were more successful. She vaguely remembered that her father used tauntingly to laugh at her because of her poor marksmanship.

These associations also dealt with inability and ineptitude, but they were recollections of early childhood when, playing with other children, she proved inferior. In the manifest dream, she was a good shot, she hit the mark that she wanted to hit. She was no longer clumsy, incapable, and inferior, but was a person who understood her business and did it right. Before falling asleep, she was desperate because she felt she was not doing well in her analysis. In the dream she consoled herself by expressing: "I can do everything well, not only the analysis, but dancing, playing, and target shooting." Thus the dream was a fulfillment of many wishes.

However, the dream reached into even deeper layers. The clock, which called forth the associations "kill music," "kill time," led to the idea "time is money" and thence to the thought of wasting money, which referred in particular to wasting her mother's money if she did not do well in her analysis. This, in turn, reminded her of her repeated losses of umbrellas, brooches, handbags, and of her frequent dreams about losing handbags. This led to a strange reminiscence. She had been a precocious child, had read everything she could lay hands on, and was very inquisitive. Once while rummaging in her mother's cupboard, she had come upon a popular book on pregnancy and birth. In it she read feverishly about the umbilical cord and the placenta, but could not understand what she had read. She appealed to her mother who answered her questions as best she could. As children often are, our patient was insatiable in asking questions. She wanted to know what happened to the umbilical cord and the placenta after birth. To this question the mother answered that it was cut off. Then she asked whether the umbilical cord had been cut off after *her* birth, too, and whether her grandfather, who was a physician, had done that. Next she wanted to know how the umbilical cord and the placenta were shaped. Not satisfied with her mother's answers, she tried to find answers by herself. She imagined the placenta to be a sack, a *handbag* in which one may keep money or other small things. When she pictured this bag to herself, it seemed soft and smooth. It reminded her of the scrotum of a boy with whom she had played between her third and fourth year. "It felt so soft when I touched it," she exclaimed; indeed, in the analysis, the recollection of her early play with the boy's genital was vividly reproduced. In this connection she mentioned that in her childhood she had been very tomboyish; she had competed with boys and had tried to imitate them.

In her imagination the umbilical cord was a pipe through which urine and blood flow. Through the boy's penis, urine likewise flows as if through a pipe; accordingly, in her infantile way of thinking, the umbilical cord became a representation of the penis, as the placenta was a representation of the scrotum. She further imagined that both penis and scrotum were cut off from her when she was born and thrown away, and that it had been her grandfather who had done this.

In the dream, she had a pistol, well known as a penis symbol. Her childhood resentment that she was not a boy, that she did not possess a penis, was, in the deepest, unconscious layer, the root of her inferiority complex. In the dream, she possessed a penis and could hit the bull's eye, could aim well (thus urinate like a boy). *She fulfilled her infantile wish.*

I regret that I must stop here since the complete understanding of the dream would require a knowledge of the dreamer's entire life history. Besides, every dream is bottomless in at least one respect.

The manifest dream was short, containing a single scene. The latent dream thoughts were numerous, complicated, branching out in many directions. Through her associations, the dreamer brought to the surface thoughts about losing time, about her inability to dance and to play the piano, about her inferiority feelings and her resentment at not being a boy, about her guilt feelings in relation to her father, and so on. More than one wish, idea or emotion was represented, yet was not apparent in the manifest dream. It is, indeed, characteristic of all dreams that the manifest dream is a product of *condensation* of the latent dream thoughts. For example: the clock represented Father Time, the patient's own father, the analyst; the pistol and the shooting represented killing her past, her father, the analyst; also, exhibiting her penis, showing off, and overcoming her inferiority feelings as if she were demonstrating that she had a penis and could accomplish anything—dancing and playing the piano.

In a single simple dream scene, even in each one of its elements, contradictory thoughts and wishes are compressed and unified. It is only in the unconscious that contradictory elements can coexist and be expressed in a single picture or scene just as if they did not represent opposite strivings.

It is not difficult to understand that the dream has to be extensively distorted if so much is compressed in a single short scene which actually proceeds in several dimensions, with events taking place within a short span of time which in reality were years apart. In attempting to unravel this dream, to undo the distortion—that is, while analyzing it—we noted how many meanings it implies. No dream has but one meaning. In psychoanalytic terminology, this multiplicity of meanings is known as *overdetermination*. In other words, each dream element may contain several ideas, thoughts, and wishes. The work done in the dream in expressing a multitude of strivings and thoughts in one dream element is called *condensation* of the dream.

Another form of distortion is achieved through the mechanism of *displacement*. Through displacement, psychic intensities are shifted from one element to another. Distortion through displacement can take a great variety of forms.

A patient dreamt that he was in bed with his wife making love to her, but felt uneasy and when he turned his head he saw his little son watching him from his crib.

The full analysis of this dream will be given in one of the following chapters. Here we shall limit ourselves to relating briefly what this analysis revealed. The dream represented the patient, when he was between the ages of one and three, watching his parents' sexual activities. Thus the dream repeats one or more scenes in which the dreamer had satisfied his curiosity about his parents' relations. In the dream he attributed his own curiosity in childhood to his son, as if he were saying: "Not I was curious about what my parents did, but my son is curious about what his parents do." He *shifted* or *displaced* his sexual curiosity from himself onto his son.

Aside from denying responsibility, displacement has still other functions. (The dream can express negation only in some positive form.) In our dream, the patient acted out his curiosity in two roles, as it were: as his father and as his son, just as in a movie, one actor may play two parts simultaneously, in a way splitting his personality. In fact, *the distortion by displacement frequently leads to the splitting of the dreamer's personality* to the effect that *several persons in the dream may represent the dreamer himself.*[1]

Actually, the concept of displacement includes the concept of condensation. When the psychic stress is displaced along a chain of associations, individual elements are left out and their energies are concentrated in another, in itself often unimportant, element. This insignificant element then becomes the representative of several elements which are not contained in the manifest dream. Thus the dream becomes short but rich in content. The dream is then the product of the work of condensation and as such is an allusion to numerous thoughts and ideas hidden behind it.

It is likewise the effect of the work of displacement when ideas and thoughts are interchangeable and may replace each other on the basis of trifling resemblances. It quite frequently happens, for instance, that one person replaces another because of a similarity in the color of hair, or because both were seen on the same occasion. It is just that one does not always distinguish sharply between individual objects in the dream; a part may represent the whole and vice versa; one situation may replace another regardless of whether they belong together logically or as to contents, time, or place. The dream is concerned only with *suitability for plastic representation.* In order to express a thought the dream displaces its elements or condenses them until they can be expressed in a plastic-dramatic form. It serves the same purpose when the dreamer transforms words into things or shifts words around and condenses them until they are new, incomprehensible word formations.

It is the displacement of the psychic accent which invests the dream with those peculiar features which cause it to appear basically so different from psychic activity in the waking state. Whereas in the waking state thinking is directed by principles of logic and demarcates the individual objects as well as persons from each other and from the subject himself, and does not confuse time and space, none of this is true of the dream. Here images are interchanged, a part is taken for the whole, and thinking is not directed by principles of logic but by the rules of condensation and displacement. This type of psychic activity is encountered in some primitives and in small children; it appears at the very begin-

---

[1] The mechanisms of displacement as well as of condensation appear frequently in everyday life. They manifest themselves in parapraxes or symptomatic actions, in mistakes like misplacing, mispronouncing words and names, forgetting, losing, misunderstanding.

ning of psychic development and is therefore called the *primary process*.

The primary process, which is alien to the nature of conscious thinking, appears in the dream and governs psychic activity that does not take place in consciousness. In other words, the psychic activity that leads to displacement and condensation proceeds outside the realm of consciousness, even in those instances where the result of this process is perceived by the apparatus of consciousness. *Such psychic processes are called unconscious processes.* Some supplementary remarks concerning the primary process will be made further on.

Displacement and condensation are, indeed, the most important and effective methods for the distortion of the dream and concealment of its meaning. Other techniques, such as symbolic representation, regression, omission, have been mentioned on the preceding pages, but there are still numerous others. One technique which deserves particular attention will be shown by an example of a dream which Dr. Sidney Kahr was good enough to let me have:

On the day following a discussion of the analyst's forthcoming vacation, a young woman patient reported this dream: "I was frantically running along a road, looking for someone. When I came to the crossroad I didn't know which way to turn." The dream was extremely unpleasant. There was a frantic, hopeless feeling in it. The houses were strange, and she was unable to recognize the scene. This dream was a recurrent one, although she was unable to recall when it had first appeared. During the analytic session the patient seemed cold and detached; she mentioned casually that she planned to leave within a few days to seek employment in another state where she believed her opportunities for professional success would be greater. Then she stated, still without feeling, that she had heard that she had been deeply attached to her father until the age of three, when he left Europe for the United States. The father, she was told, had been devoted to her. Four years later, when the family was reunited with the father in this country, it was noticed that she was no longer affectionate and friendly to him. She was indifferent and avoided his company. On a number of occasions during the next few years she ran away from home.

The threatened separation from the analyst revived deeply repressed feelings of the traumatic separation from the father when she was three. With this repetitive dream she experienced again and again her painful feelings at that time and her frantic unsuccessful search for her father.

The following day the patient told her mother of her dream. The mother recognized the houses, the road and the crossroads in the dream, as the patient described them to her. This was the road which led out of the small town in which they had lived in Europe. Following the father's departure for the United States, the mother said that the child had been inconsolable and on a number of occasions had run searching for her father on this road.

The wish fulfillment of this dream took the form of anticipation, as if the dreamer were saying to the analyst: "Before you leave me, I am leaving you." But this anticipation expressed itself through the repetition of an early childhood experience. In fact, *many dreams repeat in an almost undisguised form a traumatic experience, frequently one of early childhood.* Such an experience may have been completely forgotten, yet it appears in the dream with almost undiminished intensity. *The dream then represents the only memory of a forgotten experience, which cannot be remembered in any other way.* The function of such dreams is abreaction of the trauma through reliving it over and over again.

The dream can further be disguised not only by various distortions of the latent dream thoughts, but also by distortions of affects. The term "distortion," though, can hardly be applied to affects, for the affect as such always remains an affect which can often be traced to early childhood.

The fragment of a patient's dream may serve as an illustrative example in this connection: "I cried bitterly because my father had died. . . ." In the session preceding the dream, the patient had told me that he would take the next day off. When I called his attention to the fact that the decision to skip his next session was a sign of resistance, he said that he would come. For certain reasons I did not accept his offer. When he came back a few days later, he complained that my refusal had hurt his feelings, and then reported the dream, the fragment of which I have related. This man had never cried, not even when his father had beaten him in childhood. Upon my insistence that the affect of crying must stem from some real experience, he remembered the following event from his seventh year: One evening, already in bed, he heard his mother vehemently reproaching his father for not supporting the family and for wasting money. Thereupon the child started to cry bitterly, expecting that his father would come and ask him why he was crying. Then he would tell him how unhappy the family was because the father did not love them and therefore did not care for them. (Obviously he was identifying with his mother.) The patient evidently felt my refusal to see him as a rejection of his love. This disappointment awakened the old unconscious affect of pain over not being loved by his father. In the manifest dream the loss of father's love is represented by the idea of death.

The emotion may be strong and adequate or it may appear paradoxical and incompatible with the contents of the manifest dream. In the first case, it does not contribute to the dream distortion. In the second case, the associations lead to the latent dream thoughts to which the affect of the manifest dream belongs. This form of distortion is brought about by the detachment of the affect from one dream thought and its attachment to another. Frequently, however, the affect of the manifest dream is in direct contrast to that of the latent dream; the manifest dream may express joy and love while the latent dream may be full of hate and sorrow. It also happens that the manifest dream is void of any affect while the latent one is highly emotional. Here the distortion takes place by the subduing of the affect.

Our previous assertion that the manifest dream has no meaning and acquires a meaning only through interpretation may seem contradictory, since there are dreams that are orderly and that make sense. These dreams contain speeches and reflections which seem logical and coherent. This impression is deceptive, however, as is proved by the analysis of such dreams. For the associations lead first from the reflections of the dream to similar reflections of the waking state. Indeed, the orderly and meaningful sentences in the dream stem from waking life. They are usually repetitions of sentences or words which the dreamer has said, heard, or read. However, there are also dreams that do not contain reflections or speeches but merely images and actions, yet they appear correct and orderly; in short, they seem plausible. One feels that such things may occur in reality, too, and that is indeed correct, for the rational element of such dreams likewise belongs to the thinking of the waking state. The type of thinking in the dream which is directed by principles of logic, which establishes causal connections, which does not confuse objects with concepts or time with space, is *not* characteristic of the dream. It is characteristic of the waking state. It is not subject to displacement and condensation of the primary process. Since it develops later than the primary process, it is called the *secondary process*. While the primary process is unconscious, the secondary process is preconscious.

The foregoing review of techniques of distortion does not by any means include all the methods of concealing the unconscious meaning of the dream. Other methods, however, will not be discussed here, since it is the purpose of this chapter to present only the basic principles of dream psychology. For more comprehensive information it is best to turn to the inexhaustible source of all psychoanalytic knowledge, to Freud's writings.

Analyzing the dream, transforming the manifest dream into the latent one by undoing the distortions, is best accomplished with the help of free associations. Free associations, however, must not be looked upon as identical with the latent dream thoughts. The latter are, to use Freud's simile, contained in the associations as if dissolved in a chemical solution from which they have to be extracted. The latent dream thoughts contain preconscious as well as unconscious material. The preconscious material has to be segregated from the unconscious material and correlated with the manifest dream. This operation is the precondition of dream interpretation.

It has been shown that the dream fulfills an unconscious wish and that this wish is disguised by means of dream distortion. Now the question arises: why must the dream be disguised?

All dreams contain a wish rooted in childhood which either remains unconscious or, having reached consciousness, is immediately forgotten. In either case the result is the same: the wish is kept from being conscious and, to use a technical psychoanalytic term, it is *repressed*. What are the forces that cause repression of thoughts and wishes?

In order to deal with this problem, we have to anticipate the contents of a later chapter, and merely state briefly at this point that the personality has a structure consisting of three parts or agencies: *ego, superego,* and *id.* Since other properties of these agencies will be discussed later on, we shall here treat them only superficially. The ego is preconscious; the superego contains unconscious elements in addition to preconscious ones. It controls conscience, and by exercising criticism imposes inhibitions upon the ego. The id is unconscious and contains our instincts.

When analyzing a dream, paying close attention to the way in which the thoughts and associations to the dream are being reported, one observes that the dreamer is not always capable of refraining from self-criticism, in spite of his best intentions. He omits some connecting links, does not tell everything, represents some associations differently from the way they first came to his mind; in short, he tries at the last moment to relate the thoughts so that they cannot be recognized for what they really are. This self-criticism of the patient's is often of such proportions that it defeats the attempted analysis of the dream. However, this criticism does not newly arise while the dream is being analyzed; it was always present and merely becomes more active when the attempt is made to discover the thoughts hidden in the dream. The reason for this is not hard to understand. Man has always to struggle with thoughts, impulses, and wishes which he would rather not have. As a rule, these thoughts and wishes can be controlled. But if their intensity increases for one reason or another, and they can no longer be controlled in the normal manner, self-criticism becomes so uncomfortable that it forces the ego to develop resistances against them for the purpose of keeping them in check, that is, of keeping them away from consciousness. The resistances are always present and active during the waking state, although we are usually unaware of them. They are formed by the ego under the influence of the superego.

Carried over from the waking state into the dream, the resistances are called *dream censors*. However, as the intensity of all psychic functions is decreased in sleep, the censor of the dream is less powerful than the resistances of the waking state. Therefore in the dream, elements of the unconscious id can reach the consciousness of the ego, which in the waking state are normally denied access to the ego. Another reason why the dream permits impulses otherwise forbidden to enter consciousness, lies in the fact that during sleep there is no motility, that is, no capacity to transform thoughts and wishes into action. Accordingly, the danger of carrying out a forbidden action is excluded in normal sleep.

However, while the weakened control is incapable of preventing the unconscious thoughts and wishes from entering the dream, it can still take the edge off these impulses and wishes, by forcing them into disguise before admitting them to the dream consciousness. It is as though the dreamer were saying: "I do not want to know anything of all these impulses. But since I feel too weak to fight them successfully, I at least wish to see them in a state in which I cannot recognize them." As a matter of fact, these thoughts are expressed in a form which is not comprehensible to the dreamer: in a combination of images, objects, and symbols, in a primitive, archaic language, long forgotten. Since the dreamer does not understand them, he does not feel responsible for them. Therefore forbidden impulses and wishes may find some gratification in the dream. The distortion of the dream is thus explained by the ego's need to disguise the contents of the dream, and this need is forced on the ego by the superego which, in sleep, acts as a dream censor.

The dream wish is a psychic representation of an instinctual drive; its fulfillment results in pleasure. Since the drive and consequently the dream wish originate in the id, the undifferentiated and completely unconscious agency of the personality, the pleasure derived from gratification of the dream wish, is essentially an id pleasure. But since gratification of an instinct at times meets with the resistance of the superego, as we have just learned, this same gratification may be a cause of displeasure to the ego. Thus pleasure of one psychic agency may cause displeasure or pain to another psychic agency and lead to endless conflicts. In the waking state, as a rule, this conflict is avoided by the suppression or repression of the instinctual demand. In the dream, on the one hand, it is resolved by fulfillment of the instinctual desire, thus satisfying the id, and, on the other, by disguising the wish beyond recognition, thus satisfying the ego. In the dream a compromise is achieved between two conflicting agencies of the personality which satisfies both parts.

However, such a compromise is not possible in all dreams. If either the criticism of the dream censor or the instinctual demand is excessive, the dreamer awakes with anxiety. In other words, either the dream censor as a counterpart of the superego is so inhibiting that any pleasure derived from fulfillment of an instinctual demand threatens the moral standards of the dreamer and hence must result in pain for the ego, or the instinct is so strong that the ego cannot cope with its demands and likewise suffers pain from its gratification. As a protection from such pain, the dreamer develops anxiety which interrupts his sleep. Such a dream has failed in both of its functions: since the anxiety interrupts sleep, the dream has failed in its function as guardian of sleep; since the dreamer awakes before the attempted wish fulfillment can take place, the fulfillment of the wish is frustrated. The formula that dreams contain the fulfillment of a frustrated wish must therefore be modified to the effect that each dream represents an *attempt* to fulfill a wish, usually successful, sometimes unsuccessful.

Let us turn back now to the manifest dream, taking the alarm clock dream as an example. The dreamer saw the alarm clock as if it were in the external world, whereas in fact it was an internal image. She perceived the memory of the clock, not the clock itself. This image was conscious in the manifest dream. Consciousness in the dream is an act of perception. In the waking state, too, consciousness means perception, but perception of both external and internal stimuli. Perceiving in the dream differs from perceiving in the waking state in that during sleep the perceptive apparatus of the ego is shut off from external stimuli and is therefore accessible only to internal ones. When internal stimuli are perceived in the dream, they are projected onto the external world, thus assuming a quasi-real character.

What we perceive in the manifest dream are traces of perceptions from the external world as well as memories, ideas, sensations of the internal world, combined in such a way that they are unintelligible. They can, however, be unraveled, and then we find that these psychic elements belong to different psychic layers. For instance, the clock perceived in the manifest dream was not the real clock but a reprint, as it were, a psychic representation of a part of the external world; the elements of the latent dream—memories, ideas, moods, and desires, belonging to various periods of the dreamer's life, were thus psychic representations of still deeper strivings of the internal world. Some of these elements were forgotten, suppressed, but could be remembered with more or less difficulty. This preconscious material is an allusion to the unconscious processes, an allusion from which the unconscious wishes and strivings can be reconstructed. The reconstruction then discloses the unconscious meanings of the dream. In our example, the unconscious contents of the dream are as follows: The patient believed that her father did not love her because she had no penis (inferiority feelings as to dancing, music, shooting). For this reason she felt great resentment against her father. When he committed suicide, she felt guilty as if she had killed him through her resentment and hate. In order to undo her guilt, she was ready for any sacrifice, and her life gave proof of this. In all her relations with men she permitted them to take advantage of her to an extreme degree. She finally married a man far older than herself whom she supported and whom she permitted to force her into perversions which she abhorred.

Study of the dream demonstrates that psychic processes are of different qualities: they may be conscious, preconscious, or unconscious. The characterization of psychic processes as being conscious, preconscious, or unconscious, suggests that these processes take place in certain strata or systems which are normally interconnected. "Conscious," "preconscious," and "unconscious" are conditions, each one of which is characteristic of a psychic process within a definite system of the psychic apparatus. Perceiving, for instance, belongs to the system consciousness (designated by the letters Cs), while recollecting, thinking, speaking, and all psychic activity ruled by the secondary process belongs to the system preconscious (Pcs); the instinctual urges and all psychic activity ruled by the primary process (displacement, condensation, etc.) belong to the system unconscious (Ucs). These systems seem stratified in such a way that Ucs is the deepest layer, Pcs is superimposed on Ucs, and Cs in turn is superimposed on Pcs. It is in reference to the notion of stratification that psychoanalytic psychology has been termed *depth psychology*. The concept of psychic systems is a hypothetical one. Freud compared the psychic systems to a succession of lenses where the systems are represented not by the lenses themselves, but by the spaces between them, where the rays of light form *images* of real objects.

We have learned that the material of the manifest dream does not, at first glance, show signs of stratification, that is, of belonging to one or another psychic system. However, closer scrutiny discloses that the various elements of the manifest dream belong to different systems. Words and logical sentences, we have learned, are *preconscious* and in most instances stem from recent experiences. Symbols belong to the system Ucs and stem from infantile and archaic sources. There appears to be a correlation between the time element and the psychic systems, as if the oldest experiences were deposited in the system Ucs and the more recent ones in the system Pcs. In the dream about childbirth, for instance, the dreamer's wish to have a baby with her father was very old, was infantile, while the wish to have a baby by her husband was a recent one. The deepest drives are usually, though not always, the oldest ones. Although the dream has means of showing to which of the systems an element belongs, it has no way to express the notion of time. The dream knows neither past nor future, only the present. However, it can represent the time element in terms of space. When the dreamer expresses an event of the past, for example, he sees himself small and the other persons tall, as if he had returned to childhood. Or when he sees people, houses, landscapes at a great distance, that signifies that all this belongs to the remote past. In the system Ucs the notion of time can thus be substituted for by the notion of space.

Since the psychic systems are interconnected, a psychic activity which begins in one system can pass over into another. There are, however, barriers erected between them. The resistances in waking life and the censor in the dream exercise a kind of control over the "gates" between the systems, which may be opened or closed when an element of one system tries to enter another system. Now, if the censor between the systems Ucs and Pcs permits unconscious psychic material to enter the system Pcs, this material changes its quality and becomes preconscious. If the preconscious material is to become conscious, it has to pass another censorship, the one between Pcs and Cs. Sensory organs, motility, and affectivity are attached to the latter system. When in waking life the preconscious material gains access to the system Cs, it is perceived and thus acquires the quality of consciousness. *It can then be discharged in action and affects.* In sleep where the motility is inhibited, the mental act cannot be discharged in action but can only be perceived as the manifest dream.

It has been stated that each mental system has its own specific quality. Let us examine this more closely. Every mental act is invested with psychic energy, it is *cathected* (this word stems from the Greek *katechein,* which means "to take possession of," "to invest with"). In the system Ucs this energy is *freely mobile,* that is, it is easily shifted from one psychic element to another, as exemplified in the mechanisms of displacement and condensation. When this energy charges or cathects an unconscious instinctual drive, this drive presses for *immediate* discharge in affects and motility. The free mobility of psychic energy together with the urge for immediate discharge of the cathected instincts in the system Ucs are the basic characteristics of the primary process, which is operative in the system Ucs only. Normally, that is, when the instincts are under control, it is difficult to observe this process.

In the system Pcs which is governed by the secondary process the psychic energy is *not* freely movable; it is bound to each specific element which it has once cathected. These psychic elements are not interchangeable as are those in the system Ucs; they are stable. Although nearer to the surface, that is, nearer to the system Cs than the unconscious elements, the elements of the preconscious have not the same urge to enter that system in order to be discharged. They can be kept in suspension and out of the system Cs; they have a choice, as it were, to stay preconscious or to become conscious.

The primary and the secondary processes have, in addition to the characteristics described above, other characteristics which will be discussed later on, as will the relation between the psychic systems and the mental structure of the personality.

The dream is an integral part of psychic life. A man's entire life may be contained in a dream as in a nutshell.

At this point we must stop, for further discussion of the dream requires familiarity with other topics. As mentioned above, this chapter is intended merely to introduce the reader to the basic problems of dream psychology.

Chapter III

THE TOPOGRAPHIC AND DYNAMIC CONCEPTION
OF THE NEUROSIS

Dream analysis has proved that for the understanding of mental processes it is not sufficient to make the distinction merely between "unconscious" and "conscious" processes. In practical work with patients it likewise becomes evident that not all unconscious processes advance on the same level; they are stratified. An example can best explain what is meant by this statement:

A woman patient, among other disorders, suffered from the obsessive fear that she would have to seduce children. The reason underlying this fear was unknown to her. She had had an older brother who had been mentally ill and who had committed suicide. After his death there were widespread rumors that he had seduced children. During treatment, long-forgotten memories recurred to the patient to the effect that at that time she had thought with horror that people might say the same of her. She remembered further that in her childhood she had really seduced her playmates into sexual "misdeeds."

These memories returned to consciousness easily after a short period of analysis; they were *preconscious*. In her obsessive fear, the patient was concerned with a repetition of what she had actually done with other children in her childhood. But the "meaning," the "why and wherefore," of the neurotic symptom was not yet explained by the recollection of the preconscious idea.

After her brother's death, the patient's behavior changed strikingly. Up to then she had tenderly loved her father, but now she began to hate him. The mother whom she had hated previously, she now began to treat with tenderness. She tried to take the place of the brother in her mother's life, since she somehow felt guilty about his death. She became listless, withdrew from contacts with people, and felt lonely. She was depressed, could not eat, and often thought of suicide. While in this state, she spontaneously had the idea that her despair stemmed from an experience she had had in her third year when she had played with the genitals of a

33

housemaid. This spontaneous memory was followed in the analysis by memories of various prohibitions on the part of her mother, the substance of which was the prohibition of infantile masturbation. In conjunction with these memories there was awakened for the first time the memory of her violent hate and intense wishes for the death of her mother in that period. She re-experienced this hatred now. Although it is impossible to report the whole case here—for the deeper the analysis goes, the more complicated it becomes—the meaning of the symptom can be deduced from even this short account. It is as though the patient wished to say: "For my infantile sexual transgressions and death wishes against the mother, I deserve to die as my brother did. But I am afraid that after my death many things will be brought to light, just as happened after my brother's death, and that the same kind of rumor will be spread about me." Without intensive analytic treatment the patient would never have discovered the meaning of her fear. This interpretation reveals both the deeper unconscious motivation and the meaning of the symptom.

In neurosis we have to deal with the same two kinds of unconscious as in the dream: one which can easily become conscious and is called *preconscious,* and the other which can become conscious through the work of interpretation, the *unconscious proper.* The individual psychic factors determining the neurotic symptom thus stem from strata belonging to various depths of the unconscious, just as the individual elements of the dream have their roots in different strata of the unconscious.

Neurosis and dream also show similarities of structure in other respects. As the dreamer is unaware of the origin and meaning of his dream images and dream sensations, so the neurotic is unaware of the origin and meaning of his symptoms. Just as the manifest dream disguises the latent dream, so the manifest symptom conceals an unconscious conflict.

As in the dream one "unconscious" element may belong to a different system than another since one may belong to the preconscious and another to the unconscious system, so the psychic determinants of neurotic symptoms are not equivalent in terms of the system to which they belong. They emerge from different psychic levels; some originate in the unconscious; others in the preconscious. Through certain characteristics, the individual elements of the dream reveal the system to which they belong; the same holds true of the neurotic symptom.

Let us now consider each system separately.

THE SYSTEM UCS (UNCONSCIOUS)

As previously stated, the unconscious is not accessible to direct observation. We can deduce its existence only from certain qualities which must be attributed to it on the basis of empirical data (for example, from the study of dreams and of neurotic patients).

The unconscious is revealed by its *content* and by its *manner of functioning*.

a) The content consists of representatives of instincts and concrete ideas or ideas of things.

What is meant by *instinct representatives?* The instinct itself cannot be observed directly. We see only its psychic manifestations, such as strivings and emotions which ally themselves with ideas and give rise to wishes. The instinct representatives are accompanied by certain changes of a motor and secretory nature and appear to us as affects. It is apparent that in every neurotic symptom a great number of instinct representatives are stored up as *affects*. Of this, every neurotic patient gives evidence. To mention but one example, we see from the analysis of the sleep ritual of the compulsive neurotic previously described that the *inner excitation* was the motive force of the symptom. The patient was conscious of a certain affect, of excitation, of a feeling of tension. But she traced the insomnia to her extreme sensitivity, since the slightest noise in the next room, every contact of her body with the covers, and a number of other things prevented her from falling asleep. The true cause of the excitation, dammed-up sexual energies, was unknown to her. The patient's confusion as to causes stems mostly from the mechanism of displacement: the affects enter consciousness in connection with ideas to which they did not originally belong. As a result, their origin and meaning remain hidden from consciousness. The patient then confuses the result with the cause.

Another example may clarify this statement:

Immediately before the onset of her illness, a woman dreamt of having sexual intercourse with her father. She awoke with anxiety. On the following day she developed a fear that her child would die of tuberculosis, like her father who had succumbed to that disease. The affect of anxiety was carried over into the waking state by the patient, but the content of the anxiety became different. In the dream there was anxiety over engaging in forbidden relations with her father; in the waking state, over her son's dying. The affect was detached from one idea and shifted to another.

As this case shows, the affect itself is by no means necessarily unconscious, but the idea is unconscious to which it originally belonged. When the affect is completely suppressed, it may follow an abnormal course, not appearing as an emotion, but exhausting itself in physical changes of innervation, such as perspiration, accelerated heartbeat, convulsions, paralyses, paresthesias, and the like. In other cases, especially in psychotic states, the affects appear without disguise. This applies particularly to catatonic attacks in the course of schizophrenia and to manic states.

Thus affects can take a "conscious" as well as an "unconscious" course; that is, they may or may not be apperceived by consciousness. In the latter case they are inhibited in their development, and are considered as only *potential* affects. In neurosis they are always more or less disguised, since their connection with the ideas to which they belong is for the most part broken. Hence the patients may consciously suffer from affects whose meaning is hidden from them. Every mentally ill person suffers from an excess of undischarged affects which have been inhibited in their development. Since affects are psychic representations of instincts, *every neurosis represents a part of the unconscious instinctual life and has a suppressed, we might better say, a repressed affect and wish as its content.*

Aside from affects, the unconscious contains the actual objects to which the affects belong as instinct representatives. The objects may be stored up in the psyche in the form of ideas, that is, memory traces of perceptions of objects and of sensations connected with them. The ideas of objects consist of ideas of things or concrete ideas, as well as of verbal ideas pertaining to them. The concrete ideas are formed through memory traces of perceptions and sensations which have entered the central nervous system by stimulation of the sensory organs of vision, taste, and smell, and of the motor and receptor apparatus, as well as through thoughts, mental images, and sensations and perceptions of the individual's own body (through visceral perceptions). All this represents a reflection or imprint in psychic life of the external and internal worlds of the individual. The verbal ideas are transmitted chiefly through the sense of hearing and are formed later than the concrete ideas. Only in the course of development does the child assimilate the words which he hears, and bring them into relationship with his ideas of things. At first the child does not understand the word and treats it as a thing. Even an adult may transform the abstract meaning of a word or thought into something concrete. This occurs most frequently in dreams and in schizophrenia. A day residue, a thought or a word which was heard, is changed into a visual image. The dreamer usually does not hear the words as such, but sees and feels them as things. The dream work arranges them in such a manner that they meet the demands of the censor. As a rule we are unable while dreaming to find the words which pertain to the unconscious things of which we dream. In their place, the more primitive ideas of the objects appear—preponderantly in pictorial form. Thus the dream hallucinates a thought, a wish.

In dreams, hallucinations are a normal phenomenon. They become a sign of illness only when they appear in the waking state. They occur in hysteria and in psychotic states. As in the dream, so in pathologic states they are a sign of regression from the verbal to the concrete— chiefly *pictorial—way of thinking and wishing.* The striving for objects does not appear in visual form alone, but also in dramatic and plastic manifestations on the body. Any posture, any sensation, may express an unconscious striving or thought. It is as if the neurotic were unable to comprehend or express his emotions and wishes in adequate words. Recall the patient with the uncontrollable vomiting: In the symptom she clung to the sexual experience yet was not able to express it in words.

Another patient had a peculiar, cutting pain in the eyeball. She remembered that many years earlier she had invented and carried on a strange play with a woman. The two women had tried to touch each other's eyeball with their eyelashes and during this contact to move the lids. Our patient felt a cutting but pleasant and sensual pain from this. To children "playing" often means masturbating. The analysis of the patient provided justification for the conclusion that the play of the two women was a masturbation substitute. Indeed, the patient's illness was chiefly characterized by vehement, uncontrollable self-reproach about masturbation. The pains which now appeared in the eyeball during the analysis were similar to those which, before the onset of the illness, she had inflicted on herself by masturbation. Thus, in the symptom there was a symbolic masturbatory gratification and, at the same time, punishment for it. She was unable to put into coherent words these two seemingly mutually exclusive strivings (for masturbatory gratification and for self-punishment) but was able to express them in a single physical sensation.

It is evident that neither of these two patients could find the words corresponding to their wishes and emotions. One expressed her wish by a motor change (vomiting) and the other by a physical sensation. Like the dreamer, those who have visual hallucinations experience their wishes and emotions in a nonverbal form. The same is true of the compulsive neurotic in so far as he is under the compulsion to carry out actions. In principle the same holds true of compulsive thinking. The thoughts conceived verbally are connected with ideas to which they do not originally belong; consequently the real meaning of the compulsive thoughts cannot be understood.

A patient, having learned that his father was an illegitimate child, began to brood over his own origin and to doubt that he was really his father's son. The doubts concerning his father did not last long. Soon they were replaced by compulsive brooding over religious problems related to the existence of God. Later he had doubts about everything conceivable. When the patient came for treatment, he no longer knew about the first phase in which he had doubts about his father. When these again became conscious, it was evident that he had been hostile toward his father. Consciously he doubted the existence of God; unconsciously he hated his father. In substance, "I doubt the existence of God" may be translated as "I hate my father." Conscious thinking is formulated in words which are correlated according to grammatical rules. Unconscious thinking is different—it knows neither words nor grammatical rules; for it to be understood, it must be translated into the language of consciousness. The conscious words "I doubt the existence of God" correspond, in the unconscious, to the hatred of the father, a concrete idea.

In the compulsive neurotic, verbal ideas are likewise disconnected from the concrete ideas to which they pertain, and are replaced by others. While in conversion hysteria, a hysterical illness characterized by physical changes, verbal ideas are not only detached from concrete ideas, but may even vanish completely, in the compulsion neurosis they are lost only inasmuch as the verbal ideas belonging to the unconscious ideas of objects are replaced by others. However, the common element in all neuroses is that the relationship of the ideas of things (objects) to the verbal ideas is impaired. Sometimes the words may be completely lost; at other times they may be exchanged for other words.

The neurotic has temporarily lost the verbal, preconscious ideas, especially those which might reveal unconscious strivings, but has retained the ideas of objects in his unconscious. In every case heretofore mentioned, the instinctual strivings certainly had an object, even though it could not be named by the patients. Since the individual derives his first conception of objects from his immediate environment, and since the neurotic, as we shall see later, to a certain extent has stopped in his development at the infantile stage, or has returned thereto, the true objects of his unconscious instinctual life are the parents or their substitutes.

It is different in psychoses, especially in schizophrenia. The schizophrenic has either *partially* or *totally* lost the unconscious objects, but not always the words. Like the dreamer, he uses the words as if they were things. The peculiarities in the speech of the schizophrenic are to be ascribed to this, just as are neologisms, corruptions, and the like, in the dream. Moreover, the speech of the schizophrenic is related to his body organs. It is dreamlike and betrays unconscious characteristics, in conformity with the system to which it belongs.

According to Dr. Edward Bibring, a woman patient of his, a schizophrenic, wants to say of her persecutor who is behind her that he is handsome; what she says is: "My behind is handsome."

In the neurosis, the affects and true objects which are the contents of the unconscious betray themselves in various ways, but chiefly in symptoms. As psychic expressions of the instincts the affects can be conscious as well as unconscious. For the most part they are conscious; in so far as they are detached from the corresponding ideas and displaced onto other ideas, their meaning is unconscious. They are also unconscious when they are inhibited in their progress to consciousness. They may appear in still other forms which will be discussed later on.

The normally close connection between preconscious verbal ideas and the unconscious ideas of things is not only loosened but often completely broken in the neurosis.

b) Since we shall discuss the preconscious separately, we now turn our attention to the working methods of the unconscious which are responsible for shaping the manifest dream. In the preceding chapter we called those methods the *primary process*. The word "primary" denotes the kind and manner of psychic activity which characterizes the first developmental stages of infancy and is replaced in later development by another process which is characteristic of more highly organized psychic activity, the *secondary process*.

In a dynamic sense, we understand by the term "primary process" the method of functioning of the unconscious. As shown in the preceding chapter, it is characterized by the ease of displacement of the psychic energies, and by condensation. The primary process means disorder and chaos in the system Ucs. The only aim of the id is to discharge its energy in motility (action) and emotions.

Displacement and condensation are easily detected in all the examples heretofore given. A case of phobia may be even more instructive.

A girl who was a musician was unable to pursue her vocation because of anxiety about entering a concert hall. In the analysis it soon became apparent that this anxiety was by no means a primary one. At an earlier period, she had felt anxiety when she stepped onto the stage, and still earlier, when she took her seat before the instrument. This anxiety could be traced back to several childhood experiences. The patient was a pronounced exhibitionist; in her daydreams and in her dreams at night she indulged in the most extravagant fantasies of nudity. The analysis revealed that the anxiety about appearing in public first of all cloaked an anxiety about *showing* herself publicly. But behind the fear, a repressed *wish* to exhibit herself was concealed. The unconscious wish to show herself naked was finally changed into anxiety about public appearances. The psychic energy, which gave motive force to the ideas of nakedness was displaced from these onto the idea of the concert hall.

The unconscious of the compulsive neurotic also makes use of displacement, but with the difference that in this type of patient there is the gradually increasing tendency for the psychic energy to be displaced onto the most trivial and meaningless things. (Exactly as in the dream, a part represents the whole.) Thereby the compulsive neurotic constantly departs further from the original idea. The compulsive neurotic previously mentioned at first had doubts about his father's legitimacy, later about the existence of God, and finally about whether he (a salesman), had made the correct selection of samples for his customers.

Condensation, on the other hand, is characteristic of conversion hysteria. The psychic energy of several strivings is concentrated in each of its symptoms. Hysterical vomiting, for instance, may express the wish to be pregnant, the wish to take the male genitals into the mouth, and at the same time, disgust at this idea. Every neurotic symptom is over-determined.

Two other phenomena are subject to the laws of the primary process: *identification* and *projection*. Both are effected through displacement; the former through displacement from the object onto the ego, the latter through displacement from the ego onto the object.

Identification, the displacement of the psychic stress from the object onto the ego, is a common psychological phenomenon. We are continually identifying ourselves with someone. Among other things, the possibility of mutual understanding and contact between people seems to be based on this. Identification is a process in which one person likens himself to another in some respect. The identification may be *total* or *partial*. It always fulfills an aim and often expresses something in common with the person with whom one is identifying. Identification will be more extensively discussed later. For the present, I shall only illustrate it by an example:

The patient who had anxiety about seducing children identified herself with her dead brother. Under the stress of his suicide, a feeling of guilt which had been latent in her for a long time was aroused. She was seized by the conviction that people would spread the same accusations about her as they had about him and that she would meet with the same fate. In likening herself to her brother, she at the same time unconsciously punished herself. This was the aim of the identification in her case.

Projection is as common a psychic phenomenon as is identification. It has a counterpart in the physiological world. For instance, a person who has undergone the amputation of a leg may have hallucinations of pain in the leg which he no longer possesses. We are constantly transposing inner processes into the outer world, for the psychic apparatus refers every perception, whatever its source, to the outside world. The mechanism of projection is developed to a very high degree in children and people in a primitive stage of development; they endow the inanimate world with human qualities. This attitude toward the world corresponds to the *animistic* conception of life in certain primitive societies. Among modern civilized people there is often a tendency to treat in this way an emotion which a person cannot acknowledge as his own. In the sphere of pathology, it is in paranoia that the main defense mechanism is projection; the person's own emotions are displaced onto the persecutor. We shall return to this theme in other connections.

In so far as his neurosis is concerned, every neurotic is under the domination of the primary process, only this is expressed differently in each form of neurosis. Thus condensation is characteristic of conversion hysteria; displacement of the compulsion neurosis; and projection of paranoia. In schizophrenia, even words undergo the primary process: they are subject to condensation and displacement, as they are in dreams. Identification appears in all neuroses. In the neuroses, however, it is only partial; while in many psychotic states, as for instance in fully developed melancholia, it is total.

The unconscious is marked by two additional characteristics which are encountered in all neuroses.

c) In the first place, *the unconscious does not know contradictions.* Just as the dreamer has no means of expressing contradictions, contentedly lets opposites exist side by side, and substitutes a *yes* for a *no,* so it is with the neurotic. The following hysterical delirium of a fulfilled wish may serve as an example of the representation of an actual experience through its opposite:

Although the patient had in reality lost a beloved person, he had the delusion that he was enjoying his companionship.

The negation of loss is not always expressed in so simple a manner. Often the patient avails himself of still other means of expression—not infrequently of identification. The lost love object then continues to live in himself.

The schizophrenic and the compulsive neurotic most frequently express a thought by its opposite. The word "no" does not exist for the unconscious. Therefore, in hysteria for example, the negative, the nonexistent, the unwanted, may be expressed only through a physical state or sensation. A hysterical paralysis frequently provides expression for an unwanted action, an anesthesia for an unwanted sensation.

d) Attention must be called, furthermore, to *omissions*. Particularly in the compulsion neurosis, a word or an association is frequently omitted so that the connection is interrupted or an idea blacked out. The meaning of the striving is then concealed from consciousness.

e) *The system Ucs has no concept of time.* It knows neither past nor future, but only the present. All strivings, even if they are connected with the past or the future, are always experienced in the unconscious as of the present. Experiences long past are still active in the unconscious, unchanged, as if they had just happened.

For example, a patient unconsciously is still having a bitter struggle with his father, who actually died eight years ago, as if the latter were still alive.

In his symptoms the neurotic always experiences, over and over again, wishes and emotions originating in an earlier period, with almost undiminished intensity.

f) The *symbolic language* of the unconscious should also be mentioned. In dreams, the censor has the function of preventing unendurable or offensive ideas from entering into consciousness. When an impulse succeeds in finding a symbolic disguise, it circumvents the censor and secures admission to consciousness. The same is true of symptoms. *Thus, in addition to its other meanings, every neurotic symptom also has a symbolic meaning.*

g) Finally, it must be emphasized that in the unconscious *external reality is replaced by inner reality*. As in the dream, external reality is replaced by inner reality, so it is on the whole in the neurosis.

As an example, a patient who was otherwise not fearful, had anxiety when by chance he had to go along a certain street. Another patient fainted when she saw a certain person. The causes of these reactions were, in the first instance, that the patient was unconsciously reminded by the street of something which actually always caused him real anxiety; in the second, the person to whom the patient reacted by fainting was unconsciously associated with another person who played an important role in her life.

An unlimited number of illustrations could be presented which justify the conclusion that *certain external experiences are only an occasion for the revival of an earlier, unconscious one.* The individual then reacts to the external and conscious experience as if it were an inner experience. The actual experience revives the internal and unconscious one; consequently the patient reacts to the unconscious experience rather than to the actual external one.

In general the neurotic is turned away from the external world and toward the inner life. We call this *introversion.* The neurotic, and in even greater degree the psychotic, acts toward and interprets the external world according to his inner strivings. But the difference between the neurotic and the psychotic consists in this: the former behaves passively and in general tries to evade the stimuli from the outer world; while the psychotic endeavors, by means of delusions, to change reality.

The neurotic's attitude toward reality can be understood from the development of the psychic apparatus. At the beginning of development, there is no clear boundary between inner and outer life. For the infant, and also to a certain degree for the primitive, they are identical. He projects what he experiences onto the outside world where he sees reflections of his own ego; these reflections are for him "realities." Indeed, reality for him is his inner life which comes to him directly through the instincts. Only later does the person learn to know and control the outer world, as well as to delimit the inner world from it by his own observations. The neurotic and even more the psychotic, in his psychic reactions to reality, regresses to the stage in which inner experience is as yet little influenced by outer events; that is, he reacts to the outer stimulus only in so far as it reflects his inner needs or experiences.

Thus, the contents and functioning of the *unconscious* psychic life are revealed in neurotic symptoms. While the healthy individual—an ideal concept, by the way—directs his thoughts in accordance with logical principles, adapts himself to reality in his behavior, and accordingly controls his unconscious emotions (to which for the most part he gives himself up without inhibition, only in dreams), the neurotic is largely powerless in the face of his unconscious. Since the unconscious psychic activity, which is the older and more primitive, is the psychic activity of the child which becomes overlaid by the conscious activity only in the course of development, the psychic life of the neurotic also has an *in-*

44 PRINCIPLES OF PSYCHOANALYSIS

fantile tinge. In so far as he is ill, his thinking is not logical; it is ruled by the primary process. He either finds no suitable verbal expression for his suppressed emotions, or finds it in a way which is not usual and which is foreign to conscious thinking. He frequently expresses his wishes and emotions dramatically and plastically through certain bodily changes and through sensations. He makes more use of symbolic language than does the healthy individual. He is ambivalent, full of conflicting feelings and ideas. To the extent that he is neurotic, he knows no concept of time, since for him the past and the future flow together in the present. In general, he is turned away from the outer world; the inner life predominates over outer experience. The psychotic even misinterprets and reconstructs the real world according to his own wishes and emotions.

This characterization of neurotics is incomplete, for additional criteria are necessary to complete the description.

THE SYSTEM Cs (CONSCIOUS)

The systemic conception of the unconscious has helped us toward a better understanding of some of the puzzling problems of neurosis. We shall advance a step further if we succeed in comprehending the relation of the system Ucs to the system Cs. First, however, we must attempt to give an account of what is to be understood by "consciousness." This is a difficult task. The act of becoming conscious means, as has already been stated, perception of a stimulus. Investigation of consciousness thus implies perception of the perceptive apparatus itself; the subject of investigation being at the same time its object. Many attempts have been made to investigate the characteristics of consciousness through self-observation, but the results of introspection are not reliable. The study of dreams, to which we owe so much insight, has more to offer. In dreams we see pictures, hear words, have sensations and feelings—in short, we perceive. In the waking state we also perceive, but the range of perceptions is more extensive than in the dream. In the dream, the stimuli perceived come exclusively from within; in the waking state, they come from the external as well as from the internal world.

The function of consciousness as an apparatus of perception is the same in the dream as in the waking state: *perception of external stimuli (sensory) and internal stimuli (psychic and visceral)*. Therefore, consciousness is to be conceived as a sense organ which is located at the boundary between the internal and external worlds, and serves for perception of both external and internal processes. A conscious idea is a fleeting phenomenon, although it may be repeated and can attract attention for a longer or shorter period.

In the waking state, the system Cs normally is turned toward the external world and by means of the sensory organs absorbs from it stimuli to which the individual reacts in a more or less adequate manner. Hence the system Cs has a close relationship to reality and operates upon the principle of *reality testing:* the ego examines whether the source of a psychic experience is internal or external. In dreams and in psychoses, this principle is suspended, and in neuroses its range is more or less restricted. If one sees things which never actually happened or commits impossible acts in dreams, this has nothing to do with reality. Likewise it has nothing to do with reality when a patient considers all his wishes fulfilled in delusions, or when a paranoiac believes he is a king, regards his environment as his subjects, and acts as if he had unlimited powers. Although the general tendency to alter the world is lacking in the neurotic, he too is dissociated from reality at one point or another. He cannot endure its harshness, certain demands which it makes upon him, and renunciations which it requires. *He escapes into illness,* into the realms of his unconscious fantasies, which are independent of the reality principle. What he perceives is in part reality modified by his unconscious strivings, in part disguised impulses and ideas from his unconscious.

An example of this is afforded by a patient, a comparatively young man, who as yet had had no normal relations with women, but suddenly fell in love with a married woman, the mother of six children. Her "motherly manner" overwhelmed him. Only with difficulty could he be convinced that in the person of this woman he was loving and idealizing his mother, from whom he had been separated when he was five years old, and whom he consciously hated. He distorted reality in conformity with his unconscious ideas and wishes.

In all the examples previously mentioned, only a *partial denial* or distortion of reality can be observed. *Complete negation of reality occurs only in psychoses. Thus the function of consciousness with respect to reality fails partially in the neuroses, totally in the psychoses.*

But why does the sick person turn away from external reality to internal or psychic reality? Certainly, since reality is often unendurable, flight from it would not always be without justification; does this imply that the unconscious is easier to tolerate? We have already learned that the nucleus of the unconscious consists of the psychic representatives of instincts. An instinct which has reached a certain intensity produces tension which exerts pressure for release. In general, tension is accompanied by unpleasure, and release from tension brings pleasure. The instinct thus strives from unpleasure toward pleasure. Its tendency toward pleasure forms wishes, the aims of which are experiences which will provide gratification. Since the instincts form the nucleus of the unconscious, the whole system Ucs is ruled by the *unpleasure-pleasure principle,* in contrast to the system Cs, in which the *reality principle* operates. The sick person who evades the influence of reality thus submits to the pleasure principle which dominates the unconscious. Some unconscious pleasurable material may enter consciousness yet not retain the pleasurable feeling tone which it had in the system Ucs; it may become unpleasurable when entering the system Cs.

Since the phenomenon of the transformation of pleasure into unpleasure in the process of changing from one psychic system to another is to be considered more exhaustively elsewhere, I shall only point out here that the unconscious has a *progressive* tendency, according to which the unconscious strivings endeavor to gain admission to the system Cs, and there to initiate motor and emotional reactions. In other words, the psychic energy accumulated in the Ucs pushes upward in order to be discharged in actions and emotions. The psychic apparatus may thus be compared to a primitive being who, upon perceiving a stimulus, makes a reflex response to it.

On the other hand, it is known that an individual does not always react to every stimulus. Sometimes very intensive stimuli are not perceived although they are directed toward the system Cs. It seems as if a special device were inserted in the system Pcpt-Cs. (The abbreviation *Pcpt-Cs* expresses the especially close relationship of the system Cs to perception.) The function of this device appears to be the protection from certain stimuli. Freud calls this device the *protective barrier against stimuli.* It is situated in the system Cs at the border between the external and internal worlds. Freud submitted the hypothesis that the entire system Pcpt-Cs, with its protective barrier against stimuli, is to be found in the cerebral cortex, which phylogenetically is situated at the border between the external and the internal world. Indeed, the central nervous system develops from the ectoderm, which at the beginning of embryologic development lies between the internal and external worlds, and only later turns inwards. Besides, the sensory organs are differentiated projections of the central nervous system, which maintain contact with the external world. An external stimulus which might perhaps be too strong for the psyche is intercepted by the protective barrier against stimuli, toned down, and then admitted to the system Cs in smaller quantities. In short, its energy is distributed economically. The protective barrier against stimuli accordingly has the ability to control quantities of psychic energy. When the protective barrier permits a stimulus to pass into the system Cs, that phenomenon is initiated which in our terminology we designate by the word "conscious." *The energy of the stimulus which enters the system leaves no traces there, but is completely spent in the act of becoming conscious. The system Cs thus has no memory. In the system Ucs the process is different. Here a stimulus leaves memory traces which may always be revived and then may enter consciousness.* Through the protective barrier against stimuli an economic distribution of the psychic energy released by the stimulus in the ego is achieved. Consequently the tension of the psychic energy is reduced to a low level of tension, thus permitting the psychic apparatus to come to a state of rest (the *Nirvana principle*). Thus the process of becoming conscious is a special case of the function of the protective barrier against stimuli, since with it a release of tension is achieved.

As the protective barrier against stimuli is situated at the outermost border of the psychic apparatus and is in intimate contact with the external world, it seems as if there had been need for protection from external stimuli only. Yet we know that great quantities of energy are stored up within the psychic apparatus which normally cannot be discharged freely. The feats of strength performed by a psychotic in a frenzy give evidence of the devastation that the unfettered energy can cause. There must, therefore, exist a protection against internal stimuli just as there is one against external stimuli.

The patient in the case of phobia already mentioned, protected herself against her exhibitionistic impulses by her fear of appearing in the concert hall. She had repressed her fantasies of nudity and instead was afraid of being looked at. The exhibitionistic impulse was projected onto the outside world. The protection was achieved by projection of an internal demand. Similarly, in paranoia, the instinctual impulse is projected and then actually exists for the patient in the outer world. The protective barrier against stimuli can perform its function with reference to internal stimuli only when they are projected and externalized.

In the majority of cases, however, as in hysteria and compulsion neurosis, the patient does not protect himself against an unacceptable drive by projection, but by inhibition. Like some external stimuli, such a drive is not admitted to the system Cs, and it then takes an unconscious course. Hence there must be a protector against the forces streaming from the interior of the psychic apparatus analogous to the protective barrier against stimuli from the external world.

THE SYSTEM PCS (PRECONSCIOUS)

Heretofore we have distinguished between two psychic systems, the unconscious and the conscious. The latter is the perceptive system and is closely related to motility and affectivity. In the course of development, however, something is interposed between these two systems which complicates the psychic apparatus. This is the *preconscious (Pcs)*. On the one hand, it contains derivatives of the unconscious; on the other, it stores up impressions from the external world. Hence it is connected with reality as well as with the unconscious. Thus, for instance, the dream makes use of an actual experience, a thought from the waking state and the like, in order to express unconscious wishes.

In order to come to a better understanding of the preconscious, we shall try to reconstruct its development. We have learned that pleasure and unpleasure are perceived and discharged in a reflex-like manner. In infancy, when the psychic organization is still very primitive, this process is regulated in the perception-discharge system (Pcpt-Cs). However, the individual is constantly subject to the influence of his environment which compels him to control and modify his reactions. At first he learns to use words, then to speak coherently; he assimilates commands and prohibitions and thus gradually becomes a member of society. In this way the external influences are internalized and deposited in a special psychic system, the preconscious, which is situated topographically between the system Cs and the system Ucs. Within this system there develops a special agency which exercises moral and logical criticism. It controls the strivings coming from the unconscious, permitting some of them to pass on into consciousness and not admitting others. In a later chapter we shall see that this agency coincides in part with the function of the superego.

In general terms this agency manifests itself as the censor in the dream, and as resistance in the neurosis, and in the mastering of our mental life in the waking state. It appears only in the course of the development of the psychic apparatus and regulates the discharge of the internal stimuli, that is, the instinctual stimuli. Thus it plays the same role with regard to internal stimuli as the protective barrier against stimuli does to external ones, but it seems to be present in two sites: at the boundary between Ucs and Pcs, and between Pcs and Cs. For instance, an unconscious emotion in the dream first appears disguised as a preconscious idea, and then it is once more transformed when it enters into consciousness. The resistance (censor) in its entirety may be compared to a protective barrier against stimuli transposed to the inside.

In neurosis, the resistance (censor, in the dream) inhibits the discharge of those unconscious drives which are repressed; that is, those which were once conscious but had to be expelled from consciousness, or those which were never conscious because they were not admitted to consciousness. The compulsive patient already mentioned exhausted his energy in constant doubts about God, which were a substitute for his hatred of his father.

In some psychotic disturbances the resistance seems to have lost its effectiveness against the onslaught of the repressed unconscious ideas, since there frequently occur discharges of energy which are so violent that the patients become dangerous to themselves and others.

Through the insertion of the system Pcs, resistances are formed within the psychic apparatus. These resistances prevent the unconscious strivings from progressing into the system Pcpt-Cs and may lead to the formation of neurotic symptoms. We shall return later to the problem of resistances, which are numerous and have various origins, as well as to the problem of repression. Here I might briefly call attention to two facts: First, not every unconscious striving may lead to neurosis, but only a repressed (warded off) one. Secondly, the strivings of the individual psychic systems may come into conflict with one another whereby we obtain some insight into the interaction of unconscious forces.

The system Pcs holds the key to the perceptive apparatus of the system Cs and its motility and affectivity. If its regulating agency fails in its function, motor, visceral and emotional reactions are disturbed. In neuroses there is then *too little* psychic energy made available for the ego (or system Cs); in psychotic states, often *too much*. While a normal person is more or less in control of his strivings and adapts his behavior to reality, this is not the case with the neurotic. He does not permit his strivings to become conscious; he is either inhibited in his emotional life or his behavior takes a wrong turn. The energy stored up within his psychic systems cannot be discharged successfully. Consequently his psychic life is marked by constant tension and unrest. The psychotic, especially the schizophrenic, frequently perceives elements from his unconscious which are not ordinarily perceived, and commits acts which threaten himself as well as others with destruction. Thus while the resistance is too vigilant in the neurosis, in some psychotic states it seems to cease to function or to be "pervious" to all energy flowing out from the internal sources.

Accordingly, the system Cs generally has little sensitivity to external stimuli in psychoses (in states of delirium, catatonic stupor) and is more or less cut off from reality; in neurosis this system is much less disturbed.

THE SECONDARY PROCESS

We have learned that the unconscious is subject to the primary process, and that the preconscious is governed by the *secondary process*. This process establishes the conception of the sequence of time, the formation of logical relationships, the filling of gaps in the train of thoughts, the introduction of the causal factor. The secondary process is at work in the waking state as well as in the dream. The better it functions, the more logical thinking is. The process of thinking is initiated by preconscious thoughts and becomes conscious only when these gain admittance to the system Cs. In dreams, the secondary process is usually in operation, for every dream is subject to a *secondary elaboration*. Indeed, the dream often contains words, thoughts, ideas, which are carried over almost unchanged from the waking state. The dream, which has previously concealed its meaning through the dream work, is made plausible to the dreamer through these additional elements and thus further disguised. The secondary process serves a similar purpose in psychic illness, as is most plainly shown in psychoses.

A schizophrenic had the delusional idea that the world was perpetually changing. People were being transformed into animals continually lower in scale until finally they would be converted into lifeless beings, which then once more would undergo transformation in reverse order into men. And so it would continue endlessly. He borrowed this idea from his knowledge of the Hindu doctrine of the transmigration of souls and the Darwinian theory of evolution which he had grafted onto his dominant unconscious fantasy, to the effect that he was able to re-create and regenerate eternally the whole world out of himself. A fantasy which appears nonsensical to conscious thinking was thus rationalized through the use of acquired knowledge.

Something quite similar, though in less absurd form, occurs in neurosis. For what neurotic does not believe he knows a reason and has an explanation for his illness, an explanation based on the knowledge acquired from everyday life? For example, the obsessional neurotic's compulsion to wash may be rationalized by the idea of the danger of infection. The information concerning infection stems from the preconscious knowledge; in the unconscious, the washing compulsion means defense against and satisfaction of certain forbidden impulses. The preconscious knowledge is thus grafted onto unconscious ideas. One has, therefore, to distinguish between what is due to the secondary process and what is intrinsic to the illness. Unconscious strivings and representations of things, that is, ideas enter consciousness by way of the preconscious. In some psychotic states, on the other hand, the unconscious strivings and ideas circumvent the system Pcs and force direct admission to the system Cs. Or else, they succeed in reaching consciousness only after the primary process has modified the preconscious thoughts and thus stopped the secondary process from functioning.

In hysteria the instinctual drives which manifest themselves in illness are usually unconscious; in compulsion neurosis and in many schizophrenias they are close to consciousness. Yet even in these two forms of illness, we cannot speak of true consciousness. Indeed, the rationalizations of the compulsive neurotic stem from preconscious material. If the compulsive neurotic rationalizes his obsession to wash, by explaining that he feels dirty, it signifies that his anal tendencies, although close to consciousness, still cannot be perceived except in disguise and as a defense. Schizophrenics are often quite manifestly perverse but rationalize the perversity with words detached from their actual meaning.

For an idea to become conscious, it is not sufficient for it simply to pass from the lower system to the next higher one. The system Cs must be cathected in order to perceive the oncoming preconscious material. In other words, this system must be sensitized for perception. Unconscious ideas can also become conscious without the help of preconscious *verbal* ideas, but with the help of tactile impressions, certain motor innervations, and so on, as is the case in the deaf-mute.

Fantasy Activity

Our auxiliary conception of the localization of psychic functions in various psychic systems furthers the understanding of neurotic phenomena. But in the interests of clarity we have proceeded somewhat too schematically. Not every psychic process can be classified without further consideration, according to this scheme, for it may belong partly to the system Pcs, partly to the system Ucs.

For instance, fantasies and daydreams may be conceived of as such mixed phenomena. To be sure, they are conscious in form, but they betray their unconscious origin not only in that they disregard reality and time, and frequently contain symbols, but also through their content. Fantasies and daydreams are common to everyone but play no important role in practical life so long as they are inactive, that is, so long as they are not cathected with psychic energy. If they receive an influx of psychic energy from unconscious instinctual drives, they become active and may express themselves in many ways. They may be acted out in daily life, they may be sublimated in artistic creations. They may also be repressed and form the *unconscious nucleus of the neurosis*. We shall explain in detail elsewhere the origin of these fantasies, their nature, and the role they play in illness.

REGRESSION

The topographical-dynamic concept of psychic life brings us closer to the understanding of another phenomenon, that of psychic *regression*. Regression is a process in which the psychic activity turns back to an earlier, lower, and simpler manner of functioning, one which it has previously surmounted. We distinguish *topographic, temporal,* and *formal* regressions. The first designation means that a psychic activity which normally proceeds in a higher system, under altered conditions recedes to a lower one. A good example is a dream or a neurotic symptom where a thought of the system Pcs is expressed in terms of the system Ucs. The second implies that a present experience, reviving an experience of the past, is felt and reacted to as if it were this experience of the past, of childhood. With this is connected the third or formal type of regression. Thoughts, for instance, are experienced pictorially or words as animated objects; the thinking process becomes archaic. One form of regression is linked with another; usually all three appear together.

Chapter IV

THE INSTINCTUAL LIFE OF THE NEUROTIC

Even a superficial investigation of the symptom of the first-mentioned patient, who suffered from nausea and vomiting, reveals that her illness was in some way related to sexuality. The sexual problem was likewise significant in the illness of the compulsive neurotic. And the phobic patient who was afraid to make a public appearance as a pianist suffered from exhibitionism. In short, whenever one investigates a patient more thoroughly, one always encounters difficulties in his sexual life. We are aware, however, that the sexuality of these sick individuals does not entirely correspond to the usual conception of sexuality. Our conception is altogether different from the general and customary one. Although many physicians admit that in certain cases sexual problems are involved, in other cases they doubt whether everything that psychoanalysis considers as sexual really is sexual. Analytic concepts are, however, based upon observations and statements of patients who, as soon as they have gained confidence in the analyst, begin to tell him about their sexual life. The uncertainty in judging whether a phenomenon is sexual or not is undoubtedly connected with the fact that the conception of sexuality in psychoanalysis differs essentially from the conventional one. The deeply rooted opinion that "sexual" is identical with "genital," a view shared by the laity and scholars alike, is erroneous, and every unprejudiced observer must recognize that the concept of sexuality does not simply coincide with the function of the genitals.

Sexual need asserts itself not only in the striving for genital union between the two sexes; it affects the whole organism and has moreover a psychic component. The concept of sexuality is much wider than has been assumed. Because it has a psychological as well as a physiological component, it would perhaps be better to call it psychosexuality. Furthermore, it is not true that sexual activity begins only with the ability to reproduce. These two functions appear at different stages of development. The first, the sexual function, begins at birth, or perhaps even during fetal life;

the second, the function of propagation, appears only with maturation of the sexual organs at puberty. Recent biological research supports this point of view. For example, Steinach has discovered in the genital glands two morphologically different constituents: the spermatogenic cells and the interstitial tissue, the former a generative, the latter a formative substance. The spermatogenic cells mature at puberty and serve the propagative function; the interstitial tissue is active from the beginning and determines the sex of the individual, and has its effect on psychological and physical development. What Freud had long since disclosed through objective research by psychological methods is now gradually confirmed through biology.

GENERAL REMARKS ABOUT THE INSTINCTS

What are we to understand by "sexual instinct"? In general terms, it is an instinct like any other and is distinguished by certain characteristics. Psychoanalysis foregoes the enumeration of a whole catalogue of possible instincts—self-preservative, nutritional, sexual, and reproductive instincts, a herd instinct, a drive for knowledge, and the like. On closer examination it is apparent that it is not necessary to list so many individual instincts. They may be divided into two large groups: the *sexual* or *life instincts* and the *destructive* or *death instincts*. The instincts are difficult to comprehend in their psychological aspects, for they are on the *border line between psychology and biology*. Thus they may be studied from two points of view, from the biological, which is the concern of the biologist, and from the psychological, which is the subject matter of our discussion. Psychological studies can naturally deal only with psychological facts and make them the starting point for their investigation. From them we derive our data concerning the nature of instincts.

The instinct as such is a biological phenomenon which has psychic representatives. Only through these can the nature of the instinct be recognized. We have learned in preceding chapters that the psychic representatives of the instincts are unconscious impulses, strivings, wishes, ideas, and fantasies, which are affectively bound up with one another. They seek to enter consciousness as preconscious material, and demand expression in action. Considered from a biological viewpoint, the instinctual forces which are active behind these representatives may be reduced to the general formula of a continuous stimulation, arising largely from changes in the hormones, products of the endocrine glands. The instinct thus represents a biological stimulus which impels the organism to certain reactions. The reaction of an individual to an outer stimulus is simple and clear: either it is accepted and assimilated in one way or another, or it is rejected through defense or flight. If the stimulus is an inner one—and an instinct is—defense or flight is not possible as with external stimuli. The simplest and most primitive reaction to such an inner stimulus is activity to bring about an adequate gratification. Thirst and hunger, for example, can be satisfied only through drinking and eating; sexual needs only through sexual activities. The instinct causes tensions within the central nervous system which spread out over the whole being; it is urgent and irresistible in nature and constantly repeats itself. So the intensity of the excitation continually increases, until it decreases after satisfaction of the instinct, the energy of which is apparently exhausted in the act of gratification. While the individual is restless and tense before this gratification, afterwards unrest, excitement and tension diminish or disappear. One no longer wishes to eat when hunger is appeased; after sexual satisfaction, one turns away from one's object, and after an outburst of rage or anger, one is exhausted and calm. In other words, after the instincts are satisfied, the individual turns away from their aims and needs; he strives for rest. After a certain time, the same process begins anew; the instinctual urge increases, the inner tension grows, the urge toward gratification becomes irresistible and, when the aim is attained, again there appears the inner emptiness and need for rest. We can also describe this perpetually repetitive process in the following manner: man strives from a state of rest, through unrest to rest again, as if the instinctual life were dominated by a *compulsion to repetition.* In the repetition compulsion is expressed the striving to repeat something previously experienced which is still burdening the psychic apparatus, until the instinctual stimulus has momentarily exhausted itself and the person can again achieve a state of rest. The repetition compulsion follows the tendency to free the psychic apparatus from disturbing instinctual stimuli, to keep it free of excitation, in a state of low tension.

This repetition compulsion, common to all instincts, permits us to understand the fact already mentioned, namely that *in every neurotic symptom an earlier state is again experienced,* that children untiringly repeat the same play, that stereotyped behavior appears in the course of certain mental diseases, and so on. The phenomenon of repetition compulsion can be compared to the inertia by which inanimate matter is ruled.

Alongside the repetition compulsion and independent of it, the *pleasure-unpleasure principle* governs instinctual life. This principle is opposed by another, the *reality principle*. If one is hungry and has no money to buy food, he might be tempted to steal in order to appease his hunger. Most people will restrain themselves, because they would otherwise come into conflict with the law and besides they may still have some hope of procuring food in other ways. Since hunger is a highly unpleasant feeling of an urgent nature, the reasons for suppressing it must be important. We have just seen what they may be: on the one hand, fear of punishment; on the other, hope for satisfaction at a later time. Thus rational motives force the individual to take into account real circumstances in relation to the desired goal, to compare the anticipated pleasure with the consequences of gratification, and if need be, to postpone its achievement. Those who can limit their striving to what is actually attainable and who know how to postpone the fulfillment of their needs or wishes are acting according to the reality principle.

We continually make such concessions to reality. This involves a delay of gratification or even its renunciation. The more completely the ego is organized, the better it is able to endure unpleasure and to evaluate the results of an action, and the freer it is in its capacity of making decisions, the more it functions according to the reality principle. Thus the reality principle serves the interest of the ego.

The pleasure-unpleasure principle, on the contrary, is in the service of the instincts, which are direct manifestations of the unconscious id. An instinct causes tensions which are accompanied by partly pleasurable and partly unpleasurable feelings. This is especially true of the sexual instinct. An erection, for example, is pleasurable and painful at the same time. With an increase of sexual excitation, the tension increases and becomes wholly unpleasurable. This condition becomes so unbearable that the individual is forced to seek release from these tensions and liberation from the painful feelings. But relaxation can be brought about only by an adequate gratification which brings pleasure at the same time. The pain of tension which accompanies the increase in the intensity of the instinctual drives changes, with the discharge, into the pleasure of relaxation. In short, the instinct strives from initial unpleasure to pleasure.

The pleasure-unpleasure principle indicates the increasing intensity of the instinctual demands and brings about the discharge of the dammed-up energy. It fulfills an important task, for it regulates the *distribution* of instinctual energy, thus becoming an economic factor in psychic life. It regulates the course of the emotional life and protects the psychic apparatus from tensions which are too great. In psychic illness, the regulatory function of this principle is disturbed.

The objection might be raised that the repetition compulsion likewise leads to exhaustion of the instinctual energies, which would eliminate the reason for distinguishing the repetition compulsion from the pleasure-unpleasure principle. But if we consider that in the repetition compulsion it is merely the striving for rest which finds expression, while the pleasure-unpleasure principle follows the tendency to avoid pain and to attain pleasure, it becomes evident that the two principles are independent of each other and that the repetition compulsion is in effect operative even "beyond the pleasure principle."

Thus two principles govern the instinctual life: the repetition compulsion and the pleasure-unpleasure principle. Where they appear in pure form, they are independent of each other and may pursue aims exclusive of one another. If an individual is controlled by the pleasure-unpleasure principle, he will always be seeking new impressions, striving for contact with others, welcoming new experiences, living for rich variety and novelty—indeed, *creating* something new. To put it briefly and in ordinary language, such an individual enjoys life in all its aspects.

If an individual is subject to the repetition compulsion, he lives in the past, repeating earlier experiences. He seeks no new sensations and avoids new impressions, preferring to repeat and cling to old ideas and reactions. He is *conservative* in every respect, while the pleasure-unpleasure principle presses toward ever new experiences, thus creating progress in life. The compulsion to repetition is resolved in a state of complete rest, not by an agreeable experience only, as is the case with the pleasure principle, but also by unpleasure.

We may thus call the instincts which are under the control of the pleasure-unpleasure principle the *life instincts,* those that seek new experiences and drive one individual to union with another, thus creating new life. They comprise the sexual instincts, whose fulfillment gives the greatest pleasure. As the sexual instincts express themselves not only in physical attraction and the creation of children but also in higher, tender love, the life instincts may well be comprehended in the wider concept of the powerful "Eros" as described by Plato. Those instincts, on the other hand, which are subject to the *pure* repetition compulsion, are averse to new experiences and are essentially conservative; since they seek the past, they work against the life instincts which strive for new experiences. They tend toward eternal rest which often finds its extreme expression in suicide. These instincts may be called *destructive or death instincts.*

There is a certain similarity between the repetition compulsion and the *law of inertia* which governs inanimate matter. This law expresses the tendency of all inorganic matter to remain in a certain stable condition or to return to this condition. In the psychic sphere, the repetition compulsion seems to correspond to this physical law, reflecting the conservative nature of certain instincts. As Freud has stated in a hypothesis based on reasoning too complex to detail here, organic matter has grown out of inorganic matter; inanimate matter has been infused with life under some unknown cosmic influence. When animate developed from inanimate matter, there remained a tendency to return to the former state of complete rest, which is identical with death. This retrogressive process is checked, however, through the sexual or life instincts, which drive toward the creation of new life. The death instincts are those which strive for the state of complete rest; the life instincts those which strive for ever new experiences, disturbing rest. As we shall see later, the death instincts may, for certain reasons, also be called the *ego instincts*.

As a rule neither life instincts nor death instincts appear in pure form, independently of each other; they are fused, and their interaction results in the phenomenon called life.

At first glance the classification of life instincts and death instincts may seem strange. Its heuristic value is inestimable, however, for it brings us closer to a comprehension of many phenomena which are completely unintelligible without it. It is thus, at the least, a very useful working hypothesis, and at present we could not get along at all without it.

THE SEXUAL INSTINCTS

Since the death instincts are not easily accessible to observation, we shall first consider the life instincts, that is, the sexual instincts.

The sexual instincts have a source, an aim, and an object. We shall not concern ourselves with the sources of the sexual instincts, since they are of an endocrine nature and are in the province of the biologist. The analyst must understand, however, that the most severe psychic disorders may arise not only from disturbances within the psychic apparatus itself, but also from even the slightest irregularities in the operation of the glands of internal secretion. Conversely, psychic disturbances can affect the internal secretions. For example, we know that psychological factors may influence menstruation, increase blood pressure, thus acting like adrenalin, increase the blood sugar content, thus disturbing the functioning of the pancreas or the liver, and so on.

Of the *impelling force* of the instincts there is likewise not much to say, for the idea of something driving and urging, and therefore active, is inherent in the very concept of the instincts. *The instinct is always active,* regardless of whether its aim is active or passive. The fact that we speak of active and passive instincts is to be ascribed only to a careless way of speaking. The sexual instinct of the male is active, but that of the female is not passive. Only her aim is passive, namely to receive the man, while his aim is active, to subjugate the woman. The aim of an instinct is to achieve gratification by means of an adequate action.

Perversions

The object and aim of the sexual instincts are not stable nor are they inseparably welded together. Normally, the object of the sexual instincts is the other sex, and their aim is the union of the genitals. But there are deviations, both in aim and in object. The fetishist, for example, can obtain his sexual gratification by means of an inanimate object; the homosexual finds it only in a person of the same sex. The sexual aim is not always attained through genital union of the two sexes with discharge of sexual substances, but may also be reached on other objects than persons of the opposite sex, through stimulation of other parts of the body than the genitals, for example, through looking, exhibiting oneself, embracing, kissing, and the like.

Within certain limits, deviation from the final sexual aim is normal. It is a preliminary activity, called *forepleasure,* and serves to increase the *final* pleasure. But if forepleasure becomes the *exclusive* form of sexual activity, then it becomes a perversion.

Descriptively, the perversion results from the separation of the sexual object from the sexual aim (sexual satisfaction need not invariably be obtained from an extraneous object); from the change of objects (satisfaction need not always be achieved from a heterosexual object; it may also be from an object of the same sex or a fetish); from deviation from the aim (the aim is not always stimulation of the genitals but also of other erotogenic zones) going beyond natural anatomical satisfactions (in which shame and disgust are overcome); and from failure to advance beyond the state of forepleasure. Perversions are to be differentiated in regard to the object and to the aim, although in actual practice no such sharp line of distinction can be drawn.

Erotogenic Zones and Component Instincts

The genital is the central sexual organ, and specific sexual gratification is obtained through its stimulation. The perversions indicate, however, that the same aim, with genital discharge, can likewise be attained through stimulation of other parts of the body. Other organs are connected with the genitals and have, in addition to their own physiological function, also a sexual function. They therefore represent erotogenic zones in which sexual impulses arise and may be satisfied by adequate stimulation. In addition to the genitals, there are many favored erotogenic zones, as for example the eyes, the mucous membrane of the mouth, the mucous membrane of the rectum. The sexual excitations which arise within these zones, or from the respective organs, are called *component instincts. The sexual instinct is not confined exclusively to the genitals; it may also have extragenital manifestations; it consists of individual component instincts.*

The Sexual Instinct and the Neurosis

After these brief explanations, there need no longer be such great uncertainty in distinguishing that which is sexual in neurotic symptoms. We are now justified in assuming that the nausea of the first patient mentioned was not merely a simple reaction to a sexual attack, for the mouth and throat are erotogenic zones which may be involved when there is sexual excitement. It cannot be a mere coincidence that the girl reacted to the sexual situation with disorders of the digestive system. Through her behavior she revealed that her digestive tract was "sexually" sensitive to a high degree. The patient who was afraid to appear in public had repressed her scoptophilia and exhibitionism. Through her anxiety she protected herself against gratification of her component instincts which were unconscious. Similarly, the other patient through her anxiety protected herself against the compulsion to seduce children sexually. Thus we see in each case that sexuality, either in the genital sense or as a component instinct, is concealed behind each symptom. *Every neurotic symptom represents a part of the suppressed sexual life of the patient.*

The Relation of Infantile Sexuality to Perversion and Neurosis

The sexual instinct, then, is more complicated than appears. The reproductive instinct and the sexual instinct are not identical, although they have a common organ, the genital, for carrying out their aim. The aim and object of the sexual instinct do not coincide. The sexual instinct consists of individual elements, the component instincts. Normally these are expended in the forepleasure (kissing, looking, touching, etc.). The component instincts are relatively undisguised in perversions; in the neuroses they are distorted. By observing children, one can easily see that their sexuality is exhausted in the function of the component instincts. In children the genital function is less developed than in adults; instead, other organs and erotogenic zones are the centers of sexual excitation. In adults, as a rule, the component instincts recede proportionately to the maturing of the genital function; if they persist in part, the genital function is reduced. For the child every fulfillment of physiological needs is accompanied by gratification of the component instincts. The sexual needs go even beyond the physiological needs. The infant sucks for pleasure even when he is not hungry; the child soils himself not only to relieve a natural need, but also in order to stimulate his anal erotogenic zone. In short, as measured by adult standards, one might say that the child's sexuality is polymorphous perverse.

This impression is further supported by the fact that children's sexual aims are independent of the object. Their aim is not to satisfy themselves through union with another object; rather, they secure pleasure by stimulating the erotogenic zones of their own body. We call this kind of satisfaction autoerotism. Since the component instincts govern the sexual life of children but disappear in the regular course of development, we cannot properly speak of "perversions" in childhood. *The manifestations of the component instincts are indeed a natural phenomenon in childhood.* However, the predominance of component instincts in an adult indicates a perversion.

As the neurotic perseveres unconsciously in his infantile sexual life or reverts to it, he is a latent pervert, although consciously he rejects any perversion. Hence we may consider the neurosis as the negative of the perversion. A brief example may be related here:

A patient came for treatment for psychic impotence, not because he himself had any desire to be cured but because he had been induced to come by his family physician and his wife. Although he had been married three years, his wife was still a virgin. He had accomplished coitus twice in his life. Once he had been compelled to do it by a woman and had performed intercourse lying on his back, thus being *passive* and unconsciously playing the feminine role. On the second occasion he fantasied that his partner was a schoolboy friend. The actual sex partner at this time was an aunt of the schoolmate with whom he had shared the same bench throughout his schooldays, and whom he had loved very much.

Thus this man who, consciously rejected every sexual activity, was given to perverse fantasies of which he was sometimes aware, but which he did not wish to recognize as disguised homosexual wishes and inclinations. Consciously he rejected any sexual striving; unconsciously he was homosexual, perverse in respect to both aim and object.

The characterization of the neurosis as a negative of a perversion is valid, however, only to a certain extent. The full perversion, as will be shown later, is as complicated as a neurotic symptom and has its own history.

The Concept of Libido

Before we go further, we must become familiar with the concept of libido. Libido is a biological concept by which we mean the energy of the sexual instincts, that is, of certain biochemical processes which are for the most part unknown. Since the sexual instincts are of a somatic nature, the concept of libido cannot be formulated in psychological terms. As the quality of the instincts has psychic representatives, so has the energy of the instincts psychic forms of expression. We speak of heterosexual and homosexual libido, of anal or sadistic libido, and the like. By this is meant the energy which is at the disposal of a specific instinct.

The libido is subject to a developmental process. In general, the sexual instincts are dependent on objects of the external world. If this were true of every phase of development, the reconstruction of libido development would be easy. But in childhood the sexual instincts are for the most part autoerotic, independent of the external world. Since, moreover, adults have a tendency to deny sexuality in children, much material of infantile sex life escapes direct observation. However, the behavior of the libido in some mental illnesses fills in this deficiency. The paranoiac, for instance, rejects the external world more or less completely; instead, he overestimates his own ego in the fashion in which usually only a beloved person is overestimated, and frequently satisfies all his component instincts in the same manner as is ordinarily seen only in small children. From this behavior we may conclude that he chooses his own ego as the object for his libido. The conduct of the libido of schizophrenics is thus similar to that of children. Upon these and other facts the hypothesis has been constructed that the libido need not always be directed toward an object in the external world but may take the ego as its object. The state in which the libido is directed toward the ego, we call *narcissistic*. Since in narcissism the ego is the object of the libido, in the narcissistic phase of development the object coincides with the subject. For this reason, this libido may also be called *ego libido*.

For a long time the sexual instinct was considered as being opposed to the ego instinct or self-preservation instinct. But with the formulation of the concept of narcissism, it was recognized that the self-preservation instinct contains a sexual component and is not always opposed to the pure sexual instincts. The self-preservation instinct is a "narcissistic" instinct whose function it is to maintain the integrity of the personality and to protect the ego from injuries *(narzisstische Kränkungen = narcissistic injuries)*.

We assume that the human being comes into the world with narcissistic libido. This kind of libido does not yet know any objects in the external world. In the course of development it gradually finds external objects, until at the end of the full sexual development it has for the most part changed into *object libido*. The complete fusion of the libido with the ego, narcissism, is a primary condition but by no means a lasting one. It represents merely a phase of development and expresses the *relationship* between the ego and the libido. Since narcissism coincides temporarily with the flowering of most of the child's component instincts which strive for autoerotic gratification, *autoerotism* is the kind of sexual gratification that is adequate in the narcissistic stage of development of the libido. After the narcissistic stage of libido development has been passed, masturbation continues but is accompanied by fantasies about objects.

Developmental Phases of Libido Organization

Since the sex glands develop from the germ plasm and since the human being comes into the world as a perfectly formed and differentiated sexual being, and since, furthermore, the sexual character is dependent on the nature of the libido, the assumption is justified that the libido begins its development during the prenatal period. While in the womb, there are no objects at the disposal of the libido; consequently we must assume that before birth there exists a unity between that which we may call the precursor of the ego and the libido, a hypothesis which is confirmed by observation of the newborn infant. Just as the individual, after birth, progresses from a state of self-containment to a condition of lively relations with the world, so too his libido strives toward objects, from the previous narcissistic state. However, it should be emphasized that a certain degree of narcissism is of necessity retained throughout life, protecting the individual from many injuries.

Directly after birth, the aim of the narcissistic libido is the autoerotic satisfaction of the component instincts. Although all the component instincts are already active in the first years of life, they govern the child's sexual life in different ways and degrees. The predominance of one or another group of component instincts imposes its stamp on the child's sexual life at each stage of libidinal development. On the basis of this predominance, two major phases may be distinguished from one another in the early years of life: first the oral, and second, the anal-sadistic phase.

The Oral Phase

In the oral phase, the libido is linked with the instincts of self-preservation, especially with the drive to eat. Since food is to be found only in the external world, one might be inclined to ascribe to the oral libido from the beginning tendencies which strive toward objects. However, it can be easily established that the infant experiences stimulation of the oral zone which is quite independent of the need for food. Without being hungry, he sucks his tongue and puts everything he can grasp into his mouth. He sucks his own hands, his toes. When he cries because of bodily discomfort, he is quiet as soon as he gets something to suck. Moreover, as is known to every infant nurse, in the first weeks after birth the infant has scarcely any relationship to the outside world; he perceives hardly anything of this world except the person who nurses him. In the first weeks he experiences bodily sensations of pain and pleasure which he reveals to others by crying, screaming, smiling and the like. Just as his own body is a source of pleasure to the infant, so is his mother's breast. But he is not yet able to localize these sources in space. He does not yet differentiate between stimuli from the outer world and sensations from within. Hence at first the mother's breast, although an object in the external world, is conceived of as belonging to the ego. Since, in this first period of life, an object of the outer world (the mother's breast) virtually coincides with the ego, this first phase of libido organization has no object; it is narcissistic. The distinction between internal and external worlds begins when the child has had repeated experiences in which discomfort has been relieved and changed into pleasure through an object (the mother's breast). Accordingly, it is the instincts of self-preservation which first bring the individual into pleasurable contact with the outer world. As a result of the primary union of the libido with the ego, these instincts are strongly charged with sexual energy from the very beginning.

They strive toward the external world because their gratification is dependent upon it. However, since for the child this world does not yet exist as clearly separate from himself, the libido remains attached to the ego.

But the child soon becomes acquainted with deprivation; he no longer receives the breast at every expression of discomfort. Consequently there results a damming up of libido which is accompanied by feelings of tension and unpleasure. These feelings force the libido away from the narcissistic position toward an object in the outer world, determined by the need for food. Since, however, not all of the libido stored up in the ego can be completely gratified by taking food, the excess of libido seems to become independent of the process of nourishment. Moreover, the infant has other libidinal needs aside from food, as for instance, seeing, touching, hearing the mother. Hence the narcissistic tie of the libido to the ego is loosened in favor of strivings toward an object which is not associated with the need for food. When the muscular development has reached the point where coordinated movements can be carried out, these strivings are satisfied when the child *takes hold* of the object. Even the act of sucking is performed with the striated musculature of the oral apparatus: first the infant clings to the mother's breast by sucking, and as soon as he has teeth, he bites and wounds the breast. Thus there is the tendency to incorporate the breast, to "eat it up." The oral phase of libido organization, in which the desired object is "destroyed," is called *cannibalistic*. The first desires, therefore, are stilled by the "destruction" of the pleasure-giving object which, though only intimated, is yet psychically *real*. We find traces of this phase in the customs of many savage tribes and also in the unconscious thoughts and feelings of modern civilized peoples; for example in the figure of speech, "I'd like to eat you up," we encounter remnants of the oral phase of libido organization.

Another factor at the beginning of development favors the striving toward an object: the child is *helpless*. The child must therefore either be cared for by the mother or some mother substitute, or perish. The child experiences numerous stimuli in being cared for (in being kept dry, bathed, cleaned); through this care he comes into contact with a person who gives him love. He returns this love, when for instance, he clings to the mother, smiles at her, and so on. The child attaches himself to the mother and longs for her. If she does not respond, he cries; if she comes to him, he is happy.

Thus from the first there are two factors which lead the libido toward objects: first, the dual function of many organs, through which a physiological need and a component instinct of the corresponding erotogenic zone may be satisfied simultaneously; second, the child's helplessness, which gives rise to the need to turn to the person who takes care of him.

Although in the oral phase, the pleasure-giving object is incorporated and destroyed, yet there already exist, in embryonic form, the preliminary conditions which in the course of normal development must lead to finding objects in the outside world.

The Anal-Sadistic Phase

Certain elements of the oral phase of libido organization form a transition to the following phase, the anal-sadistic one. The infant sucks with the help of the musculature of the mouth. Thus at the beginning of extrauterine life the first instinctual needs are satisfied with the aid of muscular action in the region of the head. In fact, from the very beginning, the muscles are the implements of the instincts. As early as the oral phase, the infant tries to help himself while sucking by holding onto his mother's breast with his tiny hands. As the muscles of the extremities and the torso gradually develop and as sucking ceases to be the only method of obtaining food, the muscular system begins to serve other instincts besides the oral ones. Now the child not only tries to touch every object in order to put it into his mouth, but also seeks to grasp, to hold, and to destroy it. He develops toward the outside world an unmistakably aggressive attitude. In the oral phase, every desired object was "destroyed" through eating; now the child takes the object into his possession or even destroys it through muscular action. Although this aggression does not yet have the characteristics of the later sadism, it will soon develop into sadism. While the aggressive tendencies govern the child's psychic life, the anal zone becomes very active. The child obtains pleasure from the stimulation of the rectal mucous membrane and adjacent parts of the body. The function of the terminal part of the intestines is now exceedingly pleasurable, just as the entrance to the digestive tract was in the oral phase.

Through holding back the feces as well as through frequent evacuation, the rectal mucous membrane and the surrounding parts of the buttocks are stimulated and serve to give pleasure. The developmental phase of the libido in which the function of evacuation and the tendency toward aggression are highly charged with sexual strivings is called the *anal-sadistic phase*. It ends in the second or third year of life.

In these first two developmental phases of the libido, the oral and the anal-sadistic, the genitals play no role worth mentioning as a sexual organ. For this reason, this whole developmental period may be called the *pregenital* phase of libido organization.

The Phallic Organization

As early as in the nursing period, the excitability of the genitals as an erotogenic zone sets in. Through stimulation of his genital the child obtains pleasure, the infantile masturbation observed by unprejudiced pediatricians and nurses. However, the genitals attain their specific importance only when the first two phases have been more or less surmounted and the genitals become the leading sexual zone. As the individual erotogenic zones slowly lose their sexual excitability, in normal development it passes over to the genitals. The component instincts are absorbed by the genitals and integrated into a higher unity in the genital function (*amphimixis*, according to Ferenczi). After puberty the residues of the earlier developmental phases find expression in preparatory activities, that is, in forepleasure such as looking, touching, embracing, kissing. They serve merely to stimulate the genital strivings, achieving final satisfaction through genital discharge. Thus the genitals become the *central organ for discharging the entire libido.* In childhood, however, orgasm in the adult sense does not occur, since the production of seminal fluid and, of course, ejaculation are still lacking. Sexual excitation is gratified through masturbation and finds its culmination, in the boy, in the secretion of mucous from the urethral glands, and probably in vaginal secretions in the girl.

The phase of libido organization in which the genitalia through absorption of the component instincts become the central sexual organ begins in about the third year of life and lasts into the fifth or sixth year; it is called the *phallic* phase.

The reason for calling it the phallic phase is that in boys the penis develops as the leading sexual zone, and in girls, the clitoris, which is analogous to the male organ. In this phase there thus exists for both sexes only *one* organ, the male organ, the penis. At first the boy actually knows only one sexual organ, his own, which he esteems very highly as the site of the greatest source of pleasure. He therefore attributes a penis to all other living beings including women, and even to inanimate objects. In this phase his sexual drives are discharged in genital masturbation; his sexual strivings now have a decidedly active, masculine character.

It is less clearly evident what the parallel relationships are in girls. The clitoris is an organ analogous to the penis in the evolutionary sense. Therefore, it may be assumed that it is the seat of similar sexual sensations. In the infantile-genital phase, the girl masturbates with the clitoris. Thus she too passes through a "phallic" phase but it lasts for only a short time. During this period her sexuality is active, resembling masculine sexuality. Since her "male" organ, the clitoris, represents merely a rudimentary penis, the "masculine" strivings of girls never reach the same intensity as do those of boys. Still another circumstance contributes to the checking of her "masculine" strivings. As I have been able to ascertain from analyses, in early childhood many girls masturbate at the vulva. One of my female patients described a fantasy which had developed between her fourth and fifth years, that a bottle was screwed into her genitals. In this fantasy the "bottle" was a penis-breast symbol.[1] It seems that sexual sensations in the vulva compete with those in the clitoris, and therefore from the beginning tend to inhibit the "masculine" (clitoral) sensations of girls. However, it must be emphasized that the girl does not yet have any clear idea of the genital orifice; she confuses it with the rectal opening and with the mouth. Just as there is a tendency for an erect phallus to push into a cavity, so there is the tendency for a cavity— and such are the vagina, the anus, and the mouth—to receive something. The masculine aim is active; the feminine aim is passive. Activity or passivity thus also is determined by the anatomical structure of the reproductive organs.

The boy likewise for a long time knows nothing of the existence of separate sexual and anal openings in women; even many adult men have no clear conception of anatomical facts. In addition, in the male child the genital sensations seem to be fused with anal, that is, with cavity sensations. Thus in childhood the sexual life of the boy is permeated by impulses with a passive aim, as that of girls is with active ones. But the passive aim preponderates over the active one in girls, while the opposite is the case in boys. (The concepts of activity and passivity will be discussed more fully later on.) Thus the biological bisexual anlage in both sexes may still be clearly recognized during the phallic phase. This insight derived from psychic behavior appears to be in accord with recent research in the field of endocrinology which has discovered a male hormone in the female ovary, and a female hormone in the male.

---

[1] This fantasy, however, may have been produced by artificial stimulation. As an infant, the patient had acquired a genital infection, and for years was treated with irrigations by a physician.

Bisexuality persists throughout life. It is more pronounced in childhood and puberty than in maturity; if development is normal it becomes
invisible in later life. It is often concealed behind friendship, social activities, and the like. If heterosexual activities are for some reason blocked,
homosexual strivings automatically appear. The flaring up of homosexuality in the army or in prisons is commonly known. In symptoms of
neurotic illness, a homosexual component is almost always found to be
present.

The Oedipus Complex

In the phallic phase, the child for the first time selects a clearly defined
sexual object. His sexual feelings are now coupled with images of this
object; fantasies about it accompany his masturbation. This gives rise to
his early conflicts. Conflicts do not, however, set in suddenly, nor do they
appear for the first time in the phallic phase. The first conflict is experienced by the child when his voracious demands are kept within certain
limits by the mother or nurse, and later when he is trained to cleanliness
and encounters opposition to his aggressiveness. *These* conflicts, however,
arise chiefly through opposition to the outside world, while the "sexual"
conflict of the phallic phase arises without sufficient external cause. It
develops by itself, as it were, from within, apparently primed by a
hereditary factor. In the course of countless generations it has apparently
changed from a real, external conflict to an inner, psychic one.

This conflict belongs to the sphere of the so-called *oedipus complex*.
The designation "oedipus complex" is adopted from the stirring legend
which relates that Oedipus killed his father, married his mother and had
children with her. For this he was severely punished by the gods. What is
recounted in this ancient legend was once reality; today it is repeated in
fantasy only as a psychic attitude. The period between the third and
fifth years of life is the time in which the oedipus complex attains its
climax. The simplest and most schematic form of the oedipus complex
consists of the boy's loving his mother and hating his father. If the boy
only hated his father and did not at the same time love him—that is, if
there were no bisexual anlage—the conflict would be less complicated.
It could then be expressed in overt hostility against the father and thus
become a purely external conflict. Actually, however, it is not merely the
boy's fear of his father, but just precisely his ambivalent attitude toward
him which intensifies the conflict and provides the most important basis
for the development of the oedipus complex.

The oedipus complex is a *psychic configuration* which arises in a certain developmental period and later on abates. All attempts to minimize or deny its importance must fail in face of the facts.

The oedipus complex has several forms. We differentiate between two main forms—a *complete* and an *inverted oedipus complex*. The complete oedipus complex may be positive or negative. In the complete positive form, the mother is loved, and the father, whose place the boy usurps in fantasy, is done away with. In the inverted form, the mother is hated, the father is loved. The *simple, positive* form is rare. In the neuroses we find a great variety of combinations. The oedipus complex forms the *unconscious nucleus of all neuroses,* around which all the other complexes and fantasies revolve. It would be tempting to describe specific forms of the oedipus complex as characteristic of each type of neurosis. Thus far, however, we are not able to do this, for firstly, its development in each individual case is not yet sufficiently clear, and secondly, individual forms of the oedipus complex cannot always be clearly differentiated from each other, since there are also mixed forms. One gets the impression that in some cases the oedipus complex was normal in the beginning (simple, positive form) but that at an early age it was driven into other paths and changed into an abnormal form retaining some attitudes from the preceding period. I have been able to observe this most clearly in cases where love for the mother was transformed into hatred when, for example, the boy had been disappointed in her. This resulted in an inverted oedipus attitude out of which there ultimately developed a turning away from women toward men, that is, one type of homosexuality. The boy may also identify with his mother and in this way come to love his father. Normally, however, the boy identifies with the father; the girl, with the mother. The result of these identifications is a strengthening of masculinity for the boy and of femininity for the girl. It is not quite clear how it happens that there is identification at one time with the parent of the same sex, at another time with the parent of the opposite sex. It is assumed that a constitutional factor forms the biological basis for bisexuality, at one time exerting pressure toward identification in the direction of the masculine, at another time of the feminine strivings. In any case, *the contents and form of the neurosis bear the stamp of the form of the oedipus complex.* In other common variations of the oedipus complex there appear substitutes for the parents, such as nurses or older siblings, upon whom all the strivings of the primary oedipus complex are focused.

One might assume that the oedipus complex should not develop in children who at a very early age have lost one or both parents. But experience shows that in such cases the child creates parents in his fantasy and develops the attitude of the oedipus complex toward these fantasy figures. For instance, if the child has no father, he creates a father in fantasy to whom he attributes almost god-like qualities. If the father is alive but a weak person, then it frequently occurs that the child seeks out some firm man and substitutes him in his fantasy for his own weak father. In similar ways, the child may fantasy the so-called "family romance," which has as its leitmotif his origin from other, usually more distinguished, parents. This same theme also appears in fairy tales in manifold variations.

In another context it will be shown how the oedipus complex is mastered. Here we merely state, in conclusion, that in the succeeding period of sexual development, the latency period, the oedipus complex becomes more or less dormant, flaring up again with the increase of libido at puberty. Then there develops a severe conflict with the mature sexual instincts, and later psychic health or illness depends upon the outcome of this conflict.

The Castration Complex

In the phallic phase, the instinctual life is further complicated by a new factor. As a reaction to the incest wish implied in the oedipus complex, there arises the fear of losing the penis. The ideas centered around this fear and the emotions linked with them are called the *castration complex*. In addition to the castration fear (fear of losing the penis), there may also exist a wish to lose the penis, even a feeling that it has been lost, hence we differentiate between an *active* and a *passive* castration complex.

Weaning and the evacuation of feces may be considered as precursors of the castration complex. Since in the first developmental period the mother's breast appears to the nursing infant as a part of his own body, it can easily be conceived that withdrawing the breast (weaning) is experienced by the infant as a loss of a part of himself. This supposition is confirmed when one analyzes patients who have been weaned late, at about three years of age. In fact, such children experience the withdrawal of the mother's breast as a loss and a lasting injury to the ego. The same is true of evacuation of feces, except that the contents of the intestines actually pertain to the ego, whereas the mother's breast pertains to it in a psychic sense only. The experience of these and other losses prepares the ground for the idea of the loss of the penis, the castration complex. Indeed, it sometimes happens that birth, the separation from the mother, *in retrospect* is *fantasied* as "castration."

Some authors consider all these real or fantasied losses equal to *true* genital castration. If the concept of the castration complex is thus extended, its specific significance is completely lost. Most certainly, in the unconscious, a single similarity, even a very slight one, is sufficient to cause the substitution of one set of ideas for another. For example, the loss of an object, a trifling injury and the like, may, in the unconscious, have the meaning of castration. But these injuries are merely used by the unconscious as *representations* of castration. If the concept of the castration complex is not to become meaningless, it must be understood in the genital sense, even though castration may be symbolically expressed by many different losses and injuries, as for example, by the cutting of the umbilical cord.

The child discharges the sexual strivings of the oedipus complex in masturbation. This preoccupation with the genital often evokes a threat from someone in the environment that the genital will be lost. Usually the threat of castration comes from a female who takes care of the child; however, she may add weight to the threat by asserting that the father will punish him. At first this threat may make no impression on the boy. Later on when he has actually made the observation that a girl has no penis, the old threat is revived. It seems, however, that this individual experience is not even required to activate the castration complex. For there was a stage in the history of mankind when castration was carried out symbolically in religious rites immediately after birth or at puberty, and there are even now peoples who still adhere to such customs. The castration complex seems to be inherited, just as the oedipus complex is.

The castration complex finds fertile soil in the child's interest in the difference between the sexes. At first the boy regards every human being as masculine, believes that everyone has a penis. He is greatly disappointed when he finds out that a girl has no penis. He believes then that she has been castrated—and when he is under the influence of an actual castration threat or the spontaneous awakening of the castration complex— fears that the same may happen to him. He cannot, in any event, reconcile himself to the idea that even his mother has no penis. He therefore develops the fantasy that an adult woman has a penis concealed in her body (the fantasy of the "phallic mother"). If he fails to relinquish this hermaphroditic conception of women, he will experience disappointments in them in later life and will reject them as sexual objects. Another frequent result of the awareness that women have no penis is contempt for women. The boy, out of pride in his possession of a penis, regards the girl as an inferior creature. It may, however, also happen that, as a consequence of the bisexual anlage, the boy accepts castration. This occurs if the feminine passive inclinations prevail. In this case, he has *feelings of inferiority* which severely impair his masculinity; he may become feminine, homosexual and passive. (The castration complex is, of course, by no means the only source of inferiority feelings.) On the other hand, the same underlying attitude may lead to an overcompensation of the disturbed masculinity. Then the boy is excessively proud and defiant and protests in every conceivable way against the castration which he imagines threatens him.

If the boy accepts the idea of the "castrated mother," he may develop pity for her, and gallantry. Recently a patient reported this charming story: When she was somewhat depressed one day, her seven-year-old son tried to comfort her by saying: "Don't worry, I will give you my penis."

In girls, the castration complex is called *penis envy*. In order to compensate for her lack of a penis, the girl either fantasies that she possesses a penis, or believes that it has been cut off but will grow again later. Most women see in the bleeding of menstruation, proof of their previous "castration" and are very much distressed by this idea. Just as the boy's acceptance of castration is the most important basis for his feelings of inferiority, so the woman also feels inferior, if she is not able to give up her penis envy. If she rebels against the supposed castration, she develops the so-called "masculinity complex" and behaves, in many respects, like a man. Just as the boy through acceptance of "castration" becomes feminine, so through rebellion against "castration" the girl becomes masculine. Normally, however, the girl gives up the wish for a penis, and it is replaced by the wish for a child.

Thus any disturbance at the phallic phase will decisively influence the child's attitude toward his genitals. If the castration complex has not yet appeared, it will be activated; if it is already in existence, then the child responds with attitudes and fantasies which stem from it. The way in which the child masters his infantile sexuality and deals with his castration complex will be decisive for his health and character. If this complex is not overcome, it will play an important role in the structure of the neurosis. Although it is not represented in the same way in every neurosis, we encounter it in every neurosis since it plays a significant part in symptom formation.

Fantasies

The question of sex differences, which is crystallized in the castration complex, is closely related to still another question which troubles the child, i.e., the question of the origin of human beings. The child's preoccupation with these problems is called *infantile sexual investigation* or curiosity. The ideas which children elaborate regarding birth, are quite varied. In their birth fantasies they try to satisfy their infantile sexual curiosity, to answer the troubling questions in their own way. In the phallic phase, the most frequent birth fantasy is the "water theory." (The fable that the stork brings the baby from the pond is a variation of this theory.[2]) This fantasy is associated with urination, since in the phallic phase urination plays an important part in sexual gratification.

Most children doubt the stork fable, and yet, unable to form any accurate conception about the circumstances of birth, they elaborate numerous variations of birth fantasies, according to their age and predisposition. If the oral component of sexual development is especially developed, then the conception of birth through the mouth will evolve. This conception is expressed even in some religious rites. If the anal disposition is particularly strong, the idea that the baby is born through the anus will predominate. As mentioned above, the child does not yet know that there is a special sexual opening in addition to the anal aperture; he thinks they coincide (the cloaca theory of the female genitals and of birth). Some individuals adhere to such theories as these until about puberty or even later. These theories also express themselves in the contents of the neuroses.

Fantasies in childhood are numerous and varied. Individual fantasies differ inasmuch as they are dependent on actual experiences. However, among them there are typical fantasies with which the child, according to his predisposition, reacts to certain experiences. To this group, for example, belong the previously mentioned "family romance," as well as the fantasy of "the mother with the penis." Besides, we know there are fantasies for which no real experiences provide a basis. They develop, as it were, by themselves; they are inherited and are therefore called *"primal fantasies."* It makes no difference to the unconscious whether an experience is real or not. A fantasy, too, is an experience. In the majority of cases, however, certain real experiences are woven into the fantasies and then form the individual basis for the primal fantasies. It frequently

2 The fable of the stork solves the child's curiosity about birth as well as the castration complex. In the fable, the stork brings the baby from the pond and bites the mother in the leg. If water is a symbol of the mother's womb (amniotic fluid), and if "bitten in the leg" means a symbolic castration, then the child's answer to the questions about the origin of man and the difference of the sexes would be: the child is born by castration of the mother.

happens that an event experienced years before is not worked into a fantasy until long afterwards.

We have already learned of certain primal fantasies like those of castration or birth. To this class also belong the fantasy of *overhearing parental coitus*, the fantasy of *being seduced by an adult*, and the *mother's womb fantasy*.

Concerning the first, a great many children actually have had an opportunity to witness parental intercourse. But some patients who certainly could never have observed parental intercourse report it as a memory.

Such "memories" are revealed, by analysis, as fantasies which belong to the group of primal fantasies just mentioned. The same is true of the memory of seduction by an older person. Many children have really suffered a trauma of this sort, but many who have not believe they have had such an experience. That the womb fantasy can hardly correspond to an actual memory requires no further proof.

Why such fantasies are formed is in itself a problem. The fantasy about seduction by an older person may perhaps originate in an unconscious memory of the child's early experiences when he was cared for by an adult. Through this care by his mother or nurse, the child is stimulated over and over again; his mouth, his sense of smell, his buttocks, skin, and genitalia are excited. All these stimulations are experienced in a passive way. When this bodily care is gradually discontinued, the child longs for the renewal of the pleasurable experiences. In creating the fantasy he repeats them and gratifies his infantile sexual need.

The fantasy of overhearing parental intercourse possibly has its source in "infantile sexual investigation." Supported by infantile sexual curiosity, these fantasies may perhaps appear more intensively in instances where the curiosity finds no satisfaction whatsoever in reality. The origin and meaning of the womb fantasy seem to be still more complex. Certain factors are especially effective here, factors which are also operative in the other fantasies. Their meaning is manifold: longing for the mother, escape from the difficulties of life by returning to her, identification with the mother (in the boy, a driving force toward homosexuality), sexual curiosity, and the like.

In considering all these fantasies, one cannot fail to recognize that they arise where a real satisfaction is lacking. The need itself creates its satisfaction in the form of fantasies, which in the unconscious are just as real as an external experience. In other words, if a need is not met by a real experience, the individual procures this experience in fantasy.

The necessary experience is not one selected at random, but is always fully determined, corresponding to the phase of development of the libido organization at the time. Each libidinal phase has its own means of expression, its own language. The infantile need of each developmental phase obtains adequate expression in its particular fantasy. Since infantile psychic life is part of the unconscious, the fantasy offers a means of expression for unconscious strivings and wishes. If these infantile unconscious fantasies are preserved and become active in later life, then they play a part in neurotic symptoms by supplying the material for their unconscious contents.

The Period of Sexual Latency

At the beginning of the fourth or fifth year, the sexual development of the child is interrupted. Sexual life enters a period of rest, which is called the *latency period*. There is no absolute latency, since this phase of "second childhood" is interrupted now and then by sexual feelings, even in normal development, but in general it is a time during which the child is spared the involvements of sexuality, and the instinctual energies are used for building up the ego. This period is characterized by defense against sexual feelings and a struggle against masturbation which is carried on in a manner suggesting the ceremonial in compulsion neurosis. At the same time a partial resolution of the oedipus complex leads to the formation of the psychic agency called "superego" and the establishment of aesthetic and ethical standards. Besides, efforts at mastery of and adaptation to the external world become apparent. In other words, in the latency period the sexual energies are diverted to other, nonsexual aims; they are sublimated. There will be an opportunity later to say more about sublimation.

Thus, normally the latency period is to a certain extent "asexual." However, as previously stated, there are children who enjoy this period of rest in a limited measure only. This applies especially to children who are predisposed to neurosis. They are sexually precocious, "nervous" or "naughty." They carry on their infantile sexuality in the form of masturbation, in mutual looking and exhibiting, in unrestrained sexual investigations and the like, or else in reaction formations which the educator commonly considers bad behavior, and finally in manifestations of illness, such as difficulties in eating, enuresis, anxiety, nightmares (pavor nocturnus), and in other forms which are frank neuroses. From all of this it appears that *every adult neurosis has an infantile prototype.*

THE INSTINCTUAL LIFE OF THE NEUROTIC

The infantile neurosis supplies the matrix, as it were, for the neurosis of the adult.

It is not a normal phenomenon when the child is disturbed by *excessively* strong sexual feelings during the latency period. The child has entered a period of his life in which he is in need of rest, and if he is continually stimulated he cannot master his sexual desires because of the immaturity of his ego. However, this does not imply that such children will necessarily become neurotics, for their faulty sexual development may be remedied during puberty.[3]

Puberty

The latency period lasts approximately from the sixth to the tenth or eleventh year of life. About this time, prepuberty begins; puberty itself starts at about the fourteenth year.

With the beginning of puberty at a time when the reproductive faculty also matures, the sexual development of early childhood is repeated in condensed form and the oedipus complex is reactivated. The infantile sexual aims, however, are abandoned; in both sexes there follows the final differentiation into masculine and feminine. The girl renounces her masculinity, the clitoris loses its excitability; the boy finally overcomes his castration anxiety. Both sexes abandon the sexual objects of the oedipus complex and are now free to choose nonincestuous objects. The component instincts now lead only to forepleasure which is preparatory to the sexual act. In a word, the *genitals assume exclusive leadership (primacy) in sexual life and at the same time become the organ for the carrying out of the reproductive instinct.* Since the reproductive instinct is now an integral part of the sexual instinct (Eros), the preservation of the species appears guaranteed. Although the psychological conditions for reproduction, in the form of wishes for a child, are already present in both sexes in early childhood, satisfaction of the reproductive instinct is impossible before puberty since the biological conditions are lacking. The sexual instinct, on the other hand, can be satisfied earlier, before puberty, through masturbation. Only in puberty

3 In the latency period, at least two major divisions can be discerned: (1) from five to eight years, (2) from eight to ten years. The first period is characterized by defenses against genital and pregenital impulses as well as by increased ambivalence. Reaction formations against pregenital impulses initiate certain character traits. In the second period the ego is exposed to fewer conflicts. It is devoted to a greater extent to the task of coping with reality, and there is less temptation to masturbatory activity. (See Berta Bornstein, "On Latency." *The Psychoanalytic Study of the Child*, Vol. VI. New York: International Universities Press, 1951.)

do both instincts attain their full maturity and unite into a single striving, directed toward the same aim.

The duration of puberty differs with race, social conditions, and individual disposition. It may cover a very short or a very long period. A protraction of puberty is to be observed in individuals who have difficulty in adapting themselves to reality, for instance in some types with asocial behavior.

If, because of environmental or inner psychic reasons, the individual at puberty does not succeed in outgrowing the oedipus attitude, in giving up the component instincts, and in following the primacy of the genitals in sexual life, then the most varied disturbances of the love life arise. Homosexual impulses which almost regularly appear in puberty may become fixated and persist throughout life. If the component instincts have not receded, they remain in the form of perversions. All types of impotence for the most part make their appearance directly after puberty. The majority of neuroses and psychoses start at puberty. It may also happen, however, that pubertal development is apparently accomplished successfully, yet illness breaks out later. But then a thorough investigation of the patient's past always shows either that because of inner reasons puberty did not run its course as smoothly as it had seemed, or that the development underwent severe disturbance from external causes.

Naturally, the more normal the sexual development has been the more easily puberty runs its course. Nevertheless, there is considerable evidence that faulty sexual development in childhood can be compensated for by a strong influx of libido at puberty.

The diphasic onset of sexuality occurs only in the human being, and has important consequences for his later development. In the latency period sexual life more or less comes to a stand-still. The ego begins to become organized, raises barriers against the emergence of sexual feelings, and seeks to resolve the oedipus complex. In puberty, the powerful advance of sexuality threatens to destroy all these gains of the ego which meanwhile has become intolerant toward the crude sexual emotions. It defends itself against the onrush of instincts, struggles with the urge to masturbate which reappears in puberty, as well as with the fantasies associated with it. Thus there is a severe conflict between the demands of the ego and those of the instinctual life. Health or illness depends upon the outcome of this conflict. There are, in addition, other difficulties which are to be considered as precipitates of developmental disturbances from all the three earlier stages of sexual organization.

If the stored-up strivings originating in the pregenital phases go beyond a certain intensity and assert themselves in puberty, they are even more vehemently rejected than the genital strivings which are now reaching maturity.[4]

Developmental Disturbances of the Sexual Instinct

The disturbances of sexual life are based on the fact that a striving of an earlier developmental phase appears in a later one, becomes predominant, and strives for autonomous gratification. In these instances, we are concerned with infantile strivings which take effect either at puberty or later, with the onset of illness. The developmental disturbance may have an effect on the instinct itself or on the individual's attitude to the object of the instinct; usually, however, both disturbances are coupled together.

It is evident that all these disturbances of infantile sexuality will not have identical consequences for further development. Disturbances in the genital phase will influence the development of instinctual life and the

---

[4] A more comprehensive presentation of the problems of puberty may be found in the extremely lucid book by Anna Freud, *The Ego and the Mechanisms of Defense* (New York: International Universities Press, 1946). Here I should like to call attention to two forms of defense characteristic of puberty as presented by Miss Freud: (1) *Asceticism.* The adolescent may alternately indulge in instinctual excesses and repudiate vehemently any instinctual need. In this latter phase he renounces all gratifications, denies himself any pleasure that life may offer him. In case this asceticism is not given up, the adolescent may appear psychotic, pseudo schizophrenic, or may even actually become psychotic. Miss Freud stresses the fact that there exists a definite antagonism between the sexual instincts and the strivings of the ego which appears to be of a constitutional, inherited nature. If that is the case, then "the asceticism of puberty must be interpreted . . . as a manifestation of the innate hostility between the ego and the instincts . . ." (p. 172). (2) *Intellectualization.* With the increase of instinctual energy in puberty, the adolescent becomes not only more moral and ascetic but also more intellectual. His intellectual interests are keen, many-sided, and yet seem to satisfy some kind of fantasies. Adolescent thinking seems to correspond to daydreaming on an intellectual level. The adolescent apparently tries to solve the conflicts between instincts, conscience and reality by overintellectualization, that is, by speculating about love and hate, life and death, politics, the social order. Miss Freud says: "This intellectualization of instinctual life, the attempt to lay hold on the instinctual processes by connecting them with ideas which can be dealt with in consciousness, is one of the most general, earliest and most necessary acquirements of the human ego . . . . it means that the intensification of intellectuality during adolescence—and perhaps, too, the very marked advance in intellectual understanding of psychic processes which is always characteristic of an access of psychic disease—is simply part of the ego's customary endeavour to master the instincts by means of thought. . . . The focussing of the intellect on instinctual processes is analogous to the alertness which the human ego has found to be necessary in the face of the objective dangers which surround it" (p. 178).

form of the illness in different ways than will disturbances in the pre-genital phases. And a disturbance in the oral phase will cause a different course of illness than will a disturbance in the anal-sadistic phase. These disturbances may be called forth by an accidental experience, that is, by an external factor, or by inhibitions in development, an inner factor. In both instances, the child's sexual behavior depends on the developmental phase of the libido; that is, the child will react in a manner characteristic of the phase of his libido organization at the time. The reaction patterns which then appear for the first time may be retained throughout life and influence the form of illness. Every neurosis receives its specific traits from the way in which the ego reacts to the instincts.

An instinct once gratified has the tendency to repeat itself. This tendency is just one of the manifestations of the repetition compulsion, with which we have already become familiar. In disturbances of instinctual life, the repetition compulsion is one of the factors which causes the phenomenon called *fixation* (of instincts). It is based on the tenacity characteristic of the instincts, that is, on their adherence to a definite kind of gratification if its intensity has either exceeded the degree adequate for the individual or has lasted longer than usual. Every psychically ill person suffers from fixations.

In the anal-sadistic phase, the child reacts to sexual stimuli with anal-sadistic impulses, wishes, and fantasies. If for any reason he becomes fixated at this stage of libido organization, these reactions are continued throughout life. They will also take part in the formation of the character as well as the development and content of the neurosis. For example, one of the typical reactions to developmental disturbances in this phase is the fantasy of being beaten, particularly on the buttocks. Such fantasies are subject to numerous transformations, exercise a decisive influence on the sexual life of the mature person, and have a characteristic expression in the neurosis. If, for instance, the child in the anal-sadistic phase of development has a chance to observe coitus, or if the sadistic tendencies predominate in him *a priori,* then he will form a conception of violent and cruel sexual intercourse, which not only may lead to sadism but also may invest his whole character with a harsh, cruel note. Under the dominance of the anal component, the child will retain the so-called "cloacal theory," the idea that the sexual opening in both sexes coincides with the anal opening, and will cling to the theory that children are born through the rectum. After puberty, the boy will show a preference for the buttocks of his sexual object; his perineal region will be especially sensitive; he will have a passive-femine attitude, in contrast to the boy who develops sensitivity of the glans penis, which urges him to activity. Usually, the anal and sadistic strivings do not appear in such pure form, but rather in mixed forms.

This is by no means an exhaustive enumeration of the disorders of the anal-sadistic phase and their consequences. I have merely indicated that fixations at one of the developmental phases of the libido may bring about manifold variations in psychic behavior. Analogous changes can result from disturbances in the oral or cannibalistic phase of libido development. Their traces and the fixations of this phase are equally well characterized by certain reactions and behavior patterns. The oral zone will then acquire the meaning of a "sexual organ," unconsciously in the neurosis, consciously in perversions. Numerous fantasies are developed, such as oral impregnation and birth fantasies, fantasies of children being eaten by the parents, especially by the father, as in myths, and many more. Special emphasis is placed on the female breasts in the object choice. Cannibalistic fantasies may appear, disturbances of eating and swallowing in illnesses of a hysterical type, refusals of food in illnesses of depressive character, voracity and so on.

In a previous connection, we have emphasized that the sexual energies are easily displaced and may be directed toward other, nonsexual aims (sublimation). With disturbances of the sexual life, the ability to sublimate is more or less lost, but the sexual libido as such is often displaced onto other nonsexual organs or functions, thus sexualizing them. In the discussion of the development of the sexual instinct, we have learned that the erotogenic zones lose their sexual excitability and displace it onto the genitals. In certain disorders of the genital stage, the libido takes a reverse course. If the ego rejects the genital strivings, they disappear from consciousness. They are retained in the unconscious, to be sure, but their energy is displaced onto other, nonsexual parts or organs of the body; the earlier erotogenic zones are again invested with libido. In such instances, the genital more or less loses its position as the central sexual organ; in its place other parts of the body or organs acquire heightened sexual, especially *genital* significance. This kind of displacement is characteristic of conversion hysteria. In this connection I might refer to the girl with the symptom of vomiting. She was confronted with unexpected sexual demands. Normally two reactions would have been possible: the girl would either have yielded to the man or refused him and run away from him. But she chose something different: vomiting. In all similar cases, analysis reveals with complete uniformity that behind such symptoms there are concealed unconscious sexual fantasies in which the mouth and throat play the role of the genitals. The vomiting expressed disgust which was aroused by the unconscious wish to take the male genital into the mouth. In such cases, the sexual sensations in the genitals are prevented from entering consciousness, but other parts of the body are unconsciously erotized instead; the *sexual excitation is displaced from below to above,* so that the organ which is erotized plays the role of a genital.

How is this process to be understood? It is typical of the hysterical person that his genital strivings are not admitted to consciousness and are shut off from their normal paths of discharge. There results an accumulation of libido, which causes unpleasant tensions. In order to avoid these tensions, the libido is withdrawn from the genitals and takes possession of a nonsexual but predisposed organ (in our patient, the throat), here to be discharged in an incomplete and, for an adult, inadequate manner. Not only is the sexual significance of the genitals displaced to another organ, but this organ itself takes on genital qualities. This process of displacement of genital libido we call *genitalization.*

Such a genitalized organ is then disturbed in its specific physiological function. *Disturbance in the distribution of libido thus leads to a disturbance in the function of a nonsexual organ.*

In hypochondria, an illness which appears especially at the beginning of schizophrenia, the damming up of libido in the organs gives rise to unpleasurable sensations, just as erection causes unpleasurable tensions, which however simultaneously bring pleasure. The difference between a conversion-hysterical and a hypochondriacal symptom consists in the fact that the fantasies concealed behind the hysterical symptom are directed toward an object of the external world, while in hypochondria the object of the fantasy is the person's own body, specifically the organ which arouses feelings of unpleasure and anxiety. Probably in a similar way, through an accumulation of libido in the organs, some of the organic illnesses develop.[5]

The displacement of the total libido may not only take place in the sphere of the body but also may extend to higher psychic functions, which likewise become erotized through displacement. This applies to the ideational and thought processes of the compulsion neurotic, the speech of the schizophrenic, and the like.

If a component instinct proves to be especially resistant and does not participate in the general development toward genital organization, its

[5] At the time of this English edition, they would probably be called psychosomatic neuroses or psychoses.

energy is imparted to the genital function which meanwhile has developed. There are individuals who perceive sexual excitation first in the anus, or in the mouth, or as an urge to urinate, and only gradually in the genitals. In some cases, however, the extragenital excitations may be so intense that they are exceedingly detrimental to normal sexual relationships. For example, in the history of those who suffer from *ejaculatio praecox* we frequently find enuresis mentioned, which represents an infantile form of sexual satisfaction, "urethral erotism." In *ejaculatio retardata*, on the other hand, anal strivings inhibit the discharge of semen. Thus the component instincts may establish the path for the genital function or inhibit it to a certain degree. Again in other cases, the sexual relationship can be consummated only with the help of fantasies belonging to the pregenital stages, the sadistic, anal, oral. If these are conscious, they border on perversions; if they are unconscious, they form an integral part of the neurosis.

As previously stated, not only can the genital libido be displaced onto higher psychic functions, but also the component instincts can invade nonsexual psychic regions and disturb their functions. In a speech disorder of schizophrenia, coprolalia, words are played with as if they were feces. Stuttering is a speech disorder which in most instances arises through a displacement of anal libido onto the throat and mouth and onto the act of word forming. The following short illustration will show on what remote regions the pregenital libido can encroach.

A patient had difficulty in following her vocation; she would stop short while playing the piano. Analysis revealed that it had happened first while she was playing a certain "trill"; she had become disturbed, anxious, confused, and had to stop playing. This trill was of a type called a "bouncing trill." Her father was a man of strong anal disposition, a very unrestrained person who often "broke wind" in the presence of his children and differentiated it according to its key and timbre. The kind of flatus which delighted him most he called "bouncing trill." The patient was strongly fixated on her father; it came about that in her early childhood she thought of coitus in terms of anal functions. The fantasies based on these ideas disturbed her unconsciously when she played the piano.

One might have the impression that those parts of the instinct which were disturbed in their development continued to be just as intense after the fixation had occurred as they had been before that point and that they obtruded into the illness which broke out at a later time. We have already learned that this is not always the case, since, as a rule, those component instincts which are constitutionally very strong or those which do not partake of the general development of the instincts are rejected by the ego. If the subsequent defense against the rejected instinct is not successful, the child as well as the adult reacts with anxiety or with other neurotic symptoms, since the ego cannot tolerate those instincts. It is, on the other hand, also possible that these morbid disturbances of childhood will be overcome, yet flare up again at puberty for a very short period, and then disappear forever. If, however, an illness breaks out after the earlier phases of libidinal organization have been overcome, the instincts which were previously at rest and apparently mastered, are reactivated. The instinctual life of the ill person returns to an earlier phase of development. This phenomenon we have already noted as "regression". We will gain understanding of it, however, only after having discussed the relations of the instincts to objects as well as the relation of the sexual (life) instincts to the destructive, or death instincts.

THE DESTRUCTIVE INSTINCTS

It has been comparatively easy to gain insight into the behavior of the life-preserving sexual instincts; in their striving to unite with another individual they are clamorous. The destructive instincts work in the opposite direction; they do not strive for objects, they are silent, they operate within the personality. Their manifestations, therefore, are less accessible to observation than those of the sexual instincts. Nevertheless, there is one representative of the destructive instincts that is accessible to observation, namely sadism. The objection might immediately be raised that sadism cannot be considered a representative of the death instinct, for in the first place, sadism is undoubtedly accompanied by libidinal strivings; and secondly, the external world, not the sadistic individual himself, is destroyed by sadism. The first objection is justified in so far as sadism hardly ever appears as an isolated drive but is fused with sexual instincts. The second objection carries more weight, since it can be refuted only on the basis of inductive reasoning, hence indirectly. The very fact, though, that there are illnesses in whose course the individual works toward his own destruction with irresistible force gives considerable support to the assumption of primary death instincts.

The danger of suicide in melancholia is well known. In religious ecstasies and catatonic states, self-mutilation not infrequently occurs; the patients develop a destructive fury directed against their own person which seems uncanny to the observer. Besides these extreme cases, there are relatively milder manifestations including those whose fate it is always to fail and to be unhappy. It is as if they were under the spell of a demonic power which compels them to choose over and over again what must bring them failure or even destruction. Let us recall our assumption that the infant, in the first months of his life, does not feel the mother's breast as a foreign body, that he "eats" it and incorporates it; destroys it, as it were. Let us, furthermore, recall the fact that the infant does the same with parts of his own body—he stuffs his hands and his toes into his mouth, he sucks them and gnaws at them. In view of these facts, a primary tendency for self-destruction lies within the realm of probability. According to Freud, this tendency is a biological one which is operative even in the monocellular organism, but which becomes clearly perceptible only in multicellular ones. Freud calls this deeply hidden but always operative destructive instinct *primal masochism.*

What is the relationship between primal masochism and sadism? We have assumed that at the beginning of development the libido is bound to the ego as primary narcissism. The concept of the death instincts calls for a further assumption, that primal masochism likewise has the ego as its object. The individual, in his first phase of development, thus appears to be under the influence of two opposing groups of instincts. The destructive instincts, however, do not always operate in a pure state in opposition to the life instincts, for they may also enter into union with the narcissistic libido stored up in the ego. Thereby the death instinct acquires an erotic tinge, becomes pleasurable, and changes into *actual masochism.*

We have stated at several points that every living being strives toward eternal rest, toward death, as it were. This striving for rest, however, can be disturbed by two factors: by internal or by external stimuli. The reaction to such a disturbance of rest may be very violent. Often a person who is awakened from deep sleep flies into a rage; an infant disturbed in his rest will cry, scream, and kick. A schizophrenic in catatonic stupor very frequently reacts to stimuli from the external world with outbursts of rage and fury which may lead to the destruction of everything within reach. Thus there are conditions in which every external stimulus is painful and is warded off by *destruction.* This tendency of the ego toward warding off stimuli persists throughout life. In the course of development it first gradually diminishes, but in the later, declining part of life it again increases; it manifests itself in the *conservative,* rejecting attitude toward new impressions and experiences. It seems, therefore, as if the human being, from the very beginning of his existence were on the defensive against stimuli from the external world, with aggression aiming at the destruction of this world.

But the state of rest is disturbed also from within, through the increase of libido. Libido then strives away from narcissism toward the objects of the external world. As soon as the narcissistic libido begins to change into object libido and to seek objects in the outer world, it apparently deflects the destructive instinct from the ego. The aim of the new form of aggression and destruction is no longer only defense against external stimuli, but in contrast to this, also contact with the objects. Destruction and aggression thus acquire a libidinal component. They are, consequently, another manifestation of primal masochism which has been projected into the external world. Aggression now appears in relation to the libidinal objects as sadism. Every object of the libido is at the same time under the influence of sadistic strivings. Hence sadism might be looked upon as masochism *projected* into the external world.

Just as the genital is the organ for the carrying out of the mature sexual instincts, so the *striated* musculature of the extremities and the trunk is the instrument of sadism. It is difficult to determine whether masochism likewise employs this instrument. If, however, we take into consideration the fact that there are conditions in which for instance through a spasm of certain blood vessels inner organs die, then the smooth musculature appears also to be one of the instruments of masochism.

A female patient suffered from attacks of "dying off" of her fingers (Raynaud's disease). They would become pale, anesthetic, and extremely painful. Apparently there was spasm of the blood vessels supplying the fingers. The patient also suffered from disturbances in defecation. While defecating, she would suddenly feel a cramp in the anus; the feces would either remain in the rectum or would be cut off. During menstruation she had pain and the feeling that her blood could not flow because the feces were stopping up her anal or vaginal cavity. (She was unable to distinguish between the two cavities; she evidently clung to the cloacal theory.) If she had a stool, then her menstruation was ample and painless. She fantasied that her anus (or her vagina) was enclosed by barbed wire and that in her first coitus the man's penis would be caught there and cut off and would remain in her anus. Then, in her fantasy, she felt compassion for the man and thought of all possible ways of saving him. This fantasy was so real to her that she had cold water and a towel prepared on her wedding night, to stanch the man's bleeding.

Further analysis revealed that her fingers symbolically represented the penis. Besides, she called her fingers "sausages" (in the sense of sausages of feces), which shows that she also identified them with the fecal mass. The "numbed" fingers, in the patient's unconscious, represented both the wedged-in penis and the cut-off column of feces.

The spasm of the intestinal musculature thus had been displaced onto the walls of the blood vessels of the fingers. The processes at the end of the intestinal tract had been replaced by processes in the peripheral parts of the body, with the aim of destroying the organ. The destruction was accomplished here, as in other cases that I have had the opportunity to observe, by means of the smooth musculature, through a spasm of this musculature. According to Freud, sadism as a representative of the destructive or death instincts is dependent on the functioning of the musculature. It makes no difference whether the voluntary, striated muscular system or the involuntary, smooth one is involved. (Besides, the striated musculature of the mouth apparatus is continuous with the smooth musculature of the intestinal tract.)

As our case shows, if the smooth musculature within the body is affected by sadism, it transmits its excitation to the peripheral musculature. The processes then occurring at the periphery appear to represent some kind of an autotomy whose prototype is the anal ejection. According to Abraham, ejection may also coincide with destruction (in our case the periodic "dying off" of the fingers would correspond to the tendency to ejection).

The Relation of the Destructive Instincts to the Phases of Libido Organization

The destructive instinct is already operative in the oral phase where the gratification of hunger coincides with the annihilation of the coveted objects. This phase, therefore, has been termed *cannibalistic*. Every increase of libido in this phase causes, in the first place, a state of tension in the erotogenic zone of the mouth. This tension is felt by the ego as a disturber of rest. Since the ego can perceive inner stimuli only through projection, the libidinal stimulus tension is transposed into the external world and identified with the nursing mother's breast. In this phase, the mother's breast is *a priori* the object of libido. The cause of the disturbance of rest seems to be transposed into the external world where the object itself actually is. If this source of stimuli is destroyed, the condition of rest which is always sought after, is restored. The peace-disturbing, unpleasant, as it were "hostile" external world subjectively ceases to exist, and the libido returns to the ego until the next increase in tension. Thus, at the beginning of development, *relations to the external world are regulated through the destructive instincts, which strive to keep all stimuli away from the ego.*

During the anal-sadistic phase which follows, the child is no longer dependent upon the oral apparatus alone to destroy the unpleasant object or to incorporate the desired one. In the musculature of the trunk and the extremities he possesses an apparatus which enables him to fulfill both tasks. He becomes *active* and *aggressive*. The child wishes, on the one hand, to destroy the object; on the other, to take possession of it. In this phase, in which the erotogenic character of the anal zone is still predominant, the child is better able to express a feeling of possession by retaining the feces than through muscular actions of his extremities. It is difficult for the person who is caring for the child to exercise any influence upon the child's function of elimination; that is to say, that whenever he himself wishes to do so, the child puts into action the sphincters and the necessary abdominal muscles. The child in his own wordless, unconscious language is able in this way to assert his own will and to express what he is willing to retain and what he is willing to give away. At this phase, indeed, children are accessible to love only to a slight degree. In general they are very difficult to train, as all their emotions of love are accompanied by aggressive impulses which are expressed in defiant rejection of the external world.

The instinctual life of the child during the first two phases of the sexual organization is determined in part by the destructive instincts.

As the destructive tendencies express themselves differently during the oral phase than during the anal-sadistic one, so they also express themselves in a different manner during the infantile-genital or phallic phase. Destroying, annihilating, and inflicting pain, are coupled with pleasurable genital sensations. *The sadism of the earlier phases now becomes genital.* We may call its previous forms pregenital. In the genital phase, sadism in the form of hatred appears for the first time in contrast to love. However, where the course of development is normal, the sadism (and hate) soon becomes restricted by love, and what remains of the sadism is only the activity required for taking possession of the object. Embracing, for example, is a variety of this activity.

Ambivalence

According to what has just been said, one might believe that during the first phases of development the destructive instincts are the only ones that are operative. But this is not the case, for the positive, sexual instincts also are striving for activity. The infant desires the mother's breast, not only to free himself by the act of sucking from the unpleasurable tension caused by a stimulus, but also in order to experience pleasure through the closest contact with the object which gratifies the stimulus. That the object, after fulfilling its task, psychically ceases to exist for the infant is perhaps due to the fact that at this age only one active organ, the oral apparatus, exists for both libidinal and aggressive strivings. In a single act two opposing instinctual aims are gratified. *At all stages of development we encounter such a contrast of the instinctual aims. This contrast is called "ambivalence".* In the oral phase, it seems to appear *united in one act.* Abraham, however, differentiated one further preambivalent, purely sucking, oral phase. But it seems to me that we are not yet prepared to make such exact demarcations.

The anal-sadistic phase is the one in which ambivalence is most evident. Here every libidinal desire coincides with aggression and the will to destroy; every positive impulse is accompanied by a negative one, to such an extent that frequently the positive impulse can appear only in the form of the opposite, for instance, beating has the meaning of "loving." In the next phase, the infantile-genital or phallic phase, ambivalence expresses itself in the existence, side by side, of the opposites, love and hate. Not only is the emotional life split in two, but also concepts and ideas are accompanied by their negatives. At the genital phase of development, the contrast of life and death instincts reflects itself in love and hate. If hate, or rather its primitive precursor, destruction, is an expression of rejection of the external world, then the meaning of love, or rather of its precursor, libidinal craving, can consist only in the tendency to draw the desired and pleasure-giving object as close to the ego as possible. Destruction and hate are reactions of unpleasure to stimuli of the external world and lead to repulsion and removal of the objects. Sexual yearnings and love are, on the other hand, pleasurable reactions and lead to drawing close, holding to the object, and uniting with it.

Reduced to its most essential feature, ambivalence reflects the tendency toward the rejection as well as toward the acceptance of the external world.

Development of Object Choice and Restriction of Aggression
(Fusion of Instincts)

Each phase of development of the libido has a psychic equivalent. The psychic precipitate of the oral phase is called *identification*.

In the chapter on the dream it was indicated that sleep represents a return to the mother's womb, and that with birth an instinct to sleep arises, an instinct to reunite with the mother from whom the newborn infant has just been separated. Identification seems likewise to represent a tendency to reunite with the mother.

The first reunion of the newborn with his mother is brought about through the act of sucking at her breast, and is coupled with hunger. This first reunion is a physical process. If the child does not get the breast when he needs it, he sucks his fingers, probably hallucinating the breast. Then we may say that he identifies his own finger with his mother's breast. His finger is part of himself and at the same time it is for him the mother's breast. Thus identification is considered a psychic derivative of infantile oral activity.

If we could speak of "object choice" in this early stage of infancy, we would say that the first object choice is an *anaclitic* one, in which the individual leans on another object for gratification of hunger, bodily needs, for protection, and the like. All these needs, in early childhood, can be satisfied by the mother or nurse. The child's needs bring him into closest contact with the mother; child and mother form an almost complete union. Consequently the object (mother) is psychically merged with the ego. As a result the ego acquires more and more characteristics of the object; in this way the first foundations are laid for future influence and training.

Thus the first tie of the child with the mother, the first object relation, in a sense, takes the form of identification. And, indeed, later on it is often difficult to discern the difference between object relation and identification. The only criterion is the fact that love expresses the wish to *have* the object; identification, the wish to *be* the object.

Identification may be a subject identification or an object identification. That is, either the subject changes according to the pattern of the object, or the object changes according to the pattern of the self. In the latter case, we speak of it as *projection*. Indeed, it is at times difficult to differentiate between identification and projection. There are situations in which object relations, identifications, and projections may be confused.

The choice of the object of identification depends on the sexual anlage. Normally, the boy identifies later with the father, and the girl retains her identification with the mother. Crosswise identifications after puberty lead to homosexuality in both sexes.

Identification is *ambivalent;* it carries positive feelings for an object as well as negative ones. "To be like" can express love as well as hate; one would like to resemble an object at one time out of love, at another time out of hate, out of the wish to replace it, or to resemble it for both reasons together. In other constellations, one may wish to possess the objects in order to love or in order to destroy it.

There are other roots of identification, aside from the oral one: the eye, the nose as the organ of smell, the ear, and so on. By means of the eye the pleasure-giving mother is perceived; tactile stimuli on the skin during body care are perceived; when the infant sucks at the mother's breast, he smells her, he *inhales* her odor (on a higher level, this may be transformed into spiritual identification; the "spirit" and "in-spiration" play rather a large role in the fantasies of mankind.) The identification through the ear is likewise very important: the child repeats his mother's and father's words and then takes over their commands and prohibitions. Indeed, auditory identifications (through speech) become the main basis of the superego, as will be shown in a later chapter. Although the stimuli affecting all these sense organs may, at times, be unpleasurable, they are still in part pleasurable, and for this reason are sought for. (The human being "sucks" in the environment with all his pores in a manner yet unknown.)

The memory traces of these perceptions become fused with the pleasure-giving person who has been taken into the ego by identification. There then arises in the ego, from innumerable memory traces of perceptions and feelings, a composite picture of a pleasure-giving person who demands that the child restrict aggression and control excretory function. Through the libidinal relationship with an object of the external world (the nursing person) the child first learns to know his environment and to renounce part of his aggression.

In the oral phase, the relation to the external world is expressed by identification, an ambivalent process. In the anal-sadistic phase, the ambivalence is even stronger. The relationship to the external world is expressed mostly in anal and destructive terms. The destructiveness stemming from the oral phase is augmented by the development of the musculature and the child's ability to walk. Almost anything within the child's reach is destroyed. The excretory function, too, now enters into the relationship with an object. The feces are either retained as an expression of self-assertion, stubbornness, and spite, or they are yielded as a sign of love and compliance. Retaining or yielding the feces thus becomes a means of dominating the person who is taking care of the child. As in the oral phase the unpleasurable is eliminated by vomiting, so in the anal-sadistic phase, it is eliminated, ejected in the act of defecation. The anal product, the excrements, though a part of the child's body with which it likes to play, is nevertheless at the same time considered a foreign, animated object. "Feces are not a corpse, they are a 'living being,'" said one patient. Some children are afraid of the feces, as if they contained a danger. We learn from adult patients and from folklore that this "danger" consists of ghosts, of the devil threatening the subject. These fears seem to be precursors of a later persecution mania. If we take into consideration that the destructive instincts are at first operative internally as masochism, and later become diverted toward the external world as sadism, we may conclude that sadism is projected masochism; in other words, projection is first visible in the anal-sadistic phase.

Some children also fear that they will lose a part of their body with the evacuation of feces. In his anal and muscular activities the child expresses not only aggression but also sexual pleasure. With the passage through the rectum—an erotogenic zone—the scyballum becomes libidinized and is felt as a sexual organ. Thus the fear of losing feces may be considered a precursor of the later castration fear. In the anal-sadistic phase, the anal as well as the motor activities are certainly highly libidinized. Therefore, from their activities in these spheres of the body children derive sexual, that is to say, pregenital pleasure.

Inasmuch as the aggressive instincts become progressively more fused with the libidinal ones, the child learns to control his sadism as well as his anality. The destructive strivings are still better mastered in the next phase, the phallic one, in which a further step is taken in the direction of adaptation to the environment. Though identification is still continued in this phase, the boy's libidinal relationship to the objects is chiefly characterized by projection since he equips with a penis the woman that is his libidinal object in the external world. The boy's own genitalia become intensely cathected with libido and identified with the ego. In this phase, the girl's relations to objects are determined by her penis envy. In her wish to have a penis like a boy, she identifies with him. At the end of this phase, she gives up this identification and develops the wish for a child.

This developmental phase in which the objects of the external world are cathected with libido only in so far as they actually or in fantasy possess the same genitalia as the subject, or resemble him, is a narcissistic one. The object of the external world is a reflection of the subject (animism). I might mention here that children like to look into the pupils of a beloved person's eyes and discover, with pleasure and wonderment, their own image there.

The transition from the anal-sadistic to the phallic phase seems to be facilitated by projection and to be effected by gradual displacement of the libido from the feces to the penis. What remains of the oral and anal-sadistic elements of the preceding phases, merges with the genitals. These become the dominant and leading erotogenic zone.

In the genital (phallic) phase the object is desired by the derivatives of all the component instincts—oral, anal, sadistic and so on. At first the object was incorporated by the ego through identification; finally it is found again in the external world as a reflection of the ego. Since in the phallic phase a part of the ego is projected and found in the loved object, this type of object choice is predominantly narcissistic.

Toward the end of the phallic phase, the narcissistic attitude toward the object becomes more and more restricted. The object is recognized as an independent being, is endowed with but a small amount of narcissistic libido, and desired for itself. Also the positive striving toward the object is much less opposed by negative strivings. Every thought and every wish revolves around the newly found object, in order to gratify through this object the sensual and tender feelings. Love emerges which only then brings to consciousness the existence of the contrast between the feelings of love and hate. "Love" in the earlier phases was *partial* (Abraham), not only because it was mixed with opposing emotions, but also because the object was merely desired by component instincts; furthermore, not the whole object, but only a certain part of it, was yearned for. Bibring's investigations also prove that at first the object comes into relationship with the erotogenic zones and is emotionally and associatively bound to them. (*Not* the *mother but* the mother's *breast* is desired with the *mouth.*) At the phallic phase, on the other hand, the love is *total,* because the whole object is striven for with the *entire libido* which is concentrated in the genital strivings.

In observing the development of object choice, one notices that the destructive instincts and hatred gradually recede in favor of love, Eros. Ambivalence, the manifest expression of the simultaneous negation and affirmation of the objects of the external world, decreases slowly to give way finally to a more or less unified, positive attitude toward the loved objects.

During the libido's earlier stages of organization, the sexual instincts are not yet fused with the destructive instincts; and the destructive instincts predominate; therefore true object choice cannot occur. In the genital phase, the two kinds of instincts are fused, and therefore object choice and love are no longer obstructed. Love is derived from the transformed sexual instincts; hatred from sadism. Hatred originates from an earlier phase of instinct life; love from a later one. Love means the overcoming of sadism. It is evident that both groups of instincts which first appear separately and work in opposition to each other, in the course of development lose much of their contrast and even form unions with each other. Freud calls this process the *fusion of instincts*.

As a result of this process, whose nature is still entirely unknown, the *destructive instincts, if not completely paralyzed by the sexual instincts, are to a great extent restrained by them.*

After the restriction of the instincts of destruction through Eros, there are still many difficulties in the love life which have to be overcome. These consist in the working over or assimilating of the oedipus complex and of the castration complex. In both these complexes the life and death instincts cross each other.

The "love object" of the boy in the oral phase is the mother's breast; in the anal-sadistic as well as in the genital phase, it is again the mother. But in each of these phases she is desired with different component instincts, and the more highly the sexuality is organized, the more many-sided and yet unified the object becomes. The love object for the boy always remains the mother; actually she is rediscovered in each successive phase of development. In the phallic phase, all sensual strivings are concentrated in the genitals, and in masturbation they are brought into relationship with the mother. The incestuous attitude toward the mother is, however, complicated by bisexuality and the relation to the father.

The bisexual anlage, as previously stated, is determined by heredity. The boy feels drawn toward the father as well as toward the mother. The relation to the father, however, is ambivalent; love is mixed with hate. The ambivalence is further increased by jealousy, because the father is felt as a rival. At the height of the infantile-genital phase, the entire oedipus complex appears, comprising unlimited love for the mother and an ambivalent attitude toward the father. In the oedipus complex, love and hate thus meet; love instincts and death instincts cross each other's paths. The conflict within the oedipus constellation becomes intensified through the castration complex, which has meanwhile appeared. This complex, as previously emphasized, is inherited and flares up spontaneously at the moment when the genital strivings threaten to endanger the existence of the family. The consequences of the castration complex are significant for the further development of the boy. The threat to the genitals involves a danger to the entire person, since the genitals are narcissistically prized and identified with the ego. By renouncing the function of the genitals, the boy saves both the genitals and the ego which is identified with them.

The second motive for the renunciation of the genital strivings lies in the dual nature of the oedipus complex which is both *active* and *passive*. Yielding to the heterosexual impulses, the boy wishes to take the place of his father, in order to possess his mother; or else, pursuing his homosexual attitude, he wishes to occupy the place of the mother in order to be loved by the father. Both kinds of sexual gratification are again opposed by the narcissistic evaluation of the genitals. In the first case the boy would be exposed to the danger of castration by his rival; in the second, he would have to accept the feminine role and resign himself to the lack of a penis. In order not to expose the genitals to danger, he prefers to renounce his *incestuous striving for the mother*. His heterosexual strivings are obstructed, as it were, and the libido is dammed up. From the analyses of adults we know, however, that the blocking of libido is not well tolerated and that the libido always seeks to find an outlet when difficulties stand in its way. The libido evades its original aim, searches for new paths, and seeks to gratify itself there, where it is attracted. At the moment when the boy begins to renounce gratification through the mother, the direction of his libido is set forth. It strives toward the father, for he not only hates but also loves him. Thus the tendency arises to gratify his homosexual love through his father. But the consequences of this gratification would be very serious for him, since if his father should accept him as a sexual object, he would become like his mother, castrated and feminine.

Now, the castration complex, as well as the oedipus complex, is both active and passive. Besides castration anxiety, there exists a wish for castration. The wish for castration, which in fact corresponds to a passive masochistic striving, is at the service of the homosexual inclination toward the father. The boy wishes, perhaps, to be a woman, to be castrated. This is in direct contradiction to the character of masculinity. The boy who has developed normally is opposed to the wish for castration and the passive feminine role. Castration anxiety wins predominance and becomes so intense that he also renounces his libidinal strivings toward the father. His instinctual life is now as follows: the unambiguous libidinal strivings toward the mother as well as the ambivalent ones toward the father are blocked and are apparently unable to find a way out. As we have already emphasized and shall discuss in more detail later, the libido is always able to find a way out whenever it is denied gratification. It returns to earlier developmental phases, *regresses* and, in order to attain its aims, reactivates old paths that have already been abandoned. As the boy's attitude toward the father is ambivalent, and since love and hatred may find gratification in one single act with the aid of identification, the boy has recourse to identification which, although it reaches its zenith at the oral phase, yet does not completely disappear later. *In short, the boy identifies himself with his father.* In this way he gets psychic gratification through him, not only libidinally because he comes in contact with him, but also sadistically since he, as it were, "devours" him psychically and destroys his existence as a separate being in the external world. The result of the process of identification is that the images of the psychically "swallowed" father and all the emotions pertaining to them are merged with the ego. Here they separate themselves from the other parts of the ego and form the nucleus of what later becomes the superego.

The incestuous love for the mother also changes into something else at the end of the phallic phase. The gross sexual quality of the libido is lost. It is desexualized to a certain extent: the sexual strivings are replaced by sublimated tender feelings. The boy saves his penis by withdrawing libido from the objects of the oedipus complex. *The castration threat thus leads to the destruction of the oedipus complex.*

The beginnings of the superego develop from ambivalent feelings toward the father.

The aggressive impulses turn against the ego; they deposit themselves in the ego and help form the *superego*. Out of this nucleus there develops the image of the strict father who continues the prohibition against incest and thereby inhibits the sensual drives of the boy. The destructive instincts thus enter into close relations with the ego, establish themselves there, as we shall see later on, and work against the erotic strivings; in a word, they operate within the ego. This particularly close relationship with the ego is the reason why the destructive instincts were previously designated as *ego instincts*.

Through identification with the father, the boy's masculinity is strengthened, his struggle against his incestuous desires is given support.

The entire process of the working over or assimilating of the oedipus complex has rescued the genital; at the same time, however, it has paralyzed its function. *The latency period begins.* The genital feelings being excluded, the boy's love for his mother is no longer sensual; it is tender.

The sensual strivings are called *direct* and *uninhibited.* Those strivings from which the genital feelings are excluded are called *aim-inhibited* and *tender.* The latter derive in part from the bodily care of the pregenital phases, from nursing, feeding, cleaning, hugging, in which sexual gratification occurred extragenitally. In the course of development these strivings have lost their sexual significance. If development is normal, the nucleus of the superego and the aim-inhibited and tender love for the mother have evolved from the attempts to assimilate and thus to resolve the oedipus complex. They are remnants of this complex. The final object-choice, in which both currents of strivings, the sensual and the tender, flow together, takes place later, in puberty. For a time there is a stop to the complicated process which, at the end of the phallic phase, has initiated the formation of the superego and resulted in the exclusion of the genitals and the establishment of aim-inhibited or tender love. With the *mastering* of the oedipus complex the first *sublimations* begin. In place of the uninhibited and ungovernable instincts, social feelings begin to develop and other broader intellectual interests appear. This signifies the beginning of the latency period.

The development of the girl's object choice is somewhat different, for in her the castration complex is formed before the oedipus complex has developed, whereas in the boy it is formed after that time. The boy's reaction to the castration threat is primarily flight from the danger. In the girl the shock of the castration complex is caused far less by the castration threat than by the incontrovertible recognition that she does not possess a penis. As with the boy, various reactions are possible. The girl either accepts the lack of a penis, hoping however to recover it sometime, or she denies the lack of a penis and behaves as if she were a man. Nevertheless, a feeling of inferiority almost always remains which expresses itself, among other ways, also in the fact that the girl becomes dissatisfied with clitoral masturbation and gives up masturbation earlier than the boy does. The renunciation of masturbation is apparently made easier by the fact that the active masculine strivings which are grouped around the clitoris are checked by the passive feminine ones which are localized in the vaginal entrance. In consequence of this first passive masochistic thrust, the girl seems to consider the lack of a penis, the "castration which has already been performed," as a just punishment for violating the prohibition against masturbation. As a result of penis envy, in addition, the relationship to the mother is weakened, since every girl holds her mother responsible for her lack of a penis. A situation now arises in which the girl begins to leave the masculine line, but has not yet reached the feminine one. As a result of the beginning of the development of femininity and the estrangement from the mother, the mother is no longer the libidinal object to the degree that she previously was. This attitude seems to have some bearing on the girl's giving up the wish to possess a penis. Instead she again cathects the feces with libido and develops the wish for a child. In fact, the girl returns to a former phase of libido development, the passive-anal one, a feminine phase, but one which derives genital qualities from the clitoris. In this phase the feces are intended for the mother; now, however, in the regression to this phase, the feces are intended for the father, and represent symbolically a child which the girl offers him as a gift.

The clitoris still retains some excitability, but the anal sensations are apparently displaced to the vaginal orifice and the girl begins to love and desire her father genitally. However, the love grows into full maturity only in puberty, aided by a second phase of passivity. In the boy, with the maturing of heterosexual love the ambivalence toward the father tends to change to unmixed hostility and he is regarded as a rival. Similarly, the ambivalent feelings of the girl toward her mother flare up at this time. But as the boy overcomes the feelings of rivalry and castration anxiety through identification with his father, so the girl rids herself of these feelings and of penis envy by renewed identification with her mother. Thereby her femininity becomes strengthened, as does the masculinity of the boy through identification with the father. While the girl *develops* the oedipus complex because of the castration complex and its subjugation, the boy's oedipus complex, on the contrary, *perishes* because of the castration complex. The normal boy responds to the castration complex with active resistance and destruction of the oedipus complex, while the normal girl accepts the loss of the penis—which is as a matter of fact merely a fantasy—takes to passivity, and sets up the oedipus complex. By means of the castration complex the man strengthens his masculinity, the woman her femininity; but in the man the oedipus complex is primary; in the woman, secondary.

Since the terms "masculinity" and "femininity" have frequently appeared on the preceding pages, we should perhaps try to define them more precisely. This is a difficult task, particularly in view of the fact that feminine as well as masculine character traits are represented in both sexes. We have already dealt with the concept of bisexuality in which masculinity is expressed by activity and femininity by passivity. It would thus seem as if the concepts of masculinity and femininity were essentially reduced to those of activity and passivity, respectively. While it is possible to express the idea of activity in terms of muscular innervations, motions, actions, and their psychic representatives, it is almost impossible to formulate the idea of passivity. Since the libido has active as well as passive aims or ways of gratification, it is the passive aims of the instincts that present the main problem for definition. *Genuine passivity* is rooted in the infantile fixation to the mother; perhaps it is caused by the prolonged dependence and helplessness of human beings or it may even stem from the prenatal state in the mother's womb. *Genuine passivity is a helpless state of expectation which makes the individual susceptible to shocks (trauma) and is, therefore, dangerous.*

If the sexual aim of the man is active, his object must be a woman, since his expanding penis in sexual excitement must seek an object suitable for penetration. If the woman's sexual aim is passive, that is, to receive, the penis can give satisfaction since her sexual organ is a cavity. The object choice thus seems largely dependent on the aim. In fact, the man can *completely* satisfy his aim only with a woman, and the woman only with a man. The anatomy is decisive.

Although the early history of the oedipus complex is less transparent in man than in woman, nevertheless, comparison of their developmental history leads to the conclusion that the sexual development of the woman is much more complicated than that of the man. The woman must make two changes: one is the change of the leading zone of the genital, the displacement of clitoral excitability to the vaginal orifice; the second is change of object, that is, giving up the mother and cathecting the father with libido. Consequently, the woman is more predisposed to psychic illnesses than the man, a fact which is perhaps balanced by the greater social demands made upon the man.

With this reference to pathological conditions I will close this section, in which an attempt has been made to reconstruct the development of object love. It was necessary to devote some time to these problems, as otherwise we would not have had a proper basis for our further discussions. In discussing pathological processes we must always refer to the normal (though fictitious) as a standard for comparison. Even though some of the statements made above may not yet seem completely established, I am convinced that further efforts will succeed in correcting such errors as are at present unavoidable.

General Observations About Disturbances of Object Choice

The inclusion of the destructive instincts in our theory stresses the complications of instinctual life. However, it brings us closer to an understanding of some phenomena which until now had defied explanation. Although we still lack precise knowledge of the finer structure of instinct life, we have been able, by following its development up to the stage of definite object choice, to conceive of how the two groups of instincts disturb each other and oppose each other's strivings. We have seen how, at the end, despite all obstacles, they fuse to such an extent that the destructive instincts recede in favor of the life instincts. The fusion of the two groups of instincts, however, never succeeds completely, because certain parts of the destructive instincts merely hide behind the life instincts; they become invisible, as it were, as they amalgamate with the ego. At the infantile-genital (phallic) stage, for instance, they appear in the form of the castration complex. The anxiety called forth by the castration complex disturbs sexual relations in such a way that it not only inhibits the genital function but also excludes the love object from consciousness. The anxiety inhibits the direct, sensual sexual strivings, while it permits the existence of the indirect, tender, desexualized strivings, that is, those which have been transformed under the influence of the destructive instincts. If such a split love life persists in men after puberty, they suffer from *relative impotence;* those whom they love they are unable to desire sensually, and those whom they desire sensually, they cannot love. One form of frigidity in women is, by and large, due to similar causes. Sexual prohibition, penis envy which opposes her feminine role, hatred toward the beloved man, and the fantasy of castrating him, frequently result in the absence of sensation in sexual intercourse.

Even in the simplest form of impotence, the man rejects a real love object out of fear of incest and castration anxiety, although he unconsciously loves objects from the oedipus pattern, and seeks situations which provide him with opportunity to experience, over and over again, his oedipus complex which he has not yet overcome (hysteria). In other forms of neurosis there is not even an unconscious relation to a heterosexual object; the patient loves, consciously or unconsciously, a homosexual object, an object of the same sex, thus a narcissistic one. In other cases, again, there exists a positive tie, though it is disturbed, and the relation to the object is but an ambivalent one (compulsion neurosis). In psychoses of psychogenic origin, in schizophrenia, for instance, relations with objects are almost completely absent. It is usually impossible to maintain personal contact with such psychotics, as they have lost the psychic representations of objects even in the unconscious. In other words, the neurotic, with his sexual emotions, of whatever kind they may be in the individual case, is bound to objects in the unconscious, while the psychotic in advanced stages withdraws the libido from the unconscious objects and turns it to the ego, thereby increasing his narcissism. The neurotic is able to transfer libido from the unconscious objects to other, real objects. If these can satisfy his unconscious requirements, he may give the impression of being truly in love.

The psychotic, on the other hand, at certain stages of his illness is indifferent to the whole world, if not actually hostile to it; in his unconscious, he has no object love to dispose of. The attitude toward objects of the external world, therefore, is considered the most general mark of differentiation between neurosis and psychosis. Hence the latter are called *narcissistic* neuroses; and the former, *transference* neuroses. But since the neurotic, like the psychotic, leads an inner life turned away from the external world, since he is *introverted,* this differentiation might seem useless. In neuroses, however, the libido clings to fantasies whose contents are objects of the external world, while in the psychoses, the object of the fantasies is the ego itself. The introversion of psychoses differs from that of neuroses by its defective object cathexis.

The healthy person has, on the whole, firm and unambiguous libidinal relations to his objects; in pathologic conditions, the ties become loosened —in the transference neuroses in the preconscious, in the narcissistic neuroses in the unconscious. In the latter, moreover, the object libido is converted into narcissistic libido.

It is apparent that at one end of this series, in the healthy person, the destructive instincts do not make themselves perceptible in pure form; while at the other end, in the psychotic, they control the instinctual life in a distinctly recognizable form. Approximately in the center of this series stands the compulsion neurosis, in which increased ambivalence proves that the destructive instincts are not subdued. In schizophrenia, the destructive instincts appear entirely undisguised in aggression against the external world and against the patient's own person. In melancholia, the destructive instincts are directed against the ego. Accordingly we see in the healthy person and in the hysteric, who is still close to him, that an abundance of libido strives toward objects and that the instincts of destruction are hidden. In the compulsion neurosis, the libidinal relationship to the object is evidently disturbed by sadism, that is, by destructive instincts. In the psychosis, object-libido is more or less absent, and the destructive instincts are uninhibited. It seems that the less the objects of the external world are cathected by libido, the more intense the destructive instincts are; in other words, defusion of instincts goes hand in hand with decreasing object libido. Inversely, as we know, a fusion of instincts takes place along with increasing object cathexis.

We may thus draw the conclusion that the degree to which object relations are reduced may indicate whether a case is a mild or a serious one.

Fixation, Regression, and Defusion of Instincts

In the discussion of the disturbances of sexual life we encountered the concept of *fixation*. We recognized fixation as an expression of the repetition compulsion of the instincts. We learned that the death instincts, because of their conservative nature and their irresistible strivings for rest, are subject to the repetition compulsion. But it is not quite clear why the sexual instincts (libido), which pursue the opposite tendency, should obey the same compulsion. It might be that in the fusion of instincts not all the parts of the death instincts which join the sexual instincts at each stage of development are neutralized. Thus the sexual instincts might also be stopped in their development and compelled to remain at the stage then reached. Normally, the tendency to remain stationary is overcome through further development, but in certain disturbances of instinctual life the principle of inertia wins out, and the instincts or certain parts of the instincts adhere to the stage of organization reached at that point. The place where the single part of the instinct is arrested or fixated may of course be camouflaged by the forward movement of the entire instinct development, but it always forms a point of attraction and thus a danger for the matured libido. If this point is strengthened by an influx of libido, then *the ego is compelled to repeat the infantile ways of gratification, ways which have apparently been abandoned but which earlier were experienced with more intensity and over a longer period of time than in normal development.* A fixated instinct, therefore, is always a weak point in the development of instinct life. If the libido faces difficulties which oppose direct gratification and yet cannot be guided into the path of sublimation, then it flows back to these weak points, to the points of *fixation.* Such a flowing back of the libido we call *regression.*

The regression of the libido should not be mistaken for historical or topographical regression. These latter are purely psychological conceptions, which mean that higher psychic functions are taking place on a lower level and that instead of being governed by the laws of the system Pcs, they are governed by the laws of the system Ucs. But the *regression of the libido* means the retreat of sexual energy, and is, accordingly, a biological conception. It is true that as a rule psychological regression coincides with regression of the libido, but it is not necessarily always so. It happens, for instance in schizophrenia, that the libido regresses extensively, but that the psychological process takes place in the conscious or preconscious. This is the case with delusional ideas.

The conception of regression of the libido must also not be mistaken for *withdrawal of the libido*. The former means a flowing back of the libido to a former position, while the latter means a withdrawal of the libido from a certain object or situation. Regression is, of course, accompanied by a withdrawal of libido, but the difference between the two processes is an important one. With the withdrawal of libido, only the attitude toward the object changes; in regression of the libido, the sexual organization also changes. The energy cathexis may be withdrawn either from the preconscious ideas of objects, as in neurosis, or from the unconscious objects, as in psychosis. In regression, the libido stops retreating at the point at which it is fixated; in hysteria, at the infantile-genital (phallic) stage; in compulsion neurosis, at the anal-sadistic stage; in psychosis, at an even lower level. In neurosis, when the libido has by regression reached the points of its fixation, it again cathects the objects from the unconscious system. The quality of the sexual libido now again flowing to the objects will therefore depend upon the degree of regression.

In hysteria, the genital organization does not change with regression; the libidinal strivings accordingly retain a genital character in the unconscious, though no longer in the conscious. In compulsion neurosis, the sexual organization is changed; the object is again cathected with anal-sadistic libido. In psychosis, the libido withdraws also from the *unconscious* objects; it is not transferred to the objects again after the regression has taken its course, or if it is, it is only for a very short time. In that case, sexual life shows a manifestly perverse character. After regression, therefore, the libido may, according to the type of illness, either cathect the objects again, or not. Although it cannot be overlooked that a certain parallel exists between libido withdrawal and libido regression, it is clear that *the extent of the libido withdrawal depends upon the power of resistance of the object cathexis, while the depth of the regression is dependent upon the sexual organization,* that is, more precisely, upon the *actual fixation.*

One more point has to be considered in this connection: Since these two processes (withdrawal of the libido and regression) are reciprocally related, it is evident that the changed sexual organization must influence the patient's attitude toward the external world, and vice versa.

The meaning of regression is that the libido—in consequence of difficulties encountered—retreats to former positions and cathects the fixated points. As these points gain additional energy by this process, they become active and send out strivings, which try with more or less success to gain gratification. But as there can be several points of fixation, the libido will not always return at once to the deepest fixation point, but will, step by step, cathect first the fixations which are nearer to the surface, and then the fixations which took place on a lower level. In such cases, the illness may first take the form of hysteria, then become a compulsion neurosis, and finally develop into schizophrenia or melancholia. So, through the increasing flow of libido to the fixation points, the illness may become more severe and more extensive.

The libido in its retreat will first cathect and strengthen the previously inactive fantasies which it meets first: The regression will therefore in the beginning have merely a historical character, as does the dream. The objects of the libido-cathected fantasies belong to the oedipus constellation. Thus, through regression, the oedipus complex is reactivated in manifold variations in all psychic illnesses. The form of the oedipus complex probably will be one factor in determining the type of neurosis, but —as previously stressed—we are not yet able to determine the form of the neurosis from the form of the oedipus complex. The simple, positive form of the oedipus complex appears more frequently in hysteria than in the other forms of neurosis. Since in this illness the libido does not retreat further than the infantile-genital level—the fixation apparently having taken place at this stage of development—neither the sexual organization of the patient nor his attitude toward objects changes considerably. The entire unconscious infantile conflict merely becomes intensified. In hysteria, thus, there results, from the withdrawal of libido and from the regression, the following situation: Those strivings of the libido which are directed to the objects of the oedipus constellation, as well as the genitals, are excluded from consciousness; but the objects as well as the genitals continue to exist in the unconscious.

The compulsion neurosis, on the other hand, manifests a changed attitude toward the objects and an altered sexual organization, after the regression has occurred. As a result of the flowing back of the libido to the anal-sadistic stage, anal-sadistic strivings dominate the sexual life of the patient, and his attitude toward the objects becomes extremely ambivalent. The compulsive neurotic either renounces his genital function completely, or else his genital strivings are interspersed with strivings of the pregenital stage, and he has coitus with the aid of anal and sadistic practices and fantasies.

In compulsion neurosis, therefore, the genital organization is regressively traversed, but it is not destroyed as in schizophrenia; the genital strivings which represent the unimpaired part of the phallic organization merely make use of the anal-sadistic urges and ideas, and do not return to this stage of development. Hence the compulsive neurotic is neither impotent nor manifestly perverse.

One might raise the question as to why the return of libido to a developmental phase in which the destructive instincts are still so powerful does not lead to the giving up of the objects altogether, that is, to a psychosis. Experience shows that the compulsive neurotic very early in life develops a strong attachment to a particular person in his immediate environment. This tie remains firm and continues to exist at the time of a fixation which occurs somewhat later in life. Only the regression that sets in with the outbreak of illness is capable of threatening even this tie.

Through analysis it was possible to trace a patient's extremely close attachment to his grandmother back to the latter part of his second year of life. The grandmother was actually the only person that the patient had really loved, up to the outbreak of his illness. At the age of sixteen, three years after the onset of his illness, he witnessed her death. It was a winter's night. He was in a room adjoining hers, studying and brooding, and, as was his habit, drinking hot tea. From the room in which his grandmother lay dying, he heard groans, a rattling in her throat, and then suddenly there was deep silence. He felt certain that his grandmother had just died. But this did not make the slightest impression upon him; he did not move, nor did he inform his family of what had happened, as he was afraid that the general excitement would disturb his studying and tea drinking. Only after he had finished his tea and stopped brooding, did he wake his family. But then he was seized with horrible remorse and despair. For a long time he reproached himself for his brutality toward his grandmother, the only person he had ever loved.

It seems, as this example demonstrates, that in the compulsive neurotic, a libidinal attachment to an object is formed at a time when the rest of the sexual development is not yet correspondingly consolidated. In other words, the choice of an object occurs in advance of the sexual development and is impaired only when the regression occurs. The early libidinal attachment as well as the unrelinquished part of the phallic organization might be considered the decisive factors which cause the compulsive neurotic's resistance to a complete detachment of libido from the objects. It is true that after the regression, his attitude toward these objects is ambivalent, but still he fights continually for the possession of the object, which continues to exist for him, in contrast to the psychotic.

If the object choice is a narcissistic one, the regression may lead to a psychosis. In narcissistic types of loving, the libido is at first withdrawn partially; this means that the heterosexual libidinal object cathexes are withdrawn and what remains of the libido regresses to the phallic-narcissistic stage. The object is then loved as a reflection of the patient's own person. In this way, the second preliminary stage of loving, the "projective" one, is revived. From this attitude toward the object there often develops a paranoid delusion of persecution. The persecutor corresponds to a rejected homosexually desired object. The unsatisfied homosexual desires are a source of intense suffering to the paranoiac. He feels tortured by his persecutor in every possible way. The nonpsychotic, manifest homosexual suffers likewise through his difficulties in satisfying his sexual needs, but his suffering does not reach the point of a delusion of persecution. His constitutional inclinations are very often intensified through his excessive castration anxiety. Out of castration fear, he turns from the woman to the man. Indeed, overt homosexuality in many cases represents a successful flight from castration. Though both active and passive toward his love object, the manifest homosexual is mostly active. The paranoiac, on the other hand, does not actively take flight from the castration threat, nor is he active in his desire for his love object; he is passive. The tortures he has to endure on the part of his persecutor have the symbolic meaning of castration. In the paranoiac, in contrast to the homosexual, castration is *accomplished,* as it were. The paranoiac has a passive attitude toward castration. He even strives for it in a *masochistic way.* This might seem inconsistent with the fact that the persecutor is warded off with hatred and aggression, that is, with sadistic impulses. Sadism and masochism, however, are essentially not opposed; they are merely different forms of appearance of the same destructive instinct which is, in sadism, directed outward against the object world, in masochism, inward against the ego. In *delusions of persecution a passive homosexual tie is defended against by means of sadism.* In this connection one more factor must be mentioned: as a rule, the persecutor comes from behind and is often identified with feces. Some authors, as for instance van Ophuijsen, speak of an anal persecution. This makes me think of a fantasy which has been related to me in almost the same words, by two patients from different countries and different social levels.

Both patients were inclined to interpret the world around them in a slightly paranoid way. Each patient reported the same fantasy in connection with the discussion of the castration complex. The content of the fantasy is briefly as follows: A person perceives, while defecating, that his stool has disappeared leaving no trace; under the impression that the devil has robbed him of his stool, he becomes insane. One of these patients even tried to make me believe that his schoolmates, using the devil's trick, had actually driven a hated teacher insane.

For further illustration of the relationship between castration anxiety and anal persecution, an episode may be related from the analysis of a schizophrenic:

This patient, whose aggressive homosexual attitude toward me had been apparent for some time, refused to discuss it with me. Since the theme constantly intruded into his thoughts and he always sought to avoid it, I told him at last that his refusal to discuss it would be of no avail, that at this stage of the analysis he could not avoid discussing my person. The reaction to my encouragement was a completely unexpected one. He was seized by a severe attack of anxiety. Terrified, he threw himself to and fro upon the couch, uttered inarticulate sounds, perspired, touched his head, then his genitals, and finally held his abdomen. His great anxiety prevented him from uttering a single coherent sentence. All of these movements gave the impression of protective and defensive measures. The following day I tried to find out something about his attack. I learned then that while I was encouraging him, he was seized with the overwhelming fear that I meant to kill him. In order to protect himself against my attack, he covered his head with his hands. Immediately this anxiety changed into the fear that I was threatening his genitals, and he tried to protect them with his hands. Finally this anxiety developed into the utterly unbearable idea that I meant to force my arm into his anus with the object of disemboweling him. Further investigation revealed that his fear of my aggression corresponded to his own sadistic homosexual aggression against me. The patient's fear of death at this point corresponded on a deeper level to castration anxiety, and still deeper, to a passive anal and masochistic striving for sexual intercourse with me, which appeared in his consciousness as my intention to castrate him.

There are some kinds of obstipation in which the feces are retained out of fear of anal castration (identification of penis with feces).

This episode also demonstrates the speedy withdrawal of libido to ever lower positions, out of fear of the patient's own instinctual impulses. The libido withdraws in a direction opposite to the normal, progressive course of development.

It is evident that in paranoia the narcissistic libido regresses to the anal-sadistic stage, where the destructive instincts again become dominant. Loving falls back to the projective stage.

There is a certain type of jealousy characteristic of paranoia, and in practice we must often distinguish this form from genuine competitive jealousy; therefore I should like to insert at this point a short but instructive example of such a delusion:

A patient complained of his wife's jealousy, a jealousy as baseless as it was boundless, and asked me to speak to her. She came for analysis, but after three weeks the treatment had to be discontinued for external reasons. In this short time, however, I learned enough to get an idea of her instinctual trends.

To begin with, I might mention that her husband had first fallen in love with her, though he had known her since childhood, when he saw her in riding breeches. This fact alone characterizes the mutual object relationship of this couple.

She had had many love affairs and was never able to attach herself permanently to one man, with two exceptions: her first husband and her second, the present one. Though both treated her badly, she remained attached to these two men. She had many women friends and had erotic relations with some of them.

Since the birth of her child, she suspected that her husband was deceiving her with a woman whom she hated intensely. No argument could convince her of the baselessness of her suspicion, and, in a delusional way, she found new evidence for her accusations over and over again.

This delusion had originated as follows: While she was pregnant, she had introduced her husband to a woman who was at that time her intimate friend, and advised him to have sexual relations with that woman during her own confinement. Later on, long after he had completely severed relations with this woman, the patient refused to believe it, and plagued him with violent jealousy. He did not know what to do to appease her. To put her husband to the test as to whether he still loved her supposed rival, one evening she put on a blond wig resembling the hair of her former friend, and thus disguised, went to bed. When her husband came home, and in the dark, lay down unsuspectingly beside his wife, she threw herself upon him, tried to perform sexual intercourse in the masculine position, and began to beat him. Through this "masquerade" she unmasked the meaning of her jealousy. She had become acquainted with the woman under suspicion in a curious way. She had seen her dancing in a bar and was so fascinated by her strikingly fair hair, her reckless manner, and her vivacious movements that she nodded to her, addressed her after she had finished her dance, and at once became friends with her. Thus she was the one who introduced the woman whom she herself loved, to her husband, and then persecuted him with jealousy. Analysis, of which only a beginning was made, brought to light two facts which explained this passionate attraction. The patient's own hair was strikingly blond until about her tenth or twelfth year, and darkened only after the beginning of puberty. Blond women always attracted her. Secondly, she herself was reckless, energetic, and in many respects masculine. Thus in her friend, she loved her own person. As she felt deceived by her friend, her love changed to hatred which, however, seemed more the expression of a defense against the homosexual attachment than a desire for revenge. In this case, as in genuine paranoia, with a narcissistic object choice, a regression to sadism occurred. In the absence of the real object, her friend, the sadism was displaced onto her husband.

This is by no means an exhaustive analysis of the case, but it nevertheless serves as an illustration of a part of our theory.

In another illness, melancholia, a narcissistic attitude toward the objects is likewise present. But here the libido regresses to the oral stage, from which a different picture results than that seen in paranoia.

Psychologically, identification is the object relationship in the oral stage of libido organization, in which the desired object is incorporated by the ego. Through this process the object disappears from the external world but is again established in the ego. At this ambivalent stage of instinct development, the destructive instincts predominate and turn against the object which has been absorbed by the ego, thus turning against the subject himself. This explains the suicidal tendencies of the melancholic. But the destructive instinct is directed not only against the subject's ego but also against the environment. Although, for example, the refusal to eat is an attempt at death through starvation, it is also a defense against oral-sadistic strivings directed against the external world. This defense is a proof of the presence of aggressive tendencies, as is the tormenting attitude of the melancholic toward his environment. Exaggerrated anxiety over relatives indicates an aggression which has been warded off, for if anything actually happens to one of them, the patient is unmoved.

If the object relationship is even looser than that described above, or if, as occurs frequently in advanced paranoia, the narcissistic libidinal cathexis of the object is withdrawn, there follows regression beyond the genital organization, and the sexuality breaks down into its component instincts. The most varied pictures of schizophrenia develop from this. While the sexual life of the paranoiac is marked by the defense against homosexuality, and that of the melancholic is dominated by defense against oral strivings, the sexual life of the schizophrenic is manifestly perverse. His emotional life becomes ambivalent to such a degree that negativism results, in which denial and destruction prevent any positive emotion, and both will and action are completely paralyzed. The destruction predominates to such an extent that the attitude toward the external world becomes overtly rejecting and hostile. If there is a libidinal relation to objects, it exists only in so far as it is built upon a narcissistic foundation and as it manifests itself in connection with a part of the body or the function of an organ.

To cite an example: As I entered the room of a catatonic female patient who smeared and ate her feces, I asked her why she did this. She replied that she was having the best meal of her life, that with the excrement she was creating a wonderful monument of pure gold to Kaiser Wilhelm, no, to father, and that she had just given birth to a child; after all, her excrements were the most valuable part of herself. Thus she established relations with the world on an anal-narcissistic basis.

The most important insight gained by considering the chain of development here discussed is this: With regression reaching ever lower levels, it is not only the sexual life which breaks down, but also the entire instinctual life. In studying the progressive development of instinctual life we gained the impression that it becomes step by step more unified. The component instincts are organized in the genitals; the death or destructive instincts are fused with the sexual instincts, and their effect is therefore weakened beyond recognition. In the retrograde process, regression, the destructive instincts appear more and more distinctly and, in some illnesses, work directly against the sexual instincts. The conflict of ambivalence between love and hate again sets in. In some forms of illness, the destructive instincts again take control of instinctual life to such an extent that negation of life is the result. It is in the compulsion neurosis that the dominance of sadism in the form of cruel impulses comes closer to breaking through than in any other neurosis. In the negativism of the schizophrenic, each positive striving is cut off at its start by the opposite striving. In some stuporous states in schizophrenia, this process goes still further. Every stimulus from the external world is felt as a disturber of peace and as an enemy, and the response is an act of aggression. In the delusion of persecution, the prior love changes into hatred; the hate is projected and the object is pursued by the destructive instincts. In melancholia, the destructive instinct turns against the person himself.

This process, in the course of which the libido is desexualized and the destructive instincts are again freed, we call *defusion of instincts*. The defusion of instincts runs its course parallel to the regression of libido and leads, in extreme cases, not only to the destruction of object cathexis, but also to the destruction of the subject. The extent of the defusion of instincts depends upon the depth of regression. Since the fixations determine the course of regression, the extent of instinct defusion must depend on the time of the formation of the fixations as well as on their extent. As, furthermore, the fixations develop under the influence of inertia or the repetition compulsion of instincts, the defusion of instincts might be viewed as an achievement of the destructive instincts, which were already at work when the fixations were formed. It seems, therefore, as if the repetition compulsion would facilitate the defusion of instincts.

At this point it should be emphasized that in every form of neurosis a temporal and an economic moment are to be distinguished. The former depends upon the stage of libido organization at which the decisive fixations have taken place; the latter depends upon the quantity of instinct energy (libido) which has been drawn off and bound by the fixated instinct.

If one studies the sadism which is freed with the defusion of instincts, it is easy to establish that, in most illnesses, it is turned against the subject himself. We have frequently spoken of the self-torments of the compulsive neurotic, the suicidal impulses of the melancholic, and the like. When sadism meets with the narcissistic libido accumulated in the ego, it is transformed into real, erogenous masochism. A dream of a compulsive neurotic woman illustrates this:

The patient, her physician (a gynecologist), and his wife are seated at the table. Under the table she presses her thighs together and masturbates, wondering apprehensively what the physician would say were he to find out about it. While she is tormenting herself with self-reproaches, she experiences the greatest pleasure and has an orgasm. (Otherwise she was frigid.)

The gynecologist represents her father who was likewise a physician, a surgeon. Whenever she hurt herself in childhood, her father treated her. The pain of occasional minor operations was a source of sensual pleasure to her. In order to be treated by her father again and to experience this pleasure, she deliberately injured herself frequently. She spent her childhood alternating between sadistic aggressions, followed by severe self-reproach, and masochistic pleasure. She had been conscious of her sadism since childhood, but the masochism was unconscious and appeared for the first time during analysis, in this dream.

We have already learned of another kind of masochism, the passive-feminine type which arises with the acceptance of the castration threat. This is likewise unconscious.

The third kind is called *moral masochism*. It is formed as a psychic supplement to the destructive instincts turned against oneself, and finds its expression in the feeling of guilt or in the unconscious desire for punishment. We can go no farther with this until we turn to the psychology of the ego. But in order to give some idea of the intractability of the resistance that the need for punishment often exerts against any attempt to overcome it, I shall relate very briefly the following portion of a case history:

A patient came for treatment in order to gain the strength to divorce his wife, who treated him miserably, and to marry another woman whom he loved. Analysis soon revealed that he was suffering from severe masochistic fantasies of being chained and beaten. He had been an officer on active duty in the old Austrian army. Although he was a good and a conscientious soldier, his behavior nevertheless brought him into conflict, not only with his superiors, but also with the law. His misconduct led to the loss of his rank, and finally to several years' imprisonment. The punishment did not by any means break his spirit, as might have been expected; on the contrary, he felt relieved, and behaved so well while in prison that he was granted many privileges. After having served his prison term, he built up a new life under the most adverse conditions, became exceedingly correct in every respect, and at the time of entering upon treatment, occupied a responsible and important position in public life. But he still gratified his desire for punishment unconsciously in his married life. His wife made his life unbearable. In spite of this, he could not part from her; even the analysis was unable to change this. His need for suffering was stronger than all the other necessities of life.

Later, we shall deal more exhaustively with the feeling of guilt. Now I should like to add only that it exists in most psychic illnesses but may be lacking in certain manifest perversions. Wherever the feeling of guilt is present, it can contribute to the unconscious gratification of masochism, as in the rather common fantasies of being beaten. Masochism, in whatever form it may appear, means suffering. Every neurosis contains to a certain degree a need for suffering; in one form of neurosis the masochism is stronger, in another it is weaker. Sometimes it is conscious, at other times, unconscious. But in every neurosis, the need for suffering is present and inhibits to a greater or lesser degree the enjoyment of life.

A sharp delimitation of the three varieties of masochism is not always possible. But it is certain that in some cases one form, and in others another form predominates and gives the illness its characteristic guise.

We have now reached a point where the instinct life cannot be understood without more precise knowledge of the processes within the ego. In closing this chapter, I shall attempt to give a very brief outline of the instinct life of the neurotic, although it is exceedingly difficult to find a characterization which applies to all forms of neurosis.

The most general characteristic is that, as a result of the inhibited discharge of the instinct energies (damming up of libido), the instinct life of every neurotic is under great tension. It is like a barrel of gunpowder, which may easily explode if it is not adequately protected. Secondly, the ability to sublimate is often diminished, since the sexual instincts, in consequence of fixation, drive for repetition and therefore can be displaced upon other, nonsexual aims only with great effort. Instinct life is not unified in its strivings. Even if the destructive instincts have been subdued in the course of instinct fusion, the libido has reached the genital stage undisturbed, and the object choice has been made, it may happen that at maturity a synthesis between the sensual and the tender strivings cannot be accomplished. If the neurotic has not reached the genital stage at all, or not completely, the sexuality breaks down on encountering reality, a defusion of instincts takes place, and the destructive instincts regain their previous power. They come in conflict with the sexual instincts; in severe cases they even control the entire psychic life. If the oedipus complex has been overcome, it flares up again in illness with all its consequences: incest wishes, feelings of revenge, castration complex, and so on. In every neurosis a more or less severe disturbance in relations with the objects of the libido prevails. This disturbance may, in the psychoses, lead to a complete estrangement from and hostility against the external world.

Chapter V

THE PSYCHOLOGY OF THE EGO

The study of the instincts has afforded us important insight into psychic life. In general, it has made it possible to recognize the forces of instinctual origin which are operative there, and in particular, what disturbances of those forces are reflected in illness. Thereby, however, only one aspect of psychic life in general as well as of illness itself is comprehended, for instinct life is also decisively influenced by the reactions of the ego, as, conversely, the reactions of the ego are altered by the instinct life. Hence, for a full understanding of psychic life, we must consider another component of the personality: the ego.

Usually the psychic representatives of the instincts, which, as we know, arise in the unconscious, have to traverse the entire scale of the psychic systems and to undergo certain modifications in order to gain access to consciousness and action. Only when the instinct energy has increased so greatly that it overrides all obstacles does it transform itself directly into states of consciousness and into actions, as for example in sexual ecstasy or in psychotic states.

The ego thus influences the form in which the instinct, through its representatives, reaches consciousness and is converted into action. The ego, therefore, can either permit the instinct to express itself directly in action or it can inhibit and modify the instinct. In any case, the course of the instinct will be dependent on the nature of the ego strivings. The ego works, as it were, as a medium in which all the stimuli of the inner world are refracted. But it also receives stimuli from the outside world which it has to digest and modify. The ego is, as it were, situated at the border between the inner and the outer world, and, from the topographical point of view, it coincides *partly* with the system Pcpt.Cs. of the psychic apparatus. However, one must guard against the assumption that the entire ego is conscious, for there are psychic processes which occur within the ego and which are by no means conscious. Most of our moral evaluations and inhibitions, for example, are among these. Therefore, we must assume that a part of the ego is unconscious.

In outline, Freud long recognized the unconscious parts of the ego as the censor of the dream, but only in his later work did he distinguish them more precisely from the conscious ones. Previously the conscious ego strivings were considered the antithesis of the unconscious, that is, of the representatives of the instincts. Now, however, since an unconscious component is recognized within the ego, the contrast between "conscious" and "unconscious" is no longer identical with the contrast between ego and instincts. As the instincts arise in the unconscious, and as a part of the ego also is unconscious, it is necessary to differentiate between the unconscious instinct life and the unconscious part of the ego. Since we, furthermore, discuss the unconscious in a descriptive, a dynamic, and a systematic sense, the concept of the unconscious no longer has a single meaning. Therefore Freud decided to designate the unconscious by the indifferent term "id." The former contrast between "conscious" and "unconscious" is now replaced by the one between ego and id. While the ego consists of conscious and unconscious components, the id is unconscious throughout, and comprises all of the impulses, drives, instincts, desires, and passions of the human being. These impulses and instincts have no uniform object or aim; they are not organized, they are not concentrated in *one* striving, they operate independently of one another. The id has no organization; it is chaotic.

The indifferent word "id" is also meant to hint at the fact that we are actually impelled by our instincts, that we are subject to them, and that we finally do what we must do, and only in very special circumstances that which we consciously wish to do. This is often expressed by people who say that they think, feel, and act the way they do, not because they have chosen this particular way of thinking, feeling, and acting, but because something within them is thinking, feeling, willing, and acting.

The ego *has an organization;* it is able to concentrate its own strivings as well as those of the id in a uniform aim, and to give its will a definite direction. Furthermore, it is a representative in the psychic system of the external world, but besides that, it is also in the service of the strivings of the id. The id, a representative solely of the inner world, is egotistical and gives no consideration to the strivings of the ego. If we state that the ego is at the service of the strivings of the id, we must modify this statement to a certain extent. For even though the id shows its strength by imposing its will on the ego in some measure, still the ego is not entirely helpless, as it forces the id to weaken and to change its strivings; it is even able to prevent those strivings from achieving action and consciousness.

The Ego's Function of Perception and Reality Testing

Every analyst learns by experience sooner or later that a time comes in the course of analysis when the flow of material becomes scanty, when associations stop, when the patient occasionally becomes mute altogether and behaves strangely. Not only does the course of treatment come to a standstill, but understanding the patient's psychic life is made immeasurably more difficult, if not altogether impossible. This seems strange, since the unconscious drives—now we would term them the strivings of the id—have a tendency to progress, to reach the system Cs. of the ego, hence to become conscious and to be converted into action. This tendency of the id to "reveal itself" makes use of every means at its disposal to get in touch with the outside world and to attain gratification through the medium of an object. But the ego opposes this self-revelatory tendency of the id with so-called "resistances," which veil and inhibit the strivings of the id. The resistances, however, can be comprehended and defined only when the function of the ego and its relation to the id is understood.

The function of the ego as a factor of resistance has long been known, in the neuroses as well as in the dream. We distinguished between a motor (acting) ego, a perceiving, and a censoring and inhibiting ego. The study of some psychoses, the postulation of the death instincts, and the separation of the ego from the id, enable us to come closer to an understanding of the structure and function of the ego.

If one disregards for the moment all of the finer nuances of the ego and attempts solely to recognize its most general function, it is difficult to delineate sharply between the strivings of the ego and those of the id, since all human activities are the result of strivings of the id as well as of those of the ego. These performances are phenomena of the interaction of both strivings. According to Freud's hypothesis, the ego is a part of the id; it arose from the id, and has been differentiated from the id.

To put it graphically, the ego is located on the border between the inner world, the id, and the outer world, reality. The ego's task is thus given by its topographical position. On the one hand, it has to perceive and assimilate stimuli from the external world; on the other, it has to intercept stirrings of the id in the form of feelings and sensations and to direct and discharge them onto objects of the external world. To be perceived means, as we have already learned, to become conscious. The organs of perception are the sense organs—the eyes, the ears, the sense of touch, and so on. What is perceived does not comprise only outer stimuli but also inner, mental processes (ideas, wishes, thoughts, strivings, sensations, and fantasies). External stimuli are intercepted by the sense organs and led to the central nervous system. Here they leave traces in the form of memories and ideas whose nature depends upon the particular sense organ which has received the stimulus (sight, hearing, touch). These precipitates in the psyche of external experiences, together with the internal processes, such as thinking, imagination, feelings, emotions, and visceral sensations, form what we call the psychic body scheme or image. The nucleus around which all concepts of one's own ego are grouped is the *body ego,* whose main function is perception.

The id does not directly perceive stimuli from the outside world. However, it registers stimuli from within as visceral feelings, coenesthetic feelings, and oscillations in the tensions of its instinctual needs. These oscillations become conscious through the medium of the ego as feelings in the pleasure-unpleasure scale. Besides, pleasure and unpleasure can be sensed without being consciously perceived.

Perception, certainly, is not the ego's only task. Although the impetus to volition stems from the id, action is accomplished or thwarted by the ego. It is obvious that the ego controls access to motility. The id has no access to voluntary motility; its needs and urges can only be carried out and satisfied with the help of the motor apparatus of the ego. Through motility one can determine whether an object exists in reality or in the imagination. If, for instance, one is doubtful as to whether an object is really there or is only a delusion, one has only to stretch his hand out to establish the reality or unreality of his sense perception. The investigation as to whether a perception (of an image, or a voice, and the like) is due to an external or an internal stimulus, is called *reality testing.* In the higher developmental stages, reality testing is not accomplished through motor activity only, but also by thinking and deliberation. The task of the ego thus does not consist merely in perceiving, but also in testing whether what is perceived is in the inner or the outer world. Reality testing develops very slowly; our entire orientation in the outside world and our mental health depend upon its functioning correctly. In hallucinations and delusions, for example, it fails altogether. Reality testing also provides the basis for the development of adaptation to reality.

The id cannot perform the task of testing reality because it has no contact with the external world. The id knows only internal, psychic reality. The two main instincts, the life and death instincts, are operative there. Although they are fused, each has an affinity to particular organs or systems of organs: the erotic instincts, to the sex organs; the aggressive instincts, to the motor system. Their only aim is satisfaction and discharge through adequate changes of the respective organs. At times, these instincts may suspend or even destroy the organization of the ego, or they may alter its functioning (for instance, in hallucinations).

Returning to the ego, we have seen from the foregoing that it possesses a receptive, defensive, and inhibitory apparatus for mastering and distributing the psychic (inner) and the real (outer) energies. This apparatus corresponds essentially to the protective barrier against stimuli which has already been discussed. The ego, furthermore, has various means at its disposal for communicating with the outside world, as for instance, language. Through all this it is enabled to adapt itself in every situation to the stimuli of the outer world as well as to those of the inner world.

The most important tasks of the ego thus are to perceive, to act, to adapt itself to reality, to ensure self-preservation, and to replace the primary process of the id by the secondary process of the ego.

Just as the id is ruled by the pleasure-unpleasure principle, by the urge to relieve its tensions through satisfaction, so the ego is governed by the reality principle, by the need for safety and self-preservation. It masters the dangers that threaten its safety by introducing two factors: the reality principle and anxiety. The first implies the development by the ego of certain intellectual activities: it compares the present state of affairs with memories of past experiences, evaluates the possible consequences of intended actions, and selects one which is expected to assure the greatest success without giving rise to feelings of unpleasure at the same time. Anxiety signalizes dangers threatening from without as well as from within. The internal danger, which essentially consists of an excessive amount of instinct energy, can damage the ego in the same way as an excessive external stimulus. It can destroy its organization and reconvert a portion of the ego into id.

The id has no means to ensure self-preservation, nor has it anxiety. True, it can produce the physical signs of anxiety, such as increased cardiac action, vascular changes, perspiration, increased or inhibited motility, but it cannot make use of them to produce the *conscious* feeling of anxiety. This is probably due to the fact that the id has no organization and cannot generate coordinated action. For the id is ruled by the primary process. The ego has an organization; it is not chaotic, but is ruled by the secondary process.

The aim of action adapted to reality is to change the outer world so that it can be brought into harmony with the strivings of the id, the ego, and the superego. The ego therefore must have not only a perceptive apparatus but also means enabling it to influence the external world and to inform this world of its wishes and strivings. These purposes are served by impulses and counterimpulses which originate in the id but have to pass through the ego. In the ego they call forth differences in tension of the musculature (the ego is, indeed, in the first place a body ego) and thus form the incentive for *willing*. This, in turn, may then bring about or prevent an action. It seems that the development of language is also based on such an impulse which later on is transformed into willed action. Speaking as well as not speaking, a certain bodily posture, the position of a limb, a gesture, even the tension or relaxation of a single muscle may have a meaning and a purpose. In the healthy person, the purpose of the intended actions is easily recognized. In states of illness, it is more difficult to understand the seeming "senselessness" of certain actions, but these, likewise, have a purpose. Every psychiatrist with even a slight psychoanalytic orientation has known for a long time that catatonic mutism or stupor has a meaning.

A patient who was not psychotic assumed a peculiar position during his psychoanalytic session. Throughout this time he lay stiff on the couch, his thighs pressed tensely together. The meaning of this position became clear in the course of analysis. His mother had died when he was nine years old. While reciting a prayer over her grave, in accordance with Jewish ritual, he suddenly felt an urge to defecate. In order not to soil his mother's grave, he pressed his thighs together and, with stiffly erect posture, brought the prayer to an end. As the analysis showed, he checked his impulse to soil my couch, by stretching himself and pressing his thighs together. At his mother's grave the patient knew why he pressed his thighs together; in the analysis, he did not know. It had to be made conscious to him, for the muscular tension had lost its *conscious* meaning.

The ego thus may perform actions which are consciously perceived, whose motive and hence also meaning are unconscious.

In a young woman, menstruation ceased and her abdomen began to enlarge; she was happy at the prospect of having a child. She showed so many symptoms of pregnancy that she misled, unconsciously, even experienced obstetricians to such an extent that they set the date for her child's birth. She had been married for some time. Her husband wanted a child and threatened to divorce her if she failed to become pregnant. Instead of having a physician examine her and treat her for her sterility, if this could be done, or else resigning herself to her fate, she abandoned reality completely and pretended to herself as well as to others that she was pregnant; or rather, the patient did not pretend anything, but her ego brought about such changes in her body that her wish for a child seemed to be fulfilled.

The ego is thus able to alter the body through certain changes so that a wish appears to be realized. Normally a person tries to change the outside world when he wants to gratify a striving of the id. Such a change is termed an *alloplastic* one. But if, instead, a change occurs in the ego, this is called *autoplastic* (Ferenczi). Our patient made no attempt to be treated for her sterility; instead, she changed herself from within.

All neurotics, to a greater or lesser degree, lose the capacity for gaining gratification by altering reality—in so far as reality can be subjected to their will. They change themselves and in this way achieve some gratification. They *regress* from alloplastic to autoplastic reactions.

The following comparison is illustrative: When a healthy person wishes to build an airplane, he begins by making calculations and drawings and conducting experiments until he succeeds in constructing a satisfactory airplane. One of my psychotic patients, who wished to have an airplane, lay on his back, and with his eyes closed, flapped his arms, and thus, believing he had built an airplane, he experienced a delightful sensation of flying. While the healthy individual tries to learn the laws of nature in order to influence it and to make it serve his purposes, the other one changes himself merely through his wish. The former tries to adapt his action to reality; the latter tries to change reality in a magical way.[1] In illness, adaptation to reality fails, for a wish to change the outside world ends in a *change in the ego*. The reality-testing faculty is then affected, for in so far as the ego is a perceptive ego, its task is the testing of reality, that is, of discerning whether a stimulus belongs to the outer world and corresponds to a perception, or whether it belongs to the inner world and is equivalent to a sensation or a feeling. If the patient believes he has built an airplane by flapping his arms, he has certainly lost his reality-testing faculty.

---

[1] The fantasy of flying is one of the oldest fantasies of mankind (Icarus). First there was the flying fantasy and then came the flying machine. It would seem as if fantasy created reality—which often is true. In many instances the development from fantasy to reality is accomplished not by repressing the fantasy but by ridding it of its id components and applying it in real life according to the prevailing scientific and technical possibilities. Of course, many fantasies also contain bits of reality which can be obtained through analysis. Other fantasies are inherited, as we learned earlier. They appear when a need for them arises, when reality fails to satisfy certain needs of the id.

MAGIC AND OMNIPOTENCE

Not only mentally ill people employ magic. As a matter of fact, we all still practice magic. The demarcation between the performance of magic and action adapted to reality is not always sharp. Language, for example, in many instances still has a magic connotation. It happens frequently that we cannot resist the eloquence of a good speaker, although all our logic opposes his arguments. We are simply "enchanted" by his words. Every religious prayer, every good popular speaker has a "magic" effect. "Through the word, the *Logos*, the world was created." In dreams, to children, and to primitives, the word is something material, which is treated like a thing and which possesses magical qualities. The schizophrenic practices magic with language in the negative and the positive sense. His silence frequently means that he does not want to destroy the world with his words. At one time he wants to harm the world by speaking, at another to redeem it. One is reminded of the curse and the blessing of the normal person. The "magic" power of words plays a more important role in psychically ill people and in children than it does in the normal adult.

Speech is a means of expression. Its purpose is communication; its object is another human being. Language is a function of the ego in the service of the id. Its task is to influence others. A schizophrenic said that he could speak to me only when he loved me; when he did not speak, it meant that he did not love me, and I had better leave him alone. At another time, he thought that with his words he was fertilizing the world. It seems that the energy derived from the libido of the ego is used also for the formation of language.

Sperber assumed that language owed its origin to the sexual instincts. If this is really the case, we can more easily understand why some people, regardless of the contents of their speech, speak whenever there is a chance to do so. They seem to cling to other people with words, as if they wanted to hold onto them by talking. These are usually people with poorly developed object libido, who with the magic of words attempt to dazzle the other person and to bind him to themselves. This phenomenon is not infrequently encountered in the schizophrenic at the beginning of his illness. For him talking is frequently a substitute for love. Other people, again, speak very guardedly, with long, abrupt pauses, omit many connecting links, disrupt the sentence structure, and form neologisms. Through transposition and changing of words they apparently want to conceal their secret impulses. Thus, through the medium of speech, positive as well as negative magic is unconsciously practiced.

Speech is a substitute for action. The same executive organs in general are necessary for speaking as for any other action. Although the word is formed centrally in the cerebral cortex, still its instrument of operation is the peripheral musculature, specifically that of the larynx and the mouth. As a rule, speech is set in motion, like any other organ function, through aim-inhibited sexual strivings, desexualized libido. Thus it is the expression of sublimations which begin very early. But if the speech-forming ego becomes flooded with libido, in other words, if the cerebral cortex or the speech apparatus (larynx, mouth) or both at the same time become eroticized, a disturbance of the function of speech is the result. This disturbance is expressed in a regression of the ego, in relation to speech, to its magical phase of operation. This is seen most clearly in schizophrenics and compulsive neurotics, in whom language becomes sexualized.

However, not only language, but also ideas, the thinking process, acting, in short every psychic activity, may have a magical tinge (magic effect of the motion pictures).

In his autobiography, Maxim Gorki describes an experience with a peasant whom he taught to read. After the peasant had learned to read and was beginning to understand what he read, he wondered how it was possible that something which did not exist, nevertheless existed; while nothing is to be seen or heard in reading, yet the reader sees people, woods, and fields, hears talking and the singing of birds, as if all this were reality. Finally he exclaimed with rapture that, after all, this was only magic. In a similar manner, the hysteric has fantasies and believes he experiences them in reality, the compulsive neurotic thinks that with his ceremonial he will prevent a misfortune, the paranoiac believes he influences the world in a positive or negative way by some complicated actions, and so on.

As a rule, magic is accompanied by a feeling of *omnipotence*. Leaving aside the superstition of the healthy individual, faith in his own omnipotence and magic appears clearly in the compulsive neurotic, but more extensively and intensively in the schizophrenic.

As an example, I should like to mention a patient who constantly rubbed the skin of her chest and kneaded into small lumps the scraped epidermis, which looked like dirt. Upon my asking what this meant, she replied that she was making human beings out of earth, like God; no, that she, herself, was God. The patient had displaced her position in the world; she had lost reality testing. She identified herself with the earth and with God. The boundary between her ego and the external world had grown indistinct; she felt herself omnipotent and believed she was able to create the world autoplastically and magically out of her own body. This patient was suffering from a delusion of grandeur; her feeling of omnipotence took the form of megalomania.

Megalomania corresponds to excessive self-esteem, as we have already mentioned in another connection. One's own person is overesteemed, as otherwise happens only with a beloved object. The delusion of grandeur is explained by the fact that the libido is withdrawn from the objects and turned to the ego. The feeling of omnipotence is therefore a precursor of the delusion of grandeur. The feeling of omnipotence increases self-assurance like a great, passionate love, which gives the individual the belief that he is able to conquer the world. The difference between being in love and the feeling of omnipotence (and the delusion of grandeur) is that the the latter appears when real objects are lacking, and the ego becomes the object of the libido. A condition for the appearance of the feeling of omnipotence is, therefore, the erotization of the ego.

While the feeling of omnipotence involves the entire ego, magic applies only to certain functions and organs. The genitals, for instance, are considered as a magical instrument (phallic worship, charms, magic wand). Any other erotogenic zone may likewise be endowed with magical qualities. The magic of excrements, for example, even today plays an important part not only in the rites of primitives and in popular medicine, but in the dreams and fantasies of adults, as well as in the games of children.

"The magical power of breathing" played the chief role in the symptomatology of one of my patients. He believed that through his mouth he was spreading bad odor and infecting the air. The analysis led to an infantile game in which he and his sister breathed on each other under the blanket. At that time he thought he could produce a child in that way.

It appears that narcissistic libido gives the feeling of omnipotence to the ego and invests the erotogenic zones with magic.

But there is also magic involved in the belief that one can do harm by a curse or an angry glance. Furthermore, some compulsive neurotics and schizophrenics believe, and at the same time fear, that with the semen ejaculated during masturbation, with the exhalation of breath, with the evacuation of the bowels, and the like, they create evil spirits, that even with a single thought they may harm the world. The fact that magic is in the service not only of the positive and productive but also of the negative and destructive instinct forces may make us doubt whether omnipotence and magic are dependent at all upon the libido. We must bear in mind, however, that where negative, that is, negating and destructive magic appears greater, as in the compulsion neurosis, a libido regression with instinct defusion has occurred. If the destructive instincts, in some way as yet unknown to us, join with libido, then these instincts likewise display the power of magic—not in a positive sense, however, but in a negative one. Positive magic thus serves the sexual instincts, the Eros; negative magic serves the sexualized destructive or death instincts, that is, sadism; but both are in the service of the id.

Both forms of magic as well as feelings and thoughts of omnipotence appear in the history of mankind as products of primitive peoples' animistic conception of the world. They are also to be found among children and in a great many mentally ill people. At the animistic stage of development, "inner" is as yet mistaken for "outer" (the outer world is a reflection of the inner world). The "ego boundary" is not sharp, it is blurred. The ego still does not discriminate precisely between the inner processes and those which are going on in the external world, and is unable to resist sufficiently the onrush of the strivings of the id or to modify them. For the separation of the ego from the id is not yet complete; the ego still forms an only partially organized and differentiated part of the id. Omnipotence and magic therefore belong to that stage of development of the entire personality in which the ego is but slightly differentiated from the id, in which the id, so to speak, is still "close to the ego"; this is another reason why frequently it is barely possible to distinguish a striving of the id from a striving of the ego.

Although the impulse for magic originates in the id, magic appears in the ego. Every neurotic turns to one form of magic or other; magic plays a part in every neurosis. Magic also seems to answer in part the question of the "purposefulness" or of the unconscious meaning of the neurotic symptom, which, as we know, is not completely explained through the discovery of the *causal* connection alone.

Ferenczi distinguishes four stages of omnipotence and magic. According to him, the first is the phase of *unconditional omnipotence,* which is supposed to pertain to the fetus in the mother's womb. This phase is purely hypothetical, and as we have no means of ascertaining its existence, there is no reason for considering it further. The assumption of Tausk that the schizophrenic in catatonic stupor returns to the mother's womb might be considered as supporting this hypothesis.

The second phase, that of the *magic hallucination,* is more tenable;

it is also assumed by Freud. In this phase every impulse, every wish is supposed to be magically realized. If, for instance, the infant is hungry, he will procure gratification for himself by the mere idea of sucking, if he is not gratified in reality. Although we cannot say with certainty whether in fact the process in the infant goes on in this way, we find analogies in the adult; we have only to think of the dream, where the wish is also fulfilled magically. Fantasies, daydreams, are likewise magical wish fulfillments which represent a correction of reality. By means of the same "magic," what is wished for is psychically realized in the hallucinations of some hysterics and schizophrenics through visual excitation.

The third phase is, according to Ferenczi, *omnipotence with the aid of magic gestures.* The reaction of a child to a somatic need is to kick and scream, that is, motor activity. At such an expression of displeasure, the nurse appears and satisfies the need. On the basis of this experience, the child develops the magic of gestures and conduct. The hysterical symptom, too, in which the unsatisfied needs are similarly fulfilled by means of magic gestures, may be conceived of as unconscious magic.

In the next, the fourth stage, the *omnipotence of thought* appears. Its beginnings can be traced back to the origin of speech. At first speech consisted of unarticulated sounds, which became endowed with a magical significance, and even today there are still remnants of it to be found in children and in schizophrenics. The sounds were at the very beginning attached to ideas, which likewise had a magical significance. In the course of development, words were associated with these instinctual sounds and ideas which, through this union, likewise acquired a magical character. It seems that the words were at first fused with optical and auditory ideas, later separated themselves from these ideas in a complicated process, and then combined with each other in a certain order, independent of the concrete optical and auditory ideas. A correlation of verbal and other ideas which have thus become independent, a correlation which follows certain laws, we call thinking. The magic and omnipotence attributed to sounds and to ideas in the preceding phase are taken over to the next one, and transferred onto thinking. It is chiefly the compulsion neurosis that reaches back to this stage of the development of the ego. Omnipotence and magic of thoughts play an important part in this form of neurosis.

In psychic illnesses, the inhibition in the ego's development may occur at any stage; the particular stage at which the inhibition has occurred will put its imprint on the attitude of the patient toward reality. Thus the ego may also return to the stage of omnipotence and magic. In the

symptomatology of some schizophrenics (as in catatonic stupor) unconditional omnipotence and magic apparently predominate; in paranoia,
the magical overevaluation of the entire ego and of the "demoniacal"
external world seems to prevail; in hysteria, the omnipotence of ideas
and gestures; and in the compulsion neurosis, the omnipotence and
magic of thoughts.

THE IDEAL EGO

The as-yet-unorganized ego which feels as one with the id corresponds
to an ideal condition, and is therefore called the *ideal ego*. For the small
child, up to the time when he meets with the first opposition to the
gratification of his needs, his own ego is probably the ideal. In certain
catatonic and manic attacks, in a number of those psychoses which lead
to mental deterioration, and also to a certain though lesser degree in
neuroses, the individual achieves such an ideal condition, in which he
grants himself everything pleasurable and rejects everything unpleasurable. Every person in his development leaves behind this narcissistic ideal,
but in fact always strives to return to it, most intensively in certain illnesses. When this ideal is again attained in the illness, the patient, in
spite of his suffering and the feelings of inferiority, feels more or less
omnipotent and endowed with magic powers, which in symptom formation he again places at the service of his morbid strivings. We must not
forget that every sypmtom contains a negative or a positive fulfillment
of a wish, which aids the patient in realizing his omnipotence.

In fantasies of "returning to the womb" the individual strives to
achieve this "ideal" state of his ego.

ATTEMPTS AT ADAPTATION TO REALITY

It is difficult to define in an exact, scientific way, what "reality" is. From
time immemorial, philosophers have grappled with this problem, and
nowadays physicists try to determine the meaning of reality. However,
for practical purposes, we can deal with that which everybody knows or
feels as "reality," just as he knows and feels what a perception is, although
it is almost impossible to grasp the essence of this concept. There is an
"internal" reality and an "external" reality. Desires, feelings, emotions,
thoughts are part of the internal reality, all that occurs in the external
world and stimulates our sense organs belongs to the external reality.
Both are dependent on changes which take place internally or externally.

As long as there is complete conformity between the ego and the id,
and as long as the individual practices magic freely, he is certainly not

adapted to reality. At the developmental stage of omnipotence and magic, the ego is still little differentiated from the id; inner stimuli are felt as overpowering and irresistible. Some schizophrenics feel the onrush of the instincts as an irresistible magic power to which they must submit unconditionally, while the compulsive neurotic, who likewise feels this compulsion, does not submit to it. Most mentally sick people as well as primitives believe they must employ magic in order to master their instincts and the stimuli of the outer world. The average healthy person gets along without magic, and is able to meet the demands of the inner and outer world with actions adapted to reality. In the remissions of schizophrenics it may be observed that parallel to the strengthening of object relations and to the consolidation of the ego, their own omnipotence and magic are ceded to the objects. But also in analytic treatment it occurs that the feelings of omnipotence are displaced onto the analyst. In ill people and children the renunciation of omnipotence and magic is only conditional. Children hope to regain it when they grow up. Neurotics expect to regain it through treatment; they expect to attain everything imaginable from the treatment—to become great artists, scientists, in short, individuals who command inexhaustible means for achieving everything they want and for conquering the world. The faith in one's own omnipotence is apparently so strong because man is not willing to renounce his narcissistic ideal ego completely. Schizophrenics, for instance, in whom many psychic processes go on consciously which are unconscious in others, seek consciously with all possible means to establish again their ideal ego, which they believe they have lost in their illness.

How, then, does the individual succeed in renouncing his narcissistic ideal ego and the concomitant omnipotence?

The ideal ego pursues the pleasure principle. It is a pleasure ego. Everything which gives pleasure is turned toward the ego and taken into it; everything unpleasant is rejected and projected and attributed to the hostile-seeming outer world. However, this kind of reaction to pleasure and unpleasure cannot be maintained. In the first place, it is not possible to eliminate every unpleasure (for instance, the one caused by hunger) merely by hallucination, and to attain gratification magically. Instead, the ego is forced to perform an action which *really* gratifies the need, and thus puts an end to the instinctual unpleasure. In the second place, one cannot continually be protected from the external world only by negation, by hallucination, or by projection. The external world, in spite of all its unpleasantness, cannot be completely denied or permanently escaped from. Therefore a mechanism must be developed which permits an unpleasant stimulus to be perceived. For through the accumulation of experience (memory traces of perceptions), the individual learns to recognize which stimulus causes pleasure and which, pain. This knowledge, which is based on reality testing, makes possible purposeful action. In order to be equal to the demands of life, the individual must progress from the unrestricted pleasure principle to the reality principle.

Between perception and action adapted to reality, thinking is gradually interposed, which sets the stage for action and may even take its place. Through greater life experience, that is, through the precipitates of external impressions in the memory traces of the system Pcs., which occasionally can be raised to the intensity of perception, there is formed in the ego an image of the external world which may not differ much from it. All the processes, whose nature is still not clear, which operate on these traces and form the process of thinking, take place within as if they were performed on the objects of the external world, but independent of it.

Changes which are made in the raw material of thinking through the "thinking process"—perhaps the "unconscious" mathematics, according to Ferenczi—may therefore correspond, to a certain degree, to the wished-for real changes in the external world. As in the animistic stage, the external world is an image of the inner world, so the opposite may be the case at the stage of coherent thinking. As soon as an identity is established between the result of thinking and the external reality given through the sense perceptions, purposeful willing and acting may begin. Thus a "thinking organ" develops which has the task of bringing into the sphere of the system of perception the result of thinking which has been achieved in an unconscious way in the system Pcs., just as the musculature brings objects of the outer world to the ego. If one wishes to see, to touch, to feel, to smell, an object of the outer world, he must put his musculature into motion in order to reach the object or to bring it into contact with his sense organs. Analogously, through the perception of thinking, the result of thinking is brought into the sphere of the "sense organ," the consciousness.

A special case of thinking is the function of judgment, an intellectual function preparatory to action adapted to reality. According to Freud, the judgment function of *negation* is a transitional phase between ignoring and recognizing. Recognition occurs in that state of psychic striving in which stimuli of the external world are searched for and are supplied to the perception system for the purpose of apperception, a state, therefore, in which the external world is affirmed by the ego. Hence the act of recognition is under the influence of impulses which strive for contact and union with the objects of the external world. It therefore derives its energy from the life-preserving sexual instincts, from the Eros. Ignoring, on the other hand, arises from a state in which the stimuli of the external world, which are always disturbing the sought-after state of rest, are perceived as unpleasurable. In this condition, the ego pays no attention to them, and shuts off its system of perception from them. Negation goes a step farther. It corresponds to the general tendency of the ego to eliminate, eject, and destroy the unpleasurable stimulus, just as recognition and affirmation follow the tendency to take in everything pleasant, to unite it with the ego. The function of judgment may therefore be traced back to instinct activity, whether its result is a positive or a negative one. Confirmation and recognition arise as a result of the life instincts, while ignoring and negation are the result of the destructive instincts.

In the negativism of the schizophrenic, destruction finds its most extreme expression. We know that the schizophrenic strives to free himself from all the acquired experiences of life through the withdrawal of libido from the ideational representatives of objects in the ego. Thus, with the progression of his illness, the schizophrenic strives also to give up orderly preconscious thinking, the elements of which are memory traces of stimuli from the outer world, likewise deposited in the ego as raw material. Herewith a libido regression and defusion of instincts takes place. Therefore, it could be assumed that the judgment function of negation regresses in schizophrenia to negativism in which the death or destructive instinct acquires direct access to the motor and perceptive systems of the ego.

This negative and destructive attitude toward the "strange and unknown world" seems to be the primary one. Indeed, children and primitives also flee from new stimuli or destroy their sources. How does the individual overcome this negative attitude toward the outer world? The answer to this question is made easier by consideration of the pathological condition of turning away from the external world.

The patient in catatonic stupor has his eyes open, and yet his look is vacant, and when he is addressed, he does not react, and one receives the impression that he *actively* avoids taking notice of the external world. Patients of this kind at times seem to be unaware of their real environment because they are able to "look through" an object in front of them as if it did not exist, and to stare at a hallucinated something which "they see behind it." Likewise, they frequently do not react when they are addressed by others, but at the same time they react to hallucinated voices. These patients therefore perceive internal stimuli, as if they were received by the sense organs. Instead of reacting with perception to external stimuli, they often react with a negative hallucination. The system Pcpt-Cs. is more or less closed to impressions from the external world. The most primitive function of the ego, the faculty of consciousness to receive stimuli from the real, outer world, in short, *the faculty of perception, is disturbed*. This is first expressed in "indifference" toward the world, in a kind of relation to it which indicates that no libido is striving toward it; in other words, the sensory organs receive no energy cathexis in order to gain impressions of the outer world.

If we stimulate such a patient, he reacts with a defensive motion or becomes aggressive. We interpret this as a rejection of impressions of the external world, which the patient apparently considers hostile and which arouses him to defense through destruction. The only sign of life which these patients give is frequently merely the fulfillment of their vegetative functions. Whatever gives them pleasure, such as the gratification of the most primtive, direct sexual instincts and ego functions, is affirmed; anything else which does not give them direct pleasure and which stems from the outer world is so strongly rejected that it even leads to negative hallucinations, and if this is still not sufficient, it is pursued with hatred and rage, thus with destruction. Only the inner world is acknowledged by the ego; everything else is denied or destroyed.

If these patients take notice of the external world, they are very uncertain as to what they perceive. They are frequently confused not only about the relations of two objects to each other, but also about the relation of their own person to any object. They are sometimes in doubt as to whether they are themselves or another person. The disturbed conception of the external world and of its relationship to themselves as a rule is accompanied by another phenomenon, *transitivism*.

This is conditioned by the vagueness of the "ego boundary." Normally we are able to distinguish between inner experiences and those which are given through external perceptions. This faculty is lost in transitivism. Here all psychic processes take their course in both directions: from the inner to the outer world, and from the outer to the inner world. What goes on within, the patient believes he perceives in the outer world, and changes in the outer world seem to him changes of the inner world. Animism, with its omnipotence and magic, here has its greatest triumphs. While, in the catatonic stupor, the relations to the external world are characterized by negativism—the world is denied, destroyed, and wiped away by negative hallucination—in transitivism these relations are governed by the conflict of ambivalence, with which the struggle for the existence of the object world seems to be closely connected. A patient expressed the following complaint: "I want to love you, but at the same time I must hate, bite, beat you. I do not know what it is that makes it turn out differently from what I wish." The conflict between the life instincts (Eros) and the destructive (death) instincts was very acute in this case. But, while in stuporous states the object world is completely denied, in transitivism attempts are made to affirm it; however, these attempts are again and again thwarted by the destructive instincts.

But how do those schizophrenics who strive for recovery free themselves from this conflict? In what way do they attain not only unequivocal acknowledgment of the external world but also adaptation to it?

Schizophrenia begins with a feeling of the "end of the world." It is a feeling of catastrophe, in which the world appears to the patient colorless, hazy, even dead, empty; reality is thus lost to him. The "end of the world" may be explained in general by the withdrawal of libido from the objects of the external world and the concomitant defusion of instincts. For the withdrawal of libido results in regression, in which the destructive instincts are freed. Instead of a libidinal relationship to the outer world, a sadistic one now appears, which really threatens the environment. This the patients seem to perceive, since to them "the world is dying." The feeling of catastrophe calls forth the desire to regain the lost world, to turn the libido again to objects. For this reason the further picture of the illness is characterized by the so-called *restitution,* the rebuilding of reality. Although not all phases of this restoration of reality are known, some can be reconstructed to a certain degree from the course of the illness.

The libido withdrawn from the external world cathects the ego, whereby the ego becomes enlarged by the quantity of libido which was attached to the objects. The results are omnipotence and magic (animism), megalomania, loss of the ego boundary and of reality testing. With the withdrawal of the libido, a defusion of instincts occurs, through which the destructive instincts are freed. Not only is the libido no longer carried to objects, but objects are even warded off with aggression and destruction. The destruction, however, is not aimed exclusively at objects, but also at the ego, as is demonstrated by the rejection of food, attacks of rage in which the patients injure themselves, and the like. Yet there is no doubt that some libidinal object relations are still present. This is apparent in the psychic contact which can sometimes be established with such patients. But the exceedingly acute ambivalence conflict soon destroys these relations again through the destructive instincts. If this phase is not permanent, it is succeeded by a stage which also can remain fixed; in this stage the destructive impulses which were stored in the ego are displaced onto the outer world; they are projected. A paranoid, hypochondriacal (physical) delusion of persecution develops. The content of this delusion is that the animate as well as the inanimate objects pursue the patient with every conceivable torture, the aim of which is a sexual one, against which he tries to protect himself in the most fantastic ways. The animate objects as a rule are homosexual in character; the inanimate ones seem always to represent symbolically the genital apparatus of the patient. As we have learned, the homosexual object is an object with which the subject is identified and into which, at the same time, the subject projects himself. The homosexual pursuer is therefore an object chosen upon an early narcissistic basis, just as the genitals projected into the objects of the outer world are likewise a narcissistic object.

In the "transitivistic" phase, the outer world and the ego flow together. The illness is initiated by the withdrawal of libido from the objects, and as the later development shows, the objects are also taken into the ego; they are introjected into the ego through the process of identification. While, in the catatonic stupor, no libidinal object relations are present, and in the transitivistic phase, attempts to establish such relationships appear which are, however, defeated by the destructive tendencies, in the paranoid state, a narcissistic, thus *a libidinal relationship to the outer world* is formed upon a *masochistic* basis. (The patients are tortured by the persecutors.) Even if the world still appears to the patient full of dangers, which he perceives perhaps better than the healthy person, still an important step toward adjustment to the world has been accomplished, because here the existence of a world, though narcissistically tinged and excessively hostile, is acknowledged.

In a case of schizophrenia, I could observe quite clearly that all those persons—a number of fellow patients, nurses, and the physician—who had been "added" to the ego of the patient in the acute phase were projected at the beginning of the remission, in the form of a hostile but erotically tinged power. But soon afterward one of these objects, the physician, was loved by the patient. The patient submitted himself to his guidance and leadership; he even went further and endowed him with his own omnipotence and magic. The patient also became more friendly with his environment. The "reconciliation" with the physician (the father) terminated in the acknowledgment of him as a superior being and in an expectant masochistic submission to his influence.

Even though the "healing process," the rebuilding of the destroyed object world, may halt at this stage, it nevertheless represents progress in so far as through it the lost reality is to a great extent restored. It is clear, further, that with the aid of projection, a *distance* between the ego and the objects which were merged with it is re-established, since the objects are again found in the external world and are perceived as phenomena of this outer world. Hence the most primitive functions of the ego again become effective, as for example, perception, the demarcation of the inner world from the environment, the acknowledgment of a reality existing outside of the ego.

Perception of the object no longer causes fear of a threatening danger, but becomes a *masochistic pleasure. Since the patient's own omnipotence is also relinquished to the object, and a tendency to regard the object with consideration appears, we may consider this process as the beginning of an attempt at adjustment to reality.* In the course of development of the adjustment to reality, aggression changes into a passive sufferance of the world; unpleasure is affirmed and accepted, according to Ferenczi. Since with this process sadism turns against the patient's own person and merges with the masochism of the ego, suffering itself becomes pleasure. If, with further development, masochism also is curbed, then the *overcoming of the suffering brings narcissistic pleasure.* The process in which sadism of the id changes into masochism of the ego usually takes place when the patient's libido begins to turn again to objects; this process generally ends with an at least partial reconstruction of reality. We conclude from this that a new fusion of the defused instincts occurs, whereby the destructive instincts are again mastered. According to Ferenczi, it is love in the broadest sense of the word; thus *Eros,* through restriction of aggression, leads first to *affirmation* of reality and later to adaptation to reality.

The gradual adaptation to reality in the process of recovery of the schizophrenic coincides with the libidinal cathexis of objects; it seems to take place in a way similar to the development of object choice in the child, which we have attempted to reconstruct. The lack of objects, combined with an accumulation and damming up of libido within the ego, gives rise to a longing for an object, which again drives the libido to objects and directs attention to reality.

The ego is at first merely an organ of reception and discharge. In the course of development toward adaptation to reality, the ego reaches a stage in which the aggressiveness against the outer world is deposited in the ego itself; the sadism of the id changes into masochism of the ego. But the masochistic affirmation of the painful perception of the outer world represents at most a recognition of reality and in no way a genuine adaptation to reality; this would require active measures according to the reality principle.

There is a form of illness, *depersonalization,* which shows that the recognition of the reality of sense perceptions is dependent on another factor, namely on a certain agency in the ego itself.

Depersonalization is a state of illness in which the world and all that is perceived appears changed and strange to the perceiving ego. This condition may be compared to the "end of the world" in schizophrenia, for there, likewise, not only the world but also the subject's own body appears changed and strange.

We assume that the loss of reality in schizophrenia results from the complete withdrawal of libido from objects and from the defusion of instincts accompanying this process. Essentially the situation is the same in states of depersonalization, which frequently appear after loss of an object or loss of love. The perception of the loss of a love object or the lowering of libido quantities is accompanied by the feeling that the reality of the perceptions and sensations of the ego has been lost. That destructive instincts are released is indicated by the painful complaints of patients in this state. This can be understood only in the following way: Since the complaints of the patients may be interpreted as castration complaints, and since persons who suffer from particularly severe states of depersonalization also show other signs of increased narcissism, the conclusion is therefore justified that identification of the ego with the genitals occurs. The destructive instincts freed with the loss of libido are stored up in the ego and threaten the ego as if it were a genital. Since depersonalization, whether of shorter or longer duration, appears almost always in consequence of a sudden loss of love, we may say that the feelings of estrangement are the direct result of the *sudden* transposition of the libido from the object to the ego. However that may be in finer detail, in any case a loss of the feeling of reality of sense perceptions and ego sensations accompanies the loss of object libido. We have just mentioned that at the height of the illness in schizophrenia, reality is lost, while in the remission, when the libido again begins to turn to objects, reality is acknowledged. Two conclusions result from this statement: First, for the recognition of the outer world there must be assumed a certain ability of the ego to turn libido toward objects. This formulation already has forced itself upon us in the discussion of the development of the ego from the rejection of stimuli from the outer world to their acceptance in a positive sense. The second conclusion leads to a new point of view: In depersonalization the ego perceives, but the reality of the perception is somehow not acknowledged by another part of the ego. It seems as though this part wished to ignore these perceptions altogether. The perceiving ego suffers from this rejection.

The recognition of reality and adaptation to it thus are dependent not only on the nature of the perceiving and acting ego, but also on an agency in the ego itself, which takes a certain position regarding the experiences of the ego and has to sanction them in order to render them fully real. That may perhaps explain in part why denying reality, not telling the truth, is considered immoral. At this point we must interrupt this discussion and turn our attention to this agency. We shall soon see how it influences the adaptation to reality.[2]

SELF-OBSERVATION

What is this agency? At first it seems to coincide with primary self-observation, but it has certain critical faculties, too. We have already encountered this agency in the dream, where it appears in two forms, first as endopsychic perception of ideas and sensations, thus as a function of the perceptive system of the ego; and secondly as an inhibiting, selecting, and criticizing faculty, which observes and influences our thoughts, wishes, and emotions. The latter is, generally speaking, situated in the system Pcs. (preconscious) and is called the dream censor.

In depersonalization, self-observation seems to be subordinate to this new faculty. Impressions from without as well as from within are first perceived by the ego; then what has been perceived is observed by this other faculty of the ego and is either approved or disapproved. This "inner observation" corresponds likewise to some kind of perception, but it differs greatly from the vividness of the sense perceptions of the ego. It is something else, but it is almost impossible to express in precise words what it actually is. Perhaps the difficulty of describing it might be

2 Of course, the problem of adaptation to reality has not been treated exhaustively in our deliberations. I recommend to those who have a deeper interest in this problem Heinz Hartmann's papers on the subject, particularly "Ich-Psychologie und Anpassungsproblem." *Internationale Zeitschrift für Psychoanalyse und Imago,* Vol. XXIV, 1939. Translated in part in: *Organization and Pathology of Thought,* edited by David Rapaport. New York: Columbia University Press, 1951.

explained by the fact that this inner faculty is stimulated only indirectly, by stimuli which have traversed the sensory organs of the ego; whereas the sense apparatus of the ego comes into direct contact with external, real impressions as well as with the inner instinct forces of the id. This new agency perceives merely traces of impressions, not the impressions themselves.

The impressions registered by this agency do not correspond to actual sense perceptions. Hence we may assume that another criticizing and observing faculty gradually splits off from primary self-observation, a faculty which is not endowed with sensory qualities. This assumption is supported by the following consideration: The infant in his earliest days perceives very little of the outer world in an *active* way. But from his very lively expressions of pleasure and unpleasure we are fully justified in concluding that he perceives his inner processes very well. It is known that in schizophrenia, active attention is disturbed; active turning to the external world, affirmation of this world, even if it is at the moment unpleasant, requires that the objects be cathected by libido. With a decrease of interest in the external world, self-observation increases (schizophrenia and depersonalization).

In self-observation the libido withdrawn from the external objects turns to the processes within the ego. Self-observation increases particularly in the hypochondriacal phase of schizophrenia. Anxiety which accompanies the hypochondriacal sensations induces the ego to put an end to their painful presence. Hence the task of self-observation as a function of the ego is to signal pain and thus to regulate the course of pleasure and unpleasure feelings. Self-observation is a primitive function of the ego and is most active when the libido is accumulated in the ego. An ego saturated with libido, in other words, a highly narcissistic ego, is not reponsive to external stimuli. Animals, for instance, neither hear nor see anything while in heat; the human during orgasm perceives only his pleasure, and nothing of the outer world. In the dream as well as in schizophrenia, active attention is directed to inner perception, that is, to self-observation. While in the neuroses self-observation likewise becomes more sensitive, it does not always reach consciousness, since impulses which might bring unpleasure are often checked at their onset. One might say: A mentally ill person is hypersensitive to unpleasure.

SUPEREGO (EGO IDEAL)

It would be incorrect to assume that self-observation is wholly transformed into attention. A part of it remains in its original form, while another part changes into the criticizing, selecting, restricting agency which watches, registers, and censors all processes within the ego, that is, the perceptions, sensations, and feelings. From this agency, logical and moral self-criticism develops.

In the average normal individual, the self-observing and the criticizing ego flow into each other; they work together harmoniously, at least within certain limits which vary with the individual. What the one does is not contradicted by the other; what one wishes is carried out without opposition from the other. Normally these two components of the ego cannot be distinguished from each other. Only when a severe conflict arises does their separation become apparent.

In depersonalization, for instance, there is an evident split in the ego. Perceptions, thoughts, and sensations are no longer felt as belonging to the ego; they appear alien. In the dream, this split frequently goes even further. The observing faculty is often represented by a figure in the dream; it is thus split off from the dreamer's ego and is projected onto another person. A psychic faculty which usually is inside the ego is suddenly transferred to the external world. In schizophrenia such a manifest splitting of the ego is the rule. In the delusion of being watched, for instance, the observing faculty is projected upon people who are everywhere, who spy on the patient, lie in wait for him, see and know everything he is thinking and wishing, and who gain a sinister power over him from which he cannot escape.

The healthy person is subject to a similar power. As long as this power is within the ego, it can scarcely be perceived; however, it can be perceived, when it is projected onto the external world. The paranoiac, who makes more use of projection than does the healthy person, becomes conscious of his own observing and criticizing faculty through projection. That inner processes are in fact perceived in this way, can easily be demonstrated in daily analytic practice. If, for instance, a patient complains unjustifiably that the analyst is angry with him and unfriendly, one may be certain that the patient is projecting his own hostile impulses onto his physician, or more correctly, that he feels within himself certain forbidden impulses, which become conscious to him only when projected upon another person.

This power is an internal one in the healthy person and in the neurotic, and an ostensibly external one in the psychotic, especially in schizophrenics, since it is transferred to the outside world. To schizophrenics, this power is usually something disagreeable, even hostile. We recall from earlier discussions that primarily every stimulus coming from the outside is felt as hostile and is warded off by projection. Since the ego of the schizophrenic regresses to an earlier stage of development, we could understand the projection of the inner impulses if we could assume that these are, in fact, felt as hostile powers. We have often made the comparison between the schizophrenic and the child. We know that at one time the child regards the person who takes care of him as a source of pleasure and at another as a cause of pain, an enemy, according to whether the person gratifies his instinct needs or fails to satisfy them. In normal development, not only is the primary resistance against the influences of training (by the mother or her substitute) overcome, but these influences are accepted and absorbed by the ego where, without being particularly noticed, they become effective in the further course of life; they become or remain unconscious. In paranoia, they emerge into consciousness with the aid of projection, but they are rejected: they reappear (as persecutors) in the external world, from where they came. Thus we conclude that the observing and criticizing faculty which has been erected in the ego develops through the absorption of certain external, mostly painful impressions. In schizophrenia this faculty becomes conscious again, and is rejected by projection.

Certain experiences with schizophrenics favor the assumption that the delusion of being observed is derived from scoptophilia, that is, from an erotized ego function which has changed into exhibitionism and as such has been projected onto the external world.

A nonpsychotic patient had believed from earliest childhood that by merely looking at his father, brothers, and later on, at other men, he would be able to castrate them, just as he feared he would be castrated by the glances of others. The same man tormented himself with self-observations and harsh self-criticism. Historically, it was possible to establish that at first he had been afraid of the faultfinding (and probably angry) looks of his mother, as the castrating person. (That such a thing as a hateful glance exists is well known. Belief in its magic is expressed, for example, in the superstition of the evil eye.) As a child, the patient apparently acquired this look through identification; indeed, one is always ready to react to enmities from the outside with hostilities from within.

Thus the sadism of the destructive instincts may turn against the subject in the identification and, fused with the exhibitionistic component instinct, may appear as masochism. The glance, turned inward, becomes a criticizing and spying faculty. Primary self-observation as a regulator of pleasure-unpleasure feelings is now joined by the new spying faculty which may oppose the remainder of the ego. It stems from the external world, from the power of the parents or their substitutes. It can be recognized best in depersonalization, where it is still internal, but nevertheless denies the reality value of the perceptions and feelings of the ego. The denial is, as mentioned earlier, a derivative of the destructive instincts.

Although the attempt to bring this faculty into relation with the individual erotogenic zones might appear somewhat hazardous, the fact cannot be denied that besides the elements of the visual sphere, elements from the auditory sphere also are contained in it. The auditory hallucinations of paranoiacs, in which they are accused of every imaginable evil deed, are well known; accusations and insults are heaped upon them. They are jeered at, and, by words, are incited to evil actions. (Positive voices will be discussed in another connection.) By listening attentively, one can often learn that these are words which come from the patient's early childhood and which were used by persons with whom he had libidinal relations. Through the "voices," orders and admonitions are given to him; the auditory hallucinations in an obvious way express the criticism of the parent or parent surrogate. Being spied upon in the delusion of observation, and the hearing of voices in the delusion of persecution, form a part of that critical faculty which in paranoia is projected onto the external world, and which in the healthy individual remains inside, noticed but little by the conscious ego. In the dream, it is called censorship and represents, in sleep, that psychic faculty which in the waking state exercises a selective, inhibiting, criticizing influence upon the intentions, wishes, and impulses of the individual. Topographically we have localized it in the system Pcs. Just as, in the dream, the criticizing words rarely become conscious, so, in the waking state, self-criticism only infrequently becomes conscious in words, and if it becomes conscious, it rarely has the same intolerable intensity as in the auditory hallucinations of the paranoiac. It is not consciously perceived; It is preconscious. The individual thus has absorbed a foreign being into himself not only through "looking," but also through "hearing." He has developed in himself a special faculty which, as it were, sees and hears inside, without, however, in a mentally healthy person reaching the intensity of direct perception. This faculty gains an irresistible power over the ego, from which it is detached only in the paranoiac delusion of persecution. All control and criticism which an individual, almost without noticing it, directs against himself, all of the self-reproaches which are more or less conscious are, in the paranoiac, attributed to an object in the external world. It represents, in a way, the projected conscience of the ill person.

The loss of conscience in schizophrenics is to be considered as a phenomenon which accompanies the loosening of their social ties and the abandoning of their ethical and aesthetic inhibitions. Since, at the same time, the schizophrenic feels punished, tortured, and magically influenced, the sadistic tendencies in the projected conscience are unmistakable. As, furthermore, the tortures and torments represent realized punishments, it seems that the sense of guilt is gratified by them; they are, to some extent, a counterpart to the conscience. It is significant that, in the phase of identification, the feelings of guilt are particularly strong, apparently because the objects are psychically destroyed. In the attempt at restitution in the phase of projection, the feeling of guilt is slighter, for through projection the objects are restored in the external world; they are endowed with the sadistic impulses of the patient and now are felt masochistically. But the schizophrenic defends himself against the return of these objects (as perceptions) because, belonging once more to the external world, they again call forth painful feelings. The ego has become more primitive and rejects every external stimulus. The ego has lost its organization; it is disintegrated, and a faculty which was previously within it is now outside, and is openly in opposition to it.

The origin of the controlling faculty of conscience is herewith disclosed. It develops as a result of the incorporation into the ego of the authorities of very early childhood. The delusion of persecution is therefore to be considered as an attempt at freeing oneself from the tormenting conscience. The conscience, however, again appears in it, partly as a threatening and partly as an executed punishment. The word "conscience" means "co-knowledge," participating in knowledge by means of inner knowledge, that is, through inner hearing and seeing. As already mentioned, the conscience does not possess any sensory qualities, as it does not perceive directly, but only through the intervention of the ego, which alone commands the apparatus of perception.

This new purely psychic agency differentiated from the ego is called *superego*. It develops from the absorption into the ego of stimuli from the external world with the aid of the sensory organs, through seeing, hearing, and so on. Later on, it separates from the ego (body ego). In the preceding chapter we learned that the first beginnings of the superego could be derived from the identifications which are formed in connection with the taking in of food. We must now extend the conception of identification, for the impressions of objects are absorbed into the ego by means of *all* the sense organs. Here they detach themselves from the body (perception) ego, amalgamate with each other, and thus form an independent structure, the superego.

At the beginning of the oedipus situation one cannot yet speak of a superego. It develops as a reaction to the oedipus complex. The boy mentally incorporates his father; he becomes, as it were, his own father. An ego change now takes the place of the former object relationship (of love and hatred for the father), a change which enables the boy to restrain his sensual strivings toward his mother and the aggressive ones toward his father. The sensual love for his mother is transformed into tender love; the aggression against his father changes into acceptance of the father's authority; the sadism finds modified expression in activity; in short, the boy begins to sublimate and to adjust himself to reality.

While in the ideal ego the impulses of the id are accepted without opposition and are granted satisfaction, this harmonious accord of the strivings of the ego and the id is disturbed by the formation of the superego. The superego inserts itself between the ego and the id. It ends the harmony which until then existed between them and influences the strivings of the id as well as those of the ego. In so far as the superego reflects the demands of society, it is the representative of society within the ego. The superego gains power over the ego. Hence the latter is compelled to adapt itself to the demands of society. Since society cannot consider the needs of the individual and since the superego becomes society's inner representative (Alexander calls it a rigid law code of all times, buried within the individual), it is characterized, as is society, by some severe, even harsh traits. It demands of the individual renunciations to the point of self-sacrifice. It is like a judge, a higher authority, which not only compels the individual to renounce certain pleasures, particularly those of a sensual nature, but also imposes punishments for violating its ideal demands. The ego, which commands the executive power, either carries them out or does not do so, according to its ability to resist.

How has the superego acquired this rigorousness? We know it is formed through identifications. According to our previous discussion, identification is the psychic equivalent of the oral phase and is ambivalent, for it can express hatred and love at the same time. In the oedipus situation, the boy protects himself most easily through identification against the father who is loved and hated at the same time. When the father is incorporated into the ego, the libido is withdrawn from him. In a different context, we have pointed out that with the withdrawal of libido, a defusion of instincts takes place, in which the destructive instincts are freed. As a result, the libido is desexualized. The destructive instincts then turn to the ego and are deposited there. The ideas of the father absorbed by the ego are held together by the sadism which was formerly directed against the father in the external world and now is effective in the ego. The psychic structure which has thus developed stands apart from the ego, more or less independently, as the superego. The sadism of the id which was aimed at the objects thus aids in forming the superego. This sadism of the superego, then, with individually varied intensity, takes the ego as an object. The real or supposed severity, which characterized the authorities who have been absorbed in the ego, continues to exist, but has changed from an outer to an inner one.

In the oedipus situation, a real superego did not yet exist. It developed only as a reaction to impulses which arose from this situation and had no prospects of succeeding in reality. The ego adapted itself to the necessities of real life in such a way that instead of useless object cathexes, a useful change in the ego itself took place. The superego, then, is a successor to the oedipus complex. The strivings of the id, which would have become a danger if they had remained unchanged, were subdued, taken into the ego, and desexualized. Their energy, which is free-floating while in the id, now becomes bound in the superego, which aids the ego in its struggle against the impulses which have become forbidden. The superego, accordingly, develops through identifications and derives its power from the energies which belonged to the objects whose cathexes have been withdrawn. But as the source of these energies lies in the id, the superego derives its power indirectly from the id. It is therefore connected with the id as well as with the ego. It can be influenced by both, just as it is itself able to influence the course of excitations in them. Reflecting its origins, it is at the same time the representative of the external world and of the id. Because of its position between the two worlds, it is confronted with the task of mediating between them, that is, of co-ordinating the strivings of the ego and of the id so that neither an inner, psychic, nor an outer, real conflict may arise.

But such an ideal accord is hardly ever achieved either in the mentally ill or in healthy individuals. In ill people it frequently fails because of the excessive demands which the superego makes on the ego. Melancholia is an outstanding example of the reaction to such a demanding superego. It is an illness in which the conscience, a function of the superego, seems to be especially involved. The patient suffering from melancholia subjects himself to innumerable self-reproaches; he is abject, feels unworthy, heaps all sorts of penances and punishments upon himself, even to the extent of suicide. It seems as if, in the melancholic, a force were especially developed, the aim of which is the patient's destruction. The melancholic rejects food, becomes stingy and frugal, and fears that he is ruining his family. Aside from mild delusional ideas which sometimes appear, the picture of melancholia is similar to that of mourning.

While the person who is mourning for the loss of a loved one succeeds, after the lapse of a certain time, in detaching the libido from the lost object, and returns to a normal state, the pathological mourning in melancholia has a cruel feature. The cruelty is directed chiefly against the melancholic's own person, although disguised traits of cruelty against the environment are unmistakable. Indeed, in severe depressions, a crime may be committed which to the ill person is a release and a redemption. In mourning as well as in melancholia an object cathected with libido has been lost. While in the normal course of mourning the withdrawal of libido from the object and its use elsewhere can be accomplished without a defusion of instincts (as, for instance, through displacement upon other objects), this cannot be done by the person inclined toward melancholia, because he starts with an excessively severe superego. The illness breaks out after *a disappointment in love* in the broadest sense of the word.

Being very narcissistic, such an individual cannot endure the injury to his self-esteem and withdraws his libido from the loved object. In an excessively ambivalent person—and the melancholic is very ambivalent—we know that with the withdrawal of libido there occurs a defusion of instincts whereby the destructive instincts are freed. While his ambivalence leads him to react to a disappointment by giving up the object, at the same time he identifies with the object. Since the object is incorporated in the ego, the distance between the image of the object and the superego disappears, so that the object becomes more accessible to the superego's aggressions. The sadism of the excessively severe superego is now directed entirely against the formerly loved person, with whom the ego of the melancholic has become one through identification. In suicide the melancholic wishes the death of someone else, but his identification with the other person leads to the destruction of himself. Of course, the excessive severity of the superego is not the only cause of melancholia;

in citing the example of this illness we intended merely to show what serious consequences may result from an oversadistic superego.

It is not always after a real loss of love that melancholia appears. I have seen melancholia set in after professional disappointments or after the patient had had to give up an aim to which he had devoted his entire life. This type of patient has, on the whole, loose object relations, but the demands of his ideals are exaggerated, and if he loses his only purpose in life, his constant readiness for identification and the originally strong sadism of the superego come to the fore. The excessively sharp and demanding conscience of a certain type of individual is rooted in this sadism, and not in genuine libidinal object relations. There are, for instance, fanatical reformers, moralists, ascetics, and the like who, to begin with, are not "good" people. The life histories of St. Ignatius Loyola and of Tolstoi may be mentioned as examples.

Also in other forms of mental illness the severely critical superego affects the attitude of the ego. In the compulsion neurosis, for instance, the libido has regressed to the anal-sadistic stage. But compulsive neurotics are not manifestly anal and sadistic in their behavior. On the contrary, they are excessively clean, conscientious, and considerate, and are tormented by self-accusations and self-reproaches. It appears as if the ego, influenced by the criticism of the superego, defended itself against the strivings of the id, with reaction formations. These patients do exactly the opposite of what the ego would like to do under the influence of the id, and punish themselves with self-torment and renunciations. In obedience to the demands of the superego, the ego renounces a striving of the id by changing itself through reaction formations. The superego here fights on two fronts: First, it attempts to inhibit the strivings of the id (with the aid of the ego); and secondly, it compels the ego to place itself in the service of the superego.

That the melancholic and the compulsive neurotic present such different pictures of illness in spite of the similarities of their superego structure may be attributed to two causes. The melancholic is inclined to narcissistic identification (loss of the object through absorption into the ego); the compulsive neurotic, on the other hand, despite his pronounced ambivalence, never completely gives up his object. Secondly, through the deeper regression and defusion of instincts in the melancholic, more destructive instincts are freed than in the compulsive neurotic, destructive instincts which enter the service of the superego and strengthen its sadism.

Mania, which often alternates with or follows melancholia, is perhaps the most striking proof of the inhibiting and oppressing influence of the superego, since it shows the personality when freed from this influence. Mania can be described as a euphoric state in which all social inhibitions are abandoned; or, expressed in our terminology, all identifications are dissolved. Freed from the necessity of taking his environment into account, the patient at every moment seeks anew to gratify his instinctual wishes. The manic is not subject to any commands, prohibitions, or restrictions. He feels free in every respect. He perceives no protest against the strivings of the id; the ego carries them out without inhibition. The manic state is the true opposite of the melancholic state. In pure mania, hardly any influence of the superego is to be detected. Since in most cases mania succeeds melancholia, it appears that mania represents a protest against the ill treatment of the ego at the hands of the superego in melancholia. Mania shows that a relinquishment of the identifications which had resulted in the formation of the superego is accompanied by a falling away of social inhibitions.

In the obsessional neurosis, the influence of the superego effects the inhibition of anal-sadistic strivings and causes reaction formations in the ego, whereas in hysteria, it manifests itself in the rejection of the genital libido.

It would be a one-sided evaluation of the significance of the superego, were one to ascribe to it only aggressive-sadistic intentions. A scrutiny of its development reveals that libidinal forces are also at work in its formation. The small child does not learn to control his vegetative functions by himself; he has to be taught to do this. A stranger cannot induce him to exercise sphincter control. Only for the familiar and beloved person who is taking care of him will he give up his feces at a specified time. He does so because the beloved person wishes it. He takes as his own wish, the wish of an object that is cathected with libido; he identifies with this object and acts accordingly. He is praised for this, and besides has the narcissistic gratification of having accomplished something noteworthy. Ferenczi speaks of a "sphincter morality." Probably, each developmental stage has its appropriate "ethics." A child on a higher stage of development will try not to cause any more pain to the beloved person when he senses that he has hurt her.

Although it cannot be denied that frequently a success in training is achieved through fear of punishment, still it must be stressed that the first acceptance of restrictions of the instinct life, especially of the component instincts, is usually based on love. When instinct gratification is renounced out of fear of losing the love object, this object is absorbed by the ego and cathected with libido; it becomes a part of the ego. In contrast to the ideal ego, it is called ego ideal. Out of love for this ideal, man clings to it and submits to its demands. Whereas the ego submits to the superego out of fear of punishment, it submits to the ego ideal out of love. The love, however, is not sensual, for when object libido changes into ego libido, desexualization occurs, which may be followed by sublimation. The narcissism of the ego ideal is a *secondary* one.

If the ego ideal and the superego are representatives of the outer world in the ego, it is easy to see that social actions and instinct renunciations do not occur out of hate or fear of punishment only, but that they can also be brought about through love. Identification is, indeed, ambivalent.

If, furthermore, the ego ideal is an image of the loved objects in the ego, and the superego is an image of the hated and feared objects, why is it that both concepts are confused and one is used for the other? The historical development of these two concepts is responsible for this. When Freud first formulated the concept of the ego ideal he stressed its libidinal aspect, perhaps keeping in mind also the tender ideal love surrounding it. Later he placed more stress on the sadistic side, the severe, demanding one, "standing-above-the-ego"—the superego.

In practice it is difficult sharply to separate these concepts from each other. The ego ideal seems to contain more maternal libido, the superego, more of the paternal; in reality both are fused. Furthermore, just as there are some destructive elements to be found within the ego ideal because the libido is desexualized, there are also libidinal forces at work in the formation of the superego, since it develops through identification with the ambivalently loved father. The predominantly maternal ego ideal starts to develop as early as the pregenital stages, but the predominantly paternal superego is observed first in the genital stage. The impetus for the formation of the superego is the danger of castration, a danger which threatens the entire ego in consequence of its identification with the genitals. By taking the father into his ego, the boy not only escapes the danger of castration but also gains a protector in the image of the father absorbed by the ego. The superego is formed not only because of hatred but also because of love and fear for the endangered narcissistic ego.

Just as the ego ideal (the superego) is loved by the ego, so the ego is loved by the superego (secondary narcissism of the ego). It is therefore comprehensible that the ego tolerates much at the hands of the superego. The ego frequently permits itself to be tormented by the superego because it is rewarded for this by love and protection. The instinct restric-

THE PSYCHOLOGY OF THE EGO

tion first demanded by the objects and later by the superego (ego ideal) is accepted because it is compensated for by narcissistic gratification. (There is, for example, the gratification of being a decent person.) With a primary disturbance of the relationships to objects and of the formations of ideals which are dependent on them, as in paranoia, an attempt is made to compensate for the lack of love with the aid of projections in delusional ideas. The persecution in ideas of reference and in hallucinations do not always contain a negation in the form of prohibitions, criticism, insult and the like; there are also appreciative, seductive "voices" praising the patient and admiring his beauty, kindness, and perfection.

Individuals raised without love become uncommunicative, inaccessible, inconsiderate, and gratify their instinctual demands more or less without inhibitions. One type of asocial individual develops from a childhood without love. Finally, persons with a well-developed superego frequently change after a disappointment in or a devaluation of their ideal. They lose their social feelings and become ruthless and cruel to their former friends. Apparently the narcissism of these individuals has been hurt, and they therefore rid themselves of their ideals and take revenge on the representatives of these ideals in the external world.

One might assume that those who have been raised with great love would develop a mild and indulgent superego. This is not usually the case, for love received restricts the aggression which, prevented from discharge, turns inward and reinforces the superego. An apparently paradoxical condition develops in which the parents' lenience and indulgence results in an excessively strict superego.

It makes a difference whether one has become a social being through hatred or through love. In fact, both factors play a role in the formation of social ideals, only in some cases one factor predominates, and in other cases, the other. If hate predominates, there will be an inclination to severity and asceticism; if love predominates, life will be more enjoyable. The superego-ego ideal is, indeed, a complicated structure with many ramifications; in one set of circumstances the more severe superego will prevail, and in another, the more lenient ego ideal.

It is by no means superfluous to stress the libidinal component of the superego, for this helps us to avoid a one-sided view not only of its meaning in the neurosis, but also of the role it plays in the adaptation of the individual to the social community. The ego obeys the superego not only out of fear but also out of love. The superego is, indeed, a derivative of the father.

Let us recall once more what has been said about the superego: it consists of the deposits of traces of life experiences, thus to a certain extent, of reality. But it not only represents reality in the ego, but also supports the ego in its struggle against the external world as well as against the id. We remember from its developmental history that it has evolved from the conflict between the instincts and the demands of the external world. Hence it is a product of the adaptation to reality and in turn becomes in itself an important agency which aids the ego in its further adaptation to reality. The example of hypnosis may serve as a negative proof of this. With the exception of the contact with the hypnotist, in hypnosis, every contact with the external world is cut off. The hypnotized person obeys all the orders of the hypnotist who is raised to the position of superego and is now—from within—able magically to nullify reality testing or to create a "reality" through a word, a glance, a gesture. This example shows clearly how the attitude of the ego can be changed *also* under the influence of the superego. Adaptation to reality is thus dependent not only on the ego but also on the superego. The latter has to sanction the perceptions, thoughts, and sensations of the ego, if they are to be felt as *real*.

The ego, however, is not dependent only on reality and the superego; it is also subject to the influences of the id. The same is true of the superego, which in turn influences the id. Thus there exist numerous communications between the psychic systems: first, between the ego and the id; secondly, between the ego and the superego; and third, between the superego and the id. Impulses which arise in one psychic agency may, in consequence of these permanent communications, make themselves known immediately to another one and, if necessary, influence the course of the excitation in the third. An impulse in the id is made known to the ego, and thereby the superego takes part in the excitation at the same time. If it is not in accord with the impulse of the id, the superego inhibits the executive organs of the ego and prevents them from carrying out the id impulses. In this way a harmonious cooperation of all the psychic agencies is made possible. It may also occur that the communication between the agencies is interrupted. If such an interruption is complete, a disintegration of the entire personality may result, and the ego may be placed at the mercy of the intentions of the id, as for instance in schizophrenia. But if the connection is not completely destroyed, if for instance it is interrupted only between the superego and the id, and not between the ego and the id (compulsion neurosis), then the superego is able to influence the strivings of the id only indirectly, those of the ego, directly. The ego receives impulses from the id; these, however, because of the uninter-rupted contact between ego and superego, are influenced to such a degree by the superego's immediate criticism that the intended actions of the ego are thwarted or modified. It may, furthermore, occur that the ego yields to an idea, wish, or impulse to which it is otherwise opposed, and does not recognize its own opposition. For the various components of the ego do not always develop uniformly. The parts of the ego which lag in their development may, like the instincts, become fixated; as a con-sequence of this faulty development, the fixated parts of the ego undergo repression and become separated from and unrelated to the rest of the ego. A condition results in which one part of the ego no longer under-stands another part. This kind of split in the ego is typical of the neu-roses, as we shall see clearly later on.

To cite an extreme example, I should like to mention a woman who was well educated and fastidious. She had lofty conscious ideals but fre-quently committed actions which contradicted her moral and aesthetic standards; she masturbated anally and occasionally played with her feces. When I called her attention to the contrast between this behavior and her good breeding and exaggerated cleanliness, she could not understand me. She replied in a stereotyped fashion: "But these are *my* feces." It is evident that a part of the infantile ego had been retained and had lost its connection with the other, very fastidious one.

Later I shall discuss this more fully. At this point I wish only to men-tion that the ego ideal—superego—may, in the course of time, undergo a change in accordance with the milieu and social conditions, though in most cases its unconscious portion (nucleus) is not touched. In conclusion I must stress that there is also a "negative superego," which compels the individual to aspire to an ideal opposite to the object of identification (for instance, a need to be unlike one's father). As far as I can see, how-ever, this ideal is a secondary one, grafted upon the primary one, and as a rule goes hand in hand with a more or less distinctly apparent split in the intentions of the superego (ego ideal).

In summary, one may say that the id represents the biological inher-itance; the superego, tradition or historical inheritance; and the ego, actual reality.

THE SYNTHETIC FUNCTION OF THE EGO

Freud ascribes to the sexual strivings of the id, the Eros, the tendency to join other objects, with the aim of creating a new unit. An analogous tendency may be seen in the ego, a tendency which finds expression in its faculty of binding, unifying, creating. This tendency of the Eros, however, has sexual aims, whereas in the ego it is devoid of sexual meaning.

The ego, once a part of the id, has, in the course of development, become separated and differentiated from it. The strivings of the id aim not only at union with the objects but also at reunion with the ego. The tendency of the id to reunite with the ego, and vice versa, never ceases; in other words, a tendency is always at work to undo the differentiation between ego and id, to merge once more. This tendency can be observed in dreams, in certain psychotic states, and in neuroses where the repressed part of the ego joins the id.

When the ego and id are united, complete narcissistic gratification is achieved. This state may be assumed to prevail in the first year of life, when full harmony seems to exist between id and ego; that which the id desires the ego carries out. When the expected gratification is not forthcoming, the harmony is disturbed.

As long as there is no superego, the relationship between ego and id is fairly simple. When the superego develops, this relationship becomes rather complicated, for the ego must carry on activities on several fronts. First, it coordinates the autonomous and contrasting instincts of the id and gathers them for unified action. (The ego does not tolerate contradictions.) Secondly, it brings the strivings of the id into accord with the demands of reality. Thirdly, it reconciles the demands of the superego with those of the id as well as with those of reality. Thus the ego exercises the function of a mediator within the personality as well as between the personality and the external world.

On the basis of the material obtained in psychoanalytic treatment, it seems that the first tangible manifestation of this ego function is the superego. The superego is the heir to the oedipus complex. The oedipus complex consists of certain relations of the child with his parents. It is resolved in such a way that its objects (father and mother) are replaced by the superego; that is, a relationship to objects of the external world results in a change of the ego. The psychic representations of these objects are assimilated by the ego and held together by the bond of feelings and affects attached to them. The ego then *creates*—out of the infinite number of perceptions, impressions, feelings, emotions pertaining to the psychic representations of the objects—a new and, under certain conditions, independent formation, called the superego. This new psychic agency is thus formed through assimilation and integration of quite a number of traces left in the ego by external and internal stimuli. In this assimilation and integration the ego exercises a function which is called its *synthetic function.* *The synthetic function of the ego thus manifests itself in the assimilation of internal and external elements, in reconciling conflicting ideas, in uniting contrasts, and in activating mental creativity.* Another manifestation of the synthetic function of the ego is the *need for causality,* which, in its primitive expressions, becomes apparent even before the formation of the superego. Though not an instinct, this need has an instinct's compelling force. I do not intend to enlarge on this problem as such, because the problem of causality belongs to the domain of philosophy. I will discuss the *need* for causality, a psychological problem, the need to connect two facts in such a way that the second seems determined by the first. The strength of this need can perhaps best be illustrated by the example of a posthypnotic suggestion. The hypnotized person in question was given the order to go to the corner of the room, to pick up an umbrella that had been placed there, and to open it five minutes after awaking from the hypnosis. When he had executed this order, he was asked why he opened the umbrella. He replied: *"Because it is raining."* (As a matter of fact, it was not raining.) The need for causality is obviously so strong that when the cause is missing, it is invented.

The seeking for connections in a chain of events in which the last link is determined by the first, seems to be at the root of causal thinking. This process is certainly a preconscious psychic activity. If the "causal" relation discovered is an illusion, not a fact, then its finding is called rationalization. It seems that rationalization in the waking state corresponds to the secondary elaboration of the dream. The secondary elaboration reconciles contrasts which are too sharp, fills in gaps and gives the appearance of plausibility to illogical mental processes of the dream. The secondary elaboration takes the lead where the dream work has not been successful in disguising sufficiently the latent dream thoughts, and gives the manifest dream a certain logical appearance. Where repression is least successful, as for instance in schizophrenia, where the repressed material succeeds in directly entering consciousness, rationalization is most prominent. As the ego, due to its tendency to unify and connect, cannot bear contradictions, things or ideas, which in no respect belong together, are brought into "causal" relation indiscriminately. Rationalization, which in psychoses takes the form of delusions, bridges the gap in the thinking activity caused by the split of the ego. (The ego cannot bear lacunae in its consciousness.) The younger, the less logical, the more primitive or the sicker a person is, the more easily will he find "causes."

As indicated before, the need for causality is as urgent as if it were the derivative of an instinct. It manifests itself in childhood in the form of curiosity. First, the child asks questions about the origin of things and mostly means thereby the origin of human beings. Later on, if the child is not intimidated, he also asks about the difference between the sexes. The child's curiosity is in fact curiosity driven by a sexual instinct. One would almost be inclined to consider infantile curiosity a component instinct. Sexual instincts are a manifestation of Eros, which represents the totality of all life instincts. Their aim is to unite two beings to create a new one. The compulsion to search for the actual cause of the physical world, the need for causality, appears to be analogous to the creative quality of Eros. (When one individual unites with another, a new being is created; when the explorer discovers the cause of a phenomenon, he often can re-create the phenomenon.)

Both the creativeness of Eros and the need for causality of the ego strive for a connection between two links and the creation of something new; one process, however, is the manifestation of the id, the other, of the ego. It seems justified to assume that the need for causality is a sublimated derivative in the ego of the Eros. What appears in the id as a tendency to unite two beings, manifests itself in the ego likewise as a tendency to unite, not objects, however, but ideas, thoughts, memories. As long as this tendency for synthesis remains in the id, it has a sexual connotation; when it enters the ego, it is sublimated and one of its manifestations is the need for causality. Altogether, the synthetic function of the ego represents a principle of the highest order in mental life.

For the tendency of the ego toward uniting, binding, and creating includes also a tendency for simplification, generalization, interpretation, and finally understanding. In schizophrenia, incoherent, even contradictory ideas are connected, which makes the thinking of these patients appear so bizarre. It shows the patients' attempts to escape from the chaos in which they find themselves by forming a conception of life with unity and no contradictions. By generalization they try to reconcile contradictions; they merge the memory traces of past experiences with actual perceptions and form a new *Weltanschauung* (philosophy of life), adapted to their particular psychological needs. Actually, it is the philosophy of a mind deranged: out of range of reality. They interpret the world in their own way and satisfy their urge to "understand" the world, which gives them a certain degree of satisfaction and sometimes reduces their anxiety considerably. As a rule, their philosophy of life is essentially a cosmological one, based on the problem of the genesis of man; the world which they feel lost, is reborn, created again in their minds with the help of synthesis. The problem of the genesis of man is thus generalized and reduced to a simple formula in the idea of the creation of the entire world.

The tendency to simplify and generalize, to integrate and the like, reveals that the synthetic function of the ego is subject to an economic principle, which induces the ego to economize expenditure of effort. In the id the psychic energy is free-floating, in a state of chaos; when this energy passes over into the ego, it changes into bound energy so that the contents of the ego become stable, coherent. While there is chaos in the id, order reigns in the ego: the primary process of the id is replaced by the secondary process of the ego, the unconscious of the id becomes in part preconscious in the ego, where it can be harnessed by its synthetic function. Synthesis thus brings about not only unity of the whole personality but also simplification and economy in the ego's mode of operation.

The younger the child, the more primitive the adult, the less his ego is integrated, the more easily it can tolerate contradictions. The higher the mental development, the more integrated the ego is, the more it strives for unification. The synthetic function of the ego fails when the personality disintegrates completely, as for instance in psychosis. Yet, when the integrity of the ego is most seriously threatened, but a measure of constructive energy is still available (as in the paranoid forms of schizophrenia), the synthetic function of the ego is immeasurably stimulated; everything is indiscriminately connected and merged, systematized, all of which finds its final expression in delusional ideas. Thus the ego's synthetic function is overextended. (The generalization, simplification, and systematization of the schizophrenic's delusional ideas, then, are reminiscent of some philosophic *Weltanschauung*.)

The delusions of paranoia give the impression that they represent not only an attempt at reconstruction of reality but also an attempt at sublimation. In fact, artistic, scientific, and social creativeness, that is, sublimation, is dependent on the proper functioning of ego synthesis. Indications of sublimation can be recognized very early. By its cleanliness, for instance, the little child gives up direct instinct gratification in favor of higher aims (love of mother). Full sublimation, however, does not occur before the resolution of the oedipus complex and the institution of the superego. Indeed, out of libidinal relations to objects of the external world there develop nonlibidinal relations, such as morality and social feelings, new feelings synthesized out of the feelings of the oedipus complex.

A woman's choice of her profession may serve as an example of sublimation: She was allowed to study medicine, after having overcome great resistances on the part of her father who was himself a physician. After her first year of study she married. Although she was an enthusiastic student of medicine and had passed her examinations with honors, she wanted to give up her studies after her marriage. First, however, she sought to induce her husband, who was studying in another field, to change to the study of medicine. The motive for her wish to give up the profession she had voluntarily chosen was revealed in the following train of thought: If her husband became a physician, she would not have to become a physician herself, since indirectly, through her husband's profession, she could maintain the only remaining relationship with her father. The sublimation occurred here in a way similar to what occurs in the formation of the superego: The absorption by the ego of the libidinal object and the accompanying instincts, the renunciation of the object through identification, and the turning of the instinct from its direct aims. Object and instinct were combined in the ego, the former as an idea which had become unconscious, the latter as an aim-deflected instinct, hence as desexualized psychic energy. In our patient this energy found discharge first in her studies and later in her profession. After she had found her object and was able to discharge her instinct in a direct way, she was willing to put an end to the sublimation.

It is obvious that the problem of sublimation in particular as well as that of synthesis in general is not exhausted here.

The main task of the synthetic function is that of mediating in internal conflicts. The attempt at solution of the conflict may result in sublimation, change of character, neurosis, or psychosis. Some of these solutions will be discussed in another context.

In conclusion, it should be stressed that the ego, due to its development from the id, is replete with derivatives of aggression in all its manifold forms as well as derivatives of libido. The latter manifests itself in its constructive synthetic function which impels the individual toward harmonious unification and creativity in the broadest sense of the word.

REACTION FORMATIONS OF THE EGO

In a sense the superego can be considered a reaction formation of the ego, a complicated reaction to the oedipus complex. The fully developed superego in turn stimulates the ego to further reaction formations. The ego has to change its structure according to internal and external needs. It has the difficult task of maintaining itself in the face of three kinds of influences—the superego, the external world, and the id. Although its core is stable, the structure of the ego as a whole changes according to the influences to which it is subjected. Instead of reacting to these influences, that is, perceiving and discharging or abreacting them, the ego assimilates them and creates something new. Consequently it will contain traces of the external world, of the superego, and of the id. Here we see the synthetic function of the ego at work. These reaction formations contribute much to the shaping of character; this aspect, however, will not be discussed here any further, for it will be taken up in a later chapter.

At this point I want merely to stress that very early there develop reaction formations of the ego which also contribute to the final structure of character. I should like to deal with only two of these numerous early reaction formations: disgust and shame.

It is difficult to say when the first signs of disgust appear, but certainly not before the end of the first year. According to Freud, feelings of disgust seem to have developed very early in the history of mankind, probably at the time when man raised himself from the ground and assumed the erect posture. As a consequence, the olfactory nerves received fewer stimuli and the sense of smell underwent *organic repression*. This repression protected man from returning to a previous state of development in which the male was sexually aroused by the odor of the menstruating female. As observation shows, it also protects him from enjoying the smell of human excrement. Nevertheless, the smell of the human body still in some degree enhances sexual attraction.

Disgust is closely connected with the physiological function of the digestive system. It starts with nausea and salivation and culminates in vomiting, in which the stomach contents are ejected through antiperistaltic muscular movements. Disgust thus is the opposite of appetite and hunger, in the physiological as well as in the psychological sense. Hunger aims at introducing something into the stomach, disgust at eliminating something. Disgust at sexual activity is hidden behind many hysterical symptoms. For instance, tracing certain fantasies of female patients suffering from *globus hystericus* and nausea, we learn that they wish to take the male genital into their mouths. Disgust in this case is a reaction formation of the ego to an oral sexual impulse. In other cases, as in melancholia or in compulsive neurosis, such oral impulses manifest themselves in coprophilic fantasies, fantasies which are acted out in perversions and in schizophrenia. If we bear in mind that there are primitives who in observation of certain rites eat corpses and excrement and that, furthermore, the time is not long past when excrement was considered an important remedy in folk medicine, the conclusion is justified that disgust is a consequence not only of the repression of the primary olfactory sense, but also a reaction to coprophagic and cannibalistic impulses. This conclusion is confirmed by the fact that the more intense the conscious disgust is, the more coprophagic and cannibalistic are the unconscious fantasies. It may be true that the reaction of disgust becomes reinforced and generalized under the influence of the superego and that then it spreads to everything forbidden; but, primarily, it seems to have developed very early, even before the formation of the superego.

Although the origin of the sense of shame is just as obscure as that of disgust, it is evident that it too represents a reaction formation, specifically to exhibitionism. Where the sense of shame is excessive, there is excessive exhibitionism in the unconscious. The erythrophobic, that is, the patient suffering from fear of blushing, is extremely bashful. We have learned from analyses of such patients that their faces have become "genitalized," that is, they have acquired erotic qualities and play the role of genitals. Erythrophobia is thus a reaction to the repressed wish to show the genitals. This wish, however, is accompanied by the fear of losing the genitals. Hence erythrophobia is a reaction to fear of castration if the genitals are exposed. The delusion of being watched represents "negative exhibitionism," that is, a state of mind in which exhibitionism is warded off. Translated into the conscious language of a normal person, the meaning of the delusion would be: "It is not *I* who wish to show myself (to be seen); the other person wishes to see *me*." In other words: "I want to show myself (my genitalia)."

The analysis of the exhibitionism of a male patient revealed that he was afraid of losing his genitalia merely by being looked at, just as he was unconsciously convinced that he robbed other men of their genitalia by looking at them. In another case, looking had a conscious sadistic purpose. The sense of shame would thus be an equivalent of the fear of castration. This is in accord with Freud's conception that man acquired the sense of shame when he assumed the erect posture, as a consequence of which the genitalia could no longer be hidden and hence required protection.

Two objections could be raised against this conclusion. First, that the woman has no penis, hence could not have castration fear, at least not to the same extent as the man. Secondly, that shamefulness in all human beings does not refer only to the genitals but to everything else as well.

To this we can reply: male exhibitionists show their genitals, but I have never heard of women exhibiting their genitals, at least not in our culture. The entire body, which is far more erotized than that of the man, is to them a substitute for the "missing penis." Having no penis of which they can be "proud" like the boy, they exhibit the entire body; normally they do this more frequently than the man does his genitals. Finally, girls masturbate on the clitoris, the rudimentary penis; they meet with prohibitions just as boys do, and these prohibitions replace the castration threat. The prohibition against masturbation and showing the genitalia is extended to all bodily functions and leads to the concealing of all other sources of pleasure (erotogenic zones). The more gratification they offer, the more anxiously they are hidden. It may be mentioned here how interested many children are in watching the excretory processes and how anxiously they hide them when they have become adult.

It follows from all this that shame is a reaction formation of the ego to the wish to exhibit. Castration fear is the motive power of this reaction formation.

The fact that bashfulness, disgust, anxiety, and the feeling of guilt are often mistaken for one another proves that they are somehow related. "Ugly" is often used for "disgusting" or "bad." "Beautiful," "good," and "clean" have become almost synonyms. The transgression of the bounds set by shame and disgust calls forth the same feelings of guilt as does a moral transgression. They have a common origin; they develop from inhibitions of certain excessive instinct strivings, and they represent reactions of the ego to these instincts. The deeper the layers of psychic life into which we penetrate, the more difficult it is to distinguish them from one another. The reaction of shame becomes more and more a general reaction to nonsexual strivings and helps to hide all kinds of feelings, thoughts, and ideas. We are *ashamed* of an immoral thought or an immoral deed, probably because our entire instinct life has been prohibited.

These reaction formations are weaker in perversions and in certain psychotic states. It is open to question whether this is due to a primary incapacity of the ego to offer full resistance, or to the overpowering demands of the instinct, or else to the weakness of the superego. Generally shame and disgust are increased in neuroses, decreased in certain states of schizophrenia, in manic states, and in perversions.

The Feeling of Guilt

Whereas shame and disgust are easily recognized, this is not always so with the feeling of guilt. It appears in numerous forms: as a feeling of discomfort, as a sense of dull inner tension, as an urge to offer gifts or to spend money, as courting the favor of others, as exaggerated helpfulness. Some patients have the feeling that, in spite of all their efforts, they are unable to give from within all that they wish to give in order to free themselves from a terrible tension.

The feeling of guilt may also appear in a variety of expressions of a somewhat different type: as constant anticipation of impending disaster, as inferiority feeling, as humility or suffering, as a wish to be punished, as readiness for sacrifice, as a compulsion for purification.

The first group of expressions of the feeling of guilt is clearly directed to the outside world, seeking reconciliation with this world, whereas the second group is directed to the ego, representing an attempt to punish oneself.

If shame and disgust are defense reactions to exhibitionistic and anal-oral instinct needs, we must ask ourselves whether the feeling of guilt likewise is a reaction to some instinctual demand.

In the care of the small child the primary concern is the regulation of the intake of food and of evacuation, thus the restriction of the oral and anal instinctual aims. Disgust seemed to us a reaction to those aims. We may now state that the mastery of the instinct life in the first developmental stages is, in the main, concerned with the suppression of impulses whose source is the entire digestive tract. We may consider as a single erotogenic zone the tract which is terminated at one end by the mucous membrane of the mouth, at the other end by the mucous membrane of the anus. Its task is the intake of food and elimination. The taking in of food and its further progress in the digestive tract requires muscular activity, specifically that of the extremities—since with the help of the extremities food is brought to the mouth— and of the mouth apparatus. The striated, voluntary musculature of the mouth is continuous with the involuntary, smooth musculature of the digestive tract which advances the food through contractions and, with the aid of the voluntary musculature of the abdominal walls, evacuates it after it has undergone certain chemical changes. We know that a libidinal gratification occurs with the intake of food.

On the other hand, the musculature which is necessary for the mastication and digestion of the food is an instrument of sadism which is under the sway of the destructive instinct, as is all musculature. Sadism is connected with libidinal instincts; it is even at the service of the libido, since it brings the object within reach of the individual. With the aid of the striated musculature the object is brought close to the individual and is destroyed, and with the aid of the smooth musculature it is advanced in its course within the organism and assimilated. As soon as the object (food) has been incorporated, sadism takes effect no longer outside, but within the body. A disturbance in the course of the excitation from the moment the urge sets in (hunger) to the moment of ejection results in states of tension which are unpleasurable and, with increase of excitation, may lead to bodily pain. The libido provides the impulse for the action. The action is carried out by the musculature, the instrument of sadism. The sadism within the ego, rather the *primary masochism*, seems, under the influence of the libido, to be turned away from the ego while seeking an object for the libido, but after its gratification again to return to and settle within the ego. *The turning of sadism against one's own person seems, then, the first consequence of the desire and its gratification.*

If we assume that this process takes its course not only in the bodily sphere but also in the mental sphere, then the gratification of libidinal strivings would likewise result in the turning of sadism against one's own person. Any disturbance in the course of this psychic process could lead to feelings of tension and pain, as in the physiological process. Identifications are, indeed, psychic equivalents of the oral phase. Those identifications which lead to instinct suppression, as is the case for instance in toilet training and the restriction of gluttony, are accompanied by feelings of unpleasure and states of tension. When the child resists the influences of training and rejects the identifications, a conflict arises with the environment, but not within the ego. It is an external conflict. The child is, of course, weaker than the adult and develops anxiety. The child suppresses his oral, anal, and aggressive impulses. He complies with social standards. *Social anxiety* brings about the child's first adaptation to society. This infantile social anxiety forms the core of what later becomes the fully developed sense of guilt.

The feeling of guilt in the strict sense of the term develops not out of conflict with the external world (mother or nurse) but with the internal world. Originally, the ego develops barriers against oral, anal, and other strivings, in the form of disgust, shame, and the like. The formation of these barriers seems to be the result not of upbringing alone, but of a deeper biological factor as well. All of these factors begin to appear in the preoedipal phase as an inhibition of pregenital drives of the component instincts. After the integration of the pregenital drives in the phallic phase and the establishment of the oedipus complex, the superego begins to emerge. From here on the feeling of guilt in the strict sense serves to inhibit not only the pregenital drives but also the genital one and the aggression. The feeling of guilt now becomes a moral factor. It is a state of mind which results from real or intended inhibitions imposed by the superego on the ego. In short, it is the result of a conflict between ego and superego.

Usually we do not feel that we have a superego. Only if the ego is at variance with the superego, if the ego commits actions, psychically or really, or even if it merely intends to perform actions which call forth criticism or disapproval on the part of the superego, it makes itself felt in that peculiar state of mind which manifests itself in the ego, consciously or unconsciously, as guilt and need for punishment.

Freud distinguishes—as shown above—two kinds of guilt feelings: one, which develops as a reaction to external factors, known as the primary, social feeling of guilt; and another which develops under the influence of the superego.

The primary feeling of guilt arises as a reaction to the fear of punishment when certain instinctual demands are not renounced. For the small child, punishment is identical with loss of love; one is not punished if one is loved. This feeling of guilt stems from the fear of loneliness, for man dreads to be alone. This anxiety is an objective anxiety, and the fear of the loss of the libidinal tie to a real object, therefore, has a social character from the very beginning. Hence this feeling of guilt is also termed *social anxiety*. That feeling of guilt, on the other hand, which develops under the influence of the superego, is less dependent on external factors; it arises when there is no objective reason for anxiety, when there is no conflict with the environment. In order to understand this, we must further consider the development of the superego.

Freud was of the opinion that the feeling of guilt (and morality in general) derives its power from the oedipus complex. In the primal horde, the sons murdered the primal father and devoured him in the totem meal. After the deed was committed, homosexual love for the father increased, and remorse and yearning for him developed. Remorse and longing combined in the feeling of guilt. The sons wished the father back in life—that is, they wished to re-establish him in the external world. This wish could be satisfied only with the help of projections. The fathers became gods, projected into the external world. Now the frustrated homosexual libido could be satisfied in a sublimated form, in religious worship. If the conception is correct that archaic, prehistoric experiences are inherited and can under certain conditions be reactivated, then it must be possible to discover in psychic life even today hidden traces of the murder of the primeval father.

In the development of the individual a mere thought or an impulse may have consequences similar to what once occurred in reaction to the deed, in the development of mankind. The father is no longer eaten, but he is absorbed by the ego, he is psychically devoured, as it were. This process is, as has been stated previously, the psychic equivalent of the oral developmental stage of libido and is termed identification. The father images absorbed by the ego are differentiated from the rest of the ego and form the superego. The ego behaves toward the superego as earlier the son behaved toward the father. The following dream of a patient, which has already been published elsewhere illustrates this:[3]

"I am on a street, near a semicircular *cave*, in front of a meadow, which I only sense, but, for the time being, do not see. In the cave, which is broken out of a rock wall, stands *a bed which belongs to my older brother.* I have the feeling that *my father is sleeping in a bed on the meadow and that this is a good opportunity to kill him.* Drowsy, he is being lured up to the cave, and then I notice two iron gates, one towering from below upward and the other one in the opposite direction, but they do not meet. The gate is made of vertical iron bars held together by some horizontal bars. My brother seizes Father around his waist from behind and tries to pull him through the opening between the bars. Father is awakening gradually and calls for help. Since both of us now understand that our assault has failed, I become afraid and wake up with the thought that we are lost. After falling asleep again, I see the meadow submerged under water. I notice a white shirt which is being rinsed in the water, by an arm. The shirt is entirely spread out, but between the front and back are floating light brown, soft feces of a child, which cannot be removed from the shirt. Very uneasy because the shirt cannot be cleaned, I can no longer watch."

The patient thinks that the cave with the pointed bars represents a mouth. The older brother probably represents the dreamer himself. He always wanted the older brother to show more courage toward their father; he wanted him as an ally in his fight against the father. The wish to kill the father in the dream corresponds to a frequently recurring fantasy that the father would die or that he had already died. The dragging of the father through the gate might express the wish to swallow a strong man, since, firstly, he had believed that he would be strengthened by swallowing semen, and secondly, he always fantasied an immense penis which he would take in his mouth.

He was struck by the fact that in the dream he had had a feeling that he ought to feel sympathy for his father, and he recalled that after fantasies of the death of his father he was always seized by remorse and that to comfort himself he would try to think something nice about him. "My father in the dream," he said before my interpretation, "did not die. I

[3] "Schuldgefühl und Strafbedürfnis." *Internationale Zeitschrift für Psychoanalyse,* Vol. XI, 1926. Translated as "The Sense of Guilt and the Need for Punishment," in: *Practice and Theory of Psychoanalysis.* New York (Nervous and Mental Disease Monographs, 1948) : International Universities Press, 1955.

have only retained a feeling of guilt in place of the intention of killing him." The cave, he said, reminded him also of the times when he stood for hours in front of the bear cage in the zoo, waiting in vain to see the intercourse of the animals. Furthermore, he remembered his fantasy of the big penis of the father entering into the mother and sprinkling and nourishing the child in the womb. When in later years he learned, with anxiety and disgust, how children are conceived, he had thought that the woman as well as the child within her might be terribly injured. According to these associations, it seemed to him that while in the womb he wished to swallow his father, that he wanted to suck in his entire strength and thus to kill him.

Despite its complexity, the dream shows its main theme very clearly: *the ambivalent attitude toward the father and the psychic state of mind which Freud reconstructed in terms of that of the primal horde after the primal deed. The remorse, the yearning, the anxiety, the feeling of guilt prevent the dreamer from repeating the same crime.*

The associations to the second part of the dream indicate the patient's fantasies about reviving or reconstructing the lost object by anal birth.

The validity of this interpretation is corroborated by the following detail from the analysis of the obsessional neurotic who has already been discussed:

One morning he received a sealed registered letter from his firm, which terrified him. He feared that the firm was sending him a certain sum due him and, therewith, breaking off all business connections with him, because, as he thought guiltily, he had not been working as well lately as he used to. Before opening the letter he felt an urge to defecate. *Immediately after the evacuation it occurred to him* that the sealed letter in no way implied the breaking off of relations, but contained a check covering his recent expenses, and this proved to be the case. Similar experiences were repeated regularly during his deepest depressions, when he doubted the existence of God. After a copious stool, "as soon as it [the stool] was out," an amazing number of proofs for the existence of God came to his mind, whereupon the depression disappeared. Although it angered him that the enlightenment took place just when he was on the toilet after having defecated, he nevertheless felt free of his doubt for a short period.

Here I should like to quote Róheim, who seeks to show that the mourning rites of primitive peoples represent a reaction to the primal crime. The mourning ceremony in some primitive tribes consists of certain cleansing rites which are preceded by the ejection of feces on the grave of the deceased. In melancholia, the prototype of an illness in which the conscience plays an important role, anal and oral strivings dominate the clinical picture. We owe to Abraham the proof that in melancholia, which likewise represents a kind of mourning rite, the mourning for the lost object is marked by oral and anal symptoms. In catatonic attacks, patients smearing their feces believe that they are making an offering in order to expiate their guilt and give birth again to the world which, in their delusion, they believe they have destroyed. Similarly we can see, in neurotics, evidence that feelings of guilt find a good sounding board in the digestive tract. Defecation and vomiting often lead to a discharge of the feeling of guilt. Some short examples may clarify this:

A female patient of the obsessional neurotic type had to go away on a trip. Her first words in her analytic hour the day before the journey were: "I hate to travel to Berlin, it simply horrifies me." At this moment borborygmus occurred, to which I called her attention. The patient laughed at me, saying that this noise could not possibly have any connection with the thought she had just uttered, that she was simply hungry. I did not reply, and the patient was silent, but the first sentence she uttered after her silence was: "Really, I feel guilty toward Anatol." Anatol was at that time in Berlin where he eagerly awaited her.

Another female patient suffered from states of excitement alternating with depressions, during an interruption of her treatment. She could neither eat nor sleep and was constipated. Besides this, she was seized by a compulsion to buy things. She bought a great number of things she did not need and gave them away immediately. This compulsion followed a dispute with an attendant at a public bathing establishment who accused her of not having paid the admission fee. Since this time she had to think constantly of a dishonest act which she had actually committed shortly before. Checking a bill which she had just paid, she had noticed an error in her favor. She dismissed her original impulse to return the difference immediately with the reflection that the owner of the business was rich enough anyway. It is thus obvious that the patient wanted to make amends for her dishonesty through the buying compulsion. The stress lay not on the buying but on the spending. She paid her debt, even though at the wrong place. It is clear to the analyst that here money stands symbolically for feces.

One might raise the objection that it is only in conversion hysteria that the anal-oral components of the feeling of guilt change into symptoms, since in hysteria there is the tendency generally to transform the psychic into the physical, whereas in the obsessional neurosis and in other illnesses the feeling of guilt remains in the purely psychic realm. It is known, however, that there is no obsessional neurosis without a hysterical admixture; the hysterical symptoms of the compulsion neurosis manifest themselves, in my experience, primarily in the digestive tract. Instead of giving many examples, I shall cite only one which is particularly characteristic, and also demonstrates the well-known link between anal erotism and sadism.

A patient reported a dream in which all of his relatives had died. Immediately after the analytic hour during which the dream had been analyzed, he went to the toilet. He had great difficulty in defecating. There he fantasied (I quote literally): "It was as if I had to give birth to a child. It seemed to me that the child's head could not force its way through. It was so big, it was so difficult! Then I felt an immense relief, as if I had given birth to the child." The same patient always became deeply depressed if he did not, immediately upon arising in the morning, have an ample bowel movement. As has already been mentioned, this patient suffered from a proclivity toward doubting and brooding, which had begun with doubts about the existence of God. After an abundant stool, the doubt ceased, and a thousand proofs of the existence of God occurred to him. Behind this doubt was concealed hatred toward his father. After defecation, he felt freed of his doubt and affirmed the existence of God (the father). Since he believed that in defecation he gave birth to a child, it appears that he made amends for the crime of parricide through the fantasied birth of a living being, and thus freed himself from his guilt.

Frequently individuals find relief for a guilty conscience through the birth of a child. The destruction of one human being thus can be expiated by giving birth to another one.

The incorporation of the father (the beloved object) actually carried out in primeval times seems to be ever repeated symbolically in fantasy. Through defecation, which acquires the meaning of childbirth, an attempt is made to nullify this fantasy, that is, to eject anally what has been incorporated orally. In general, one may therefore state: In the feeling of guilt is also contained the idea of *taking* and *giving*, with the stress upon the compulsion to give back, whether in an anal or an oral sense. It not only expresses the fear of loss of love, but is also based on the most primitive form of social relations, the idea of "give and take." It seems that the feeling of possession is also connected with the primary feeling of guilt.

The feeling of guilt encompasses also remorse and longing. Remorse is a tormenting regret for a deed committed. It presses for the undoing of what has taken place. This pressure is manifested in longing for the lost object; in the case of the "parricide," in longing for the lost father. Through projection of the "swallowed" father—"projection" means, precisely, expulsion, throwing out—the primitive seeks to reestablish the father's power. One may assume that the religious and social delusion of persecution in paranoia corresponds to this stage in the development of mankind.

The feeling of guilt conceals ungratified object libido which is striving for gratification, to be able again to love the object in reality. The para-noiac achieves this gratification, although in a negative sense, in projec-tion with the aid of his delusion, the religious person through his religion, and the normal person apparently by begetting children and by develop-ing socially useful creativity. Only the neurotic is inhibited in this striv-ing. Fear of the loss of love arises when object libido finds no gratification. The yearning for the lost object expresses, indeed, the striving to banish the fear of the loss of love, that is, *the fear of loneliness.* Extensive feelings of guilt disturb love relations.

The sense of guilt is expressed not only in fear of the loss of love and in ungratified striving for an object, but also in pain, humility, self-abasement, subservience, in perpetual failure; it manifests itself in ever-renewed acts of expiation and renunciation; it appears in suicidal ideas, in the neurotic symptoms of conversion hysteria, in the asceticism and self-torment of the obsessional neurosis, in the "persecutions" of the schizophrenic, in the fantasies of patients with perversions. Suffering and self-punishment permeate the whole being of these patients. The need for punishment may so dominate a person that he even commits a real crime in order to find justification for this tormenting feeling and to obtain relief through punishment. *There are, indeed, those who become crim-inals out of feelings of guilt.*

The officer of the old Austrian army previously mentioned, forged checks of his superiors, behaved insolently and provocatively until he had brought punishment upon himself. He lost his rank and was jailed for sev-eral years. He confessed in his analysis that he had been fully aware that punishment could not be avoided. Nor was there any external compulsion which might have forced him into this behavior, but he could not resist provoking his superiors and irritating them. His behavior was completely incomprehensible to him when he started to think about it. His excellent behavior in jail proves how directly his actions were aimed at bringing on punishment; he behaved so well in jail that his sentence was shortened. He emphasized that he had never in his life felt so quiet and peaceful as in jail. Even stronger proof is offered by the following: When he was free again after having served his time, he felt very depressed and lonesome. In this mood he married a woman who made him suffer terribly. He was unable to leave her in spite of all efforts. (It was for this reason that he came into analysis.) The long imprisonment had obviously not fully satisfied his masochism, and, since he could not live without punishment and found punishment through his wife, he could not leave her despite all conscious efforts.

It is impossible to overestimate the influence of the need for punish-ment, which overrides all other emotions. There are individuals whose lives consist of nothing but the expectation of punishment. In order to understand at least in part this overwhelming need for punishment, we must turn our attention again to the formation of the superego. Its starting point is the oedipus situation. When external difficulties arise, the small child renounces instinct gratification out of fear of the loss of love. The external prohibition leads to instinct renunciation; the consequences of this, however, are of greater significance than a mere inhibition of the instinct life. The prohibition is not simply accepted by the child and obeyed. The child feels it as something unpleasant, something forced upon him. The forbidding person is felt as an enemy. If the child heeds the prohibition, if he renounces the instinct gratification, some hostility against the prohibiting person remains within the ego. But this aggression cannot be discharged, for, in the first place, the child is too weak and undeveloped to cope with adults, and secondly, he also loves the prohibiting person. This love is a prerequisite for any obedience and educational influence. The release of the destructive instincts against the loved person is thus checked by love; ambivalence forms the background for the first restrictions of aggression.

As the instinct life develops further and becomes more unified, the gratification of the component instincts becomes proportionately less important to the child than the gratification of the genital (phallic) strivings. The boy selects his mother as the object of these strivings, but the genital drive toward her is checked by fear of the father's revenge, the fear of castration. The earlier prohibitions on the part of the parent or nurse are now supported by this fear; the inhibition of instinct life is thus reinforced by castration fear. While earlier this inhibition was a result of fear of the loss of love, it now takes on primarily the character of castration fear. With the earlier restriction of the pregenital instinct life, hate and aggression against the forbidding person were released. Aggression is likewise released when the genital strivings are inhibited. Its object, however, is no longer the person taking care of the child, but the father. Just as the aggression has earlier been turned against the subject, so it is also now turned against the ego. The sexual-genital desire for the mother thus becomes associated with hatred of and vengeance toward the father. But since the boy at the same time loves his father, he wards off his hatred by projecting it onto the father and thus perceiving it as hatred on the part of the father. (This may be one of the roots of persecutory ideas in paranoia.) Seeking to protect himself against the danger of castration, the boy again takes a predetermined path. He hides his genitals.

Moreover, the boy identifies himself with the threatening father and takes him into his ego, just as he earlier incorporated the disciplining person's prohibitions restricting his pregenital instinct life. The inhibition of instinct life is from now on bound up with the image of the father, which has become unconscious. The aggressions directed against him (and in part also the libidinal instincts) are absorbed by the ego together with the father images. The boy's behavior is similar to that of the primitive. But, while the primitive murdered his father and devoured him, contemporary man is satisfied merely to identify with him, that is, to incorporate him psychically. As the savage developed longing and remorse after the parricide, so does the civilized man develop feelings of guilt with his victory over the father.

As in the pregenital developmental phases of the libido, fear of external authority inhibits the primitive instinctual impulses, so, in the phallic phase, the gratification of the genital impulses is prevented by fear of castration. This fear is mastered through the formation of the superego, and thus the fear of external authority is replaced by fear of inner authority. The feeling of guilt is now less dependent on external conditions than upon processes which are going on within the ego itself and from which there is no escape.

The superego is, as we know, a special agency within the ego, and one of its functions is the conscience. Its task consists of watching over the intentions, impulses, and wishes of the ego and compelling it not only to act according to the superego's intentions but also to think, feel, and will in accordance with them. If there is tension between superego and ego, if the ego opposes the intentions of the superego in feeling, thought, or action, there arises the sense of guilt, the conscious or unconscious perception of the severity of the superego. I wish to stress once more that the conscience is a function of the superego, whereas the feeling of guilt is a condition of the ego which results from conflict between the strivings of the superego and those of the ego.

If we return to the initial situation at the formation of the superego, it is evident that it develops not only as a reaction to the fear of castration, but, in view of the genesis of this fear, it develops also as a reaction to the individual's own sadism. If one further considers that at the time of the formation of the superego the function of the genitals is temporarily suspended (latency period), it follows that the morals represented by the superego develop from castration fear, on the one hand, and bring about, on the other hand, the renunciation of masculinity which for many people involves aggression and sadism. I should like to cite here part of the case history of an obsessional neurotic.

The patient's mother had gone on a trip. A week after her departure, the father was supposed to join her. The patient became excited. He reproached me for the long duration of his analysis and demanded an exact statement as to when it would be terminated. I replied, jokingly, in a hundred years if he continued to act that way. He left furious, without telling me that this was the day of his father's departure. The following day, he started his analytic session by saying that he "would rather not have had to come today," because he was afraid of me. In reply to my question as to what he had done, I received the answer that he had bought a revolver the preceding day, loaded it, released the safety catch and held it in his mouth for an hour without being able to make the decision to discharge it. Afterward he had fantasied that he threw himself in front of the train in which his father was supposed to leave the same evening. The meaning of this fantasy was—as he became aware while reporting it—to deprive his father of the pleasure of joining the mother. Besides, these were not the first suicidal fantasies in which he sought to take revenge on his father. After the attempt at suicide, he accompanied his father to the railroad station spontaneously and was so affectionate toward him that it surprised the latter. Nevertheless, he could not restrain himself from telling the father that he was very unhappy and indicating that he would seek a violent end.

Immediately after returning from the station, he was overcome by intense feelings of remorse and decided to mend his ways from now on, that is, to stop masturbating, to give up his sadistic fantasies, to sell the sadistic books of which he owned a large number, to make no more attempts at suicide, and to carry through his analysis conscientiously. Upon my request that he hand over his revolver to me immediately, he went home and, without the slightest objection, brought me the weapon with all the cartridges. (Ordinarily he was immensely stingy; that day he even paid for a cab.) For a while the analysis proceeded satisfactorily; the patient felt better and better, even during the days following the return of his parents.

He became so "moral" that he granted neither himself nor others any liberties. While on a visit, the father related a sexual joke. The mother reprimanded him for this, and the son supported her, which did not happen as a rule. On the same or the following day he passed flatus when leaving the bathroom. He was in despair because his mother might have heard it. Gradually increasing fury against his father accumulated in him. The following now occurred: he committed an error in his father's office (where he was working), and expected to be reprimanded by him. Instead, his father was friendly and excused his error. To this he reacted with despair, vehement self-accusations, and renewed thoughts of suicide. To me he threatened that he would again start to masturbate, to buy sadistic books, to go to prostitutes and beat them. In fact, he soon afterward met a prostitute who permitted him to beat her. The pleasure, however, was not as great as he had expected. The following night he dreamt of one of his schoolmates who had owned a little black dog. In his dream, the dog attacked him and he crushed him in his hand. The dog reminded him of a Negro who, according to the newspapers, had been lynched because he had tried to rape a white woman. He had always liked this schoolmate very much, and he often masturbated with sadistic fantasies about him.

He usually masturbated with sadistic fantasies. He doubted that the analysis would change this; he hoped, on the contrary, that it would turn him into an overt sadist, *for, in his eyes, sadism was an indispensable attribute of manhood which he did not want to renounce, except when he was tormented by the feeling of guilt.*

Now we understand why he changed so suddenly after his attempt at suicide, why he became so "moral," and was so ready to hand over his weapon to me. After the aggressions against the father preceding his attempt at suicide, he felt guilty. In the suicidal attempt he apparently turned the aggression against himself and sought to atone for his guilt by renouncing every sexual activity and giving up his genitals. (Giving up the revolver was a symbolic castration.) In his hypermoral behavior he became more and more submissive toward his father, and his feeling of guilt manifested itself in humility, renunciation, subservience, self-castigation, constant expectation of or, rather, longing for punishment. During such periods he had no sexual sensations nor erections. He was, as it were, castrated.

In other cases also I observed that the clinging to sadism had the purpose of warding off fear of castration, and that sadism was a proof to the patient that he had not lost his virility. Since, however, with the feeling of guilt the sadism is not discharged on objects, but is turned toward the ego and there strengthens the need for punishment, it is comprehensible that morality is so often associated with emasculation, that is, psychic castration. Not only does the castration complex develop when the feeling of guilt exists, but the reverse is also true, that feelings of guilt are a consequence of the castration complex.

The renunciation of aggression, which leads to the formation of feelings of guilt, is compensated for by masochistic gratification. We have already differentiated three forms of masochism: first, the *erotogenic* form which appears a) in those perversions in which there is a masochistic predisposition; b) in those mental illnesses in which the superego is partly dissolved, as in schizophrenia; and c) as a substitute for the need for punishment, as for example in self-mutilations and in fantasies of being beaten. Secondly, masochism appears as *feminine* masochism; it is a consequence of the acceptance of castration and flight into femininity. It is called "feminine" because it leads secondarily to instinctual attitudes

which are primary characteristics of women.[4] The third form of masochism is *moral* masochism, which is closely related to feminine masochism.
It develops, as has just been shown, under the influence of the superego,
as sadism is deflected from the object onto the ego and there discharged.
An active instinctual drive is changed into a passive one. The passive
attitude of the ego then replaces the sadistic attitude of the id toward the
external world. The melancholic, for instance, is very ambivalent. If he
is compelled to give up his love object, he identifies with it and absorbs
it into his ego. His superego, fundamentally sadistic, is now able to discharge its aggressions against the representative of the object within the
ego. The ego, on the other hand, which identifies with the love object,
enjoys this aggression masochistically. There thus exists a libidinal masochistic relationship between the ego and the superego. The superego of
the melancholic is overly severe, his conscience hypersensitive, his feeling
of guilt, therefore, excessively strong. Now, if a libidinal striving is added
to the feeling of guilt, the morality is debased to the level of masochism,
as is, indeed, the case in melancholia. The feeling of guilt thus becomes
erotized and changes into moral masochism. In religious exercises of
penance, or in heroic sacrificial deaths for God, for the benefit of the
nation or of mankind, or in certain types of compassion, this masochistic
need for suffering is gratified in a socially acceptable form.

Even where a libidinal object relationship exists, it may be maintained
through the striving for suffering expressed in the need for punishment,
especially when the object is unattainable for external or internal reasons.
Sometimes a borrowed feeling of guilt may be involved, which with its
suffering forms the only remaining bond with the once beloved person:
"We take the sins of the others upon ourselves."

Although in reality it is not always possible to make a clear-cut distinction between the feeling of guilt and the need for punishment, still it
can be stated that the feeling of guilt means longing for the lost (destroyed) object, that the need for punishment represents the wish for the
repetition of the act of aggression against the subject's ego, and that the

4 Paradoxical as it may seem, even feminine masochism may at times be a sign of
the denial of castration fear and may end in aggression. A patient, a masochist, used
to frequent prostitutes and to ask them to whip him. When sufficiently excited, he
would take the whip out of the prostitute's hand, place it in a corner of the room,
throw her down and have virile and aggressive intercourse with her. When I was able
to show him that he wanted to prove to the woman that not *she* but *he* had a penis,
he became aware that the entire performance reminded him of a circus performance in
which a girl whips horses but nevertheless remains beautiful and desirable as a woman.
He often had a mental picture of his mother threatening a child with outstretched
forefinger. This image was always accompanied by feelings of hatred for her.

expiation is the fulfillment of this wish. Thus the feeling of guilt is in the service of ungratified object libido, the need for punishment in the service of the erotized destructive instincts directed against the subject's ego. In the feeling of guilt the wish predominates to undo the forbidden deed or thought. In the need for punishment these thoughts and intentions are carried out and the actions are repeated, not, however, on the objects of the outer world, but on the ego itself. The guilt and the atonement are closely interrelated. One cannot say that the need for punishment is a result of the feeling of guilt, since the one without the other is inconceivable; both have a common root in their developmental history. Only, in one form of illness, the feeling of guilt is predominant, and in another, the need for punishment. In hysteria, where the genital organization is maintained and a striving for the object is present, even though repressed, the feeling of guilt apparently predominates as remorse, longing, and fear of the loss of love. In the obsessional neurosis, where the genital organization has been replaced by the anal-sadistic one, yet the wish for the object has not been given up, the self-destructive need for punishment predominates. In melancholia, where in addition the object libido has been lost, the destructive instinct turns inward toward the ego. In schizophrenia the feeling of guilt appears in the delusional ideas of the redemption of the world, the need for punishment as fulfillment of the destructive drives in masochistic suffering (delusions of persecution, hypochondria).

The sense of guilt not only interferes with instinct gratification, but it may also increase instinct tension and procure masochistic gratification. Most prohibitions increase instinct tension.

To summarize: the sense of guilt appears in two forms, one *external,* as *social anxiety,* and one, internal, the *sense of guilt proper.* The sense of guilt grows on the basis of ambivalence. The more intensely the person who rears the child is loved, the greater is the feeling of guilt, that is, the fear of losing the love of this person. Whereas the child, when hiding from parents or nurse, is still able to gratify a forbidden wish without expectation of punishment, this is no longer the case with fear of the superego (internal feeling of guilt). For through conscience the superego is always informed of the mental processes within the ego. Every thought, every wish, every intention is controlled, although mostly unconsciously, and is inhibited if it is in opposition to the demands of the superego. To the extent that the parents lose influence, the external feeling of guilt (social anxiety) recedes, and the fear of the superego, obeying internal laws exclusively, increases.

The more severe the father, mother, or nurse was, the more severe the superego becomes, and hence, the more intense the feeling of guilt.

One might therefore assume that the intensity of the sense of guilt is dependent on the severity of the person who rears the child. This is, however, not always valid, since an excessive feeling of guilt may develop in boys, for instance, whose fathers were indulgent and weak, or in a boy whose father was absent altogether while he grew up surrounded by women who spoiled him. The more love a child receives and the more indulgent his parents are, the more his aggression may be inhibited and changed into feelings of guilt. Thus children grow up who are exceedingly good and who suffer enormously from the excessive burden of their feeling of guilt. The aggression prevented from reaching the outside world is bound to turn against the ego and to perform its work of destruction inside. The feeling of guilt is even more severe when merely slight aggressiveness is directed against an object which is intensely loved by the child.

Another consideration must also be taken into account. It is a fact that children whose father died when they were very young so that they grew up without a father, create a father in their fantasy, and then often substitute a real man for this fantasy and develop an oedipus complex, just as if they really had a father. They also develop a superego and the corresponding feeling of guilt with all its consequences. On the other hand, children who never knew their father, illegitimate children, for instance, often grow up full of resentment, as if they had no feeling of guilt, and behave ruthlessly, as if the world owed them something. They take revenge for not having a father.

It is evident that feelings of guilt can thrive only where there is ambivalence, where hate and love oppose each other and seek a compromise. Eros brings men together, aggression drives them apart. Where two people meet or where a group of individuals is formed, these two primal instincts must clash. The result of this conflict is the feeling of guilt in all its forms, which inhibits aggression and makes it possible for individuals to live together.

Actually, we do not see the death or the life instincts in pure culture; they always appear fused in one proportion or another. In each libidinal striving there is a varying degree of admixture of aggression. Each repression of an instinct need results to a certain extent in defusion into its libidinal and destructive components. In the neurotic symptom, a compromise is formed between sexual and aggressive instincts, and the patient finds masochistic gratification in his suffering, a moral justification for his illness, as it were. Civilization seems to have developed along similar lines, for the direct sexual strivings become more and more restricted and are frequently allowed to find an outlet only in union with internalized aggression, that is, as the erotized feeling of guilt. *In short, feelings of guilt appear to be one of the products of the eternal struggle between the life and the death instincts.*

If one compares the morality of our times with the state of the social feelings of the primeval horde after the parricide, it seems that they consist of the same elements; these elements appear today, of course, in the most complicated combinations, and it is therefore difficult to recognize their origin. After the parricide, these feelings were reactions to a real deed, committed in the outer world, whereas today they are a reaction to mere wishes. Since, however, everything psychic is felt as real, these reactions even now occur as though the crime had actually been committed. Feelings of guilt, and all morality, seem indeed to prove best how men have learned in the course of development under the most painful self-conquest to become the masters of their instincts.

As Freud stresses many times, the superego preserves traditions from one generation to the next, as if the traditions represented by the superego were inherited. Since the feeling of guilt develops under the influence of the superego, we may say that the sense of guilt is also inherited, though of course shaped by individual experiences.

DISTURBANCES IN THE HARMONIOUS COOPERATION OF THE PSYCHIC AGENCIES

Through the development of the superego with all its by-products, such as guilt, punishment, and shame, the function of the ego has become rather complicated. The moral demands which have developed under the superego's influence have the effect of inhibiting, even negating, instinctual life. "Morality" regulates feeling, willing, and acting, and later on, thinking. Direct instinct life is restricted wherever the superego has succeeded in enforcing its demands. This is especially true in the neuroses. *From the point of view of the ego, it seems, therefore, as if the neurosis represented a negation of life.* On the other hand, the superego protects the ego from the danger of the instinctual demands by restricting them. Not only the neurotic but also the healthy person tries to control his instinct life and to adapt himself to reality, out of fear of the objective danger inherent in instinct life, out of fear of castration, and out of fear of the superego. There exists also a fear of losing the benevolence of the superego, which is not only aggressive but also has libidinal components and contributes toward the maintenance of the narcissistic ego. The adaptation of the neurotic is, of course, not adequate, for he adapts himself to a world which appears to him to be full of exaggerated dangers. The compulsion for this exaggerated "adaptation" stems from his over-exacting superego.

In any case, adaptation to reality takes place at the expense of the instinct life, for the more capable an individual is of controlling himself, the more he is equal to the real tasks of life.

The adaptation to reality is in general based on the recognition and affirmation of the objects outside of the ego. With progressing adaptation, no longer is every stimulus from the outside world perceived as hostile and rejected, no longer is every object which appears suitable for instinct gratification absorbed by the ego. This, however, does not yet enable the individual to have an "objective" conception of the external world, to take his place in it, and to act purposefully and intentionally. This is a complex process which accompanies desexualization of the ego functions of perceiving and performing. In the course of development toward the reality principle the individual learns not only to renounce pleasure temporarily and to postpone it until later, but also to endure pain. But not even this is sufficient for an "objective" view of the world. It seems that there is an intermediate stage where the individual's own magic has already been given up, but where magic is still ascribed to the objects of the external world. During this phase the adaptation to reality is based on a *masochistic sufferance* of the world. This phase is later also abandoned; the world is no longer credited with the subject's instinctual and narcissistic impulses; a demarcation takes place between the ego and the external world. Ego boundaries are formed; the ego is set apart from the outside world. Simultaneously with this demarcation the superego develops, on the one hand, as a product of the adaptation to reality, on the other, as a product of the mastered instincts. It is a typical compromise formation between the inner and the outer worlds. Evolved from the necessity for the ego to adapt itself to reality, the superego itself becomes the most important aid to this adaptation, for it must first *sanction* perceptions and impressions if their real existence is to be acknowledged by the ego.

From *passivity* of *experiencing*, the individual progresses to *activity*, to the mastering of stimuli coming to him from the outside and from the inside (active adaptation). At the same time speech develops, evolving from the instinctual speech of onomatopoetic sound to a pictorial and

symbolic language, and further, to the functions of judgment and thinking. Between perceiving and acting, thinking is interpolated.

It is true that the impulse to the formation of "morality," speech, and
thinking proceeds from the instincts, specifically from sexual forces, and
that traces of these forces can be found in every psychic act; yet all these
ego functions owe their existence to desexualized, sublimated libido. The
adaptation to reality is performed through the constantly repeated and
alternating libidinal absorption into the ego of the outer world and its
destruction (desexualization), as well as through the "divesting of the ego
and the external world of their magic." The ego, thus cleared and no
longer burdened by direct instinct needs, is better able to fulfill its functions, that is, to serve the entire personality. Since the process of adaptation is so complicated and takes so long, any disturbance, however small,
may divert the many-sided and useful efficiency of the ego into wrong
channels.

The adaptation may be disturbed from various sides: in the first place,
through the id. A great passion, for instance, may silence the criticism
of the superego and its inhibiting influence, and may turn the ego into a
blind instrument of the instincts. We say, "Love is blind" and speak of a
"blind rage." Love and hate disregard all obstacles and dangers. In the
second place, the disturbance in adaptation may lie within the ego itself,
when the sense of the reality of perceptions of the outer world and sensations and feelings of the inner are lost (depersonalization). If the capacity
to distinguish between the inner and the outer world is also disturbed,
the loss of reality testing occurs. The internal world becomes, more or less,
the outer world, and vice versa, which causes a literally "deranged" attitude toward the external world (hallucinations and delusional transformation of reality in the psychoses). In the third place, the disturbance
may come from the superego. It may be either underdeveloped from the
beginning or overexacting. In the first case, difficulties arise in the adjustment of the individual to the social community. In the second case, the
superego may come into conflict with the strivings of the id as well as
with those of the ego. If the id strivings are repressed, a neurosis may
develop; if the function of the ego is paralyzed, a psychosis results. In all
of these cases the relation to reality is changed, to a greater or lesser
degree.

It is clear that the primary task of the ego is the perception of reality
and adaptation to it. The adaptation represents a compromise between
the instinctual needs of the id and that which is attainable in reality.
The superego stands, on the one hand, in the service of the narcissistic

ego (as a protector against the "danger of castration"), but, on the other hand, it is in opposition to the ego, as well as to the libidinal strivings of the id. It may, therefore, come into conflict with both of them. In this conflict the ego, the superego, or the id may succumb. In each instance there is a different result, characteristic for each form of neurosis.

In states of depersonalization, this conflict has not been solved. An estrangement between the ego and the superego appears. If the body ego (perceptive ego) does not yield to the intentions of the superego, the superego ignores the perceptions and feelings of this ego.

In the transference neuroses, it is generally the id which succumbs. The superego does not admit the strivings of the id *directly* to perception nor does it permit adequate vasomotor and secretory innervations and actions by the ego. Since, however, the processes stirred up in the id press for discharge, the ego changes its organization, thus enabling the strivings of the id to procure gratification in a distorted and imperfect way in the neurotic symptoms. The superego arouses a conscious or unconscious feeling of guilt in the ego and gratifies itself in the need for punishment.

In the obsessional neurosis the ego defends itself against the strivings of the id—as a consequence of the protest of the superego—by regressing to the stage of magic thoughts and actions. The instinct likewise regresses to the anal-sadistic stage. It now turns against the subject and appears in the ego as self-torment. The id striving is thus eventually victorious, having evaded the superego, it settles in the ego as sadism. The guilt is expiated through the self-torments. In hysteria the ego, at the command of the superego, defends itself by repression of the genital strivings. The instinct, however, assumes control over the bodily innervations of the ego for its own ends and evades the superego by finding a partial discharge through magic and autoplastic actions.

In mania, the superego succumbs to the ego, for the identifications of the superego are annulled.

In melancholia, the ego succumbs completely to the superego; even to the point of suicide.

In the simple forms of schizophrenia, the ego ideals are at first broken down, because of the weak object cathexes. Hence there is no conflict between the superego and the ego or between the superego and the id. A conflict arises between the ego and reality.

In paranoia, the conflict of conscience is settled by means of projection whereupon—as in the simple forms of schizophrenia—a conflict arises between the ego and reality, thus an apparently objective conflict analogous to the one which existed at the beginning of the formation of the superego.

If one compares the part the ego plays in the formation of the neuroses with that of the instincts, it is clear that the instincts are decisive for the content of the neurosis, the fantasies, wishes, strivings, and the like, whereas the ego determines the form of the neurosis, that is, it depends on the nature of the ego whether a neurotic conflict develops into an obsessional neurosis, a hysteria, or another form of illness. Not every regression to the anal-sadistic stage of the libido, for instance, leads to an obsessional neurosis.

We shall have to return to all of these problems in another connection and in more detail, since at present we still lack important requisites for their thorough discussion.

Chapter VI

THE ACTUAL NEUROSES

Having surveyed the role of the unconscious in the neurosis, the topography of neurotic symptoms, and the significance of the instincts for the contents and that of the ego for the form of the neurosis, it would be tempting to direct our attention to the total structure of the illness. For the present, however, we must postpone organizing the insight we have thus far gained, for there are still other problems to be discussed.

DEMARCATION OF THE FORMS OF THE NEUROSES

Even today there is a great deal of confusion and uncertainty in fixing the limits of the various forms of neurosis. Neurasthenia, for instance, is used as a "diagnostic" term covering unclear ideas about the origin, causation, and contents of most of the neuroses. We must admit that it is not easy to draw a sharp line of demarcation between many of the forms of illness, and we must not be surprised if an illness in which physical changes *cannot* be demonstrated is usually designated as "neurasthenia" or "hysteria." This indicates the need for a point of view which would make it possible to recognize psychological considerations regarding illness. Psychoanalysis provides us with such a point of view, mainly by making available to us the sources of the unconscious and of instinct life. We have been able to establish the fact that neurotic disturbances are connected with the abnormal course of instinct life. Since the instincts belong to both the biologic and the psychologic sphere, neurotic disturbances may find expression in two ways: either in the psychic representatives of the instincts, as feelings, affects, ideas, and the like, or in physical changes.

One might perhaps object that such a division, into forms of illness which are based on psychic conditions and those which are based on biologic conditions, is an artificial one, since all illnesses, after all, have a somatic basis.

Psychoanalysis has no objection to raise in principle to the conception that all neuroses have an organic basis. It is only that psychoanalysis takes the view that the organic injury does not play the same etiologic role in every case; there are neuroses in which an organic factor is found primarily, whereas such a factor cannot be discovered in other neuroses, despite all efforts. One is even led to the assumption that a psychic factor is decisive not only for the neuroses but also for the course of certain organic diseases. Taking this into consideration, one must envisage the probability that all organic diseases can be influenced psychically and that some of them have a psychic origin. On the basis of its instinct theory, psychoanalysis has succeeded first in differentiating between the various forms of neuroses and then in establishing a systematic scale of illnesses, from the purely somatic to the psychically conditioned. Psychoanalysis, because its psychological method of research has advanced beyond the biologists in establishing certain facts, will probably suggest the direction for further biologic research.

Although it is very difficult and often practically impossible to draw a sharp line between the psychic and the somatic, Freud was the first to succeed in demarcating the organically conditioned neuroses, the so-called *actual neuroses,* from the *psychoneuroses,* on the basis of psychologic criteria. Thereby he also indicated the point where the psychic meets the organic.

Even though the actual neuroses are of little practical importance to the psychoanalyst—since the patients of this group seldom come to him— still they claim his theoretical interest. For the actual neurosis is present in every case of illness, and, as we shall later learn, the psychoneurotic symptoms are built upon it.

The conception of neurasthenia was, as mentioned earlier, a catch-all in which many kinds of illnesses were indiscriminately thrown together. Freud was first to distinguish neurasthenia as an independent illness from the anxiety neurosis. He included both of these illnesses in the concept of the *actual neuroses* and contrasted these with the *psychoneuroses.* In the actual neuroses he could find neither psychic causations nor psychic mechanisms; in the psychoneuroses, on the other hand, he did find psychic factors as the causative agents of the illness. He thus took an opposite and more fruitful direction than the rest of the medical profession. Even today we hear again and again the same statement: "Since no somatic disturbances are to be found, the illness is a nervous one." Freud used exactly the opposite method, in considering as not "psychogenic" those "nervous" illnesses which could not be explained in psychologic terms.

The actual neuroses can be favorably influenced by psychological means, but only indirectly, that is, through exercising influence upon the patient's mode of life. Besides neurasthenia and anxiety neurosis, hypochondria also is included among the actual neuroses. As Federn suggests, perhaps depersonalization also belongs to this group.

<h2 style="text-align:center">NEURASTHENIA</h2>

The diagnosis of "neurasthenia" is still frequently misused. If correctly conceived, it designates a rather sharply circumscribed picture of illness, which is expressed mainly in a pressure on the head, in lassitude, fatigue, painful physical sensations, and digestive disturbances. Overwork, sorrow, and the like are considered causes. On closer examination, however, this proves to be invalid, since the causal connection is the converse of this, that is, those who suffer from neurasthenia have greater difficulty in tolerating any physical or psychic burden. Ferenczi has described a transitory indisposition with the typical neurasthenic symptoms of headaches, hypersensitivity, painful sensations in the limbs, and so on, which he terms "one-day neurasthenia." It often appears after nocturnal pollutions, and is thus directly related to the sexual life. Even before that, Freud has discovered that excessive masturbation over a long period of time and frequent nocturnal pollutions lead to neurasthenia. It is not quite clear why masturbation calls forth neurasthenic symptoms.

Masturbation is, indeed, a normal phenomenon in sexual development. This is true of infantile masturbation as well as of masturbation in puberty. It is more intensive in boys than in girls; in both sexes it is subject to various modifications. Masturbation is accompanied by a conflict which is often solved through reaction formations, as will be shown later on. If this solution is successful, the reactions contribute to the formation of character traits which may be valuable for the personality. If this solution is unsuccessful, substitutes for masturbation are formed, or masturbation itself may become part of a neurotic symptom.

Besides, it seems that elements of masturbation are an integral part of normal sexual intercourse.

Usually masturbation is accompanied by the struggle to give it up. This struggle contributes to the symptomatology of the psychoneuroses. It appears as if the rituals of the compulsive neurotic were a continuation of the masturbation, on the one hand, as its substitute; on the other, as a defense against it. Masturbation seems to be much more widespread than is generally assumed. Among male patients only those who had been subject to extreme intimidation in childhood did not masturbate in puberty. Masturbation within certain limits does not seem harmful. But if masturbation goes on beyond the years of puberty and is practiced excessively, it may, on the one hand, be a sign of a sexual development which is not normal, and on the other hand, it may in itself become the cause of harm, the significance of which, incidentally, is greatly exaggerated. The exaggeration of the danger resulting from masturbation seems to have the same basis as the denial of infantile sexuality, namely, one's own sexual repression. The best proof of this is that many patients feel better immediately after being freed from the feeling of guilt linked with masturbation.

Nevertheless it cannot be denied that long-continued and excessive masturbation leaves harmful traces. But of what do these traces consist? The physical symptoms are, most likely, partly toxic and partly reflex in nature, caused by excessive stimulation of the sexual apparatus.

We know, however, that the sexual act—and masturbation is such an act—is not a purely physical process. The genitals can be excited by psychic means, just as sexual wishes and ideas can be released through excitation of the genitals; in short, psychic energies play a part in every sexual act. In masturbation, the fantasies which, as a rule, accompany the mechanical stimulation of the genitals, are fed by psychic energies. Even if masturbation succeeds in bringing about a physical gratification, still there is no psychic gratification, since the object of the fantasies is not real. The psychic energy which is not used up in that way is dammed up and probably cathects those organs which are most flooded by the sexual products. Psychic and physical injuries thus coincide in masturbation; one is inconceivable without the other. As a consequence of excessive stimulation of the genitals and of the unlimited opportunity for gratification, not even the slightest sexual tension can be endured; thus arises a hunger for stimulation which seeks ever new ways of gratification but never leads to complete satisfaction. As to the psychic aspect, the easy access to satisfaction leads to an overdevelopment of fantasy life, to an independence from the real sexual object, hence to a neglect of reality and sometimes even to a turning away from it. But the most important psychic consequence of masturbation is the increased feeling of guilt which usually accompanies it, as well as the defense struggle which may last for years and claim the entire psychic energy. The source of the feeling of guilt about masturbation is not quite clear. The prohibition alone is not sufficient to explain it, for often without a prohibition there is an intense feeling of guilt. The following fact gives a fuller explanation: masturbation at puberty is a repetition of infantile masturbation. The latter was accompanied by fantasies from the oedipus complex. Since the feeling of guilt has its roots in this complex, it emerges again with the unconscious fantasies accompanying masturbation at puberty, which have the same source. These infantile masturbatory fantasies form the unconscious core of the later neurosis.

In the chapter on the feeling of guilt we learned that the aggressive instincts, blocked from discharge, are turned inward, and changed into the feeling of guilt. In masturbation there is never a complete sexual gratification, at least not in the psychic sphere, since the real object is missing. The aggression mixed with the libidinal impulse now changes into the need for punishment. It seems that this represents the most direct source of the feeling of guilt in relation to masturbation.[1]

The renunciation of masturbation is accomplished under the pressure of the feeling of guilt after severe struggles. It frequently happens that anxiety (as a phenomenon of abstinence) and hypochondriacal or hysterical symptoms then replace masturbation. As we have already stressed, the neurasthenic symptoms form the actual-neurotic foundation of the hysterical and the hypochondriacal neuroses. A somatic disturbance which was once actually present is assimilated psychically and worked up into a psychoneurosis. If, in some quarters, the existence of a pure neurasthenia is contested and an attempt is made to demonstrate psychic mechanisms in its structure, we have no objection to that conception, inasmuch as the ego, because of its synthetic function, strives to assimilate the neurasthenic symptoms (the somatic, actual-neurotic ones), to weave them into the psychic structure, and then to use them for the building up of the psychic illness.

And now an important question arises. Freud once said that it is more interesting to find out why man loves than why he does not; in other words, to inquire how he frees himself from his narcissism. The latter

---

[1] Already the ancient Hebrews understood the meaning of masturbation. Genesis 38 says: "And Judah said unto Onan: 'Go in unto thy brother's wife, and perform the duty of a husband's brother unto her, and raise up seed to thy brother.' And Onan knew that the seed would not be his; and it came to pass, when he went unto his brother's wife, *that he spilled it on the earth,* lest he should give seed to his brother. And the thing which he did was evil in the sight of the Lord; and He slew him . . ."
Onan masturbated instead of having intercourse with the dead brother's wife, according to the levirate law. If we understand that the spilling of semen on the earth is to be taken symbolically as earth equals mother, then the whole episode means intercourse with mother, for which transgression one is killed by God (father) .

designates the primal distribution of libido; object love develops later in a very complicated way fraught with danger. In this connection the question of why a person stops masturbating is pertinent. We know two facts about this: first, the male stops masturbating not only out of feelings of guilt, but also—and perhaps mainly—out of fear of castration; secondly, the woman stops out of disappointment in her clitoris and out of disgust with her genitals.

But we see over and over again that the abandonment of masturbation is not permanent in either sex. It is often resumed when internal or external conditions cause frustration in the individual's love life, as is the case in the army, in prison, in concentration camp, or when a love relationship is broken off.

At times, masturbation is a sign of improvement, as we see in our analyses. If a patient was too intimidated to masturbate, we consider the temporary resumption of masturbation a sign of improvement.

Why is it easier for one man to give up masturbation than it is for another? Why does one man in distress fall back to his infantile habit while another does not? Freud's answer to this question is that there probably exists a constitutional factor which is intrinsic to the development and integration of the sexual component drives into the one central genital instinct, and this factor still eludes our understanding. Masturbation interferes with object love. Perhaps the spontaneous growing of the yearning for love objects breaks up masturbation suddenly.

HYPOCHONDRIA

Hypochondria is closely related to neurasthenia. It frequently accompanies the masturbation of puberty. The fear and expectation of punishment connected with the feelings of guilt attach themselves to the unpleasurable physical sensations connected with masturbation, the neurasthenic symptoms, as it were, and utilize them psychically. But hypochondria appears also in later life, long after puberty, in connection with an unsatisfactory sexual life.

A fifty-year-old man suffered from the fear that his heart would stop beating, that his limbs would fall off, and the like. He was unable to sleep, for he awoke every few minutes in order to check whether he still had all of his limbs. He suffered from *real* sensations which he perceived as painful ones in the region of the heart, the extremities, and the nose. All of these complaints culminated in the fear that he would die of "arteriosclerosis." He had heard something about arteriosclerosis as appearing at his age and now imagined that his vessels, which he thought of as some kind of tubes, would become obstructed so that some parts of his body would have to fall off. He himself, during the first hours of his treatment, without any influence on the part of the physician, connected his suffering with his irregular sexual life. For years he had practiced coitus interruptus. He felt that this harmed him; he had pains in his genitals and in his head, and various other disagreeable sensations. He several times sought to "cure" himself through extramarital intercourse, but at the last moment was always prevented by his fear of the consequences of transgression of the moral-religious laws. At last, he was overcome by the fear that the semen held back during intercourse would stop up his penis and thereby harm it in a particularly dangerous way.

What another person feels in the genitalia when sexually excited, this patient felt in his whole body. He identified his body with his genitalia. (This form of identification and libidinal cathexis of the ego we term narcissism.) The fear of losing parts of his body corresponded to the unconscious fear of losing the genitalia, thus to the fear of castration. The interference with the discharge of the sexual substances in sexual intercourse apparently led to a damming up of the libido which then spread over the whole body and there produced states of tension which could not be mastered psychically by the ego. Against the feelings of pain which then arose, the ego defended itself with the old unconscious castration fear, which found expression in the hypochondriacal sensations and fears.

Since schizophrenia is characterized by the transformation of object libido into narcissistic libido, it is understandable that hypochondria appears most intensively in the early stages of schizophrenia, at a time when the patients have not yet learned to master the narcissistic libidinal demands in any other way. The difference between hysterical and schizophrenic hypochondria consists in the fact that in hysterical hypochondria objects of the external world remain objects of the libido, whereas in schizophrenic hypochondria the subject's organs and parts of his body become, more or less, the objects of the libido.

DEPERSONALIZATION

The hypochondriac is distinguished by remarkable, though anxious self-observation. The same is true, perhaps to an even higher degree, in depersonalization. Depersonalization consists of an estrangement of the external and the internal world. The patient has lost the feeling of the reality of inner and outer perceptions and of sensations. Just as the external world appears to him strange, unreal, "ghostlike," so have his thoughts, his feelings, and the sensations of his own body lost, to some extent, the quality of being real. There is much to support the assumption that the denial of the reality of the perceptions, sensations, and feelings represents the first consequence of attempts at transposing the libido, that is, at withdrawing it from the object and bringing it to another position. This state of suspension, which is variable in intensity and duration, seems to usher in all neuroses and, therefore, to be an actual neurosis in itself. While hypochondria *often* has a psychic superstructure, in depersonalization the actual-neurotic element of the transposition of the libido is *always* accompanied by a psychic factor, namely by a disturbance of the ego, the disturbance of the feeling of perceiving. One is struck by the intensity of the feeling of helplessness and anxiety brought on by the lack of the reality of experiences in patients with depersonalization. As there is a hysterical and a schizophrenic hypochondria, so there is a hysterical and a schizophrenic depersonalization. In the hysterical depersonalization, objects are retained; in the schizophrenic, they are either lost or about to be lost.

Anxiety Neurosis

A certain degree of anxiety is associated with most actual neuroses. It appears most intensively, however, in the anxiety neurosis, where it completely dominates the clinical picture. The anxiety here appears in various forms: free-floating, indefinite, as an attack, as expectant anxiety, as worry about a certain person, as difficulty in breathing, palpitation of the heart, sudden perspiration, trembling, diarrhea, and the like. Not all of these anxiety symptoms need necessarily appear together. Anxiety may be indicated by one of them alone. In such a case we speak of abortive anxiety. It also happens that some of the physical symptoms of anxiety impress us as a conversion hysteria, as, for instance, sudden perspiration, trembling, and so forth. Just as, in neurasthenia, hysterical symptoms may be grouped around the actual-neurotic nucleus, so this is also the case in the anxiety neurosis.

Just as simple neurasthenia is not dependent on psychic causations, so simple anxiety neurosis is not psychically determined. It is caused always by the same disturbances—by disturbances in the course of sexual excitation, such as coitus interruptus, coitus reservatus, frustrated excitation, long abstinence, and the like.

In all of these abnormal courses of sexual excitation there is no discharge in orgasm, no ejection of the sexual substances, and no gratification. Neurasthenia is brought about through excessive sexual activity, anxiety neurosis through repeated disturbance in the course of sexual gratification, or through its absence. A toxic origin of some forms of anxiety cannot be excluded, for illnesses are known, Basedow's disease for instance, which are based on a dysfunction of the thyroid gland and likewise generate anxiety. According to a report by Federn, men develop anxiety after the ligation of the vas deferens (Steinach's operation). The particular form of disturbance which is caused by abnormal sexual life (that is, whether a neurasthenia or an anxiety neurosis develops) seems to depend on the kind of sexual damage involved. Besides, in neurasthenia, the sexual energy which has not been used up psychically seems to play the chief role, whereas in the anxiety neurosis, it seems to be a question of purely somatic energy.

A disturbance of the instinct life, involving either the psychic or the somatic component, seems to occur in all actual neuroses. The actual neurosis may be of long duration; it may become chronic. In that case it develops into a psychoneurosis, but not at random, since each actual neurosis corresponds to a definite form of psychoneurosis: neurasthenia to conversion hysteria, anxiety neurosis to phobia, hypochondria to a schizophrenic psychosis.

The painful sensations in the actual neuroses are mastered and worked up into a psychoneurosis through the synthetic function of the ego. Schizophrenic hypochondria may serve as an example. It is the consequence of especially painful states of tension in the organs. The changed state of the organs is felt by the ego not only as painful but also as strange. This strangeness acts as a constant irritant upon the ego and must by all means be mastered by it. The reaction of the schizophrenic to such body sensations is typical. Hypochondriacal delusional ideas develop, whose purpose it is to overcome and master psychically these disturbances, which are felt by the ego as narcissistic injuries. This is achieved, during the initial stages of the illness, usually in the following manner: The patient seeks to re-erect his ideal ego, which he seems to be losing, with the help of hypochondriacal ideas. The organ disturbance, caused by the damming up of the libido and felt as painful, is absorbed by the ego and worked over psychically; it serves then, on the one hand, as gratification of the need for punishment; on the other hand, for balancing the disturbed narcissim of the ego. *Something which was originally felt as unpleasant and alien stimulates the ego to an increased synthesis, as a result of which the ego assimilates, under certain conditions, something which it first rejected, and makes it an integral part of itself.*

The assimilating and binding power of the ego is effective in working up the actual-neurotic nucleus, not only in the schizophrenic hypochondrias but also in all other neuroses. Similarly, neurasthenic symptoms are worked up into conversion hysteria by the ego. From psychic motives the ego continues to cling to the physical sensations of neurasthenia long after they have ceased actually to exist. They form the so-called actual-neurotic nucleus of the conversion hysteria, as the hypochondriacal sensations form the actual-neurotic nucleus of schizophrenia. One can now easily understand how the ego works up the anxiety neurosis into the psychoneurosis (phobia, obsessional neurosis). This will be discussed later in more detail. It is thus evident that each neurosis is connected with a disturbance of the sexual life. This sentence, however, must not be reversed to the effect that each disturbance of the sexual life, in the broadest meaning of the word, must necessarily lead to neurosis.

The question as to why not every individual becomes ill with an actual neurosis when there are irregularities in his sexual life can be simply answered: the reaction is dependent on the constitution. Some individuals can endure sexual tension for a longer period, others only for a short period. This is dependent on the capacity to maintain the unemployed libido in suspense without important disturbances, or to sublimate it.

Chapter VII

ANXIETY

It is not only in the anxiety neurosis that anxiety appears. It is present also in hypochondria, in depersonalization, and occasionally also in neurasthenia. Furthermore, it forms an integral part of all psychoneuroses. In psychoneurosis, the neurotic symptoms usually take the place of anxiety or accompany it. A correlation exists between the two: when the symptom appears, anxiety disappears or decreases in intensity. If the patient is prevented from yielding to the symptom, anxiety appears. If, for instance, a patient suffering from a washing compulsion is not allowed to carry out his compulsion, he develops anxiety. Anxiety is justly considered one of the main problems of neurosis. Whether the origin of anxiety is psychic or physical has long been in doubt, and this problem has not yet been completely solved. Freud early recognized that a somatic factor plays an important role in the origin of anxiety. In the anxiety neurosis he saw a causal connection between the disturbance in the discharge of sexual excitation and the subsequent anxiety. No doubt this anxiety represents a reaction to a sexual injury, since sexual excitation which fails to take a normal course is replaced by anxiety. Hence Freud drew the conclusion that libido changes directly into anxiety. Later he modified his point of view and held that libido cannot change into anxiety directly, but that anxiety develops in the ego as a reaction to a disturbance of instinct life. It is of no great import whether one adheres to the former or the latter conception, for both refer to a disturbance of instinct life, which, indeed is both a psychic and a physical phenomenon. Anxiety can, therefore, at one time be of psychic origin, at another time of somatic origin; it can also originate in both spheres.

ANXIETY AND DANGER

The anxiety of the phobic patient might be considered as the opposite of the organically released anxiety of the pure anxiety neurosis; the

188

former is psychically determined. The female patient who was afraid to appear at the piano in public had sound reasons for her fear, but they were unconscious. This is similar to the situation in an anxiety dream. The dreamer senses the anxiety, but he perceives only in disguised form the inner psychic danger which calls it forth. However, the psychological difference between phobic or dream anxiety on the one hand and objective anxiety on the other is not so great as it seems at first glance. Objective anxiety is anxiety aroused by a known danger. In neurotic anxiety the danger is unknown. In phobia, by projection, the dangerous situation is made similar to the one which calls forth objective anxiety: the internal source of anxiety is transformed into an external one.

Anxiety is a reaction to a danger. But flight is also a reaction to a danger. The displacement of the inner danger into the outer world makes possible an attempt at flight for the phobic patient. This attempt to escape is successful for a short period, but by no means permanently, since one cannot flee from oneself. The phobic, therefore, must constantly employ new measures of defense in order to keep himself free of anxiety. As the danger is fundamentally an inner one, he cannot bring about changes of reality in order to meet it; he has to change himself, and that results in a restriction of the freedom of his ego.

The phobia of the anxiety hysteria is thus a reaction to the anxiety, and that, in turn, is a reaction to a danger. The question now arises as to what kind of danger this is and what task the anxiety reactions fulfill.

ANXIETY AND AFFECT

It is not easy to answer this question, and whether it can be done in a satisfactory way remains to be seen. First of all, an attempt must be made to describe in more detail the phenomenon of anxiety. Anxiety consists of internal, unpleasurable excitation—disturbed breathing, increased heart activity and disturbances in the vasomotor sphere (pallor or blushing, profuse perspiration, and so on); furthermore, of heightened or diminished activity of the muscles of the trunk and the limbs (trembling or paralysis). Motor excitation, increased breathing and heart activity, increased secretion (perspiration, crying, urination), and vasomotor changes are bodily expressions of an affect whose feeling tone depends on its nature. Affects, as was stressed in an earlier chapter, are the most direct psychic derivatives of the instincts; they are psychic representatives of bodily changes and attach themselves regularly to ideas or other psychic formations. *Anxiety is thus an affect which differs from other affects only in its specific unpleasurable character.* It has a physiological as well as a psychological side and can be evoked from either one. Somatically it can be recognized by increased activity of certain organ systems. The increased organ activity accompanying an affect shows that the energies arising from instincts are discharging. These processes of discharge, as well as the specific sensations accompanying them, are perceived in the guise of affects. Anxiety thus consists of activities in the form of processes of discharge, and of perceptions of specific unpleasurable feelings and sensations.

Although we have thus gained a phenomenological orientation as to the psychophysical process in anxiety, we have not come nearer to an understanding of its meaning. Approaching the problem of anxiety from a historical point of view may lead us a step further. According to Freud, the innervations and sensations of each affect are historically determined. Following Darwin's conception, Freud assumed that phylogenetically the affects were purposeful actions adapted to reality, representing a primary reaction to an important event, a reaction whose task it was to master traumatic experiences. In the course of development from generation to generation, these actions, through continued repetition, became automatic and unconscious, were inherited, and finally appeared as affects in the life of the individual. The hysterical attack, which, indeed, represents a maximum achievement of unconscious actions and energy discharges, may be considered as a paradigm of the affects. The emotional behavior of the hysteric in the attack appears purposeless, but if it is traced historically to its origin, it becomes obvious that the emotions had a meaning at the time of their inception. It was the first great achievement of psychoanalysis to prove that hysterical attacks are unconscious repetitions of once-adequate reactions to actual experiences. If we look upon the hysterical attack as a paradigm of affect, then affects are precipitates of archaic experiences and play the role of memory symbols in the experiences of the individual. Generally they represent attempts, not always successful, at adaptation to the actual situation. They represent inherited actions, as it were, the remnants of actions which once were suited to reality but now are removed from the influences of conscious will and are dependent on the instinctual life. *From a genetic viewpoint, anxiety as a special case of the affects would represent a reaction to a traumatic experience* and occupy a unique position among the affects through its specific feeling tone. It seems to be an affect fixated at an earlier time which is revived in response to an actual stimulus. Anxiety is then an inherited, archaic reaction to an actual stimulus.

ANXIETY AND TRAUMA

An average, normal individual is able to tolerate ordinary stimuli, to digest, to master them, and to distribute their energy economically. But if the intensity of the stimulus exceeds the usual measure, it has a traumatic effect. *An increment of stimulus energy which the ego is not able to master within the usual span of time we designate as a trauma.* The ego masters normal stimuli with the help of the protective barrier against stimuli which we discussed earlier. But if the ego encounters a traumatic stimulus, that is, a stimulus which cannot be mastered in the usual length of time, it is flooded by excessive amounts of energy, and the protective barrier against stimuli is under great strain or even breaks down. If it breaks down and if no anxiety appears, a shock reaction sets in and death may ensue. If the protective barrier against stimuli is threatened with a breaking through, the ego loses the ability to react with purposeful actions adapted to reality, and the affect of anxiety appears instead.

To our definition of anxiety as an archaic reaction to excessive stimuli we may now add that it arises when the ego loses its ability to master the increment of stimuli.

It has been noted that persons who have been overwhelmed by an unexpected dangerous experience develop a traumatic and not an anxiety neurosis. Although these patients do not show anxiety in their symptomatology, they have anxiety dreams in which they re-experience the traumatic situation. It seems as if the anxiety which failed to appear at the time of the accident is made up for during sleep so that the dangerous situation may be re-experienced with the production of anxiety. The trauma is, as it were, expected in sleep, and so the element of surprise is removed. In fact, an *element of expectation* is present in every anxiety; in many cases it seems as if the patient were longing for the anxiety. The difference is a fundamental one between the anxiety-free but dangerous situation when the traumatic neurosis is acquired (the development of the traumatic neurosis involves surprise) and the situation in the anxiety dream. The event which has a traumatic effect in the neurosis is a real fact which has taken place and cannot be undone, whereas in the dream the trauma is not objectively existent; it is sought and psychically repeated in a milder form. The anxiety which had not been felt in the real situation is now experienced in the dream. The moment of expectation inherent in anxiety has an important task to fulfill: to prepare the ego for the danger, so that it will not be taken by surprise and will be able to meet it with purposeful actions. In the case of the trauma, however, an adequate reaction is not possible, probably due to the disproportion between the quantity of the stimulus (increment of energy in a certain span of time) and the normal capacity of the ego to cope with a stimulus (the protective barrier against stimuli). The reaction is, instead, the ineffectual one of the anxiety affect. Nevertheless, the anticipatory anxiety fulfills its biological purpose: first, it enables the individual to prepare for the danger; secondly, the ego, through the wished-for anxiety attacks, which are repetitive, can discharge, for a certain time, the energies accumulated as a result of the trauma.

It is easy to understand why the ego has to be prepared for a new and excessively strong stimulus if it is not to be traumatically affected by it. Each new stimulus confronts the ego with a new task. At first the ego has the tendency not to accept stimuli because they might disturb its state of rest. This conservative quality of the ego manifests itself also in the tendency to keep its cathectic energies on a uniformly low level. Stimuli which have been experienced by the ego several times and thus have become familiar seem to be apperceived with the expenditure of less psychic energy than unfamiliar stimuli require. Moreover, the ego has already learned to estimate the intensity of familiar stimuli. The ego, affected by an excessive stimulus which is unfamiliar, is at first rather confused and *helpless*. Since the ego cannot associate this stimulus with memory traces of other stimuli, it has no knowledge of its effect and, what is even more important, lacks the activity necessary to master the energy of this stimulus. On the contrary, the ego is overcome by the stimulus and forced into a passive role. In such a state of passivity, of *helplessness,* anxiety arises. Biologically, this helplessness has a prototype in infancy and, to a certain extent, in early childhood; psychologically, in those moments when the child or the adult does not feel equal to the various external or internal stimuli. The anxiety of the infant thus would be a biological one; the anxiety of later periods, predominantly a psychological one. In biological anxiety, the threatening danger is not recognized; this anxiety is a simple reaction to the trauma. In psychological anxiety, the trauma is recognized as an approaching danger; this anxiety, therefore, is a reaction to a threatening danger.

Anxiety is a biological reaction of the ego with the aim of self-preservation. In infancy, the ego and the id are scarcely differentiated, and it is almost impossible to determine whether a reaction belongs to the id or to the ego. It is thus irrelevant whether the anxiety of the infant (and actual anxiety) is psychic or not. According to Freud's formulation, psychic processes are somatic processes which are originally unconscious. It is only in the course of development that id reactions (which are unconscious) are taken over by the ego and thus gain access to the perceptive and motor end of the psychic apparatus. In other words, when the ego is differentiated from the id, the affect of anxiety reaches the system Cs. of the ego and is experienced there and expressed by the psychic complex "anxiety."

ANXIETY AND SELF-OBSERVATION: WARNING SIGNAL

If the traumatic stimulus is new to the ego and cannot be associated with previous experiences, how is it that the ego recognizes it as a danger, that it knows, so to speak, in advance, that it has to protect itself from being overwhelmed by the excessive amount of energy of the new stimulus?

In the first place, there is a mechanism, self-observation, which watches all processes within the ego and registers them. Among the pathologic states, it is in depersonalization and in hypochondriacal schizophrenia that self-observation is most developed. The schizophrenic perceives all inner processes extremely well.

In the healthy person, the instinct processes are mastered by the ego without employing any more attention than is absolutely necessary, since the ego immediately levels down the difference in tension between unpleasurable and pleasurable feelings which always occurs when instinct needs arise. But if the course of the instincts is disturbed and if the ego has difficulties in mastering them, they become the source of painful feelings. Normally the attention of the individual is turned to the external world, but with such increased painful feelings it turns to the internal world. The feelings of the unpleasure-pleasure scale thus turn the attention from its external goals and transform it into self-observation. It is easy to believe that the infant pays less attention to the outside world than the adult because he is too intensely occupied by inner processes which he has not yet learned to discharge onto the outside world.

We may assume, also, that the individual's interest in himself (self-observation) is developed earlier than attention to the outside world. If this is true, then the attention of the schizophrenic has, analogously, regressed to self-observation (see Chapter V). The hypochondriacal schizophrenic with his increased self-observation perceives the slightest changes in his body, which are often painful. Occasionally he even states that the inner processes seem to him most dangerous and that, therefore, he feels compelled to undertake actions which at first glance seem incomprehensible to us, but which are later recognized as actions of defense. If he is successful in these acts of defense, he has no anxiety, but if he is unsuccessful or if he is prevented from performing them, he suffers from frightful anxiety. *Self-observation thus has, primarily, the task of signaling to the ego the course of the excitation from the unpleasure-pleasure series. This information enables the ego to undertake suitable actions in order to return to the state of rest.* In schizophrenia, self-observation may at one time give the signal to institute defense measures; at another time it may not even go so far. The ego feels so powerless in the face of the increasing energy of the stimulus that it regresses to a more primitive stage of mastering stimuli, where the result is anxiety verging on panic. In such paroxysms of anxiety patients commit senseless actions; they throw themselves out of the window, beat their heads against the wall, and so on. The room in which he is living seems too narrow to one patient, he wants to escape, and therefore he destroys everything that stands in his way; another patient fights because he feels himself attacked by enemies, and his attack is not an attack but a defense. Flight (and protection) from a danger, in schizophrenia, has a character similar to that in phobia. The patient projects the internal, the instinct danger outward; then he can adopt protective measures against this danger as if it were an external danger. In this sense we may speak of a protective barrier against inner stimuli, as we speak of a protective barrier against external stimuli. It cannot be overlooked that in all these patients anxiety is a signal of danger. *The danger, thus, can be signaled in two ways: through self-observation and through anxiety.* But while self-observation indicates pleasurable processes as well, anxiety signalizes only unpleasurable ones, that is, danger. Feelings of unpleasure lead to the feelings of anxiety. Normally, painful feelings initiate appropriate actions of defense against the danger, rather than anxiety.

With external stimuli, the danger is an objective one. In the neuroses and psychoses, it is an inner one, an instinct danger. The economic situation, however, is always the same, namely, the threatened penetration of the protective barrier against stimuli in the traumatic situation of helplessness. The general basis of anxiety is, therefore, an excessive augmentation of a stimulus whose excitation subsides (is discharged) through the specific painful affective eruption which is called anxiety. Anxiety is accordingly conditioned by quantitative factors; in other words, each overstrong excitation which threatens to break through the protective barrier against stimuli seems to evoke the reaction of anxiety. Anxiety as an affective reaction is, thus, purposeful. At first it is automatic and later it is introduced by the ego. We repeat once more: with the aid of anxiety, certain excessive amounts of energy are discharged, on the one hand; on the other, *anxiety as a signal of an imminent danger* leads to defensive and protective actions, although it is partly a defense in itself.

BIRTH ANXIETY

Anxiety is, as has been shown above, the archaic precipitate of an important traumatic experience. This phylogenetic conception is certainly not contradicted by the fact that there exists also an important individual experience, which no human being is spared, and which is the *individual* prototype for all later anxiety—the trauma of birth. Poets had a presentiment of its importance long ago. Shakespeare said that Macduff did not know anxiety because he was cut out of his mother's womb, and thus had not come into this world through the birth passage.

It is not necessary to present proof that the process of birth itself can have a traumatic effect. The signs by which the anxiety of the newborn can be recognized should, however, be indicated. The evidence is not direct; it is based upon analogies.

In the prenatal state, the fetus is protected from external stimuli; its nourishment is procured through the placental blood circulation. Birth imposes entirely different conditions. The infant is suddenly faced with the task of mastering external stimuli mainly of a tactile nature. He has to exchange the warm womb for the cold air, he has to adapt his blood circulation and respiration to the changed biologic conditions. The adaptation is performed chiefly through the musculature of the respiratory organs and of the heart. The cause for the beginning of the activity of breathing is a toxic one, but its significance lies in the necessity of adapting to the new conditions of life. The adaptation is achieved with the aid of changes in the innervation of the respiratory, cardiac, and vascular musculature. These changes represent purposeful actions for the mastering of the new demands of life. They are, most likely, accompanied by a specific unpleasurable feeling, as is indicated by the screaming of the newborn. Such actions, accompanied by a specific feeling, set in as a reaction to an important experience, and are called affects. Birth is precisely such an important experience. An affect which has a specific unpleasurable character and which is characterized mainly by changed innervations of respiration and of circulation, we have called anxiety. The affect of birth hence may be considered an anxiety affect. Since this affect is a reaction to a trauma, we ought to try to understand this trauma.

We have already mentioned that the innumerable new and violent external stimuli at birth may have a traumatic effect. But there is an additional factor. The fetus in its intrauterine life could gratify all its needs—the libidinal ones included—through its mother, since it was united with her. Through birth this unity is destroyed; separation from the mother occurs. The infant's needs can no longer be satisfied automatically and narcissistically through the mother, as before. Now an object is required for this purpose. Since such an object is not present immediately after birth, and since the change to the new way of mastering stimuli cannot occur so quickly (the mother may, for instance, have no milk as yet), a *tension* created by increased need arises which cannot be removed through immediate gratification. We have designated as a danger an excessive increase of a stimulus. The actual nucleus of the danger is the economic disturbance in the management of energies caused by the increase in the quantity of stimulus. Anxiety is the reaction to a danger. The newborn, thus, reacts with anxiety not only to the external trauma but also to the increase of instinctual energy, to the tension created by the ungratified need. The anxiety at birth is twofold: a reaction to the external objective trauma, which may perhaps be interpreted also as pain, and a reaction to the inner danger of instinct tensions. The former might be termed objective anxiety; the latter might be considered as a prototype of neurotic anxiety, because neurotic anxiety depends upon inner conditions. At birth an external factor coincides with an internal one, just as in later life, neurotic anxiety can be permanently maintained only if an internal condition for anxiety combines with an external one. A situation in which the conditions for anxiety supplement each other is typified by birth.

In summary, we may state that the traumatic situation at birth is a biological one based on the helplessness of the infant in the face of external and internal stimuli. Birth anxiety is the previously described automatic anxiety arising from the economic disturbance in the mastery of the stimuli. It is a necessity in the course of development, appearing at the boundary between two important periods of life characterized by entirely different conditions, and will repeat itself later on with each transition from one developmental stage to the following one (latency period, puberty). Each higher phase of development is, most likely, traumatic for the preceding one, which does not end abruptly but coexists with the higher one.

Although it seems doubtful to us that (as Rank believes) birth anxiety has psychic content, it is certain that it is later on transformed into psychic anxiety. The psychic contents make use of the original somatic mechanisms of anxiety as means of expression, just as psychic contents generally tend to make use of somatic pathways previously established. This supplying of an old automatic mechanism with new contents is the more easily performed in later life since painful experiences similar to the experience of birth are repeated in a typical way.

Let us visualize once more the situation at birth. The fetus is bound to the mother with narcissistic libido. When this unity is destroyed through birth, when the child is separated from the mother, the striving of Eros to unite and fuse is blocked. We may assume, on the basis of the repetition compulsion characteristic of all organic beings, that immediately after birth a regressive tendency sets in, a tendency to unite again with the mother. The separation, however, is an accomplished fact which, biologically, cannot be undone. This striving for reunion with the mother, this tendency to restore the unity disrupted by force, a tendency which cannot be realized, must release a most painful need tension, which calls forth the reaction of anxiety. As the fetus does not know an object in the true sense of the word, it is not possible that, at the separation from the mother in birth, the loss of the object is perceived as such. The newborn infant can merely feel the disturbance in the economy of instinct energies caused by birth. Here anxiety is a reaction solely to that disturbance. *Birth anxiety, therefore, is an anxiety of separation.* It is biological but it becomes the prototype of psychic anxiety.

TRANSFORMATION OF BIRTH ANXIETY

A certain readiness for anxiety in the infant cannot be overlooked, a readiness which increases during early childhood. Although the manifestations of infantile anxiety are numerous and varied, still we find some typical forms of infantile anxiety. Fear of the dark and of strangers are the most typical of infantile anxieties. Fear of the dark, of being alone, of a stranger, and so on, can be traced back to a single factor: to missing the longed-for person, that is, the person cathected with libido. The first, the "primal anxiety" arose with separation from the mother; now anxiety arises with missing a beloved person, thus also with a separation —now, however, a psychic rather than a physical one. Castration fear may be considered as a further continuation of this anxiety; here it is also a question of separation from a narcissistically highly valued object.

Nevertheless it is not quite clear why missing the mother should cause anxiety. Now, in the mother's womb the child is bound to the mother directly with its entire (narcissistic) libido. After birth this tie is continued, no longer biologically but psychologically, through perception with the sense organs—the eyes, the ears, the nose, the sense of touch, and so on. The child after birth continues, one might say, his intrauterine relationship to the mother, but in a different way. This tie, however, is often broken when a real satisfaction does not occur, as for instance, when the mother's breast is not given to the child. At this stage of development the child is still capable of gratifying his needs through hallucinations. The sense organs are stimulated from within; in our example, for instance, the child "sees" the absent mother and "sucks" the hallucinated breast. But the need for food cannot be gratified through hallucination for any length of time. If the child continues to miss his mother, an absence of perceptions results which causes an inner tension, as in the case of an object loss; the object (the mother) consists, indeed, of individual perceptions. Since the tension caused by the frustrated need can likewise not be removed through hallucination, it seems that the loss of perception is analogous to the loss of object at the separation from the mother. The temporary separation from the mother, however, does not always cause an increase of tension which results in a traumatic situation, since with ego development the child learns to control his instinctual needs. Although missing the mother does not always mean a traumatic situation, still the child frequently becomes anxious, apparently reminded of the first separation, and through the associative connection repeats the first anxiety. This anxiety is a reaction, no longer to a trauma, but to the danger (as an attenuated trauma) of object loss. It is, therefore, based on experience; it is a signal of an imminent danger of object loss, and is set in motion when the mother is missed. The missing of the mother and the anxiety which accompanies the absence of perception hence would be the first transition from biologic automatic anxiety to psychic anxiety (introduced by the ego itself). (On the basis of this assumption the fear of the child and also, in general, of the adult, of being alone and of loneliness could become intelligible.) The absence of perception becomes a loss of object.

When the child starts to develop affectionate feelings, a mere turning away by the mother, a threat, a reproach, is sufficient to cause fear of object loss, which soon changes into fear of the loss of love. The automatic anxiety, biologic in origin, is converted in the course of development, going in turn through the loss of perception, of object, and of love, into a psychologic anxiety, arranged and, as it were, desired by the ego. It is then no longer a simple reaction to a direct danger; it is merely a warning signal which leads the ego to undertake measures of security. The noteworthy fact is that *the danger is anticipated,* for the anxiety apparatus is set in action by the mere idea that a danger might approach. While with automatic anxiety the ego experiences the anxiety *passively,* its course is now initiated by the ego *actively.*

The transition from passivity to activity is closely connected with the psychic development of adaptation to reality.

We have discussed it before, and I wish to repeat at this point, that adaptation to reality develops in such a way that the primary passive perceiving and experiencing becomes active. Thereby experiencing becomes "more conscious," more dependent on the ego's purposes; it can more easily be controlled. Children repeat in their play certain impressive experiences as though they wanted to practice mastering these impressions. Patients suffering from a traumatic neurosis repeat with anxiety, in dreams, the injurious experience, in order to master the trauma gradually in this way. The ego, which once experienced the trauma passively, now repeats it actively in a weaker form, and the anxiety now has the meaning of a signal for help. There occurs a discharge of the increased quantities of energy which have been brought to the ego through the external stimulus or have arisen through instinctual processes. This is a form of abreacting. The anxiety represents also an attempt at defense against the danger, though this attempt fails in the neurosis.

Since anxiety has the task of announcing danger and averting it, there is no doubt that it is one of the most primitive institutions of the ego in the adaptation to reality. At the beginning it arises automatically, and its function is the freeing of the individual from excessive quantities of energy. Soon, however, anxiety is displaced from its source in the situation of helplessness to the expectation of a dangerous situation. Then follows a shift from the dangerous situation to conditions engendering danger, as for instance, object loss, love loss, castration, and the severity of the superego. In all of these situations the individual is warned of the real consequences by anxiety. (It makes no difference whether they are real in a psychic sense or in the objective world. Basically, all these dangers are real.) We shall try later to understand why anxiety is not always an adequate reaction but is, on the contrary, often very inadequate.

ANXIETY AND PAIN

If anxiety is originally a fear of a loss, a fear of separation, and a reaction to an intolerable stimulus, the question arises as to what difference there is between anxiety and pain. Pain is, indeed, likewise a reaction to an intolerably strong stimulus which finally may lead to tissue destruction, to the severance and loss of an organ which, like all organs, is cathected with libido.

In the infant, pain is not yet differentiated from anxiety; both must have a common root. Physical pain develops when a stimulus striking the periphery is strong enough to pierce the protective barrier against stimuli, that is, when the ego, which endeavors to withdraw the stimulated place from the stimulus, is powerless to do so through its reactions of defense. The ego is even more helpless when the pain arises in inner organs. Pain and biologic anxiety thus are primarily the same reaction to a trauma which has pierced the protective barrier against stimuli. It is now easy to understand that, in the infant, pain cannot be distinguished from anxiety (biologic), since the economic situation is the same in both cases. Only later on, after biologic anxiety has partly changed into psychic anxiety and this begins to appear independently beside the biologic anxiety, is pain separated from anxiety. From then on, each can appear as an independent type of reaction. Through the affect of psychic anxiety the child protects himself against too-intensive stimuli threatening the protective barrier against stimuli. Biologic anxiety and pain arise after the protective barrier against stimuli has been penetrated. Since psychic anxiety represents an attempt at an adequate action—though it usually fails—it seems actually to correspond to a defense against the piercing of the protective barrier against stimuli, hence, to some extent, against pain.

Just as we distinguish between two kinds of anxiety, a somatic and a psychic type, there is also bodily and psychic pain. Although physical pain and somatic anxiety have the same origin, there is a significant difference between these reactions. Pain is merely a sensation; in anxiety, an action is added. Physical pain as well as primary anxiety develop as a reaction to the penetration of the protective barrier against stimuli; pain, as a specific unpleasurable sensation of the excessively stimulated part of the body; the affect of anxiety, as an action of discharge. Later on, these ways of reaction separate and take their own paths. From somatic anxiety there develops psychic anxiety, and from physical pain, psychic pain.

With physical pain a narcissistic cathexis of the afflicted organ takes place, as Ferenczi sought to establish; this organ claims all the psychic energy which, as a rule, is otherwise employed. (Toothache, for instance, absorbs all psychic interest.) Even the psychic representative, the idea, of the organ can be as painful as an objective pain. Persons who have had a limb amputated often feel pain in the limbs which are in reality missing; they thus feel pain in the psychic representative of the limbs. Like anxiety, pain can be displaced from the bodily to the psychic sphere. The gradual transposition of anxiety from the physical to the psychic is connected with the development of object libido. Psychic pain, likewise, can appear only where the narcissistic libidinal cathexis of the ego (and the body) is shifted onto objects and is restricted in their favor. The object then plays the role of the subject's own body cathected by libido. When this object fails or is lost, psychic pain results.

Why is it that psychic separation from an object, its loss, through death for instance, or through disappointment, can be painful? The child, as mentioned earlier, has at birth no concept of his mother. The image of the entire personality of the mother as a definite person develops gradually only after repeated gratification of the infantile needs. When a need arises, the child wishes for a repetition of the gratification which is necessarily associated with memory images (ideas) of the mother. The child, consequently, wishes not only for the gratification but also for the reappearance of the mother. It seems that in time a shift takes place from the wish for gratification to the wish for the mother. This striving for the object which is highly cathected with libido we call *longing*. Separation from such an object causes longing. Nobody finds it easy to renounce an object from which he must completely and finally separate either for inner or outer reasons.

The melancholic, and to some extent also the mourning individual, re-establishes the lost object within the ego through identification. With each loss, first of all an identification takes place, resulting from the longing. There is, so to say, a return to the primary situation, in which the object was still a part of the ego. Since, nevertheless, a real satisfaction cannot occur, the tension increases more and more, and the object thus absorbed by the ego now acts as a part of the body which is cathected by increased stimulation. The constantly increasing libido at this "part of the body" and the insatiable longing create the traumatic situation of helplessness. It is in this situation that psychic pain arises for the first time.

Now we see more clearly the difference between psychic anxiety and psychic pain: psychic pain is the reaction to the trauma of real object loss; psychic anxiety is the reaction to the *danger* of object loss. In other words, psychic pain arises when a highly cathected libidinal tie between object and subject is broken (ideals and the like may also be substituted for the object); psychic anxiety, when such a break is merely threatened.

ANXIETY AND THE DESTRUCTIVE INSTINCT

We have learned from our consideration of the relationship between anxiety and pain that some forms of anxiety may also be looked upon as signals for help against threatening pain, against the danger of bodily or psychic destruction. In castration anxiety this danger of destruction is most apparent. There was at one time a real external danger of castration, and the anxiety was a direct reaction to this danger. Since the development of the superego involves the inclusion of the external world, the danger of castration is also internalized; the external danger becomes an internal one (as an unconscious threat on the part of the superego). Not only the purely sexual instincts but also the (internalized) destructive ones are a source of anxiety. Animal phobias must be considered as one reaction to such an internalized sadistic danger; castration anxiety is more easily recognized in them than in other phobias. In the animal phobia, that is, in disguised castration fear, a part of the sadism absorbed by the ego also finds expression, since in it aggression against the father is turned against the ego itself. Not only in animal phobia but also in other phobias sadism turned against the ego forms an important part of the anxiety. A brief example will demonstrate this. The example concerns a woman; corresponding evidence concerning a man is not at present available to me.

A female patient, whom we have already mentioned in another connection, suffered from anxiety when on the street. She was mainly afraid of open places. Her anxiety was so severe and she became so confused, that she was always in danger of being run over. She would run into a passing vehicle as if "on purpose." It was easy to demonstrate prostitution fantasies hidden behind this behavior. But the fact that her anxiety was most intense whenever she met an acquaintance in an open place, pointed in another direction. She had first developed this anxiety when she once met her brother on the street. Consciously it was almost self-evident to the patient that her fear of her brother was actually a fear of punishment. At first, however, she did not know why. This brother had been the first person to protect her against anything sexual; he had not admitted her to his own sexual play with other girls. In connection with these memories, others appeared of her fear in childhood of sex murders committed in the street. In the town where she lived, a sex murder had actually taken place; her father, therefore, had strictly forbidden her to go out alone. Although at that time she did not know exactly what a "sex murder" was, she had a dim inkling of it. She was drawn into the street by a peculiar curiosity, and constantly disobeyed her father's orders. For this and for many other reasons she was always expecting to be punished by her father, as analysis convincingly showed her. The fear of punishment which she felt when facing her brother was thus displaced onto him from her father.

In puberty she had learned what a sex murder meant. At that time she developed her phobia, but she was no longer consciously afraid of murderers on the street. Finally, in analysis she became clearly aware that as punishment by her father she expected some kind of sex murder and that her conception of sexual intercourse had always been an extremely masochistic one. She injured herself frequently in order to be treated by her father, who was a physician. When her father treated her injuries, she felt the pains inflicted by him as a sexual pleasure. If we recall that anxiety is also an expectant anxiety, we may state that in our case the punishment, the masochistic pleasure, is expected. The danger becomes pleasure.

This does not mean that I wish to imply that the other forms of anxiety are not also operative in phobias. On the contrary, in our example, fear of the superego, of the loss of love, and so on, appeared distinctly one beside the other. However, the phobia decreased only very slightly as long as its masochistic component was not uncovered. The sadomasochistic component of the sexual instincts would also serve to explain the paradoxical phenomenon that the anxiety which should protect the individual from dangers often drives him into even greater danger, paralyzes him, and sometimes leads him directly to death.

Theoretically this phenomenon may be explained by the fact that the destructive instincts are automatically strengthened by damming up of the libido or by an increase of tension due to unsatisfied needs. We know from observation of the compulsion neurosis and the delusion of persecution and delusional jealousy that love does not change into hate, but that with an increase of the need for love, the need for hate also rises. That the chord of the death instincts is sounded where there is no possibility for discharge of an increase of libido, may perhaps be explained by the fact that defusion of instincts occurs when the sexual instinct is

204 PRINCIPLES OF PSYCHOANALYSIS

blocked, and that the excess of the energy of the sex instincts is added to the destructive instincts. *This shows, too, that the free psychic energies are easily displaceable.* The increased libido becomes a danger when it finds no way of discharge and when, in addition, its energy is transmitted to the destructive instincts. It thus seems that, in the signal for help of anxiety, the death instinct also becomes active, which often, at the height of the anxiety, leads to paralysis and loss of consciousness, to the removal of the stimulus—thus to "rest." *The anxiety, therefore, is not only a reaction of the ego to an objective or an internal instinctual stimulus but is in itself of instinctual origin.* Anxiety is thus a general, inherited, affective reaction whose purpose it is, on the one hand, to defend against the onslaught of unfamiliar and excessive stimuli; on the other hand, to discharge the psychic energy and reduce it from a state of high tension to the lowest possible level, in other words, to procure rest for the ego. Behind biological as well as psychic anxiety reactions is concealed the repetition compulsion of the conservative instincts. Thus anxiety, be it biological or psychic, is always a reaction to stimuli which imply a danger and have a traumatic effect. This general conception of anxiety explains also why it appears not only in the human being but also in all other creatures. This, again, proves that it is also a reaction to an objective danger.

NEUROTIC ANXIETY

The reaction of anxiety in response to objective dangers has been acquired phylogenetically. This reaction seems to have diminished to some extent in the civilized adult, perhaps because struggles with external forces have become fewer with progressing cultural development, and man has learned gradually to master nature. The child has more objective anxiety than the adult; the primitive, more than the civilized man. Anxiety because of inner reasons, on the contrary, seems to have increased as cultural development has demanded greater control over the instincts. Even in primitive man, anxiety is often a fear of internal dangers, that is, of dangers projected from within onto the outside world (in the manner of a phobia, as for instance in the fear of ghosts), and hence independent of external conditions to a much greater extent.

Neurotic anxiety, whatever its manifestation may be, is a reaction to an instinct danger, to an inner stimulus. It may, at one time, be caused by a biological factor, at another time by a psychological one; that is, it may be either an automatic reaction, arising from the economic conditions of the instinctual situation, or a signal of pain produced by the ego.

In the former case, something is happening in the id which is analogous to the situation at birth in which the anxiety reaction automatically sets in. In the latter case, something is happening in the id which activates a danger for the ego and induces the ego to produce the anxiety signal. The former is typical of the actual neurosis; the latter, of the psycho-neurosis.

The anxiety of the actual neuroses has a somatic source. It is an adequate reaction to the traumatic situation of helplessness against the pressure of ungratified instinctual needs. This anxiety appears where the sexual life is disturbed and is a reaction to an abnormal course of the libido, but does not necessarily come from the sexual instincts directly. We have learned that the impelling force for the production of anxiety as an emotional reaction ensues through displacement of energy cathexis from the id (instincts) onto the ego. And this intrapsychic energy which can be displaced is not to be confused with sexual libido. If we wish, nevertheless, to stress the sexual origin of anxiety, we may do so only in terms of desexualized libido. The ego can work only with sublimated libido, since otherwise it is disturbed in its functioning. Although in the actual neuroses the situation is economically similar to that in birth anxiety, the anxiety of the actual neurotic is, besides, a result also of an ego function; although initiated by processes in the id, it is molded by the forces of the ego into the form of the anxiety affect.

The provocation for the development of anxiety by the ego may come from the outer world as well as from the superego or the id. In the first case, we have to deal with objective anxiety; in the second, with pangs of conscience, and in the third, with somatic anxiety. In the actual neuroses, anxiety arises, as we have just learned, as a reaction to an increase of excitation in the id. In the psychoneuroses, anxiety does not develop automatically but as a warning signal of a danger; it is accord-ingly a motivated reaction. It is a reaction to processes within the id as well as to processes within the superego. An example may serve to illus-trate this.

A woman is utterly disappointed in her husband; she withdraws from him completely and suffers greatly. Shortly afterward, she has anxiety dreams, in which she has sexual intercourse with her father, but is severely beaten by him. Then she is stricken with an anxiety hysteria. The libido which she had withdrawn from her husband became dammed up and could not be discharged. She soon found an outlet by regressively cathecting the father imago with energy. The libido which she had withdrawn from her husband activated the libidinal strivings of the id fixated on her father. These strivings, however, had necessarily to remain ungratified. This frustration caused instinctual tension which signified a danger to the ego. To obviate this danger, the ego gave the anxiety signal. It was also evident that punishment was expected, was demanded by the superego, and was taking its effect on the ego in a masochistic way. The further analysis of this case showed that three factors provoked the anxiety: danger from the superego, instinct danger, and undischarged (dammed-up) libido. In this psychoneurosis, as in all others, there was also an actual-neurotic factor, which was the starting point of the illness.

It is almost self-evident that in the psychoneurosis there exists an actual anxiety in addition to the anxiety planned and arranged by the ego. In every neurosis, the instinct life is more or less inhibited, leading to instinctual tensions, a part of which can be discharged most directly in anxiety.

This recalls Freud's earlier conception that anxiety is the result of repression. The reaction of anxiety is, in fact, a very sensitive indicator of disturbances of the instinct life. On the one hand, it is a process of discharge; on the other, a signal for help when a danger is present. Against this danger the defensive struggle—including the repression—sets in. Anxiety initiates the repression which follows. And yet, the other conception that anxiety develops with repression is also true, for, with the repression, an instinctual demand is rejected, and the libido is partly blocked from discharge. The lack of gratification creates tension in the id which may, as anxiety may, become the cause of a repression. It thus represents again a threatening danger to which the ego, in turn, reacts with anxiety. Since repression does not always lead immediately to the formation of symptoms, anxiety may arise in the interval between the repression and the symptom formation. Neurotic anxiety is, on the other hand, also an indication of a psychic conflict. The anxiety, therefore, is fundamentally independent of the repression and may develop before or after the repression has taken place; its task is merely to call the ego's attention to a danger, in order to induce it to institute *appropriate* defense actions.

CONDITIONS FOR ANXIETY

The dangers which drive the ego into reactions of anxiety are quite varied. The processes occurring in the id may lead to the danger of loss of the object, loss of love, or loss of the genitalia. Loss of love and separation from the object is the chief element of danger in women; castration, likewise the separation from a highly esteemed object, in men. Fear of the superego appears later, usually in the form of pangs of conscience. The last transformation of the fear of the superego is the death anxiety, the fear of destiny, which is a projection of the superego.

Each developmental period has its own conditions for anxiety. The first condition is the biologic helplessness of the infant. Bernfeld has pointed out that, because of this helplessness, among many primitive peoples, the mother imitates the fetal situation in the care of the child in early infancy. Helplessness after birth is a characteristic in which the human being differs from most animals. He would perish without protection. His psychological helplessness corresponds to his biological helplessness. The ego is undeveloped, helpless in the face of the onslaught of excitations. The psychic helplessness of the infant, therefore, is also a source of danger. In early childhood, the human being is unable to do anything for himself and is entirely dependent on the person taking care of him who satisfies all the child's needs. In this period the loss of the object is the danger.

The castration danger is characteristic of the phallic phase. The dangers resulting from the demands of the superego are characteristic of the latency period. Occasionally one can clearly observe how one condition for anxiety develops from another, earlier one. Not infrequently one sees how, in a compulsion neurosis, intense castration fear in childhood changes gradually until it appears in puberty as pure fear of the superego. It is much more difficult to observe directly castration fear in women as a precursor of the fear of the superego. Frequently in women, in place of castration fear, there appears fear of punishment either represented symbolically as fear of childbirth or directly as a masochistic component of the sexual instinct. If, however, it is kept in mind that often, behind the castration fear, there is concealed a wish for castration, and that anxiety is often an expectant anxiety, it follows that castration fear thus also contains masochistic elements. All these conditions for anxiety rarely appear in isolation; most frequently they exist side by side, without excluding or influencing one another. This coexistence of the various forms and conditions of anxiety is perhaps the chief reason for the lack of clarity in the problem of anxiety.

The conditions and forms of anxiety differ according to the developmental stage of the libido and of the ego. Thus, anxiety in the pregenital phase, where the part played by the destructive instincts is greater than in the following phase, may contain many more sadomasochistic elements and may perhaps be even more paralyzing than in the genital stage. In the phallic phase, the instinct danger is of a genital character, and the anxiety is a castration anxiety. Anxiety in women which appears at the object stage as a result of loss of object or loss of love refers to the danger which threatens when the protection, the care, in short, the satisfaction offered by a beloved person, is wanting. The content of the anxiety depends upon the developmental stage of the libido, that is, upon the stage at which fixation has occurred.

The form, on the other hand, seems to be dependent upon the developmental stage of the ego. One might assume that the vague anxiety which is expressed predominantly in cardiac and respiratory symptoms pertains to a very early stage, perhaps to that of the birth situation, and that it is later repeated in the actual neuroses; that, further, anxiety in which trembling predominates belongs to the developmental stage of the ego in which attempts at flight can be undertaken, but are inhibited by the sadomasochistic component of the danger. The anxiety states in which bodily symptoms are predominant perhaps belong to the genital phase and correspond to conversion symptoms. The vague anxiety without bodily symptoms, which chiefly bears the character of self-reproach, apparently belongs to the developmental stage of the ego at which the superego has already been differentiated from it and feelings of guilt already exist.

Anxiety as a function of the ego which, like the libido, can regress to points of fixation, in illness takes on the form of an earlier affect reaction which had already been mastered. In other words, the ego may have developed normally but may reach back to the old reaction of an anxiety affect when the mastering of an instinct meets with difficulties, and this instinct, therefore, becomes a danger. Hence anxiety has a different meaning in each particular illness and is based on the danger involved in the individual illness. In every illness several such conditions for anxiety will, of course, be of significance; one, however, will always dominate. In hysteria, for instance, loss of love is the chief condition for anxiety; in the phobia, the castration complex; and in the obsessional neurosis, the overly severe superego. One would be inclined to ascribe to each danger situation a characteristic form of anxiety and condition for it, and to recognize from each kind of anxiety the corresponding danger concealed behind it. The recognition of the specific danger, however, is made more difficult because of the secondary fantasies which often are attached to the anxiety but which have nothing to do with its essential character.

Thus womb fantasies appear to be closely connected with certain anxiety states. Yet they only represent very radical attempts to flee from a danger to that place where the individual feels best sheltered and protected—the mother's womb.

We are now confronted with the problem of what is the most common preliminary condition for neurotic anxiety: why does one person perceive an instinct demand as a danger and react to it with anxiety, while another does not? If we again compare phobic anxiety with objective anxiety, it appears that the source of danger in the phobia is outside the ego; the anxiety is a reaction to a quasi-real danger. In reality, however, this is not so, for the danger here is a projected one. It is psychic rather than real. The difference between neurotic and objective anxiety would thus be that the former is a reaction to a psychic danger, the latter to a real danger. But we know that the inner perception is as real to the psyche as the outer one. The difference between inner and outer becomes even less defined when one takes into consideration that instinct dangers are often objectively based on external, real conditions and that some inner dangers have at one time been external, objective ones. The anxiety reaction is an indication only of the ego's weakness in mastering the dangers, no matter where the source of these dangers lies, within or without. Some other factor must therefore be sought for as the criterion of neurotic anxiety. At first glance, objective anxiety is a reaction to a known danger, neurotic anxiety a reaction to an unknown danger, thus a danger of which one is not aware. Since, however, anxiety is most severe in childhood, before a differentiation between unconscious and conscious processes has occurred, the fact that the source of the danger is unconscious cannot play the decisive role in the formation of neurotic anxiety.

If we consider that most individuals have to struggle against the demands of the instincts, particularly sexual ones, which are recognized as dangerous, and that, furthermore, not everybody develops anxiety when disturbances of the instinct life occur, then we must realize that the limit to which an instinctual tension can be tolerated without damage is variable. Hence the limit of mastery over excitations differs with the individual. It seems that these limits are transgressed where there is a certain *readiness for anxiety*, and it is this readiness that creates the disposition for the neurosis. *This readiness would consequently depend, on the one hand, on the incapability of the psychic apparatus at the moment to master an increase of energy caused by an excess of excitation, and, on the other hand, on the excessive sensitivity to danger.* The neurotic has remained infantile in his behavior in the face of danger, for he adheres to old conditions of anxiety which have been long overcome in the normal person. The reactions of his ego to instinct needs are fixated in childhood, obsolete, and no longer adapted to the changed conditions of adult life, and this seems to be the ultimate precondition of neurotic anxiety.

Chapter VIII

THE PROCESSES OF DEFENSE

THE PROTECTIVE BARRIER AGAINST STIMULI AND THE UNPLEASURE-PLEASURE PRINCIPLE

We have learned to recognize anxiety as a signal of danger. We found it to be a useful reaction of the ego; the signal of anxiety directs the ego's attention to the danger and calls forth defensive measures. It is evident that the type of defense reaction will depend on the nature and stage of development of the ego and on the intensity of the threatening danger. The defense of a weak and poorly developed ego will be different from the defense of a fully developed and better organized one.

Every danger threatens to break through the protective barrier against stimuli or to put out of action the pleasure-unpleasure principle which acts as a protection against internal stimuli. It is, hence, in the first place, a disturbance in the economic organization of the psychic energies which is the cause for defense and protective measures. It is true, we may consider the anxiety affect the inception of an attempt at defense, but it is in itself a very unpleasurable affect, while the aim of defense is the avoidance of unpleasure.

For the average normal adult, defense is rather simple: it occurs through flight or other protective actions. A child is less able than an adult to protect himself adequately against dangers; the younger the child, the more difficult defense is for him. First of all, as long as the external and the internal world are identical for the child, he will hardly be able to localize the source of danger correctly. But even if he were able to do so, he would still have difficulty in fighting the threatening danger, because he has not sufficient mastery of the motor apparatus to carry out actions adapted to reality. All defensive reactions of a child against outer and inner dangers will therefore necessarily end in a change in him. He develops sphincter control, for example, because otherwise there would be endless conflicts with his environment.

211

The child's way of facing dangers differs from that of the adult; he must utilize entirely different defensive and protective measures. Although the technique of defense undergoes changes in the course of development and although its primitive autoplastic forms are replaced by others, still they remain in the unconscious as a precipitate of a phase of development which has been surmounted, and they occasionally reappear in the adult. Such archaic defense mechanisms, which are no longer adapted to reality, also form a part of the ego's unconscious ways of working.

The infant during the first weeks of his extrauterine life is completely narcissistic. He takes but little notice of the outer world; he sleeps constantly, as though he wished to prolong the intrauterine state. It cannot be ascertained definitely whether the sleep of infants is based on a wish to sleep, as in the case of the adult, or whether this sleep corresponds merely to a state of indifference. It is, however, unlikely that the sleep of the infant has a different meaning than the sleep of the adult. There are people who have the particular faculty of fleeing into sleep from the unpleasantnesses of life and of thus blocking the unbearable stimuli of the external world. One might assume that the sleep of infancy represents a similar flight from the demands of reality, the more so since the infant is less equal to the demands of reality than the mature person.

When one falls asleep, interest is withdrawn from the outer world, and object libido changes back into narcissistic libido. The person falling asleep is, in terms of the distribution of libido, in a state which is similar to the state within the mother's womb. The fetal position which many people assume when falling asleep, the sleeper's need for warmth, the suspension of activity of the sense organs, those organs whose task it is to maintain contact with the outer world—all of this is strongly in favor of this view. It is nothing new—only we arrive at this conclusion in a different way—to maintain that the infant continues the prenatal state, whereas the adult endeavors only periodically, during sleep, to return to the mother's womb. The motive for sleep, the regressive striving for the mother's womb, is based on a negation, a kind of rejection of the real world and an attraction to the prenatal state.

This kind of defense, this flight-like regression, is very complete in deep hypnosis and in severe pathological states, such as catatonic stupor. In the latter, by the way, mastery over the motor apparatus is lost, as is revealed by the dissociation of the muscular innervations (flexibilitas cerea).

Another primitive, general method of defense, performed with the aid of the destructive instinct and muscular activity, can again best be observed in catatonia. One of the chief characteristics of catatonia is negativism, a general tendency to nullify every positive striving through a negative one. The destructive instinct appears most clearly in negativism. If the catatonic shows any reaction at all, it is usually a reaction of violent temper and destructive rage to even the slightest external stimulus. He thus wards off external stimuli by destroying them with the aid of the motor system, "repressing" them, as it were, from his field of vision.

Thus defense occurs, at one time, to avoid the danger of the breaking through of the protective barrier against stimuli—for economic reasons; at another time, because of narcissistic rejection of the external world. Both these motives, however, are closely linked together during the first stages of development and meet in the striving for rest, for the state without excitation. Since this striving is expressed in the repetition compulsion, the deepest root of any defensive action is consequently the repetition compulsion of the unconscious id. Also considered as a general motive is the unpleasure-pleasure principle in which the tendency to avoid pain is expressed.

The defense, however, is not directed only against the external world. We know, for example, that the catatonic patient rages even without external motives, that he fights against inner as well as outer stimuli and thereby often destroys himself, as if he felt himself to be a foreign body. The infant likewise kicks and screams as a reaction to internal stimuli which he obviously is trying to ward off. In most neuroses, however, it is a question of defense against quantities of internal stimuli, namely against instinct needs. Even though these do not always represent an immediate danger, their gratification may lead to real dangers. It is striking that the ego considers sexual urges as the greatest danger.

We must, therefore, distinguish between the defense which arises when a disagreeable instinctual urge is aroused by an external perception, and the defense which appears without external motivation. There are illnesses in which the defense is mainly based on a relation to an object, and illnesses in which the defense is independent of objects. When the narcissistic stage of libido organization persists, defense against the instinctual impulses will set in even when there is no longer a relation to the love object in the outside world, as in melancholia, or when it is hallucinated, as in schizophrenia, whereas on the object stage of libido organization, defense sets in only when the object or its substitute is perceived, as in hysteria. Here the defense probably appears only when there is the necessity to ward off an instinctual impulse directed toward a particular object (phobia). Nevertheless, it is not always easy to draw a sharp line between the defense against an external cause and defense because of inner danger only.

IDENTIFICATION

Identification as a form of defense develops first out of a vague relationship to the outside world. Although the libido, on the oral stage, is directed toward an object in the outer world, still this object is not located in space, outside of the ego. When there is an increase of libidinal excitation, whose organ of discharge, during the oral or cannibalistic phase, is predominantly the mouth, gratification, the removal of the unpleasurable state of excitation, occurs normally through sucking. The stimulus is done away with when it is gratified through a real motor action, leading to relaxation. One may also consider this process as a defense, since it does, indeed, remove the unpleasurable stimulus. If such an action cannot take place, if, for instance, the mother's breast is not offered to the infant, the pleasure-giving mother, or the breast, is incorporated by the ego psychically. The child perhaps hallucinates a gratification in the act of sucking, that is, the perceptive apparatus of the ego is cathected with psychic energy, and the psychic representative of the tactile organ, of the mucous membrane of the mouth and the lips, is stimulated and gratified from within. The purpose of the introjection of the mother's breast is fulfilled if the painful state of excitation is thereby removed. Identification, which is also called introjection, is thus the most primitive way to ward off stimuli exceeding a certain intensity, which would have a traumatic effect. Defense is facilitated to a particularly high degree through the ambivalence which characterizes identification on the oral level. One might say that the libido makes use of the object in order to remove the instinct stimulus in an adequate way through the object's incorporation by the ego. The child takes possession of the object orally, as it were, and abolishes the distance between himself and the object, in order to ward off the instinct excitation and to attain the sought-for rest.

Identification as a form of defense plays a different role on the narcissistic and pregenital stage than on the genital and object stage of libido development. On the genital stage it has to fulfill one of the most important tasks in the entire life of the individual, namely to help in the formation of the superego, to deprive the strivings of the oedipus constellation of their direct instinctual character. For after the boy has succeeded in incorporating the beloved and hated father, in identifying with him, and in making his demands and prohibitions his own, he is enabled to renounce his sexual strivings for the mother as well as the function of his genitalia. Herewith the latency period sets in. Through identification, therefore, the defense against the direct instinctual demands is accomplished, for the mother is no longer considered a sexual object. This, however, is not to imply that with identification all relationships to the object and to reality cease. On the genital stage it rules out only one relationship—the sensual one. All the others remain intact; with the aid of the incipient superego social relations are further developed.

We must therefore distinguish between a *partial* and a *total* identification. With the aid of the former only a particular relationship to the object is warded off; with that of the latter, all relationships. The former is seen in hysteria, the latter in neuroses of the narcissistic type. Patients who have reached the genital stage and have formed durable object relations tend more to develop partial identifications, whereas those patients who either have not reached the genital and object stage or have reached the genital stage but have not given up narcissism, tend more to develop total identifications.

A twenty-year-old girl developed hysterical anxiety states whose content was the fear of becoming insane. It soon became evident that intense self-reproaches about masturbation were hidden behind this anxiety. The illness was preceded by a period of frequent relations with men. She was often in the position of fighting off sexual attacks, but masturbated regularly afterward. To the masturbation she reacted first with feelings of guilt which were later replaced by an overwhelming fear of becoming insane. The idea of becoming insane, which almost seemed like a delusional idea, was understandable in the light of an infantile experience. One night, when she was not quite five years old, she called for her father from her crib. Instead of her father, a twelve-year-old cousin entered her room and masturbated her. The child overcame the effect of this seduction after a few days, but in her illness it reappeared. This cousin was psychotic, "crazy," and died a few years later in an insane asylum. During puberty the patient thought that he had become insane as a result of masturbation. He therefore became a frightful warning of the consequences of sexual activity. In her illness she identified with *him*; she felt "crazy" like him, and thus punished herself instead of masturbating. Through identification she was thus able to ward off sexual impulses. It is superfluous to relate at this point more of this analysis, since what has been said is sufficient to show that an instinct demand can be warded off with the aid of identification. It is necessary to add that the other relations of this patient to the opposite sex, that is, relations without genital contact, were not noticeably disturbed. This, accordingly, is a hysterical identification.

Where object relations are loose, on the other hand, and there is increased narcissism, the entire object is warded off through identification. One of the various types of homosexuality originates in this way: the boy identifies with his mother and loves only boys, as the mother once loved him. In this case the identification has the result that the woman no longer exists as a sexual object. Through the identification, the heterosexual strivings and the object to which they pertain are completely warded off. The effect of identification is even more profound in melancholia and in certain forms of schizophrenia. The melancholic has no genuine interest in the persons around him, despite his worry about them; the stuporous schizophrenic is entirely indifferent to his environment.

The conception of identification as a defense mechanism does not exclude its other aspect, the positive one. There is, indeed, also an identification out of love, which has nothing to do with defense. As has been stressed, identification can be ambivalent, and, in the present connection, we see that the negative side of an ambivalent process can be used as a defense against its positive side. As love represses hate, the reverse can also occur: hate represses love. In any case, through identification a union is established between the ego and the object or instinct which is to be warded off. What cannot be warded off from the ego by being kept away is warded off through assimilation, synthesis. This form of defense has approximately this meaning: "If I cannot conquer the enemy in any other way I will unite with him and by this means render him harmless."

PROJECTION

Another type of primitive defense is projection. The time at which it first appears is not easy to establish; it is probably one of the most primitive psychic functions.

It has already been stated in various connections that the ego perceives inner processes, with the exception of unpleasure-pleasure feelings, only in projection. In order to become consciously aware of an instinct danger, the ego therefore would have to externalize it, that is, to localize it in space.

Just as the ego in other instances uses previously formed physiological mechanisms, so it also soon takes possession of physiological projection in order to place it in the service of its psychic strivings. It is certainly easier to flee from a perceptible danger and to take protective measures against it than from a danger which is still within, thus not perceptible. Since the small child—the younger he is, the more helpless he is—cannot at will coordinate his muscular actions, he can neither make attempts at flight nor undertake consciously purposeful protective actions against the threatening danger. He is therefore limited to the only means at his disposal, that is, to projecting the internal source of excitation into the external world. Therefore, on the lowest developmental stages of the ego, projection becomes, in itself, an action of defense, a precursor of motor flight. The result of projection is that the excitation due to ungratified instinctual demands is kept away from the ego and thus a distance is established between the ego and the source of danger.[1]

Projection also is at the service of the unpleasure-pleasure principle: the individual strives for everything that is pleasurable, and rejects everything painful, especially as long as he is a child. Projection is at first an expression of defense against instinctual stimuli which—even though of a libidinal nature—are still felt as painful when their energies accumulate and threaten to produce a traumatic effect. In the schizophrenic's delusions of persecution, the masochistic component of the instincts is transferred to the outside world through projection. The patient perceives the instinctual aim indirectly through the persecutor and feels it masochistically. Projection is often followed by very intensive motor activity. Everything possible is undertaken in order to escape the "persecutions"; even murder may be the outcome of such delusional attitudes. After all painful stimuli have been eliminated through projection, the entire environment takes on a hostile tinge, while the ego becomes pleasurable.

Although adults continually project without being aware of it, projection is far more frequent and striking in primitives and children. If a child bumps into a table, he will hit the table, as if it had purposely moved and caused him pain. It is to be assumed that in illnesses in which, besides the libido regression, an ego regression has also occurred, the mechanism of projection is revived. This can best be observed in schizophrenics. In certain stages of their illness they again animate inanimate objects and suspect dangers in their surroundings, against which they adopt the most varied protective measures, which are often unin-

[1] If, for instance, the hungry infant gratifies his need by hallucinating that he sucks at mother's breast, but after a while this gratification fails, as is to be expected, the infant may perhaps hallucinate that the mother is eating him, as if expressing: "Not I am hungry, but mother is and wants to eat me." This may be a precursor of later persecutory ideas, the background of the delusion of being poisoned.

telligible to us. The fear of danger is greater at the animistic stage than on a higher level, and it will appear more frequently where the ego has regressed to this stage.

At a higher stage of development, that is, when a differentiation within the ego has occurred, disturbances in the economy of psychic energy are no longer exclusively responsible for stimulating projection. There are also psychic motives, mainly those of a moral nature. Projection then means: "It is not I who wish to commit this or that forbidden and evil deed, but someone else." Thereby the conscience is appeased. Projection, therefore, will be motivated by other forces after the erection of the superego than before. But it will also have another meaning on the genital and object stage than on the lower levels.

While at the pregenital stage in projection as well as in identification the stress lies mainly on defense against the *instinct,* at the genital-narcissistic stage there is added the defense against the *object.* One should be able to determine whether the projection of the object has taken place before the establishment of the superego or after. In the latter case it should further be possible to determine at what point the projection sets in under the pressure of the superego and under what conditions it concerns the superego itself and dissolves it.

A projection of the instinct and of the object at the same time occurs in the development of the previously mentioned type of homosexuality. This appears in puberty, at a time when definitive object choice is supposed to take place, and reveals that the normal relationship to the opposite sex is disturbed. The homosexual object choice occurs in two acts—first in a warding off of the mother with the aid of identification, and secondly in a projection of the subject's person onto another boy. The homosexually desired object is thus a narcissistic one. It can be demonstrated by this example that, in general, loose object cathexes facilitate projection. In individuals of a narcissistic disposition a disappointment in the mother often leads to homosexuality. The defensive character of projection manifests itself more clearly in the delusions of persecution of paranoia. The persecutor is, as a rule, a previously loved person of the patient's own sex. The paranoiac wards off his own sado-masochistic impulses by projecting them upon an object chosen narcis-sistically.

One part of the ego, the superego, is built up, as we know, through the absorption of objects of the outer world. In some forms of schizophrenia there is the tendency to withdraw libido not only from external objects, but also from the superego, the structure erected within the ego through identifications. The withdrawal of libido from the superego is expressed in the projected delusion of being influenced (delusion of persecution, delusion of being spied upon). The defense against the libidinal tie with the superego and against its restraining bonds thus is the second root of the delusion of persecution. Where the demands of the conscience appear in the form of auditory hallucinations, the projection has gone farthest. It leads to the rejection of the objects of identification and, consequently, to the dissolution of the superego. The meaning of this projection is, finally, likewise the rejection of the influences of the outside world which had become anchored in the ego. It appears to be possible only in libido and ego regression with simultaneous instinct defusion.

Projection does not always lead to such serious consequences. In the phobia, for instance, it leads neither to the rejection of the outer world nor to the disintegration of the ego. Little Hans, Freud's five-year-old patient, warded off his aggressive impulses against his father through his fear of horses. He wanted to bite his father, but transformed this wish into the fear of being bitten by the horse. He projected his own impulse onto his father and then, in keeping with his age, displaced it onto an animal. The relationship of little Hans to his father did not consist merely of hatred; he also loved him. The conflict of ambivalence in the child was solved through the projection of his hostile impulses and their simultaneous displacement onto another object. The female patient who was afraid to appear in public likewise projected her exhibitionistic impulses, which arose in childhood, onto the environment. The difference between hysterical (phobic) and paranoid projection is clear: in the former, the object is retained; in the latter, the object is lost. Thus in hysteria, in contrast to schizophrenia, the relationship to the outer world is maintained. Little Hans actually only exchanged one real object for another, the father for the horse.

If we compare the dynamics of projection with those of identification, we see that they have one quality in common—the displacement of psychic energies. In identification, they are displaced from the image of the object onto the ego; in projection, from the ego onto the object or its image. The same dynamic process has two opposite end results: in the first case, the distance between object (image) and ego is diminished; in the second case, it is increased. In both cases the relation to reality is disturbed. In total identification the real object disappears, and in the second case there exists a delusional reality that is a reflection of the inner reality. *The displacement of psychic energies is the most general way of warding off dangers.*

It is a peculiarity of the psychic functions that they rarely occur separately. Although, in general, identification as a form of defense is characteristic of melancholia, and projection, of paranoia, still in most cases both forms of defense appear simultaneously, and it is not always possible to recognize what part of the defensive process is identification and what part is projection.

DISPLACEMENT

The displacement of psychic energies, however, does not appear solely in these two forms of defense. In the animal phobia of little Hans, the intolerable idea of hating the beloved father is displaced upon a horse. It is not the father who will take vengeance for the aggressive impulses, but a horse. Besides projection and identification, the simple displacement of the psychic energies from the original idea onto a substitute one may solve the conflict of ambivalence.

While, in the phobia, the substitute idea is sometimes rather closely related associatively to the idea which is to be warded off, in the obsessional neurosis, it is usually more difficult to discover the original idea. Reik offers a good example of an obsessional-neurotic displacement.

His patient suffered, among other things, from the obsessional thought of gray hair on a black background. Traced back, this obsessional thought was found to hide the idea of a donkey's ears (with gray hair) and, further back, a donkey, and even further, an insult to his father, whom he called a donkey.

In the obsessional neurosis, thus, through displacement onto the *insignificant,* through a hardly recognizable allusion, the unbearable idea is warded off and the conflict of ambivalence weakened. In advanced schizophrenia, where the primary process belonging to unconscious thinking has invaded the conscious, the tendency for displacement is even greater, the interchanging of ideas, thoughts, associations, and the like, almost the rule. Where it would not occur to a normal person to see a similarity, to the schizophrenic it is a matter of course. He uses it uncritically to express his train of thought. One might compare schizophrenic thinking (and, with certain reservations, also obsessional-neurotic thinking) to that of gifted rebus solvers. An association of sounds often suffices to evoke an apparently far-fetched visual association, and vice versa.

Changing into the Opposite and
Transformation of Activity into Passivity

The various psychic defense mechanisms seldom operate in an unmixed form, as has already been mentioned. Besides projection, identification, and the like, one can also see other forms of defense at work in *one single* act. Little Hans originally wished to bite his father; in his phobia he fears that a horse will bite him. The hostility toward the father, the sadism, is changed into its opposite, masochism, and transformed from activity to passivity. The instinct thus turns simultaneously against the subject. The following case, which will be discussed later in more detail, may serve as an instructive example of the turning of the entire sexual instinct upon the subject; this turning is the result of defense against the instinct, which was originally normally directed.

As a child of three, the patient once saw his mother nursing his younger brother. He wished to be fed at the breast too, but was rejected by his mother. From then on, deeply hurt, he turned away from his mother and to his older brother, with whom he started to masturbate. In puberty, the desire arose in him to take a man's penis into his mouth; since he did not yet dare to do this, he managed to suck his own penis. He was unable to find his way to the opposite sex; he gratified his sexual needs himself in this perversion. Here I do not wish to discuss the other determinants of the perversion, but only to show that the instinct aimed at the opposite sex may, as a result of an infantile frustration, be warded off by being turned toward one's own person, that is by inversion into the opposite and by transformation from activity into passivity.

In another, somewhat more complicated case, similar processes of defense may be demonstrated, perhaps even more convincingly.

A female patient of a distinctly visual type (she was a gifted painter) had completely repressed her sexual scoptophilia, and the corresponding exhibitionism expressed itself only very timorously in roundabout ways. Her sexual life was completely inhibited; she had had no sexual relations with her husband for the last few years. In the course of analysis she gradually lost her sexual inhibitions. During an interruption of her treatment she entered into an erotic relation with a married man. Having resumed her analysis, she imagined more and more that I despised her. From the expression on my face, from the tone of my voice, from my silence, she concluded that I condemned, rejected, and had contempt for her. No arguments could convince her of the contrary. She felt uneasy in my presence, since she felt me observing her. Evidently she was developing a delusion of being observed. Isolated paranoid traits appear not infrequently in the course of an analysis. Further investigation of her fears showed that behind my person were hidden first the deceived wife of her lover, and then, on a deeper level, her own mother. Afraid of both these women, she was convinced that she was watched by them and interpreted their behavior as contempt, reproach, and condemnation. Thus there was a clear delusion of persecution, with ideas of being observed in the foreground. In connection with a dream, relying on previous experiences, I told her that her fear of being observed (seen) contained the inversion of infantile scoptophilia and secret observation of parental intercourse. This interpretation impressed her, and she offered a wealth of confirmatory material.

She suffered, with periodically changing intensity, from a compulsion to look at men's genitalia through their trousers. This scoptophilia had been most intensive in her early childhood, when it was directed primarily at her younger brother. Ever since he was born she had persecuted him with violent aggression, which finally reached its climax in the fantasy of robbing him of his penis. At about her sixth year, she went through a short phase of intensive exhibitionism. At the same time she felt humiliated, degraded, and inferior. She would look at herself in the mirror, naked, and murmur: "It serves you right." Analysis disclosed that these words alluded to the lack of a penis. When she was naked before her siblings and parents, she would feel humiliated, but, at the same time, would also experience a certain gratification. In the feeling of being persecuted, spied on (looked at) of her later years, she experienced a punishment (a symbolic castration) as she had previously experienced it in her childhood; memories of painful yet voluptuous sensations in her genitals when her mother washed her clearly showed her masochism. Her entire attitude toward life in later years also confirmed its presence. It is thus evident that her original aggression against her brother and her scoptophilia were warded off through masked exhibitionism and sadism directed against her own person (masochism). The delusion of persecution sketched here, which was rather distinct although only transitory, thus represented in a passive form the defense against an active and aggressive instinct, directed originally to the outside world.

In certain states of schizophrenia one can observe *in statu nascendi* the transformation of instinct aims as a form of defense. I have seen patients who were very aggressive at first, raging, wanting to throw themselves at me, who then, suddenly, as though automatically, began to beat and lacerate themselves. I have seen others who recounted fantasies to me of how much they would like to eat me up, and then, at the next moment, full of fright, asserted that they were being consumed by me. It is most instructive to learn from these patients directly, if one succeeds in establishing contact with them, the motive for these inversions. These inversions are forms of defense, since the patients, according to their own assertions, otherwise would actually have to yield to their first impulses.

We cannot but ask ourselves why it is that schizophrenics, whose social ties and the considerations resulting therefrom have been in great part destroyed, cannot gratify their instincts but instead ward them off. One might assume that a part of a libidinal relationship to the outside world is still maintained in most cases and that consequently the destructive instincts are not permitted to come into action. But there are schizophrenic states in which all object relations are dissolved and yet the destructive instincts are warded off. The only possible conclusion is that there exist processes of defense which have no social bases and are independent of the superego as well as of the outside world. This has been emphasized previously in another connection. Defense at the most primitive stage seems, therefore, to be an automatic process and may, perhaps, correspond to *primal repression*. That in such cases defense against the instinct aim and not against the object is striven for is, perhaps, most clearly demonstrated by the "repression" through changing into the opposite, in those illnesses where there is the greatest tendency for regression, the psychoses. Here this form of defense is quite manifest. The hatred of the melancholic, originally directed against the love object, becomes self-hatred; the schizophrenic's looking at becomes being looked at and being overheard (spied on), and so on. Nor are such inversions infrequent in nonpsychotic conditions; the desire to beat becomes being beaten; consuming becomes being consumed. *The changes are effected not so much on the idea of the object as on the direction of the instinct.*

What is striking in the changing of instinctual activity into its opposite is that an instinct whose aim is gratification through an object is turned away from this object, gives it up, and changes into a narcissistic one. With the turning of the instinct toward the subject, the ego often identifies itself with the object and enjoys, through itself, the gratification originally expected from the object. A most striking example of this situation is offered by the patient who sucked his own penis. He identified himself with the hated brother, and, as such, he sucked his own penis; moreover he identified his penis with the beloved mother (breast). By putting himself in the place of his brother and his penis in the place of his mother's breast, he was able to gratify himself narcissistically through his own body. It is no contradiction that a twofold identification takes place here: it is merely a complication. Circumstances never are as simple as we would like to represent them. In this patient something further may be noticed: the turning to his own person coincides with the transformation of activity into passivity.

The warded-off scoptophilia means: "It is not I who is looking, but I am being looked at." In the identification with the object of his desire to look, the subject enjoys the gratification of "inverted" primary and active scoptophilia in the form of exhibitionism. The gratification is passively and narcissistically experienced on his own body. The turning to the subject's own person and the transformation of activity into passivity is not a simple process. Not all of the stages of these transformations have as yet been satisfactorily cleared up. They have been studied best in sadism, which, in the form of activity and aggression, in greater or lesser degree accompanies all instincts.

No detailed proof is needed that at the anal-sadistic stage a situation is bound to occur in which the aggressive impulses of the child have to be restricted by his environment. The sadistic impulse then turns back on the ego as though automatically. Certainly everybody has seen children turn the full force of their rage against themselves when prevented from giving vent to it against someone else. It happens with adults also that they rage against themselves if they are, for internal or external reasons, prevented from discharging their rage on an object. I was able to demonstrate to a patient that she had made all of her preparations for suicide solely because she had not been able to revenge herself sufficiently on her husband. Later I learned that her husband had subsequently committed suicide and that she had been well ever since, and had enjoyed life.

In catatonics, lightning-like outbursts of rage against themselves are an almost daily occurrence. Naturally, sadism will abandon its direct and crude forms of manifestation to the degree to which the ego has become more differentiated and refined. When the ego is more differentiated, the turning of the sadism against the subject is already indicated by exaggerated grief, worrying, self-reproach, and the like. These manifestations of sadism turned inward may appear in all neuroses. But they appear in more isolated form in hysteria than in the obsessional neurosis and melancholia. That is, in hysteria they refer to definite persons and specific situations, and do not have the serious and tormenting quality they possess in the obsessional neurosis and in melancholia, where they dominate the entire personality. In both the latter forms of illness they assume the guise of reaction formations.

Another stage in the defense against sadism is the one in which the object also changes.

A female patient masturbated genitally with fantasies of decidedly autosadistic character. Among other practices, between her fourth and sixth years, she would press her clitoris so hard that she felt pain. Then she would utter the words to herself: "It hurts." In the fantasy a man would lean over her, whom in the analysis she was able to recognize as her father, and would console her in a kindly manner, saying: "It has to be that way." Turning against her own person the sadism carried over from the preceding phase of development, she also changed the object. She identified with her father, and with him she enjoyed the pains he inflicted upon her. Later on, after having given up masturbation, she developed fantasies of a child being tormented by a physician and then beaten by a male teacher. She herself was no longer a partner in these tortures, but merely witnessed the cruelties. For the benefit of the conscious part of her personality she warded off the sadomasochism secondarily through displacement onto other objects. Originally she warded off the sadism by transforming it into masochism.

The first stage of sadism is thus aggression linked with activity against an outside object. The second stage, which may appear as a form of defense, consists of a turning against the subject which is identical with a change of object (autosadism). If the object is entirely absorbed by the ego, then the sadism is transformed into secondary masochism, which then grafts itself upon the primary masochism preceding the sadism, and strengthens it.

At this point I should like to illustrate still another form of defense with a short example.

One evening I was visiting at the home of friends who had a little daughter who was at that time not quite five years old. She had just been put to bed and was moving about there in a lively way. She undressed and exposed herself with the greatest pleasure. When she noticed me, she closed her eyes and exclaimed repeatedly: "I am blind! I am blind!" The child warded off the exhibitionism through its opposite; that is, she punished herself with blindness. Showing herself, she closed her eyes in order not to see herself. She punished her *seeing* organ.

We see in adults also that an instinctual impulse is warded off through the blocking of a corresponding component instinct (exhibitionism— inhibited scoptophilia, hysterical blindness).

From all that has been said we conclude that it is difficult to draw a sharp line of demarcation between the various forms of defense. All of them are interwoven.

Defense as a Narcissistic Protection
and the Repetition Compulsion

Undoubtedly I have not succeeded in enumerating all of the forms of defense appearing at the different stages of development. For the time being, however, we must be content with what we have been able to grasp and try to clarify it. We found that the most general condition for all of the defense mechanisms was the helplessness engendered by a state of excitation, hence a traumatic situation. The danger releases feelings of unpleasure. These give the signal of anxiety which later introduces defensive and protective measures. Through the anxiety, actually through the discomfort lurking behind it, a defensive tendency is activated which strives to balance the disturbance in the economy of the instinct energy, to master it. It looks as though in the dangerous, traumatic situation, recuperative healing processes were activated. If we consider the starting point of the processes of defense, we notice one trait which is common to all forms of defense: the libido turns away from the external world and cathects the ego; object libido changes into narcissistic libido. This is true of identification, of the turning against the subject, of the transformation of activity into passivity, and the rest. Although in simple displacement (phobia) the instinct does not seem to turn against the subject, still this displacement is accompanied by other forms of defense (identification, projection, and so forth) which are evidently in the service of narcissistic protective tendencies of the ego. In general, the situation is this: an instinctual drive whose gratification is blocked rebounds back to the ego, where, at the very beginning, every gratification would be obtained without any restriction.

Too little notice is taken of the fact that the libido, when feeling its way into the outside world, immediately, upon the first rebuff it encounters, is withdrawn to its narcissistic point of departure and takes effect in the ego. The libido, if it meets with greater or lesser difficulties in gratification, always returns to narcissism, in the neuroses and the psychoses, as well as in daily life.

Now, the effects of this withdrawal are varied, depending upon the quantity of the withdrawn libido and on the resultant instinct defusion. In the severe psychoses the withdrawal of libido is more or less complete, hence the defusion of instincts is also greater. In the neuroses, on the other hand, the withdrawal is partial, and, as in hysteria, the defusion of instincts plays hardly any role. Thus, when gratification or discharge of instincts is frustrated, the libido withdraws to the better protected narcissistic position; now one has to ask oneself which factors cause frustration. Does it depend on the external world or on the intensity of the instinctual demands? It may be caused by both. If, for example, the infant's hunger is not satisfied, the frustration is conditioned by an external factor. Since the impulse which has cathected the image of the mother's breast with its energy does not disappear without adequate gratification, the infant perhaps hallucinates the sucking and thus gratifies himself through the ego instead of through the object. The same gratification through the ego by the way of excitation of the sense organs from within may also occur in hysterical hallucinations when the object of gratification is lacking. Defense against an intolerable state of excitation, hence, may also occur through the hallucination of gratification by the desired object, thus through a wish fulfillment (the object and the gratification are not present, and yet they are experienced as present).

There are, however, frustrations which are quite independent of external gratification, since the state of excitation cannot be done away with at all through real external gratification because of the unusual intensity of the instinct. In this case, likewise, the instinctual urge turns to the ego and seeks gratification there. It thus seems as if the libido takes flight whenever gratification, for some reason or other, encounters obstacles. It retreats to an earlier position, the narcissistic one. One might say that the instincts, yielding to the *principle of inertia,* return to their earlier state whenever difficulties arise in their gratification. Since in the psychic realm the principle of inertia is expressed in the repetition compulsion, *an impulse which has to be warded off will have, first of all, the tendency to repeat itself.* Through the repetition of an earlier method of instinct gratification the defense against a present instinct need is brought about; that is, *the mechanism of defense is fixated* and made resistant against any subsequent attempts to break it up. It is the repetition compulsion, as we have already discussed in greater detail, that is the factor which predisposes to the fixation of the instinct. The repetition compulsion calls forth the most primitive form of defense, which is called *primal repression.* This primal repression is responsible for the fact that an impulse which is striving for expression can attain it only with great difficulty or not at all.

The defensive processes are unconscious processes which are governed by the laws of the unconscious, that is, by the primary process, and which have thus acquired the ability to express impulses also through their opposite. Therefore, when trying to translate a warded-off instinctual expression into the language of the conscious, we must frequently look for its opposite; for instance, behind passivity, its unconscious counterpart, activity; behind masochism, sadism; and so on. Exaggerated love or hate are quite common in hysteria, but their unconscious meaning is likewise to ward off the opposite of the one or the other.

If we further recall that the unconscious is also the infantile, then we must add that the characteristic of defense to which the neurotic has recourse is not only an unconscious but also an infantile protective mechanism. This will be discussed later in detail.

In attempting to describe the processes of defense, I intended first to discuss those forms which are independent of the differentiation of the ego and of the adaptation to reality, in order to be able later on to discuss the more complicated forms separately. I do not seem to have been wholly successful in this attempt, for it must not be overlooked that the same forms of defense appear at all developmental stages of the ego and the libido. In psychic life, nothing takes as simple a course as some people who are inclined to schematize would like. Each psychic process is linked to others by thousands of invisible threads, and therefore one is occasionally compelled to retract at one point what one has stated as an established fact at another point.

Identification, for instance, serves to procure an adequate gratification of an id impulse on the oral stage. We do not know, however, precisely what, in this process, is the defense against an instinct stimulus through the ego and what is simply an automatic process of the unconscious id under the influence of the repetition compulsion. It is sometimes very difficult to distinguish whether a process occurs in the id or in the ego. It is especially difficult when one is dealing with developmental stages of the personality in which the ego is not sharply differentiated from the id, as in illnesses where the ego and the libido have undergone a very far-reaching regression (schizophrenia). In any case, it seems that here the processes of defense take their course automatically, so to speak, with little participation of the ego. If the ego is more sharply differentiated and better organized, it takes hold of the defense processes of the id, in order to make use of them in the defense against id impulses. Thus the same forms of defense appear at all developmental stages of the ego and the libido, though they may have a different genesis and meaning in each individual case. Every form of defense develops in a very complicated way, through devious paths.

The defense against excessively strong instinct stimuli in the first stages of development occurs, in principle, in two opposite directions:

either through projection, a form of flight, or through withdrawal of the libido from the objects (turning to one's own person, as in identification, and the like). In projection, the ego protects itself through displacement onto the outside world of the threatening instinctual demand. In the other forms of defense, as for instance in the turning against one's own person, the instinct is driven back to the id. One might also picture the process in this way, namely that with increasing instinct danger the ego perceives the signal of unpleasure and forces the instinct either into the outer world or back to the id. The result is identical in either case: protection of the ego, assurance of narcissistic rest.

As long as the ego is weak and "close to the id," the defense may take its course in such a comparatively simple way. These processes of defense, however, must necessarily become more complicated when the ego demarcates itself from the id and the outside world and when it enters into a real relationship to the outside world through object cathexes and when, furthermore, the superego evolves. The ego will then have to defend itself against three influences: against the outside world (as perception), against the id (emotions, feelings, affects), and against the influences of the superego (affective thoughts like sense of guilt). In the earlier stages most of the defensive processes were automatic. Now the ego takes possession of them, thus gaining in power. The ego is no longer so helpless against the influences of the id, since the strengthening of the ego depends to a high degree on its ability to master the defensive processes. Through its relation to the superego the ego undergoes still another change which means a strengthening as well as a weakening: it is, on the one hand, supported by the superego in its struggle against the strivings of the id—it has, so to speak, a rear guard; on the other hand, it often becomes too dependent on the superego, thus impairing the ego's independence.[2]

GENERAL CONSIDERATIONS ABOUT RESISTANCE

The force with which the ego opposes the influences emanating from the id, the superego, and reality, we call *resistance*. Since the ego has to struggle against so many kinds of dependence, there are several kinds of resistance which will be discussed more fully at another point. The

[2] For instance, when a sadistic impulse in the anal-sadistic phase is frustrated, the child often harms himself automatically; later on, when the superego has developed, such a sadistic impulse is converted into self-punishment, penitence, and the like.

resistances are directed against the realization of the id strivings, that is, against their transformation into actions directed toward bringing about gratification, as well as against the perception of the instinct representative and of the external stimuli (reality), and finally against the influences of the superego. It may occur that resistances against the influences of the superego assert themselves within the ego, which otherwise is supported by the superego, and that these influences are warded off just as are the impulses of the id. The task all these resistances have in common is, thus, to keep certain disagreeable stimuli away from the ego; they introduce defenses against those stimuli. The most important of the resistances is repression. This concept is often confused with that of suppression. While in repression the ideational content is forgotten and the emotion persists either as such (free-floating) or attached to different ideas, in suppression the idea is not forgotten and the affect is controlled and subdued. Repression is an unconscious process; suppression, a preconscious or conscious one.

Now we will attempt to determine in what way the defense operates under the influence of these resistances.

REPRESSION

At the genital stage, object relationships are already established. The genital impulses strive, in the first place, toward the objects of the oedipus complex. The child's genitals, however, are not yet mature enough for sexual intercourse. Any attempt in this direction must fail because of the biologic conditions of the child. Besides, at this period the attempts at realizing the sexual strivings are opposed by the castration complex. In any case, the activity of the sexual instinct must be renounced. Either the object as a perception or the sensations which the instinct releases and which press for motor discharge may be warded off. As a rule, both these processes occur simultaneously: with the warding off of the perception, the instinct is also blocked off. For the child, the simplest method is to deny a disagreeable perception or impulse. In this respect the child always "lies." What is disagreeable to the child is simply nonexistent. The adult likewise prefers to escape unpleasant impressions. There are patients who develop a general reaction out of their infantile method of denying unpleasurable perceptions. Frequently their behavior appears as indifference and gives the impression of passivity, while it is really an active defense against painful experiences.

In hysteria, this "negation" is more or less conscious at the beginning of the illness; later on it becomes unconscious. I need only cite the first example of the girl with hysterical vomiting, who quite simply denied to herself a recent experience which she had not yet forgotten. (It was preconscious.)

In depersonalization the processes of the inner and outer world are still perceived, but the perceptions lack the vivid feeling tone which accompanies every conscious psychic process. The lack of the feeling accompanying the act of perceiving suggests that a special, highly differentiated part of the system Cs has become insensitive to excitation. Since, in depersonalization, as we already know, one part of the ego refuses to take cognizance of the perceptions, feelings and sensations of the other part, it is clear that the lack of the feeling accompanying perception may also be placed in the category of the defense processes. Depersonalization may reach various degrees; it frequently may be so slight that it is hardly noticed by the patient and is accordingly quickly forgotten.

The tendency to exclude psychic experiences from consciousness is much greater in the amnesia of hysteria than in depersonalization. In place of a perception or memory there is a lacuna; nothing of the former ideational content has remained in consciousness. The entire system Pcpt-Cs seems to be no longer sensitive to excitation by certain stimuli. In order to be capable of functioning, the perception system of the ego must be cathected with energy, a fact clearly demonstrated by the example of depersonalization. This energy can be drawn only from the reservoir of the id. If the cathecting energy is withdrawn from the perceptual system, an inhibition of function results. If we say "the objects are lost," as for example in schizophrenia, it means only that the system Cs has become insusceptible to excitation for the perception of objects. In all the cases in which the perception apparatus has become more or less incapable of excitation, it appears as if the ego were fleeing before the instinctual demands. The withdrawal of libidinal cathexis from the objects, resulting in nonexcitability of the perceptual apparatus of the ego is a general characteristic of defense. In dreamless sleep this nonexcitability reaches the point of complete withdrawal from all external and internal impressions. Whether a psychic act is conscious or not thus depends upon the cathexis of the system Pcpt-Cs.

In hysteria the system Pcpt-Cs is not accessible to stimulation by certain psychic processes; it is probable that here too cathexis is withdrawn. The libido withdrawal, however, proceeds in all neuroses silently; the process in itself cannot be seen, it can only be inferred from the results. In depersonalization, on the other hand, more of this process can be observed, and still more in the schizophrenics' delusion of the "end of the world." In some states of catatonic stupor, the libido withdrawal is so complete that not only does the outside world seem dead to the patients, but these patients also believe themselves dead, an idea which they sometimes are able in some way to communicate. It is self-evident that the catatonic loses completely his contact with the outer world; this is not true of the hysteric. Even though the libido withdrawal in catatonia is far more complete and encompasses much more than in hysteria, still it corresponds to a similar process of defense in both cases. The difference lies in the fact that the ego in catatonia because of its nonexcitability is inaccessible to the demands of the id as well as to reality, whereas in hysteria reality is not warded off.

It makes a difference whether the excitability of the apparatus of perception has been decreased through a withdrawal of cathexis in the ego or through a withdrawal of cathexis in one of the two other systems, which indirectly deprives the perception system of its excitability. We see that in sleep the cathexis has been withdrawn from all systems: during sleep neither outer nor inner stimuli are perceived. In confused and twilight states in which the external world is negated, the excitability of the outward surface of the system Cs has been decreased, but not that of the inner surface; only wishes, fantasies, and the like are experienced; thus mental, inner stimuli are perceived. In schizophrenia, cathexis, on the whole, is withdrawn from the unconscious representations of objects and from reality. Certain parts of the system Cs then become nonexcitable; the system Pcs, on the other hand, remains excitable: schizophrenics handle words as things, and verbal ideas replace concrete ideas. In depersonalization, it seems that a certain point between the system Cs and Pcs has lost its excitability; these patients perceive, but without the feeling tone pertaining to the specific perception. In hysteria, on the contrary, the excitability of the system Pcs is reduced; for hysterics, though they have lost the verbal and other equivalent representations of objects, have by no means lost the unconscious ideas of objects corresponding to them. The excitation related to the objects originates in hysteria in the system Ucs, but it cannot progress to the system Cs, because the system Pcs has become nonexcitable, and hence cannot be traversed. The schizophrenic gives up the unconscious ideas of the object; the hysteric, the preconscious ones. In consequence, the relationship of the hysteric to real objects is only barely noticeably disturbed.

Whereas in twilight states the system Cs has become only slightly excitable to impressions from the outside and more or less blocked from the real world of perceptions because of libido withdrawal from this system itself, in hysteria it does not receive excitation because the connection between Ucs and Cs is interrupted as the result of withdrawal of cathexis in the system Pcs. The nonexcitability of the system Cs in hysteria is a secondary one, in contrast to that of the catatonic stupor or twilight states. In hysteria, the ego is but little affected, whereas in catatonic stupors and twilight states, its most important function, perception, is affected.

The process in which cathexis is withdrawn from the system Pcs so that a psychic act can find no access to the system Cs and, therefore, becomes or remains unconscious, is called repression. This particular defense mechanism, which takes its course in the ego between the systems Cs and Pcs, on the one hand, and Pcs and Ucs on the other, is characteristic only of hysteria. It can, of course, take place only when differentiation between preconscious, conscious, and unconscious has become possible. All other processes of defense are qualitatively and quantitatively somewhat different. This manifests itself, for instance, in the fact that repression can be undone comparatively easily, whereas the restoration of the libido in schizophrenia is infinitely more difficult.

Since the system Pcs controls access to consciousness as well as to motor and affective discharge, the result of repression is that the preconcious idea is refused admission to consciousness and the discharge of instinct energy in motility and affectivity is inhibited. The most successful repression includes, therefore, the idea as well as the affect. This is achieved most frequently in conversion hysteria, where the disagreeable idea has been excluded from consciousness and the affect pertaining to it is lacking. The affect is prevented from progressing from the system Ucs to the system Cs. In hysterical paralysis, for instance, there are no apparent signs of either the repressed idea or the affect.

In anxiety hysteria, the repression of the affect is less successful. The striving of the id is little changed by the repression. But the object changes; its image is transformed. In the case of little Hans, the place of the father is taken by the horse. The defense mechanism in hysteria— repression—thus has a special relationship to reality: it renders the apparatus of consciousness insensitive to certain perceptions, hypersensitive to certain others, which may also be perceptions of substitute ideas. The hysteric notices, in fact, only those things which he wishes to see or which do not disturb him. He has a scotoma for other, disagreeable ones. Paradoxical as it may seem, repression is also, so to speak, an

234 PRINCIPLES OF PSYCHOANALYSIS

expression of the striving to "adapt oneself to reality," to avoid dangers, even though this striving fails. Thus it is probably a phenomenon of adaptation if the little boy renounces his sexual strivings for the mother out of fear of the father. In repression, the ego operates, indeed, under the influence of external reality and replaces the originally objectionable ideas by substitutes, as in phobia.

"Adaptation to reality" of course does not have the same meaning on all developmental stages. The dangers which threaten an adult because of gratification of his instincts are different from those which children incur. If the boy represses the sexual strivings of the oedipus complex, he is adapting himself to reality inasmuch as he adjusts himself in his psychological development to biologic and social facts. He withdraws from an instinctual impulse which, in the face of his helplessness, would necessarily have a traumatic effect, since it can be neither mastered nor gratified.

If the adult, the biologically mature person, renounces his genital functions toward nonincestuous objects for the same psychological infantile motives, then he is not adapted to reality, at least not so far as his sexual life is concerned. It becomes evident that here the first infantile repression persists and continues to have its effect. It seems that the part of the ego which originally caused the repression did not participate in the development of the rest of the ego and has itself succumbed to repression. Thus one can explain the seemingly paradoxical fact that the conscious actual ego often strives for the object, affirms the instinct, but fails when it comes in contact with reality and when it attempts to transform the desire into action. This is the case, for instance, in psychic impotence. The actual ego, thus, is limited in its freedom of activity in consequences of the repression which once took place and, therefore, performs a new repression under entirely different conditions in which a real motive for defense no longer exists. *Each new repression does not represent a new act without a psychic prototype, but a repetition of the primal repression; that is, a process of defense which has once taken place is reinforced through repeated repression.* The primal repression is strengthened by subsequent repressions. The present repression, which is called the *repression proper,* does not always occur as a result of an external cause; it can also occur for inner reasons, with an increase of stimulation.

The after effect of the original repression thus shows in the actual repression inasmuch as the originally repressed idea attracts every new idea which has any connection at all with it.

The repression, which is in fact an afterexpulsion, is nevertheless an active process. This consists in the withdrawal of cathexis from the *preconscious* instinct representatives. What occurs further is independent of the ego. After the withdrawal of cathexis in the preconscious has taken place, the now repressed idea sinks into the unconscious, where it is subject to the rules of the primary process governing this system. Displacements through identification, projection and the like carry out, indeed, besides other tasks, that of automatic defense. Now, when a repression takes place, these primary forms of defense reappear and make common cause with the repression. They are reproduced after the first act of repression and go into action again as though driven by the repetition compulsion. The attraction which the repressed prototypes of the primal situation exercise on the present situation would hence be explained by the repetition compulsion of the unconscious id. The repetition compulsion apparently comes to the aid of the repression proper (afterexpulsion). One might express it in this way: in the struggle against the instincts, the archaic mechanisms of defense come to the aid of the ego which has been weakened by the withdrawal of cathexis through repression. However that may be in its details, in any event the repression is performed in two phases: the withdrawal of cathexis in the system Pcs, and the repetition of the primary forms of defense. In reality, however, these two phases cannot be sharply differentiated from each other, at least not in the neuroses.

As has been previously mentioned, repression develops under the influence of external reality, on the one hand; under inner, psychic pressure, on the other. Among the inner causes, the most important is flight from the criticism of the conscience, the feeling of guilt. Moral demands form one of the most important causes of *actual* repression in all neuroses, only they do not play the same role everywhere. The feeling of guilt, for instance, does not dominate the clinical picture of hysteria as wholly as it does that of the obsessional neurosis. It is not always conscious in the obsessional neurosis, but it is almost always unconscious in hysteria. Nor is it as tormenting and aggressive in nature in hysteria as it is in the obsessional neurosis; the entire emotional life of the hysterical patient is not as much governed by the feeling of guilt as is that of the obsessional neurotic. The feeling of guilt generally covers fear of the superego; its nucleus, in men, is formed by castration anxiety. In women, there is also fear of the transgression of the moral demands of the superego, but the nucleus of this fear is not castration anxiety. In women it is not so much a question of the loss of the genitalia as of the loss of love (the father's). The greater faithfulness of the woman in love relationships might be explained by her attachment to the idealized father whose demands, incorporated in the superego, become her own. The psychic illness typical of women is hysteria, where fear of the loss of love plays the chief role; that of men is the obsessional neurosis, of which castration anxiety is characteristic.

Since, in the concept of the superego, the emphasis lies more on the destructive side, in the concept of the ego ideal, more on the libidinal side, and since, further, the feeling of guilt is more tormenting and aggressive in the obsessional neurosis than in hysteria, one might assume that the feeling of guilt of the obsessional neurotic is rooted more in fear of punishment, and that of the hysteric, in fear of the loss of love. In both cases, the feeling of guilt would injure the narcissism of the ego; in obsessional neurosis, through the threat of destruction on the part of the superego; in hysteria, through the threat of the loss of its protective power (as the ego ideal). Even though the hysteric is less inclined to excessive self-punishment and asceticism than the obsessional neurotic, still one must not forget that there are also hysterics with strong tendencies for self-destruction. These, however, are an exception and appear to develop on the basis of an excessively masochistic disposition. While the sadism of the superego in obsessional neurosis is turned against the ego, it seems that in those cases of hysteria where a very strong need for punishment is present, there is an erotogenic masochism.

REGRESSION

The resistance, which arises in the ego under the influence of the superego, is directed against the strivings of the id and aims at inhibiting the course of ideas (perception) as well as affects and action directed toward the outer world. But while, in hysteria, the ego turns away from the offensive and unpleasure-evoking instinctual impulse and idea by means of repression and leaves the further course of the process of defense simply to the unconscious, this is not the case in the obsessional neurosis.

Here something further is added to repression, namely *regression*. In hysteria, the defensive process is concluded when the cathexis has been withdrawn from the preconscious idea, perhaps for an external reason. In the obsessional neurosis, the cathexis in addition is withdrawn from the genital organization. Although the genital stage has been reached in the obsessional neurosis, it proves to be easily relinquished; this is in contrast to hysteria, where the genital organization continues to exist after the repression.

The point of origin of the defense is the same in obsessional neurosis as in hysteria: the strivings of the oedipus constellation. During its further course, however, the defense in the obsessional neurosis is much more radical, for it is followed by the abandonment of the genital libido position. This libido, detached from the genitals, retreats to a lower stage of development, settles where it once had been fixated, and revives the libido organization which had already been overcome or abandoned. In compulsion neurosis, the libido regresses to the anal-sadistic phase, since the genital strivings are particularly strongly rejected. The meaning of the regression, which can be clearly observed in some cases, is that anal or sadistic activity seems far less dangerous to the patient than genital activity. I should like to cite just one example:

A compulsive neurotic, after having anxiously avoided any contact with women, used to masturbate, for a time, with the idea that the hollow of his hand was an anus. He believed he was thus complying with the severe parental and religious prohibition against sexual intercourse with women before marriage. In this way of sexual gratification, however, the power of attraction of the repressed unconscious became apparent. In later attempts at masturbating in the same manner, he was seized by the fear that his penis could be pinched off in the anus. In this case it is very clear that the defense against genital gratification occurs because of castration fear, and no less evident that the same castration fear pursues the patient *regressively*, even into the pregenital stage. Although our patient proscribed any kind of sexual gratification, genital as well as pregenital, yet, after marriage, he always had intercourse from behind, but reproached himself most severely for this. The first attempt at defense seems initially to have been successful through the act of repression. But the libido escaped from the genital to the pregenital position, and regressed to the anal-sadistic stage. Since, however, the patient's conscience and his feeling of guilt did not change in the same way as his sexual organization, equally violent resistances arose against the anal-sadistic impulses as against the genital ones.

The compulsive neurotic sets the entire apparatus of defense in motion against pregenital impulses. Just as repression corresponds to a flight of the libido, so also does regression, except that the latter flees far more thoroughly. The regression of libido is the characteristic which lets us distinguish between the compulsive-neurotic defense and the hysterical defense. One might raise the objection, though, that in hysteria, also, regressions appear, even to the womb. The difference, however, consists in the fact that the hysterical regression applies only to the world of ideas, whereas the obsessional one includes the instincts themselves. Regression in hysteria leads back to *forms of expression* of a previous stage of development, whereas, in obsessional neurosis, it leads to an *actually lower stage* of sexual life.

It is the disposition which is responsible for the fact that, in compulsion neurosis, the defense takes the form of regression, but does not take this form in hysteria. The compulsive neurotic is fixated at the anal-sadistic stage. It is not only the development of the libido of the future compulsive neurotic which is thereby indicated, but also the development of the ego. We know that, with a strongly anal-sadistic disposition, an extremely severe and unloving superego develops. Therefore the superego is far more intolerant and demanding and has a greater power over the ego in the obsessional neurosis than in hysteria. The dependence of the ego on the superego is increased in the obsessional neurotic; the ego must therefore reject the genital strivings of the oedipus complex far more energetically than in hysteria.

The latency period of the obsessional neurotic is filled with the struggle against masturbation, which shows signs of the beginning of a ritual. But since, during the latency period, the self-imposed prohibitions against sexual activity (masturbation) are constantly transgressed, the conscience is constantly burdened and becomes more sensitive, whereupon an even stronger feeling of guilt develops. The tendency toward asceticism, which is characterstic of the obsessional neurotic, as a rule sets in with puberty. The final advance of the matured sexuality then meets with a resistance of the ego which is the more violent since the ego is threatened by an extremely moral, aggressive, and destructive superego, which rejects any instinct activity. The ego submits; it forces the libido to withdraw from the genitals. The libido retrogresses to earlier stages of development, but stops at the fixated point. Then sexual impulses invade the consciousness again, only they are no longer genital, but anal and sadistic in character. Regression is no longer sufficient to ward them off, because it has already fulfilled its task once, and neither is repression, because it is able to ward off only impulses on the genital stage, as we have already learned from the discussion of hysteria. Thus still another process of defense has to be put into action.

REACTION FORMATIONS OF THE EGO

Since the superego of the obsessional neurotic is excessively demanding, aggressive, and destructive, the ego feels itself threatened. In order to escape the danger of punishment on the part of the superego, the ego changes itself, by transforming the impulses of the id into their opposite and by intercepting them; this leads to reaction formations, which change the character of the obsessional neurotic.

The changes consist mainly of most scrupulous conscientiousness, exaggerated self-criticism, a tendency to asceticism, excessive moral demands on oneself, and the like. These character traits end in self-torment and self-accusation. One can easily understand that, under these conditions, an especially scrupulous consideration of the environment evolves. It is expressed in excessive compassion and readiness for sacrifice. As Federn termed it, the obsessional neurotic renders "forced labor." Besides, these patients develop excessive cleanliness. It is clear that these character changes are reactions to the anal-sadistic striving to which the obsessional neurotic has regressed in his instinctual life. Similar reactions also appear in hysteria, but they do not change the patient's character, since they apply only to a definite situation or to a specific object. The hysterical woman who, in her heart, hates her husband displays excessive affection and anxiousness about him; for others close to her, whom she does not hate, she shows no excessive affection nor anxiousness.

If we compare the part the superego plays in the defense processes of the obsessional neurosis with that in hysteria, the difference is rather clear. In both illnesses there is fear of the superego. In conversion hysteria, the ego, under pressure of the superego, withdraws the cathexis from the representatives of genital ideas; they become unconscious, repressed. But the genital organization remains unchanged in the unconscious. In obsessional neurosis, there is regression in addition to repression, whereby not only the psychic representatives of the genital strivings are warded off, but the genital itself is abandoned as the sexual executive organ. Anal-sadistic strivings, which have again become cathected because of the shunting of the libido, again come into conflict with the superego. The ego of the compulsive neurotic, in its subservience to the superego, once more sets up sharp measures of defense against the anal-sadistic impulses, apparently mastered long before, which have now come into action again, having emerged from the depths of the unconscious. These measures are the above-mentioned reaction formations.

The ego thus succeeds in warding off the objectionable, aggressive, and sadistic initial idea. The affect pertaining to it is, however, suppressed to a certain extent only. That part of the affect which could be suppressed upon the perception of the obsessional idea reappears at another point and in another form, as a sense of guilt; the patient is rarely aware of its true origin. The ego has done its duty by repressing (not perceiving) the objectionable impulse, but it seems that the superego recognizes the obsessional ideas as a substitute for the repressed one and that it communicates its knowledge to the ego, whereupon the latter feels guilty. The situation is this: the ego is able through all the means of defense, such as repression, regression, and reaction formation, to shut itself off from the id, but not from the superego. The latter is in communication with the ego and with the id, and can, therefore, transmit its knowledge of one of the systems to the other. On the other hand, there are cases in which the ego succeeds in blocking itself off from the superego, but not from the id; the feeling of guilt then is not conscious, but unconscious.

It is thus evident that the process of defense does not end in regression and reaction formation, since the forbidden impulse can no longer be fought by these means alone.

Undoing and Isolating

We have mentioned the animistic stage of the development of mankind, in which magic means were used for mastering the world. We have attributed animism to the narcissistic stage of development. At this stage, each impulse, each wish and thought can be fulfilled immediately as though by magic, and the outer as well as the inner world can be transformed in accordance with the wish. From the behavior of the obsessional neurotic it can be concluded that not only the libido regresses to a lower stage, but the ego also, which regresses to the animistic, magical stage. The superstitiousness and the omnipotence of thought and emotions of the obsessional neurotic are well known.

We have considered denial as a precursor of actual repression and have become acquainted with the amnesias as being a further step along this path. In amnesias, which are characteristic of hysteria, the libidinal cathexis is withdrawn from a specific event, with the result that this event does not exist in consciousness; it is repressed. The obsessional neurosis employs another technique of defense in certain phases of the illness. This technique consists of *undoing*. This means that an experience, a thought, a situation, is undone through magic formulas and actions; it is as if it had not occurred. The obsessional neurotic thus, in his defense, makes use of magic. Certain unintelligible forms of prayer of these patients may serve as an example. These prayers, which are like magic formulas, consist chiefly in petitions to God that he protect a certain person from evil. Further analysis reveals that the patient has to struggle against the most violent sadistic impulses within himself, directed against the very person whom he consciously appears to love. A similar defense is hidden behind the "fear of touching" seen in so many obsessional neurotics. This concerns, in the first place, the fear of touching the genitals; it is thus a defense against masturbation. The fear of touching a member of the opposite sex, in an erotic as well as in an aggressive sense, spreads to other spheres, in the obsessional neurotic. The basis upon which the fear of touching develops is ambivalence. The avoidance of contact represents, as it were, negative magic, and even today it flourishes, in peoples at a primitive stage of development, as a means of protection against evil forces. The obsessional neurotic feels these evil powers within himself and thus differs from primitive man and the schizophrenic, who project their instinctual drives into the external world and then feel threatened from the outside.

In principle, the aim of every defense, including hysterical repression, is the undoing of an event, an impulse, or a trauma. The hysteric withdraws the preconscious cathexis from the unpleasant event. The obsessional neurotic tries, in addition, to do away with it, symbolically and magically. He is thus more active than the hysteric, perhaps because of his sadism, the executive organ of which, the motor system, is libidinized. The fact that sadism plays such an essential role in the obsessional neurosis would also explain why magic, especially negative magic, is so predominant. We have, indeed, derived negative magic from the destructive instincts.

Not only sadistic but also anal libido takes part in the development of the compulsive ceremonial. Every compulsive ceremonial fails over and over again and has to be repeated anew in a sequence determined by certain rules. With progression of the illness, there is less and less possibility of concluding the compulsive thinking and acting. As I have been able to observe in several cases, the so-called "normal" course of the compulsion is disturbed by anal strivings. Some kind of defilement in the compulsive thinking and acting is felt by the patient; it is, as it were, never "clean." The compulsion, therefore, must be started anew, the train of thoughts or the action has to be cleansed until the patient gets a feeling of "relief." Thus, instinct energies from the anal sphere are displaced to the sphere of thinking and feeling, and, in the compulsive ceremonial, they are warded off in a way that is similar to the warding off of the sadistic ones through "undoing." The invasion of higher spheres by anal strivings is just as disturbing to thinking, feeling, and acting as are the sadistic strivings.

While, in hysterical amnesia, an important traumatic experience actually vanishes from consciousness, this is not always the case in obsessional neurosis. The compulsive neurotic very often is capable of recalling important experiences, even of very early childhood. Only these memories are more or less robbed of their affect and have lost their connection with similar experiences (or strivings). They stand isolated like a foreign body; almost all of the associative links leading from them to the symptoms are cut off. While, in hysterical amnesia, the libidinal cathexis is withdrawn from the pathogenic experience itself, in compulsion neurosis, it is withdrawn merely from the connecting links. In hysteria, the memory of the experience itself is lost, whereas, in compulsion neurosis, the recollection of the circumstances accompanying each such experience is lost. Hence, in obsessional neurosis as well as in hysteria, the understanding of the connection between the symptom and the salient event is lacking. The effect is the same in both illnesses: the psychic strivings on which the symptom is based are unconscious. This technique of defense, which renders a psychic process unconscious, is a counterpart of repression in hysteria and is called *isolation*.

Isolation can be compared to the concentration of attention, which, according to Bleuler, is based on the opening of new paths for desired associations and on the inhibiting of undesired ones. Isolation in the obsessional neurosis, however, serves not to open paths for new associations but only to keep undesired associations from consciousness, to inhibit them. This is achieved through special actions in the form of a ceremonial, through which the entire defense receives a motor reinforcement. Both the associative inhibition and the motor action for defense are of magical character. The result of this magic of isolation is that what actually belongs together becomes separated.

The taboo against touching, of the obsessional neurotic, is expressed in the tendency to isolate and undo, as in the above-mentioned fear of touching. Here it is a question not only of avoiding physical contact— at first in a genital sense (masturbation), later on, after regression, in a destructive sense—but also of avoiding any contact with the obnoxious ideas in thoughts, symbolically.

The forms of defense in compulsion neurosis are, accordingly, numerous. In this connection, however, we are interested only in the reaction formations. We recall that they are helpful in warding off the repressed ideas which from a deeper level repeatedly press for action. In hysteria, the process of defense is more or less completed with the formation of symptoms. This is not so in the obsessional neurosis, since there it fails over and over again and demands ever new defense measures. The ego of the obsessional neurotic, with the aid of reaction formations, develops a resistance against the ever-renewed upward push of the repressed instincts.

COUNTERCATHEXIS

In hysterical repression, the cathexis is withdrawn mainly from the preconscious idea of the instinct which has to be warded off. The repressed instinctual impulse may become cathected with energy from within, where the instinct is strengthened spontaneously, or from the outside, through the perception of an object on which the instinct is focused. Now, the hysteric develops a special vigilance which helps the ego to withdraw from the perception of the object or from the psychic representative of the repressed instinct. He may, perhaps, experience a vacancy of mind when the forbidden perception attempts to force itself into consciousness, or he may instead have scotomata for such perceptions and ideas. *Vigilance* has the special task of keeping the undesirable idea from consciousness. Such vigilance develops through the cathexis of the perceptive surface of the ego by the energy which has been withdrawn from the instinct representatives. The process is called *countercathexis.* This type of countercathexis is typical of hysteria; it may occur either through the intensification of the opposite feeling (an excess of love for a certain person may take the place of hate) or through the cathexis of the perceptive surface itself. When an object is perceived which through associations is linked with repressed material, pain may appear. The countercathexis of the perceptive apparatus which is turned to the external world is more distinctly evident in phobia than in conversion hysteria. In phobia, the ego is particularly vigilant against external impressions. The projections in schizophrenia also correspond to a countercathexis, for an object in the external world is cathected as a defense against an instinctual urge. In obsessional neurosis, the countercathexis takes place in the shape of reaction formations and leads to the intensification of some of the ego's characteristics; exaggerated compassion, for example, is developed in order to avoid sadism.

The countercathexis is an integral part of the resistances against the re-emergence of warded-off instinctual strivings. Whereas, in hysteria, the resistance derived from the countercathexis serves mainly to reinforce the defense against external perceptions, its task, in obsessional neurosis, is exclusively to strengthen the defense against inner dangers, thus against the instincts themselves. In hysteria, the countercathexis is predominantly an external one; in obsessional neurosis, an internal one. To state it more clearly, the hysteric in the first place wards off his relationship to love objects; the obsessional neurotic wards off the instinct itself. The hysteric thereby breaks off the connection with consciousness, while the obsessional neurotic does not. Common to both is the fact that they ward off the undesirable perceptions and instinctual impulses through alteration of the ego organization. Since, in the obsessional neurosis, the decisive defense occurs through regression which forces the instinct life down to a lower level, and since, furthermore, the obsessional neurotic works against his instinct life with internal countercathexis, while the hysteric accomplishes the same with external countercathexis, it appears that there is a relationship between repression and external countercathexis on the one hand, and between regression and internal countercathexis, on the other.

RESISTANCE

The countercathexis which is brought about through the displacement of the energy of the id onto the ego is called *resistance*. This definition expresses in other words what has been said previously: countercathexis keeps away from consciousness undesirable, pain-provoking psychic material. The first resistance is present simultaneously with the first repression; it is, as it were, identical with it. It is later reinforced through other types of resistance stemming from different sources, which form the afterexpulsion. There are, indeed, several types of resistance whose task it is to maintain the defense, to protect it, for the instincts, because of their continuous character, cannot be permanently banned through a defense occurring only once. The ego must, therefore, continuously furnish defense forces or countercathexis, in order to maintain the first repressions. This continuing effort, expressed in the resistance, consumes much psychic energy.

The resistance which we see at work at the very beginning of the neuroses and which plays an immensely important part in the treatment has essentially the same task, in the neurosis, as the censor in the dream, namely, to keep ideas from consciousness and to block instinctual impulses from access to motility and affectivity.

The resistances, as we have seen, are of compound nature and have various sources. Most of them are ego achievements, and, since they affect the system Pcpt-Cs, one might assume that they are conscious. They appear to develop in this system as a kind of protective barrier against stimuli, to counteract the influence of internal and external forces; but they are unconscious.

The resistance of the ego may be in contradiction to the rest of the ego, which also has other tasks to pursue than the building of resistances; we have, indeed, learned that with the first defense, that is, the primal repression, not only the instinct but also a part of the ego is inhibited. This part of the ego does not participate in the development of the rest of the ego. It may thus occur that with a changed situation later, when the ego is already equal to a danger and does not have the intention of warding it off, the inhibited part of the ego treats the danger as it did before. One part of the ego then no longer understands the other part; the ego is split. Although this process of defense is an ego resistance, it is not conscious. The process is very complicated and not yet clearly understood in all its details. It appears in three forms: first, as *repression resistance;* secondly, as resistance stemming from the *secondary* or *epinosic gain from illness;* and thirdly, as *transference resistance.* Repression resistance has been discussed. Resistance because of the secondary gain from the illness will be elaborated upon in another connection. We turn now to the transference resistance.

TRANSFERENCE

The term "transference" is self-explanatory. It means that affects and ideas are "transferred" from one object to another, from one situation to another. Transference is based on two factors: first, as we have seen in the discussion of the development of the libido, there is an urge to make contact with an object of the external world. Secondly, there is a tendency for past impressions to take over new impressions, if there is even the slightest similarity between them, and for the individual to react to the new ones as if they were indeed those of the past. This tendency can be derived from the tendency to repeat old experiences and to find, in the perception of present objects, similarities to previous objects *(Wahrnehmungsidentität).* It is as if present impressions were experienced in terms of the past. The tendency to relive old experiences in the present is realized, in the psychoanalytic situation, in the relationship between the patient and the analyst, a specific relationship which is called transference.

Transference is a phenomenon which was first recognized in the psychoanalytic situation but which, of course, also exists outside of this situation. The tendency of repressed material to be transformed into actual experience finds expression in the transference. In other words, a *readiness* for transference is always present, although it cannot always develop into real transference. The psychoanalytic situation is particularly suited for the transformation of the readiness into transference. The transference readiness of the neurotic is greater than that of the so-called normal individual, because he suffers more from frustrations, inhibitions, and repressions.

In the structural sense, the transference is based on the fact that the ego does not permit the impulse originating in the id to traverse the entire scale of the psychic systems in order to become conscious. Thereby the impulse avoids the system Pcs (that is, the preconscious part of the ego) and gains direct access to motility and action.

During psychoanalytic treatment, the repressed unconscious material is revived, and since this material contains many infantile elements, the infantile strivings are reactivated and seek gratification in the transference. As the most important relationship of the child is that with his parents, the relationship between patient and analyst established in the transference becomes analogous to, or, at times, even similar to the patient's relationship with his parents in childhood. The patient endows the analyst with the same magic powers and omniscience which, in childhood, he attributed to his parents. The traits of submissiveness and rebellion, in transference, likewise reflect the attitude of the child to his parents. The patient behaves irrationally in the psychoanalytic situation; it often takes a long time to make him see the irrationality of his behavior, which is deeply rooted in his unconscious infantile life.

Since the neurotic repeats, "transfers" into the analytic situation, everything that has not been discharged, the transference can be a *positive* as well as a *negative* one; he may love his analyst and also hate him. Transference may become a new source of resistance. It often happens that the patient cannot admit to himself his feelings for his analyst, whether out of self-respect, as for instance in the case of a female patient in love with her analyst, or out of fear of him. In both instances, the transference leads to an ego resistance which may be considered a narcissistic protection. The ego withdraws the cathexis from the strivings involved in the transference and is itself cathected by the same energy (countercathexis). This is identical with a defense against the transference; thus this form of transference resistance becomes an ego resistance. This ego or transference resistance serves to strengthen further the primary repression resistance. While, in this type of transference, only the origin of his feelings and affects is unconscious to the patient (he accepts his love and hate at their face value), there exists another type of transference in which these feelings and affects themselves do not enter consciousness, but procure expression in innumerable unconscious actions (in *acting out*). In acting out, old, repressed, undischarged wishes, experiences, fantasies, and the like are repeated.

A female patient, for example, developed a particularly intense curiosity about my private life. I could not, of course, satisfy her curiosity, but, on the basis of her associations in connection with this curiosity, I called her attention to the fact that she must have gratified her scoptophilia during a certain phase of her childhood. She was not able to recall anything about this. Before falling asleep that night, she continued to search her memory, but nothing came to her mind. Instead, she was overpowered by the desire to masturbate, to which she yielded. The following morning, while standing fully dressed in front of the mirror before going out, she suddenly opened her blouse and looked at her breasts. After having told me all of this in the analytic hour, she remembered suddenly, with immense relief, that in childhood she used to open the trousers of her brother, who was three years younger than she, and look at his genitalia.

It is thus revealed that the repetition compulsion is the last resort of the ego in the process of defense. What cannot be attained in any other way is acted out but *not remembered* until a temporary exhaustion of the instinctual energy occurs. The transference resistance may therefore stem from the ego as well as from the id; in any case, the resistance of the ego and that of the id frequently unite in the transference to form a common resistance.

RESISTANCE OF THE ID

The repetition compulsion in the form of acting out does not manifest itself solely in the transference situation. Acting out may also appear without any relationship to the transference, that is, the patient may provoke experiences in which he satisfies some id strivings without any participation on the part of his conscious ego. In such instances it becomes evident that the repetition compulsion is operating when a repressed instinct is struggling for gratification and expression but does not find it. The resistance which, in this constellation, opposes the "becoming conscious" of unconscious processes belongs to the unconscious id. Of all the resistances this is the one most deeply rooted and least understood; it seizes upon the repressed instinct and seeks to procure gratification for it, but succeeding only partly, merely repeats and reinforces the defense. An example may illustrate this point.

Upon entering my office, a patient declared emphatically that all doctors are murderers. Asked why he considered me a murderer, he answered that I was cruel to him, as I had not given him drugs at a time when he was suffering intolerable pain. I told him that he, as a physician, must know that his accusations were unjustified, but since he accused me of being a murderer, he himself must feel like one. This remark brought forth a number of memories of his cruelty to animals in childhood. Then there followed a chain of associations from which it became evident that since his early childhood he had made many symbolic or real attempts to injure his father. He remembered further that as a very young physician, he had recklessly undertaken dangerous operations for which he lacked the experience; it was just luck that no disaster had occurred. (Later on in his professional life he did not perform such serious operations, and after some time, gave up surgery altogether.)

This patient, from childhood on, had committed acts of cruelty whose meaning remained unknown to him until recently. These cruel deeds were aimed at his father.

Thus he repeated sadistic actions which were disguised symbolically and in other ways; he repeated an id striving whose meaning became conscious only in the analysis. His sadism was repressed, of course; that is, the cathexis was withdrawn from the psychic representations of this drive, consequently its meaning became unconscious. The repressed striving then tried to gain access to motility and to be acted out, to be repeated in actions. Obviously, this repetition added resistances on the part of the id to the repression, introduced by the ego.

RESISTANCE OF THE SUPEREGO

Finally, there is the resistance on the part of the superego which works in the following way: the superego prevents the ego from enjoying libidinal gratification on the object and turns its aggression upon the ego. This aggression becomes bound to the ego and operates within it, causing suffering, renunciation, self-reproach, self-punishment, and the like. When the ego submits to the strict demands of the superego, it often derives masochistic pleasure therefrom, because the aggression of the superego fuses, in some way, with the repressed libidinal strivings within the ego. The resistance of the superego which reinforces the original repression now itself becomes a source of libidinal gratification for the ego, by way of masochism. The feelings of guilt or the need for punishment caused by the superego bring about narcissistic gratification; hence morality is erotized. It is striking how often people suffering from self-imposed deprivations enjoy their suffering and behave as if they were saints. Some even praise themselves for this suffering.

We have now become acquainted with three sources of resistances: the ego, the id, and the superego. The resistances of the ego are further divided into three categories: the transference resistance, the repression resistance, and the resistance of the secondary gain from illness, which will be discussed later. We must therefore take into consideration five kinds of resistances. In the next chapter the various processes of defense are illustrated with clinical material.

In summary, we find that defense is a general concept which comprises all the mechanisms for the protection of the ego from experiences and instinctual strivings that involve danger. The mechanism of repression stands in a special relationship to consciousness and is characteristic of hysteria. Regression has a special affinity for the obsessional neurosis and other illnesses of a certain type, as for instance melancholia. We have further seen that the mechanism of defense at the genital stage and after the establishment of the superego is different from that on earlier developmental stages. It seems that repression is the defensive response on the genital stage of development, whereas reaction formations seem to bear a special relation to the pregenital stages of organization.

If repression proves to be too weak a protection, then there set in regressively other, older defense mechanisms, such as projection, identification, repetition compulsion, and reaction formation. In the struggle of defense, the external world and certain parts of the ego may be lost (schizophrenia). The defense then takes place between the ego and the id, in more primitive forms.

Through the resistances erected in the service of defense, the connection and the free communication between the individual psychic systems are interrupted. The ego is weakened, since it is restricted in its freedom and its ability to make decisions and since the dammed-up instincts constantly exercise high pressure. It is as if a fragile vessel were filled with dangerous explosives.

It is true that through repression (defense) the neurotic adapts himself to instinctual dangers, but only in so far as he flees from them and renounces real adaptation and gratification. His ego loses its unity and strength.

The defense mechanisms set in when the synthetic function of the ego becomes inadequate. The ego is always striving to bind and to mediate. If the instinct demand is so strong and the superego so intolerant that gratification in reality is impossible, then the ego loses its synthetic capacity to a certain extent. In order not to be disturbed continually (in order to procure rest), the ego shuts itself off from the instinct demands or from the demands of the superego, as the case may be; it represses. Repression and defense, in general, are signs that the ego is not always able to maintain its role as a mediator between the id and the superego.

Chapter IX

THE PROCESS OF ILLNESS

REPRESSION AND NEUROSIS

Repression has proved to be a mechanism of the ego for mastering anxiety, a mechanism of protection against instinctual impulses. It is not identical with symptom formation, since not every repression necessarily leads to illness. It may happen that the cathexis is withdrawn from an instinct striving which is not ego-syntonic, that is, one which meets with the ego's opposition, and yet no illness results. We know that with repression the mental representatives (ideas) of the instinct disappear from consciousness, and the unfolding of the affect is inhibited. Since the unconscious instinct representative is no longer cathected, it becomes inactive and incapable of having any noticeable effect on the systems of consciousness and motility. But, as we have already learned, the energy withdrawn from the instinct may attach itself to the ego, where, forming countercathexes, it is employed to reinforce character traits of the ego or is used for sublimation.

As long as the individual is able to sublimate, his psychic equilibrium is not disturbed by the repressions which have occurred in the course of his life; of course he is able to sublimate only if the repressions have been successful, as described above. I should like here to refer again to the female physician whom we have mentioned in discussing sublimation.

We recall that this woman physician wanted to induce her husband to study medicine and wished, herself, to give up the profession. She was prompted by the idea that she herself could give up medicine, if thus, through her husband, she could maintain contact with her father. Her husband, however, did not change his profession, and the patient herself became a competent physician. It was not the failure of this wish which led to her illness. She became ill only later, after a succession of experiences which deprived her of any pleasure in her profession. Unfortunately I cannot, for obvious reasons, undertake a more complete description of this case. I merely want to show, with its help, that a

251

repression can be well tolerated as long as the repressed instinct is gratified through sublimation. Our patient procured the sublimated gratification through her attainments, by way of the gratification of her narcissism, and indirectly through the attention of her father which these attainments brought her.

But the more she experienced conflicts, the less she was able to master her instinct life. With ever-increasing frequency, old instinct demands, until then repressed, made themselves felt, though she was not completely aware of their significance at that time. She tried to fight them, but without success. The illness began when external difficulties arose which absorbed her energy so much that her ego failed in the face of inner demands, that is, instinct demands.

In every neurosis we encounter a more or less similar situation. The external difficulties of life weaken the ego in its ability to defend itself against the instinctual strivings of the id. *The repression then fails,* the warded-off strivings of the id again become active, and the ego is unsuccessful in opposing them. This *inner failure* leads directly to the neurotic symptom. The illness begins, then, with the actual conflict and an external frustration which is then replaced by an inner failure. The actual conflict must not be mistaken for the actual neurosis, as sometimes happens. The actual neurosis is a somatic illness; the actual conflict is a psychic process. It is true, though, that an actual conflict often results in an actual neurosis and, consequently, in a psychoneurosis. Inversely, a conflict which has been dormant for years may become acute and actual, because of the psychic constellation, without direct external cause, and may lead to the frustration of the instinct demands, to actual neurosis, and later to psychoneurosis. It is a vicious circle, in which the starting point of the factor precipitating the illness cannot always be determined with certainty. The relationship between actual neurosis and psychoneurosis will be further discussed later, in another connection.

PRECIPITATING CAUSES OF ILLNESS

Individuals become ill from causes which appear quite commonplace such as grief, worry, overwork, disappointment in love, and the like. Each one of us has to endure frustrations, failures, and misfortunes, yet not everyone has to pay for them with his health. Though we are not able clearly to define the concept of psychic health, still we consider relatively healthiest that person who is best adapted to the real demands of life, who knows how to bring his instinct demands and his ego demands into such accord that neither inner nor outer conflicts develop from gratification of the two kinds of demands. The most general precondition for becoming ill is thus the failure to adjust oneself to the real demands of life. These demands are as numerous and as vast as life itself. A disappointment in love may play the same role as a gambling loss. In the first case, the instinct fails to be gratified; in the second, the ego is frustrated in its exaggerated feeling of omnipotence, hence its narcissism is injured. The fact that one person is able to endure disappointments in love, gambling losses, and the like, without becoming ill, and another person is not, implies that the real difficulties of life are not in themselves sufficient to produce an irreparable disturbance in the balance of psychic forces. There must be something additional which is independent of external conditions, to prepare the ground for neurotic reactions.

Persons whose love life is restricted and dependent on certain conditions remain well as long as these conditions are fulfilled. If, for instance, a homosexual is forced to renounce his specific sexual gratification, he becomes ill. Although the occasion for his pathologic reaction is an external denial, it is caused by the restriction of his instinct life, which makes object choice difficult.

External frustration may lead not only to neurosis but also to psychosis; seclusion from the world, severing contact with reality, may have the same effect (for example, prison psychosis). In the neuroses, the external frustration affects predominantly the instinct life; in the psychoses, the ego.

It is obvious that external frustration plays only a minor role as a causative agent of the illness, at most, that of an agent provocateur. It has a pathogenic effect only if it meets a certain inner factor that is responsible for the internal frustration. External and internal frustrations supplement each other. There are individuals who become ill because of an insignificant external happening, and others in whose case such a happening is wholly lacking. The severity of the illness is by no means dependent on the intensity of the frustration.

How, then, does an internal frustration develop? To answer this question, I must go into some detail.

FANTASY AND NEUROSIS

Just as there are persons who have the faculty of escaping from the difficulties of everyday life into sleep, so there are individuals who can withdraw from the difficulties of life into fantasy. We have mentioned earlier that fantasies bear a great resemblance to dreams; they are dif-

ferent in that they occur in the waking state and are predominantly subject to the secondary process, whereas dreams occur in sleep and are
predominantly subject to the primary process.

A fantasy may be active or inactive. If inactive, it is isolated, does not
invade the general mental activity, and does not noticeably influence the
individual's behavior. Often a fantasy contains memories of actual experiences, and it, instead of the memories themselves, may be worked
into a dream. Just as the dream is not formed during the night of the
dream, but merely becomes manifest during that particular night's sleep,
stimulated by some happening of the day—having waited, as it were, for
the occasion to invade consciousness—so it is with the fantasy. Most
fantasies are formed of material from the individual's life collected from
early childhood on; yet there are also fantasies which seem to contain
precipitates of the history of mankind, and to be inherited.

A fantasy becomes active only when it is cathected with energy; then
it forces itself upon consciousness and may cause numerous changes in the
ego. It may even become part of the neurotic symptoms. If its intensity is
excessive, it may flood the entire rational ego and culminate in a psychosis. One is almost inclined to state that man becomes ill because of his
fantasies. Why these fantasies do not always lead to illness is another
question. This much can be said in this connection: individuals with
overabundant fantasies are introverted, they are frequently infantile,
and lead an existence directed away from actual life. There are among
them some individuals, such as artists, who, through their creativity,
escape a neurosis, and others who, because of their excessive fantasy and
their inability to find adequate expression for it, become ill.

What is the relationship between fantasy and neurosis? I should like
to illustrate this with an example. It is especially instructive because the
fantasy could be observed *in statu nascendi,* as it were.

A patient related during his analytic hour that early that morning,
after awakening, he had felt very strongly drawn to his wife; he had felt
such sexual excitement as he had not experienced since his illness began.
He was prevented from having intercourse by the presence of his children
in the same room. After having succeeded in mastering his sexual excitement, he developed a state of depersonalization. Everything became
strange to him—his wife, his room, his children, and himself. Immediately thereafter, he was overcome by an agreeable, peaceful sensation, a
sensation of swimming, of swimming toward me. It was easy to interpret
this fantasy, since I was familiar with the patient's past life. The sensation of swimming was a repetition of the sensation he used to experience
as a child when he indulged in fantasies about being in his mother's

womb. He imagined, in these fantasies, that he was swimming toward his father and would hold on to his penis and suck it while the father was having intercourse with his mother. That he was swimming toward me in his fantasy was explained by the transference situation in the analysis. I might add that he developed anxiety when he noticed that he was swimming toward me.

The fact that the patient was prevented from achieving sexual gratification represented the external frustration. The first consequence of this was depersonalization, a withdrawal of libido from the real situation and from the ego. Following this, the libido returned to an earlier position, regressed, and cathected old, apparently inactive fantasies. These, however, now procured access to consciousness and, as soon as they were perceived, met with opposition on the part of the ego. The emergence of old, repressed impulses, which were directed toward an actual object, created a conflict in the patient, as his anxiety indicated. To the external frustration which appeared at the beginning, there was now added the inner one. At this point, it should be noted that the *neurotic* conflict resulting from such a situation is not identical with the *actual* conflict. The latter is a conflict between the ego and an impulse which is not repressed, whereas the neurotic conflict is a conflict between the ego and an impulse which is repressed.

Such an emergence of repressed fantasies occurs usually at the outbreak of a neurosis. Not infrequently these fantasies first appear in dreams and are then further elaborated in the waking state. *The re-emergence of repressed fantasies is an indication of unsuccessful repression.*

In these fantasies the repressed material reappears which had evidently been again cathected with libido. The inactive fantasy becomes active again. The libido which has been withdrawn from the real situation at the onset of the illness returns to a previous position. The regression stops where the libido was fixated. The first stopping place is, as a rule, the phallic stage, the goal of which is the objects of the oedipus constellation. The fantasies contain—although generally in a distorted form—the impulses and object representations that have their origin in this phase and which have been revived with the regression of the libidinal cathexis. Fixation at the phallic stage is characteristic of hysteria. If, however, the fixation has occurred at one of the pregenital stages, then the phallic stage is soon abandoned. The impulses of the pregenital stages crystallize in fantasy likewise about the objects of the oedipus constellation. But because these objects become cathected with pregenital libido, the conflict grows even more acute. The defense struggle which sets in after the failure of repression leads directly to neurosis and symptom formation.

Not all fantasies are based on an actual experience of the past; some may originate in individual experiences, others in the typical experiences of mankind. Thus some fantasies may arise without a real experience as background. When fantasies, regardless of their origin, become fixated, they determine the contents of the future neurosis. An experience of very early childhood, be it a traumatic real experience or a fantasy of traumatic intensity, is called a *primal scene*. Witnessing parental intercourse, either in reality or in fantasy, is considered to be the most frequent traumatic primal scene.

I should like to demonstrate with clinical material the significance of a primal scene.

It is the case of the already-mentioned pervert, who suffered from the compulsion to suck at a man's genitals and to swallow the sperm. In his third year, his youngest brother was born. He reacted to the news of this event with rage, hatred, and despair; he ran away, cried, and was furious. When he returned, the infant was just being bathed; the baby's skin was strikingly dark brown. It seemed to the patient that the skin of the newly born brother was smeared with feces. Weeping, he cried out: "I don't want this dirty brother!" He wanted to hit him, to kill him.

This scene seems to have prepared the ground for later morbid reactions. A short time later, when his mother was nursing the infant, the boy, who was then a little over three years old, also wanted to be on his mother's lap and to suck her breast. But his mother did not permit this. She warded him off with her hand, and in doing so, raised her arm. The boy followed this movement with his eyes and noticed, on a dresser behind his mother's back, the statue of a mythological figure. The statue represented one of the three fates, Parcae, a female figure who, in one hand, held a thread at the level of her breast; in the other hand she held a ball of thread which was near the lower part of her abdomen. It seemed to the boy that the figure's breast had fallen down to the region of her genitals and had remained hanging there. Although this statue had always been in the house, he had never noticed it before. Only the new, undeniable disappointment in his mother, and the rejection, which seemed to him brutal, drew his attention to this statue. His interest in it was supported by the movement his mother made with her hand, which— as it seemed to him—was meant to express: "See, the breast is at the genitals."

This event brought to an end his attempts to gain his mother's love. Thereafter he turned to his older brother, with whom he masturbated frequently up to his fifth year. After puberty, he turned to other men, without, however, daring to practice the perversion. Instead, over a period of many years, he sucked his own penis, until, after severe inner struggles, he decided to perform the same action with other men.

The structure of this symptom is, of course, far more complicated than can be shown here. I wanted only to demonstrate what effect a primal scene can have and how it can form an integral part of the symptom. The details of this scene had to be unwrapped, as it were, from a number of fantasies in which they had been enveloped.

<h3 style="text-align:center">NEUROSIS AND PERVERSION</h3>

What fantasies did our patient produce in his childhood and how did he go on from them to the perversion?

While masturbating with his older brother, he imagined that he was lying in a bathtub, first on feces and then on the little white tails of pigs. This fantasy appears to have very little resemblance to the "primal scene." The primal scene was the refusal of the mother to give him her breast during the nursing of his brother. But there is one feature which points to a connection not only with the primal scene itself but also with the prior experience at the birth of his brother. He had seen him for the first time in the bathtub, and his brother had then seemed to him to be smeared with feces. In the fantasy, he himself was lying on feces in the bathtub. Thus he identified himself with the dirty brother, at the same time making a regression to the anal stage.

When his mother found him masturbating, she threatened to tell his father. The latter, however, much to his surprise, did not punish him, but only said that he was a pig, which was, for him, identical with dirt and feces. The small tails entered the fantasy as a symbol of the penis. Their white color was associated with the white color of his mother's breast. The masturbatory fantasy thus contained an oral and an anal component. It is not necessary to stress the fact that the fantasy of the bathtub is a symbol of the womb and contains a birth fantasy. The details were determined by the experiences of this particular individual.

When he noticed that his father did not condemn his masturbation as severely as did his mother, that he did not threaten him with castration as she did, he gained confidence in his father, and turned to him. This attachment was strengthened by his competitive attitude toward his younger brother, since his father preferred the latter.

During the period of this competition, he often had the opportunity to overhear parental intercourse. Through various impressions, the idea took hold of him that his mother, during intercourse, sucked his father's penis and that his father was thereby soiled. Comparing this idea with his later perversion, one sees that, so far as his orality is concerned, he no longer identified with his brother, but with his mother. The brother is not sucking the mother's breast, but the mother (patient) is sucking the father's penis. It is not the mother who becomes the object of his libido, but the father. In regard to anality, he identified himself with his father. It is not the brother who is soiling himself, but the father (patient). This second component is at first not clearly manifest in his perversion.

Overhearing parental intercourse, he had the impression that his father was cruelly torturing his mother. He suffered severely, had sleepless nights, and wished longingly that the father would take him in place of his mother, in order to spare her the suffering. He was ready for any sacrifice, and actually, he did make sacrifices in later life.

Just as he had experienced disappointments in his mother and his father—his mother refused to give him her breast, and his father did not use him for passive-homosexual and masochistic purposes—so, also, his older brother had broken off his erotic relations with him, in his fifth year. The patient followed his brother around, but the brother no longer wanted him. Coprophagic fantasies and anxiety dreams began to appear. He dreamt that his mouth was filled with something gritty, like sand, which had a disgusting odor.

His younger brother had, apparently, a distinctly anal disposition and was difficult to train to sphincter control. At first, his mother did not scold, but cleaned him up without punishing him. Our patient considered this a proof of love and, now and then, imitated his brother, in order likewise to obtain a proof of love from his mother, that is, to be cleaned up by her. Later on, however, a harsh struggle to break the brother of his habit was begun, in which our patient participated eagerly. His soiled underwear was tied around the little brother's mouth, in a manner similar to the way in which young dogs and cats are housebroken. Later on, the patient reproached himself violently for this and was haunted by the horrible idea that he would be punished in the same way (see the coprophagic fantasies). His feeling of guilt became so overwhelming that he imagined hellish sufferings and inflicted pain upon himself by burning his skin and by injuring himself in order to test how much pain he would be able to endure.

The feeling of guilt was linked with marked feelings of inferiority, which referred primarily to his genitals. For he was convinced that he had completely mutilated his genitals through masturbation. His greatest concern, the leit-motif of his life, was to undo this "mutilation." His oral fixation showed him the way. The largest genital that he had ever seen was his father's. He wanted to incorporate this in order to become a bigger and stronger man. This led to the fantasy that he was biting off his father's penis and swallowing it. This fantasy, however, could no longer gratify his real need; he was driven on to the act itself. Then he actually tried to suck at a playmate's genital, but was interrupted by his older brother, who forbade this sexual activity. Because of this, he was more impressed by the brother than by his father, who ignored his masturbation and said nothing about it, except for the one time when he had called him a pig.

Actually the father played a subordinate role in this home. Shortly before the youngest son was born, he lost his entire fortune. The patient remembered the despair of his mother at this time, and, although he did not understand what the loss of the fortune meant, still, his father, who up to then had impressed him as very powerful, lost all of his authority in his eyes. This attitude was supported by his mother, who constantly abused the father and complained of having to do the housework and of having to take care of the children herself. Moreover, his father continued to decline, earned nothing, and was exposed to all sorts of humiliations. His brother, on the other hand, only a year and a half his senior, played a manly role. He stopped masturbating with the patient, forbade him sexual play with his playmates, and was, himself, physically as well as mentally a capable person. The entire striving of the patient was now directed toward growing up quickly in order to earn a great deal of money and to free his mother from her hard work and worries.

The birth of his younger brother was an easy one. This provided an opportunity for the mother to talk about the birth of her oldest son, which had been a very difficult one, endangering her life. His mother's stories were elaborated by the patient into ideas of his mother's tremendous suffering, of how she was literally torn by the birth of his brother. He was even envious of the difficult birth of his brother and sorry that he was not his brother, that he had not inflicted the same pain on his mother and had not exposed her to the same danger.

That the patient's manifest masochism corresponded to latent sadism was proved by the deepest fantasy, which was the last to become conscious. The contents of this fantasy was that he was in the womb, rather in the mother's rectum, and that he was biting off columns of feces which he identified with children and with a penis.

The older brother, of whom he was now jealous, also impressed him very much. He therefore entered into competition with him, a competition which differed from that with his younger brother and with his father. He wanted to become as able physically and intellectually as the older brother. Not only did he soon attain this goal, but he even surpassed him in every respect. He became a high-spirited, physically very skillful boy, intelligent, gifted, and mature beyond his age. His relationship to his parents apparently consisted, at this period, in his deriding them, defying them, and trying to anger them.

At about his eleventh year, he fell in love with a girl of the same age. Since, however, his playmates teased him about this, he soon gave up his affection for her. At puberty, the drive to the other sex awoke in him, but he mastered it, ever mindful of his mother's warning that one should not enter into relations with women, since only evil, such as infections and the like, came of them. He thus renounced the heterosexual urges out of castration fear and obedience to the mother. He began to masturbate manually, but not for long. His old drive reawakened, he felt himself drawn to men, compelled to look at the genitals of every man through his trousers, and, whenever they seemed to him bigger than his own, he wanted to take them into his mouth and suck them. He did not, however, practice this perversion. Instead, he succeeded in taking his own penis into his mouth, in sucking it, and in swallowing the sperm. Afterwards, he became afraid that the sperm was becoming putrid in his stomach and that he had a foul breath. As the analysis disclosed, concealed behind this was the fear that the sperm might turn into feces, and that he might thus bear children, which would stamp him definitely as a woman. He would thus, through the perversion, achieve the opposite of what he consciously was striving for, namely, to become a strong man.

But, if he was faced by a real temptation, if he came into contact with an active homosexual, he found it very difficult to control himself. He resisted at first, but developed severe neurotic symptoms, which will be discussed later on. Finally, he was no longer able to control himself, and, after severe inner struggles, began to practice the perversion. After each homosexual activity, however, he was overcome by disgust, remorse, feelings of guilt, and anxiety.

When we review this condensed case history, which contains merely the most essential features, we see, first, that the patient's entire life was filled with fantasies, which sought in every possible way to be converted into reality. But if he encountered either an external or an internal resistance, so that the instincts hidden behind the fantasies had to be suppressed, he succumbed to illness.

Every neurotic suffers from fantasies which cannot be realized. Only, as a rule, the patient does not even attempt to realize them, and, if he does so, the gratification is not manifestly "perverted" in character, since the instinctual striving is disguised, where it reaches the system Cs. The psychotic also suffers from the same type of fantasies. But whereas, in the pervert, these fantasies undergo manifold elaboration and are combined into a striving for a single goal, in the psychotic, several contradictory primitive fantasies exist side by side. The sexuality of the psychotic is, indeed, disintegrated. There is still another fundamental difference between the fantasy life of the neurotic and that of the psychotic. While the neurotic is able to distinguish between fantasy and reality and to control his actions accordingly, the psychotic lives in the fantasy, exclusively. For him the fantasy is reality. There are, of course, all kinds of intermediate stages. Indeed, there are persons who are considered healthy even though, for them, a wish or a mere expectation, becomes reality.

To return to our example, we can learn still more of value from it for the understanding of the neurosis.

In puberty, our patient developed normal heterosexual urges. For inner reasons, primarily out of castration fear, he avoided the other sex. The dammed-up libido then cathected the old fantasies until the component instincts corresponding to them gained such an impetus that they flooded the ego and had to be discharged in actions. All of the laboriously erected dams—shame, disgust, and guilt feelings—were broken down; the ego blindly obeyed the impulses of the id. We see, furthermore, that the libido regressed ever farther until it reached its point of fixation. The rejection of the oral wish of the three-year-old boy had probably caused this fixation. After the regression, the entire instinct life of the patient was centered about this point. This fixation, in later life, pressed toward the gratification of passive-masochistic as well as active-sadistic wishes. Both were involved with the castration complex. In the active attitude, the patient protested against the castration threat, while in his passive attitude, he submitted to it and gratified his masochism; his regression to the anal stage served the same purposes. In his childhood, the objects of his instinctual drives were more or less "conscious." After puberty, however, the patient was unaware that his impulses were still directed toward the same objects, those of the oedipus constellation. The representations of these objects were replaced by others in his consciousness. The original object representations, thus, had been removed from consciousness (repressed), whereas the instinctual impulses pertaining to them were retained, though they had undergone various transformations.

In perversion, as in neurosis, the oedipus complex forms the central point around which all instinct needs and the fantasies fed by them are grouped. The oedipus complex appears but rarely in its simple, positive form in the neurosis, and hardly ever in the perversion. Our patient does not simply love his mother and hate his father, but at the same time, he hates his mother and loves his father; in short, his attitude toward *both* his parents is ambivalent.

It is not clear without further consideration why this patient became a pervert and not simply a neurotic. At first one is impressed by the fixation of a component instinct and its persistence beyond the normal degree. But, whereas the ego succeeded in repressing the object representatives of the oedipus series, it could not prevent the instincts and the affects pertaining to them—with the possible exception of hate—from entering consciousness. Why could they not be inhibited?

His father had very early lost all authority in the family. The weakening of his position in the family coincided approximately with the birth of the younger brother. His mother was strict, domineering, and disdainful of the father. The boy, however, yearned for a powerful, authoritative father, perhaps like the one of the earlier period. His older brother impressed him with his manliness. He leaned on him, and became manly himself. He soon surpassed his brother. In puberty, when the entire infantile sexuality again awakens, he no longer had anyone, neither father nor brother, with whom he could identify. He therefore lacked any support in mastering his maturing sexuality; in other words, he missed the parent of the same sex, necessary for the consolidation of the superego. Perhaps this was the latest reason, in point of time, for his inability to master his perverse tendencies.

We have thus found as the basis for this patient's perversion: the fixation of a component instinct and the repetition compulsion, the repression of the objects of the oedipus complex without repression of the instincts, castration anxiety, and a weakly developed superego.

We know that, in the neurosis, the objects of the oedipus constellation are likewise repressed and that the fantasies are just as active as in the perversion. What, then, is the difference between neurosis and perversion?

In our patient, perversions and neurosis alternated. If he practiced his perversion, he was not ill; if he succeeded in controlling himself, he developed severe symptoms.

The symptoms centered about the intestinal tract, about those erotogenic zones whose component instincts were the driving force of the perversion. When he once was compelled to spend the night in the company of a homosexual and had, with the greatest effort, succeeded in resisting him, he became ill. His abdomen swelled up, he was unable to eat, especially unable to drink milk, he suffered from severe diarrhea, from a feeling of faintness and weakness, as if he were dying, and in a short time he became so emaciated that his life seemed endangered by advanced malnutrition. His physicians were helpless until finally one of them recognized the "nervous" basis of his illness, at which point it became possible to influence the patient with sedatives. Thus, the neurosis broke out when he was compelled to repress not only the objects but also the instinct.

Such an alternation between neurosis and perversion is not rare. I noted a striking periodicity in an obsessional neurotic, in whom extreme asceticism was repeatedly interrupted by unrestrained indulgence of his sexuality with all its perversions.

Let us again consider our patient. The chief symptoms of his neurosis were: he could not eat nor drink; he was disgusted by all food, especially milk. His perversion consisted of the desire to suck male genitals. In his neurosis, he rejected what, in his perversion, he desired. The oral instinct was active in both, although, in the neurosis, it was manifested only as a rejected wish (disgust in place of appetite). Although the object of our patient was a homosexual one, the desire for oral gratification was first directed toward his mother. The oral striving, obviously fixated as a result of the frustration, was displaced first onto the older brother and then onto the father. It occurs also in other cases that some *pregenital* striving which was primarily directed toward one of the parents is displaced onto the other one and is later discharged in certain instinctual attitudes and neurotic symptoms. The apex of the oral developmental stage of the libido is reached before the oedipus complex is established.

In our case there is some evidence that a disturbance of orality occurred

THE PROCESS OF ILLNESS

and was fixated even before the birth of his younger brother, at about his second year, at a time, therefore, when the oedipus complex was not yet established. Since the material concerning this point is not sufficiently clear, I shall refrain from discussing it further. In other cases, however, the part the *preoedipal* strivings play in the illness seems fairly clear: this persisting part of the preoedipal strivings causes changes in the oedipus complex which may perhaps at its onset have appeared to develop normally. The example of a hysteria which follows later will show quite clearly how the fixation to the mother is displaced onto the father and worked out in fantasies and symptoms.

Let us return to our subject. The difference between neurosis and perversion is now clearer. The objects of the oedipus complex are repressed in both. But whereas, in the perversion, the instinctual impulse is conscious and is realized in action, in the neurosis it is turned away from consciousness as well as away from action. The neurosis may therefore be considered the negative of the perversion.

Perversion has as complicated a structure as neurosis. It appears as if, in certain forms of perversion, the male patient tries to recapture the object which he is afraid of losing, or to build up genitalia which he feels he lacks or which he is afraid of losing. For instance, one type of homosexual believes that he will become a man through sexual relations with another man and then will be able to establish an object relationship. A type of fetishist, for instance a foot fetishist, believes that he will strengthen his weak genitals through satisfaction on the fetish. The fetish, among other meanings, has the symbolic meaning of his own genitals; these are projected onto the foot of the woman. He equips the woman symbolically with his genitals and through this symbolic relationship tries to restore the relationship with an object that is constantly escaping from him. The fetishist is ever struggling to maintain object relationships. Moreover, it seems that the pervert is trying to gain the object with sexual strivings fixated on a pregenital level.

It might appear that in neurosis the instinct life is merely inhibited. It is, however, not as simple as that, for the neurotic symptom represents more than a mere inhibition.

SYMPTOM FORMATION

What is a symptom and how is it formed? Although there are some disadvantages in using as examples fragments of psychoanalytic cases, still I must again utilize this expedient. I shall choose an example which shows certain similarities to the case of the homosexual, an example which has in part been published previously.[1]

The case is that of the patient who, after being prevented from having intercourse, developed states of depersonalization and a womb fantasy. He had been approximately normal until his thirtieth year. He had a cardiac lesion, but this was compensated and caused no symptoms. When he had to part from his business partner, who was also his friend, he became ill, but he ascribed all his troubles to his ailing heart. Although some specialists told him that his present ailment had nothing to do with his heart, he did not cease consulting them until one of them advised him to see a psychoanalyst. His suffering was marked by peculiar headaches. They consisted mainly of a pricking, stinging, burning, and itching sensation in the head and the feeling of having a tight band around his cranium. Whenever these sensations became especially acute, he felt a peculiar weakness, which he could not describe by any other words than "sensual pleasure." He was an intelligent man, but uneducated, and hence less capable of using words to disguise his feelings and thoughts than a more articulate man.

It is striking that an individual, who claims to suffer so much and who actually gives the impression of being a very ill person, should feel sensual pleasure in his suffering. Questioned about his sexual life, he gave the typical answer that everything was all right. He ascribed his illness to other causes, namely to business worries. Since the separation from his partner, his business was bad; he maintained that he now had to work too hard, and consequently had injured his already ailing heart. He forgot, however, that he had previously had to work hard and that, despite this, he had remained well. After the separation from his friend, he visited him frequently on the slightest pretext. He felt compelled to see him, without knowing why. The relationship to his wife, which had not been very good, became even worse. He had intercourse with her rarely, imperfectly, unwillingly, and without pleasure.

It soon became evident that his illness was not caused by poor business but by the loss of his friend, to whom he was strongly attached. As the analysis disclosed, he was much more attached to this friend than he could admit to himself. He surrounded him with fantasies, the sexual nature of which was unmistakable, but no intimacies ever occurred between them. He had sublimated this relationship as well as he could; he had acquiesced in all arrangements which his friend made, had taken over all the work, and had become the guiding spirit of the business, which was successful, due to his efficiency. For external reasons, however, the business had to be dissolved. He thought that the loss of his business took from him all further pleasure in working and in life, but actually it was the loss of his friend which was responsible for his unhappiness.

---

[1] See Case 6, in "States of Depersonalization in the Light of the Libido Theory." *Practice and Theory of Psychoanalysis.* New York: International Universities Press, 1955.

He withdrew more and more from other people, worked far less than before, and without success. Instead, he indulged in fantasies of many kinds, the nucleus of which, as has already been mentioned, was the womb fantasy. At first, he was unaware of its contents. He remembered merely that whenever he had suffered failure in life, even in childhood, he used to pull his blanket over his head and then would experience an agreeable sensation of floating and of warmth. The contents of the fantasy, as analysis uncovered, was the mental picture of floating in the mother's womb and of sucking the father's penis. This is a fantasy which is widespread among primitives and is based on the idea that the child is always present in the mother's womb and is nourished by the father during intercourse until it is strong enough to be born. His fantasies were accompanied by masturbation.

How did he arrive at this fantasy? He related the following event as his earliest recollection: He was ill, a physician came, his mother stood beside him, he had to take a black medicine and cried, "Wa-wa" (water). Later he supplemented this recollection by stating that his father had also been present and had held him. It developed later that, in this recollection, at least two experiences were fused. At first, it became apparent that the physician had done something to his genitals. He had fallen while playing and had injured them. He was afraid and would not allow the physician to examine him nor to touch his genitals with a brush. While relating this scene, he became uncertain. Once he claimed that his mother had held him during this minor operation; at another time, his father. For several reasons, however, it is unlikely that the father was present at that time. In his recollection he identified the physician with his father. In all probability this injury occurred in the first half of his third year. Since, from then on, he had constant fear for his genitals, the injury must have stimulated castration fear.

The black medicine which was supposedly forced upon him belonged to another experience. He was nursed by his mother for a very long time and offered violent resistance to weaning. His mother finally smeared her nipples with some foul-tasting liquid. When he took the breast into his mouth, it tasted bitter; he spat, cried, and screamed, "Wa-wa" (water).

The mother's breast and his own genitals are fused in his memory into one disagreeable experience: one can lose both if one is naughty. The loss of his genitals which he feared had been equated with the loss of his mother's breast.

He was an illegitimate child. Only in the latter half of his third year did his father come to live with his mother and establish a home with her. The boy was thus suddenly thrust into the normal and real oedipus constellation. Before that, his father had only visited occasionally. Although the boy was afraid of him in the beginning, he soon made his peace with him, and loved and admired him just as he did his mother. But the father was strict, brutal, moody and egotistic, and very uneven in his behavior toward his son.

At about this time, the first womb fantasies developed in the child. The aim of these fantasies was the father's penis, and the basis for this aim was his feeling of inferiority. He had heard it said that he was too weak and small for his age. Moreover, he had learned very early of his mother's difficulty in making both ends meet. He imagined that he developed so poorly because he did not get enough to eat, and his ambition was to become big and strong. We know, however, that at this period he had already developed an extremely severe castration complex. The root of his feelings of inferiority is probably to be found here. This might explain his idea that he would become a big and strong man through sucking his father's penis. The father's genitals were to him apparently a substitute for his mother's breast, the loss of which he had found so painful.

There is still another connection between his father's genitals and his mother's breast. He sucked at her breast until he was three years old; he remembered distinctly that he sometimes bit her and caused her to bleed while he was sucking, and that he pulled at the breast with his hands; this was one of the reasons, indeed, why she withdrew her breast from him so abruptly. He fantasied also that, while sucking his father's penis, he was biting it off, and derived great pleasure from this idea. His fantasies, thus, also contained a good bit of vengeance.

After he had to give up his sublimated homosexual relationship with his friend, he regressed to his infantile fantasies, in which he could give vent to his love and hatred for his father.

After his condition had improved considerably in the analysis, he began slowly to find his way back to his wife. We recall that once when he was sexually excited and was prevented from having intercourse with her, he developed a state of depersonalization which was followed by a floating fantasy with a homosexual aim. When he noticed this, he felt anxiety, and in the course of that day, his old symptoms returned. The dammed-up libido thus activated an old fantasy, which gave rise to anxiety when it gained access to consciousness and had, therefore, to be repressed immediately as a danger. In place of the genital impulses, sensations appeared in an entirely different part of the body, in the head. These sensations had the character of a symptom.

Why was the patient's symptom now confined to the head? Apart from the symbolic meaning of the head as a penis, our patient had still another individual reason for this displacement. Apparently in connection with his numerous water fantasies related to the womb fantasies, he was in childhood much interested in fish, especially in their heads, eyes, and mouths. He imagined that his penis was such a fish, a living being with a head, eyes, and a spitting mouth. He spoke of his penis only as a "head." It soon became clear that he meant the glans penis. His special interest in his glans was, again, explained by his castration complex. His father had made it a practice to walk around naked in the apartment during the summer months. Thus the son had the opportunity of observing the father's genitals. He noticed with envy that his father not only had larger genitals but also that his glans, the head, was free. Therefore, the boy tried to pull his own foreskin over the glans, in order to get the head free, like his father's. Once, however, he could not return the foreskin to its former position; the foreskin was swollen and formed a band around the glans, causing severe pain. A physician had to be called to put the foreskin back in its place. Now, in his illness, he suffered from a similar painful sensation, a sensation of having a band around his head. After this relation between head and penis had been disclosed, it was easy to interpret the rest of his head symptoms.

The tickling, pricking, itching, and burning, which were connected with "feelings of sensual pleasure" and which he felt in his back, also, as a shivering, corresponded to the sensations which he felt when sexually excited and which he had also been able to produce through masturbatory excitation. In his illness, he did not feel these sensations in the genitals, as in normal excitation, but in his head. Gratification took place through the symptom, no longer in the genitals through their excitation, but in another, suitable part of the body. It is, however, still not quite clear what caused this suitability. The identification of the glans with the head of a fish would probably not have sufficed to establish this symbolic equation. The burning, a particularly painful, dull sensation in his head which could not be more accurately described, was traced back by the patient to other, oft-repeated experiences of his childhood. His father was a teacher and gave his son his first instruction. Among other things, he made him recite the days of the week. The boy always stopped at the word "Wednesday," which he could not remember and for this he was beaten over the head by his father. The more brutally his father mistreated him in this way, the less he was able to remember the name of *this* day. But he thought that he was being beaten by his father, not for the forgetting of this word, but for something else. With the word "Wednesday" (in German, *Mittwoch,* that is, middle of the week), he always pictured the "middle," the navel of his mother, and he was convinced that his father was punishing him for that. (In later life, he clung to the habit of working at words which he did not understand, until he succeeded in giving them a meaning by distorting them.)

A hysterical symptom is, thus, among other things, a *memory symbol* of a *real* affective experience.

A female patient suffered from similar headaches, feeling as if her head were squeezed tight by an instrument. Besides, she felt a throbbing in her head and anxiety connected with it. In her childhood she had slept in a crib next to her parents' bedroom, with the door ajar; hearing suspicious noises, she tried to catch a glimpse of what was going on in the adjoining room. Since she was not yet able to climb out of her crib, she tried to force her head through the railing, but became caught there, and experienced pain and fear. The throbbing in her head corresponds to a sensation of "throbbing" which she feels in her clitoris when sexually excited. A pain had, thus, once actually been present and later on, was yearned for and repeated when she was in a state of ungratified sexual longing similar to her state in childhood.

In our first patient, the pervert, the sexual excitement arose in the genitals. The patient had erections, ejaculations, and orgasms—a clear example of the fact that, first, there is cooperation between the component instincts and the genitals, in the pervert, and secondly, that the sexual discharge takes place in the genitals, even though the stimulation may stem from other erotogenic zones. In our second patient, the conversion hyteric, there was consciously no trace of sexual excitement in the genitals. But he felt, in his head, pain and various disagreeable sensations, linked with "sensual pleasure," exactly the same as he had experienced previously in the genitals when sexually excited.

While, in the perversion, the instinctual impulse is conscious and active, in hysteria it is unconscious, repressed. In conversion hysteria, the sexual energy (libido) is, moreover, withdrawn from the genitals and displaced onto another organ. The·symptom in conversion hysteria arises through *displacement of the genital libido onto a nonsexual organ.* It is a substitute for an excitation which has been prevented from running its full course in the genitals. The symptom contains, furthermore, those fantasies and impulses which must not be gratified through the genitalia. A quasi gratification is achieved, consciously, with exclusion of the genitals; unconsciously, however, the affected part of the body has the significance of the genitals ("genitalization"). The "gratification" is, however, scarcely discernible, as in our case, or not at all, as in most other cases. There is no real sexual discharge. The libido, the sexual energy, remains *dammed up,* despite the attempt to find a way out in the symptom. Therefore, a real gratification cannot take place. It remains incomplete, for the course of the excitation needed for a real gratification is blocked. There is a change in the *dynamics* of the instinct life through the formation of the symptom, it is true, but none whatsoever in its *economy.*

Let us consider once more the development of symptoms in conversion hysteria.

As a young man, the patient married a woman whom he loved at the time. The marriage was unsuccessful, the wife being chiefly to blame. She was quarrelsome and distrustful, with distinctly paranoid tendencies. His home life became distasteful to him; he fled from his home and sought the company of men, without, however, being consciously aware of his homosexual impulses. In social gatherings he sublimated as far as possible—he played music and the like. He became more closely attached to his later business partner, and only through him did he become, now and then, aware of his homosexual impulses in an indirect form, through projection. (He suspected his friend of homosexual-sadistic intentions.) In his conscious life, however, his homosexual impulses were of no importance. He was well able to sublimate them through devoted cooperation in their business. After the separation from his friend, he yearned for him and finally fell ill.

After all that has been said, the statement may not be surprising that it seems to be the fate of human beings to repeat former experiences, that an important situation in life mirrors a previous one, long forgotten, perhaps never quite comprehended consciously. Whether this "repetition" is striven for primarily or is merely secondary, the result of psychic regression, cannot always be definitely determined. Usually, however, both factors probably have to combine to give the impression of inescapable fate.

This patient also seemed to be repeating an important period of his childhood at the onset of his illness. Just as he now turned away from his wife, after his disappointment in her and the loss of her love, and as he now turned to men, so had he turned to his father after the painful loss of his mother, who had died when he was five years old. Just as he met with little love in return, on the part of his father, so did he now court his friend with scant success, not daring to admit his love to his friend or to himself. Just as he now developed anxiety and longing after his separation from his friend, and felt himself compulsively drawn to his friend's neighborhood where he wandered about apparently without purpose, so had the patient developed anxiety after his father's death (he was seven years old at that time), and had wandered about as though looking for him.

The frustration of the heterosexual libido threw him back upon homosexuality, which, however, remained unconscious in the beginning. His ego still possessed the ability to sublimate. It was only after the loss of the homosexual object that the libido could no longer find a way out. The libido became dammed up and cathected the repressed, inactive fantasies. The result was their penetration into the system Cs of the ego. The repression, maintained up to the time of the external frustration, had now become permeable; it failed. The further fate of the id drives was not yet determined in this case—and it is the same in all other neuroses—for several ways were open to them. It is evident that as long as repression is effective, the state of health is more or less balanced. Only when the repression fails is the dormant conflict revived with all its consequences.

Until the complete failure of the repression, the way of the perversion and of the neurosis is a common one. From this point on, their paths separate and lead in different directions, according to instinct and ego disposition. Either the instinct demand is so strong that the ego cannot resist it, or the ego is so weak that it has to yield immediately to the slightest impulses of the id. Both conditions seem to be necessary for the development of a perversion.

If the ego is capable of offering a greater degree of resistance to the id strivings, the inner frustration is added to the external one, and *neurotic conflict* and anxiety develop. The ego seeks to find a solution of this inner conflict. It first employs the old methods; it tries again to withdraw the cathexis from the ideas and affects. This renewed withdrawal of cathexis now causes what we have called *repression proper*. In conversion hysteria, the result of this process of defense is the disappearance of the instinct representatives (ideas) from consciousness and the diplacement of the sexual energy from the genitals to another part of the body. The ego thus solves the neurotic conflict, at first, by excluding it from consciousness. If, however, psychic material disappears from the sphere of consciousness, this does not mean that it has become inactive. It may remain active; its course is merely subject to different laws than before. As soon as the ego succeeds in removing the material involved in the conflict from the system Cs of the ego, and if this material retains its charge of energy in the unconscious id, it comes under the influence of the primary process; it is displaced and condensed. *This displacement leads to the formation of the hysterical symptom.* The conflict is thus solved through symptom formation; it is brought down to a lower level of the psychic apparatus, where it is subject to other laws than those of the system Pcs. Previously it was conscious or preconscious; now it becomes unconscious, charged with a great quantity of unbound psychic energy.

One might be inclined to assume that in hysteria the repression proper (afterexpulsion) has failed, at least in part, since the warded-off instincts, in spite of all defense measures, still have found a way to certain organs, even though they have not gained access to the conscious ego. Acceptance or rejection of this assumption depends upon the point of view from which the neurosis is considered. From the point of view of the conscious ego, the conflict has certainly been solved. The ego knows nothing of all the disagreeable struggles. From the point of view of the id, the conflict seems, likewise, to be solved: the instinct strivings are more or less gratified in the symptom. If, however, the neurosis is considered in relation to the demands of real life, such a solution of the conflict is a complete failure, for the instinct life is restricted, and real gratification is impossible. The symptom also represents a failure from the economic standpoint, for the dammed-up energies are never *completely* discharged in the symptom. In terms of subjective feelings, the afterexpulsion succeeds relatively best in conversion hysteria, since not only has the objectionable idea disappeared from consciousness, but also the affect is displaced or inhibited. Hence, the path of the instinct to motility and action is blocked, and *this is essentially the aim of the defense.* In fact, the process of defense in conversion hysteria is completed with the formation of the symptom. It represents an unconscious compromise against which the conscious ego raises no further objection. The tendencies and strivings contained within it have been removed from the dominion of the perceiving and acting ego.

While the conversion hysteric is free from anxiety, in phobia, anxiety is the most striking symptom. As we know, anxiety arises when there is a conflict between the strivings of the id and those of the ego. If the purpose of repression is defense against instinctual danger, then the continuing anxiety in the phobia means that the danger has neither been warded off by the ego nor otherwise mastered through the formation of the neurotic symptom; the repression thus appears to have failed completely. This, however, is not quite the case. The situation in phobia shows certain similarities to that in perversion. The phobic individual, however, does not suffer from a conscious perversion, but from anxiety, because he is able neither to yield to the perversion nor to repress it completely.

Let us recall the phobic patient. She did not feel anxiety all the time. Anxiety appeared only when she had to play before a large audience. Analysis succeeded in showing her that the danger that lurked behind the anxiety was unconscious exhibitionism. The conscious content of the anxiety betrayed nothing of the inclination to show herself nude. Nevertheless, this anxiety was warranted in so far as it protected the patient against the upward push into consciousness of the instinct. Consciously, she feared not her perverse desires but the audience. When we learn, however, that behind this audience is hidden an older brother, a father substitute, before whom she had in childhood actually exhibited herself and whom she had consciously desired sexually in puberty, we can see that in phobia the original object is repressed, as it is in perversion and conversion hysteria.

The idea of the object, however, has *not* completely disappeared from consciousness as in conversion hysteria, but has been displaced upon *another* object in the external world or onto another situation.

In conversion hysteria, repression has forced the mental representation of the object to disappear from consciousness (amnesia). In phobia, repression has caused this representation to be displaced upon an object of the external world. Symptom formation in phobia is thus, in general, subject to the laws of displacement, just as in conversion hysteria. However, in the latter, the affect too is repressed, so thoroughly that, in some cases of hysteria, the indifference with which the symptom is endured, is striking. In perversion, the mental representation of the object is repressed, but the instinct is not only conscious but also capable of action. In phobia, the object is repressed, while the instinct is merely disguised by insignificant distortions caused by displacement of cathexis. The pervert is a slave to his instinct, while the anxiety hysteric defends himself against it. *The anxiety refers to the substitute idea,* the result of displacement. Thus the pervert represses merely the object, repressing the instinct not at all or only to a slight degree; the conversion hysteric represses both the object and the instinct; the phobic represses the object primarily and the instinct only secondarily. In the phobia, stronger emphasis is placed on keeping the ideational contents away from consciousness; they are rendered thoroughly *unrecognizable* through displacement. The anxiety is then a protective measure against the emergence of the repressed idea. That the substitute idea is related to the original idea, that this association is not a superficial one, is proved by the fact that with its appearance the situation of danger to which the ego—as always—reacts with anxiety, is unconsciously revived.

Anxiety is by no means always pathologic; it is, indeed, the most general reaction to instinct danger. Our patient had once in reality been afraid of her brother, and, at that time, the anxiety may have been justified. But what stamped it as pathologic later on was its apparent lack of motivation when it was connected with the substitute idea, which at first glance seemed meaningless. What is pathologic in anxiety hysteria is the unmotivated appearance of anxiety upon the perception of an otherwise harmless object or situation. The psychic energy in anxiety hysteria is displaced in the same way as in conversion hysteria. In so far as the original idea disappears from consciousness, the repression, in anxiety hysteria, has succeeded.

But when the substitute idea enters consciousness and is perceived, then anxiety sets in. The condition for the attack of anxiety is, thus, the perception of the substitute for the object which originally evoked anxiety. Whereas, however, in conversion hysteria, the neurotic productivity is concluded with the formation of the substitute in the form of the symptom, in phobia, it really begins with this. The anxiety affect is, indeed, the reaction which is constantly repeated in relation to the substitute, as if it were the original object. The anxiety in anxiety hysteria spreads to ever larger areas, substitute ideas of the substitute ideas are formed, as the chain of associations grows ever longer. Anxiety hysteria (phobia) stands between perversion, conversion hysteria, and obsessional neurosis. It is genital like conversion hysteria, but it has a sadistic coloring like obsessional neurosis. In the phobia, the symptom consists of the substitute idea and the anxiety. In respect to the substitute idea, it is similar to conversion hysteria; but in respect to the anxiety affect, behind which the only slightly or not-at-all distorted instinct lurks, it is closer to perversion.

The conversion hysteric, by and large, succeeds in withdrawing his instinct life from the influences of reality; the phobic does not. The ego of the conversion hysteric has nothing to fear from the inner or from the outer world; it has peace (with the exception of those cases where external perception may cause pain, analogous to anxiety; we know indeed, that the reaction to a danger may be pain or fear). The ego of the phobic, on the contrary, is disturbed by the outer world, which is actually a projection of his inner world. The neurotic conflict in conversion hysteria is split off from the ego. But, in the phobia, the conflict is closer to the ego and to consciousness, and is enacted between the ego and the external world. The conflict between the ego and the original idea, it is true, does not become conscious, but that between the ego and the substitute idea does. The ego, in anxiety hysteria, clings to the reality of the objects, only these are no longer the original objects, but their derivatives, upon which the patient projects his own impulses. The part of the ego which fears these objects is the one with which the ego reacts in the illness, that part which had its origin at a time when the boundaries between the ego and the external world were not yet distinct, when they could be mistaken, one for the other. The pathologically reacting part of the ego is split off from the rest of the ego. In conversion hysteria, one's own body, so to speak, forms the external world. Here the psychic processes (thoughts, ideas, emotions, feelings) are expressed by the body. Even though, in hysteria (conversion and phobia), the objects of the outer world are not always sharply distinguished from each other and from the subject's own body, the relations to the outside world are nevertheless not given up.

In obsessional neurosis, the situation at the outset is in many cases the same as in phobia, as is illustrated by the following example:

A young girl, a patient whom we have discussed before, and her fiancé were embracing on a garden bench. When some youths passed by, she became afraid that they might disclose to her fiancé that she was no longer a virgin. From then on she avoided this bench, and so far as possible, also this neighborhood, where she had lived throughout her childhood. If she had to go there, she became uneasy and anxious. From her fear that her sexual past might be suspected, there later developed, in a complicated manner, the obsessional idea that she was going to seduce children, in particular, her little daughter. In order not to be forced to give in to this impulse, she took special precautions and care in her dealings with children, especially with her daughter. Finally, she was unable to approach her child without being tormented by her obsessional idea. She no longer dared to touch the child, and left the care of the child entirely to her mother.

She was convinced that she would injure her child if she yielded to her impulse. Actually, her unconscious desire to injure was directed at her husband, with whom she found much fault. The injury she might do to the child would be a revenge on her husband. There were good reasons for the choice of the child as the means for her vengeance. This is the same patient whose brother, who had committed suicide, had been spoken of as a seducer of children. The youths, who had aroused her anxiety in the situation described above, were former playmates of hers. As a child she had been wild and tomboyish. She imitated her older brother in every respect, was aggressive, and actually seduced the other children to sexual play. She was discovered in this play by her mother and punished. The mother also frequently threatened that her father would punish her. The child waited for this punishment, but in vain. If her father occasionally inflicted pain on her (he was a physician), she endured the pain with pleasure.

She was idolized by her father and brothers, who extolled her beauty. At twelve years of age and even later, she still went about the house nude, in order to enjoy their admiration. She knew very well that this was no longer proper, but she deliberately pretended to be childish and ignorant.

This child, so exuberant and aggressive, so little inhibited in her instinct life, very early developed severe feelings of guilt, brooded a great deal, periodically felt very unhappy, and passed sleepless nights in self-reproach and prayer. After puberty, she changed completely. She became puritanical and did not want to be reminded of her childhood pranks and sins.

Now, when first faced with the real demands of sexual life, she did not feel equal to them. Her sexual life was under the strong pressure of her feeling of guilt. When, by chance, the young men passed by who reminded her of her childhood pranks, she was seized by the same fear that she had previously felt of her mother, her father, and her older brother. After her identification with her younger brother, the pressure of the feeling of guilt had become even greater. She tried to free herself from this state of torment; she fell in love, probably partly for this reason, but felt herself rebuffed because of the peculiar behavior of her fiancé, especially because of his indecisiveness (she, herself, was most indecisive). In her ambivalence, she turned more and more away from him. Her old wishes and fantasies were revived; they consisted of sexual aggressions directed against the playmates of her childhood. Anxiety protected her from the realization of her desires, as did her eventual marriage, to which she agreed, in spite of her inner objections. She was well able to suppress her hatred of her husband. The aggressive-sexual wishes directed against him were displaced onto the child and thus partly discharged. The child now acquired a double meaning for her: first, she represented one of the many children in her own childhood on whom she could gratify her sexual aggressions; secondly, the child symbolically represented the penis, chiefly that of her husband (regressively, that of her brother). In order to avoid the impulse to injure her child (the penis), she became extremely careful in her relations with children. This was especially true with her own little daughter, so that finally she avoided touching the child at all; thus contact with the child was eliminated and the danger removed. In a sense, she practiced magic. In this, she also obeyed a prohibition (taboo against touching) which had played an especially important role in her childhood. It was the prohibition, so often transgressed, against touching children's genitals, behind which the prohibition against masturbation was hidden. Masturbation itself had a magical meaning for the patient. The compulsive thought, "I must not touch my child," meant, in the deepest unconscious level: "If I masturbate, my mother dies." (The patient had a deeply rooted hatred of her mother.)

While, in hysteria, gratification is more or less achieved, even though unconsciously, in the obsessional neurosis, the tendency to prevent any gratification at first prevails. The reason for this probably lies in the fact that the instinctual needs in the two illnesses are different. In hysteria, there are in the foreground genital impulses which the ego has less cause to reject than the pregenital impulses of the obsessional neurosis. In the latter, it is true, the genital impulses are warded off even more vigorously than in hysteria, but the libido of the obsessional neurotic, in addition, makes a regression to the pregenital, anal-sadistic stage. At first, slight anal-sadistic impulses merely accompany each genital impulse of the obsessional neurotic, but later on, as the illness progresses, they become predominant. The defense then is directed chiefly agains these impulses. The hysteric, it is true, avoids castration anxiety, as does the obsessional neurotic, but in the hysterical symptom, the genital strivings return.

The obsessional neurotic is, as we have said, more successful in his flight from genital impulses, but anal-sadistic ones return instead. These are not admitted, but the energy withdrawn from them appears in the reaction formations of the character changes. The denial of every instinct gratification explains the tendency to asceticism of the obsessional neurotic. With the progress of the illness, the defense can no longer be completely successful. The striving for gratification finally wins out over all of the opposing tendencies. A case which I have already mentioned illustrates this point. This patient was under the compulsion to clean and rub his penis so thoroughly after every urination that he had an erection.

Symptom formation in obsessional neurosis thus follows the laws of displacement, as in hysteria and phobia. But whereas, in conversion hysteria, the instinct energy is displaced upon another, nonsexual organ, and in phobia it is shifted from the object to its substitute, in obsessional neurosis, something further occurs: reaction formations, with which we are already familiar, appear. They consist of exaggerated caution, anxious avoidance of certain persons or situations, renunciations, self-torments, and expiations of a compulsive nature. In phobia, the substitute idea is warded off through anxiety, in obsessional neurosis, through character changes in the form of these reaction formations. The ego becomes extremely intolerant toward instinct demands. In advanced cases, the compulsion consists of defensive actions exclusively, so that the symptom formation coincides with the reaction formation. The substitute idea is warded off through the reaction formation, and what remains of the affect is the very painful, frequently unconscious, feeling of guilt.

The washing obsession may serve as an example of such reaction and symptom formations. It is a tormenting urge to cleanliness which generally appears as a reaction of the ego to sexual uncleanliness (masturbation) and to anal impulses and desires, and yet, at the same time, means symbolically the same "uncleanliness." The instinct cannot be completely repressed, even in the obsessional neurosis. It always finds a way out, under the mask of a compulsion. Even in obsessional neurosis, partial gratification often takes place in the form of conversion-hysterical symptoms. The obsessional neurosis is hardly ever pure. It frequently begins with hysteria, and also during its further course hysterical symptoms appear. Hysteria often begins in childhood and is succeeded later, usually in puberty, by obsessional neurosis.

In a patient previously mentioned, the obsessional neurosis was preceded by enuresis of many years' standing. He was a pious Jew. His illness started after his confirmation, which the Jews observe on the thirteenth birthday. This celebration, in disguised form, bears the traits of the puberty rites of primitives, as described by Reik. The boy was accepted in the "community of men" and now himself became a man, which filled him with great joy. Eight days later was the Jewish Day of Atonement, on which he had to confess his sins in order to reconcile himself with God. On this day his illness began with doubts about God, to which he reacted so violently with feelings of guilt and acts of atonement that he was not able to lead a normal life for years.

Until puberty he suffered from enuresis. With the beginning of puberty, when he again started to masturbate, the enuresis became less frequent. After some of his obsessional symptoms had become weaker or even disappeared in his analysis, the bed wetting reappeared every night.

I cannot go into the detailed analysis of this symptom, but I should like to give enough of the material disclosed to demonstrate how a hysterical symptom may be worked into an obsessional neurosis. The stratification and meaning of this symptom are manifold. First, the enuresis was a substitute for infantile masturbation with incestuous wishes. Further, it was a reaction to the castration complex and a protest against the castration threat. It was to prove and confirm to him the size and power of his penis. Besides this, the urinary stream had a magical meaning for him. With it, he could reach anyone he wanted to reach, could touch a person, fertilize the soil, produce demons, and so on. In urinating, thus, his aggression also found expression ("omnipotence and magic"). By these means he could also, at the same time, soil himself and others. He felt a malicious pleasure when his mother or sister had to dry his bed in the morning. To soil with urine was to him the same as to soil with feces. His greatest concern was to produce plenty of feces, an interest which was retained as one of his foremost symptoms in his subsequent obsessional neurosis. In order to achieve this, one had to eat a great deal, and accordingly, in his eating habits, he alternated between periods of gluttony and abstemiousness. To produce large quantities of feces meant to him just as great an achievement as to produce a large urinary stream or just to urinate.

With his ambivalent attitude toward his father, at one time he would sanctify him, at another time he would see in him the personification of all human vices. In his rivalry with him, he kept surveillance over his father's excretory functions. When the father went to the toilet, he wanted to know how much he had urinated and defecated. If the father went to the bathroom frequently, the patient thought he was pretending, for he considered him incapable of defecating and urinating, since he was capable of nothing. He thought himself, on the contrary, particularly capable of carrying out these functions. On the other hand, he felt that if his father did not defecate, urinate, or eat, it was an evidence of holiness and sublimity, for then he would be like God, who had no human needs. And so his ambivalence went on: the vegetative functions were at one time in the service of the ascetic and aggressive tendencies; at another, in the service of the libidinal ones. In any case, these ideas revolved about the castration complex and the potency of his father. Incidentally, from this example one can see that the gods are the victims of the attribute of "holiness" which mankind forces upon them with aggressive intent.

It is of particular interest to note in this case how a symptom of hysterical nature can be replaced by a symptom of obsessional nature.

Until puberty, the patient suffered from enuresis. The penis was the executive organ of genital strivings, even though the excitation proceeded from the urethral mucous membrane. After the obsessional neurosis had broken through, the enuresis stopped, and its place was taken by anal and sadistic impulses, cloaked in fantasies. Before puberty, as a matter of fact, anal and sadistic impulses likewise furnished the driving force for the enuresis, but then they used the genitals as the executive organ. All of the repressed impulses were concentrated in the genitals. The morbid symptom, the enuresis, was, therefore, of genital-hysterical character. After puberty, the genital organization was to a great extent abandoned, and the anal-sadistic impulses came to light in an undiluted form, probably because the passage through the genitals was not possible. They caused the ego to produce obsessional reaction (symptom) formations such as *folie de doute,* obsessional thinking, washing compulsion. But when the enuresis now and then reappeared, the compulsive neurotic suffering was lessened.

The point of origin of the symptom formation in both types of illness (hysteria and obsessional neurosis) is defense against the instinct demands of the oedipus complex. Common tó both is the rejection of the libidinal demands. The difference is that in the obsessional neurosis there is added the defense against the pregenital anal-sadistic strivings, as a result of regression. It seems here that the libidinal strivings concentrated in the genitals meet with less opposition on the part of the ego than those pertaining to the pregenital stages, even if they succeed through a maximum of distortion in obtaining a minimum of gratification (obviously because of the increased sadism). A less tolerant superego corresponds to the less organized libido of the obsessional neurotic, a superego which does not even tolerate the substitute ideas which take the place of the anal-sadistic ideas.

It is for this reason that the compulsive neurotic always has to defend anew, and his symptomatology increases, while that of the hysteric remains more or less constant. Whereas, in hysteria, that which is to be warded off no longer has any influence on the ego, in obsessional neurosis, it is able to enter into union with the ego and to influence it. What has been warded off returns as an instrument for warding off, in the form of a compulsive action or a compulsive thought—thus in a symptom, as for instance in the washing compulsion, which simultaneously has the symbolic meaning of defense and of gratification. Considered from this angle, a gratification occurs in the compulsion neurosis, also, perhaps to an even greater degree than in hysteria. Only it takes place in the former with the participation of the perceptual ego; in the latter, without such participation. This may be a reason for the fact that the compulsive neurotic feels more responsible for his instinct impulses than the hysteric. Besides, conversion hysteria takes its course in the sphere of the body ego; obsessional neurosis, in that of the psychic ego.

The partial gratificaton of the instinct needs in the symptom yields the *primary gain from illness.* Yet, every neurotic suffers from his illness; the hysteric less, the obsessional neurotic more. The tension caused by the damming up of the instinctual energy—thus an economic factor—cannot alone be held responsible for this suffering. The obsessional neurotic does not suffer only from frustration; there is evident in his symptomatology also a trait of self-torment. This contains the aggressive and destructive impulses which in the id are aimed at the object. The sadism directed against the object is turned against the subject, diverted onto the ego. The autosadism of the obsessional neurotic takes the form of self-reproaches, sacrifices, acts of expiation and castigation, and hence serves to gratify the need for punishment. Usually the obsessional neurotic permits a gratification of libidinal strivings only if he can, by the same token, punish himself. He has to pay for the pleasure with self-torment.

The gratification of the need for punishment is not characteristic of the obsessional neurosis exclusively. The need for punishment takes its toll in every neurosis. This means that every neurotic (as well as every other person) has a superego and a feeling of guilt which is the driving force for the defense against those instinctual impulses which are not ego-syntonic. This, however, does not mean that the need for punishment has to be satisfied in every neurotic symptom under all circumstances. In some cases of hysteria, for instance, it may be missing; most hysterics develop their symptoms not out of the need for punishment, but out of the fear of punishment. The need for punishment, if it does appear, manifests itself in various forms—at one time as passivity, whose aim is masochistic gratification, at another time as opposition and protest, in order to provoke punishment, and so on.

To the question as to why in some forms of illness the hunger for punishment is stronger than in others, there are two answers. Either the indviduals concerned are of a more masochistic disposition, or their superego is stricter and more demanding. In the obsessional neurosis, sadism, which is stronger from the very beginning, coincides with a more demanding superego. The superego becomes more cruel and aggressive with the mastering of the sadistic impulses by the ego, probably in consequence of the fixation on the anal-sadistic stage and the later regression of the libido. Thus a vicious circle is formed, in which cruelty against the subject increases as the superego becomes more demanding and cruel, and the superego, in turn, becomes the more demanding and the more cruel, the more energetically the ego has to ward off sadistic impulses.

In hysteria, hate, too, may be hidden under the disguise of the symptom. One of the most frequent reactions to disappointments in love, especially in childhood, is not indifference, but hatred. Many love relations which actually have ceased to exist are clung to because of hatred. There are, for instance, depressed hysterics who cling to their partners with exaggerated love only because they have not yet been able to take revenge. Superficially, they have the appearance of melancholics.

By now it has become evident that in all illnesses, including the perversions, the ego introduces and maintains the processes of defense not only in consequence of the painful need tension, but also under the influence of the superego. The superego, however, does not play the same role in every neurosis. The quality and intensity of its influence on the processes of defense depend upon its character. If it is excessively severe, even sadistic, then the defense takes place not only out of moral anxiety, but also for the purpose of gratifying the destructive instincts whose psychic equivalent is the need for punishment. The hunger for punishment shows its power particularly in obsessional neurosis, and even more clearly in melancholia. If the superego is more lenient, more loving, then the feeling of guilt generates fear of the loss of love of the person represented in the ego ideal. There are hysterical women who hold themselves aloof from all men out of unconscious fear of the loss of the father's love.

Two factors are at work in symptom formation: a dynamic and an economic one. The former develops through the interference of the superego; the latter, through the damming up of libido, which causes unpleasurable need tensions. Symptom formation is always initiated by repression; the libido is withdrawn from the instinct representatives. Processes similar to repression are already known to us from the normal development of the personality, as, for instance, in the formation of the superego, in reaction formations which contribute to the building up of the character, and in sublimations. In all of these processes, the libido is withdrawn from the strivings of the id and is stored up in the ego. In the ego it is desexualized and appears as indifferent psychic energy. It is now used by the ego in its tasks of mastering the outer world and the id. Another part of the libido is, in the healthy person, gratified directly on the object. With the process of repression, that is, with the withdrawal of the libido from the instinct representatives, libido is dammed up. What happens now to this libido? One part is gratified directly in the symptoms, while another part is used in a different way.

In the phobia, it forms countercathexes (as has already been described in the chapter on the processes of defense), for it cathects the substitute ideas which emerge after the repression. This cathexis no longer comes from the id, but from the ego. It is no longer of sexual nature, nor does it serve to gratify the strivings of the id, but to protect the ego against the emergence of what has been repressed. This psychic energy is shifted onto perceptions stemming from the environment, in order to protect the ego against the emergence of the dangerous instinct representatives. This is also true of obsessional neurosis, with the difference that there the ego is protected not through cathexis of the environment but through its reaction formations. The tormenting, sadistic nature of the reaction formations of the obsessional neurosis may serve as an example of the defusion of instincts and desexualization of libido which accompany countercathexis.

The countercathexis in conversion hysteria is less clear. Here the entire libido appears to cathect nonsexual organs of the body ego, causing changes in the motor and sensory innervations. The entire libido is thus bound in the symptom and acts as a countercathexis. But it is not likely that defusion of instincts and desexualization of the libido take place in hysteria.

We see, thus, that here also the symptoms are formed through displacement of the psychic energy. The instincts are mastered not only through the reduction of the force of their impetus, as a result of libido withdrawal, but also through the ego's utilization of the energy withdrawn from these instincts and its employment for reinforcing the defense against what has to be warded off.

From our considerations we may conclude that countercathexis contributes considerably to symptom formation; that is, certain quantities of energy are displaced from the id onto the ego. In conversion hysteria, the body ego is countercathected; in compulsion neurosis, the psychic ego. The ingenuity of the psychic apparatus and the economy of its manner of working manifests itself in this: the same energy which otherwise is capable of overpowering the ego places itself in the service of the ego when it has succeeded in passing through the filter of the ego. Paradoxical as it may seem, what has to be warded off becomes, to some extent, the warding-off force, under the condition, of course, that it has moved from one psychic system to the other.

It seems that symptom formation is not always concluded with the countercathexis. If, for instance, the reaction formation of the compulsive neurotic no longer suffices to prevent the return of the repressed impulse, then the other auxiliary techniques appear, such as undoing and isolating, which take on the character of a ceremonial.

The symptom formation, the entire way in which the neurotic conflict is solved, depends on the organization of the ego. The neurotic conflict arises, indeed, when there is a threat to the functioning of the pleasure-unpleasure principle; the conflict can be solved by the ego only when it succeds in setting defensive forces in motion. The form of the neurosis, hence, depends on the *technique* which is used in solving the conflict, as has been stated previously in a more general way.

Thus we see that in the development of the neurosis both kinds of instincts are at work, the libidinal ones (life instincts) and the destructive ones (death instincts). In certain types of conversion hysteria, as for instance in globus hystericus, the libido is gratified in the symptom, while the aggression which accompanies every sexual instinct in the form of more or less evident sadism, is transformed into the feeling of guilt and is gratified in its manifestations.

In those conversion hysterias, on the other hand, where strong masochistic tendencies are present, libido and aggression are gratified simultaneously in the symptom, and there is no feeling of guilt. This is especially marked in those cases where no actual symptom neurosis develops and the entire instinct life is gratified in masochistic behavior.

In obsessional neurosis, the partial gratification of the libido and that of the aggressive instinct alternate as though in a compromise. In phobia, the libido is scarcely gratified, but the feeling of guilt is gratified in the form of the need for punishment, as for instance through the restriction of personal freedom.

Reaction formations, undoing, isolating, and so on, all pursue the same goal—the defense against libidinal strivings. In melancholia, there is no gratification of libido, but only of aggression. In schizophrenia, the gratification of one or the other group of instincts occurs according to the stage of development of the illness. In paranoia, in particular, the gratification of aggression against one's self is actually achieved with the aid of projection; by means of this defense, instinctual excitations can be kept at a distance from the ego.

In the normal person, the instinctual needs are gratified, so far as the real circumstances permit; otherwise they are held in check, and their gratification is postponed. Perverts, however, as well as some psychotics, do not succeed in maintaining adequate self-control. Their ego disregards all ethical, aesthetic, and social considerations in order to procure gratification for the instinct. The average healthy person is able to initiate actions serving instinct gratification and also to bring about real changes in the external world for this purpose, without coming into conflict with himself or with the environment. The neurotic stands between the healthy and the perverted or psychotic individual; he is unable to endure, for long, strong need tensions, but he is also unable to gratify these needs in reality. On the one hand, he must inhibit his instincts; on the other, he strives for their gratification. In many neurotic symptoms both goals are attained more or less satisfactorily in a single act. In order to procure gratification the normal person changes the outside world; the hysteric changes himself. Indeed, he does not strive for any real change; on the contrary, he blocks off his instinct life from the outer world and gratifies it autoplastically, acting it out on his own body, much as, in the dream, thirst may be stilled for a time through the hallucination of drinking. A woman with globus hystericus actually feels a foreign body in her throat, a feeling which results from unconscious contractions of the musculature. Another, whose wish for a child cannot be fulfilled, develops a large abdomen and deceives herself into the belief that she is pregnant. The hysteric, according to Ferenczi, *materializes* his wishes, fulfills them through his own body.

Are autoplastic measures characteristic only of conversion hysteria, or do they also occur in the other neuroses?

It is evident that, in phobia, the wish is not fulfilled through the subject's body. The patient develops anxiety and flees from the dangerous idea. The ever-increasing restriction of the freedom of movement is the result of flight from the ever-renewed danger. A normal person, threatened by some danger, may perhaps also develop anxiety and flee if he does not feel equal to the danger. But if the danger continues to become greater and to threaten his very existence, then he will finally take measures to avoid the danger. The phobic, however, changes himself instead of bringing about changes in the outer world. He flees, benumbed, as it were, by his anxiety. Besides, any attempt to bring about changes in the outside world would be pointless, since the source of danger lies within. It seems, moreover, that the phobic senses, though unconsciously, that his anxiety is a psychic one which cannot be influenced by changes in reality. In this respect, too, the phobic differs from the psychotic who believes in the objective existence of his "phobia" and, consequently, undertakes actions in the outside world designed to remove the dangers which appear to him to be real.

The obsessional neurotic, too, employs autoplastic measures in the solution of the neurotic conflict. The impulses of the id striving toward objects of the external world turn against the subject's own person, and instead of using the released psychic energy to change the external world, the obsessional neurotic changes his own character. Just as the phobic believes that he can flee from the demands of the id with the help of the motor apparatus, so the obsessional neurotic believes that he can attain the same end by means of his precautionary measures, his magic formulas, and his ceremonial. Both, in a certain sense, mistake the inside world for the outside world, for they think they can transform the outside world through changes in the ego. The patient who suffered from agoraphobia believed that she could escape her drive toward prostitution by avoiding the street. An obsessional neurotic believes he can prevent a disaster by repeating certain prayers.

Whereas the anxiety of the phobic may sometimes appear to have a rational basis, the various forms and ceremonials of the obsessional neurotic give the impression of incomprehensible magic. By omnipotence and magic is meant that the individual believes that he possesses irresistible power with the aid of which he is able to fulfill all his wishes and to change his environment. Actually, he is only changing himself. To the obsessional neurotic, a certain thought, an action, a verbal or motor magical formula has the power to fulfill every wish, to prevent every disagreeable event. In conversion hysteria, the wishes are for the most part fulfilled in the symptoms; in obsessional neurosis, in the early stages of the illness, they are for the most part rejected; thus the hysteric practices predominantly positive magic, the obsessional neurotic, predominantly negative magic. In conversion hysteria, the libido withdrawn from the repressed ideas changes into bodily innervations, with the aid of the magical abilities of the ego.

This does not yet make it quite clear how this "leap from the psychic into the physical" takes place. The remarkable affinity of the psychic to the physical in hysteria may perhaps be clarified by the following consideration. Every psychic process originates in the unconscious id and has the progressive tendency to reach the motor and sensory part of the ego and to discharge itself there. To this end it must traverse all of the psychic systems, including the preconscious.

An instinct representative (idea) can become conscious only when the unconscious idea succeeds in forming a union with the preconscious verbal idea and in procuring access to the system Pcpt-Cs by a special process, that of hypercathexis. In repression, however, the cathexis is withdrawn from the system Pcs, rendering it impassable to the currents flowing from the unconscious; a perception or action does not take place. In conversion hysteria, however, muscular contractions and spasms occur, sensations are perceived, even hallucinations appear, but all of these excitations in the motor and sensory part of the psychic apparatus possess no "quality of being conscious." Evidently a "short circuit" takes place between the systems Ucs and Cs (whereby the Pcs is avoided). With the withdrawal of cathexis from the system Pcs, that is, with repression, it seems that this system becomes insensitive to excitation, as if it did not exist. Repression establishes a state similar to that of childhood, where there is no sharp separation between conscious and unconscious. Since the nucleus of the unconscious is formed by the instincts in their entirety, ego and id would now be closer to each other.

As we know, a psychic process first becomes conscious when an unconscious idea unites with a preconscious one and is hypercathected. In repression, this whole mechanism is put out of order because of the withdrawal of cathexis in the system Pcs. In conversion hysteria, however, the instinctual impulses of the id succeed, with the aid of the ego, in obtaining expression and discharge. With a hysterical disposition the ego is thus better able than otherwise to express somatically the processes taking place in the id without participation of actual consciousness; in other words, the body ego predominates in hysteria. Since psychic conflicts are so frequently reacted to with disturbances of the genital apparatus, and since the hysterical symptoms represent displaced genital strivings, there may perhaps exist a closer relation between the genital libido and the character of hysterical symptoms, on the one hand, and the withdrawal of the libido in the system Pcs, that is, repression, on the other. The hysteric expresses his actual needs in bodily changes which may have been adequate in childhood, corresponding to the development of the infantile ego.

It is now evident that, in symptom formation, not only the libido but also the ego regresses to a lower stage of development. It is not difficult to understand why. In the rejection of instinct needs, the ego has not always identified itself with its rejecting, unconscious part. There once were phases in the development of the ego in which the ego reacted to instinct demands and to reality in a different way from the present actual ego. If at one time the libido was withdrawn from a preconscious instinct representative, it was forced to turn about, to regress, and to take up another position. The ego would then make identifications, projections, would practice magic, and so on. When the libido makes a regression following the repression, this infantile ego is revived and reacts in the old way to the present instinct demands. This explains why the hysterical symptoms, the obsessional ceremonial, and the like, are so strange and unintelligible to the actual ego. This ego regression is a different one in every form of illness; in every neurosis the ego is *split*.

A female patient, one who has been mentioned several times in other connections, suffered from trembling, a feeling of cold, and shivering. This symptom remained unclear and did not abate until its infantile determination had been discovered. As far back as she could remember there had always been a tender relationship between her and her father. In her early childhood, her father used to come to her crib and fondle her, to hold her in his arms until she would fall asleep feeling comfortably warm. If her father, however, once in a while omitted his usual visit, she became cold, shivered, and did not fall asleep until he came to her. Whether her shivering had been real or feigned, as children often simulate when they want to obtain something, could not be established beyond doubt, in her analysis. All the evidence, however, supported the assumption that the shivering had been arranged "unconsciously" at that time, in order to bring her father to her, if one can discriminate at all, at that age, between "'conscious" and "unconscious." This luring of her father into her room ended abruptly in her fourth year, as has been related previously at another point. It was not he who entered, this time, but her twelve-year-old cousin, who seduced her sexually. After that she never called her father, nor did she shiver or tremble. Only when she became ill, at the age of twenty, did the shivering and the trembling reappear.

The situation is similar in obsessional neurosis, but still there are some differences. The relation between body and psyche is looser. The symptoms have a more "psychic" character, the desires are not expressed by unconscious innervations of the body, but rather in voluntary, coordinated, usually very complicated actions, whose more or less conscious motive is caution or the wish to undo something. Between the driving forces of the id and the executive organ, the ego, a thought, a word, an idea is interpolated. There are even obsessional neuroses in which no compulsive action whatsoever takes place, and the entire process takes its course exclusively in "thoughts"; obsessional doubting is typical of this. The hysteric, on the other hand, has no "thoughts," since in the repression he has lost the verbal ideas, while in obsessional neurosis the verbal ideas have often been retained in consciousness. Most frequently they are merely "thoughts" which seem remote to the patient and yet are charged with affect.

Thoughts and words in dreams have their origin in waking life, in reality. They are preconscious. In dreams, they are subject to the primary process and are treated as if they were things. The preconscious represents a bridge connecting the unconscious and the conscious as well as the conscious and reality. The preconscious ideas are more resistant in obsessional neurosis than in hysteria. The defensive struggle with the aid of the substitute techniques (isolating, undoing) in compulsive neurosis is not directed against the ideas of the unconscious object, as it is in hysteria with the aid of repression; instead, it is directed against the substitute ideas, that is, the preconscious ideas and preconscious thinking. Accordingly, the hysteric substitutes unconscious actions for thinking. In other words, his wishes and strivings are materialized in unconscious actions, in magical bodily changes, without intervention of the preconscious.

In obsessional neurosis, on the other hand, the repressed instincts of the id, pushing upward toward consciousness and encountering the preconscious ego with its preconscious thinking (ideas), cathect it with libido; this preconscious thinking then takes on qualities of the unconscious id, is subject to the primary process and endowed with "magical" qualities; thus worked over, the unconscious material of the id enters consciousness. Hence, where the hysteric "acts" and "feels," the obsessional neurotic "thinks." This, however, sounds too vague. We must inquire whether there are not other states known to us in which word and thought are "materialized" (treated as matter).

The relationship of the hysteric to objects is, generally, a positive one. Even though the hysteric represses his libidinal impulses, nevertheless the objects remain in his unconscious as concrete ideas. When a hysterical woman expresses her desire for a child through physical symptoms, in a fantasied pregnancy, that does not mean that she wishes to be impregnated in a parthenogenetic way, as some schizophrenics fantasy, but by a certain beloved man, usually by her father. In the schizophrenic defense against instincts, on the other hand, the entire libido is usually withdrawn from objects, and consequently the unconscious concrete ideas of objects are likewise lost. This process gives rise to a feeling of the "end of the world" and is accompanied by excessive anxiety.

In order to rebuild the lost world, the schizophrenic cathects preconscious verbal ideas and thinking with energy. Words replace objects for him; they are objects to him and are treated accordingly: they are subject to the primary process, are condensed and displaced. (If words enter into union with bodily sensations and ideas, the speech of the schizophrenic is colored by a hypochondriacal tinge, and becomes the so-called "organ speech.") Words, for instance, are put together in a magical and symbolic way; words and sentences which belong together are separated, in order to prevent them from doing evil through contact, by means of negative magic. The compulsive neurotic behaves similarly; he sometimes disrupts sentences by omitting a single word which connects the first part of the sentence with the last. Individual ideas are isolated, whereby the meaning of the entire sentence is lost; it becomes unconscious.

One might object immediately that the speech of the obsessional neurotic is far less disorganized than the speech of the schizophrenic and that, for him, the world has not been destroyed through the loss of libido. The language of the compulsive neurotic is, of course, not as unintelligible as the schizophrenic's, but still his words and his thinking have similar magical character. Furthermore, the object relationships of the schizophrenic are threatened. Instinct defusion occurs with the regression of the libido in the obsessional neurosis, as in schizophrenia. The destructive instincts are freed, those instincts which oppose Eros and threaten the existence of the object. But, as analyses show, the compulsive neurotic clings to the object. It is only repressed, as in hysteria, at the onset of the illness, because of the preconscious withdrawal of libido. While, in hysteria, the idea of the object remains repressed, in the obsessional neurosis it emerges again, frequently as a substitute idea, apparently because it is again invested with preconscious libido. The schizophrenic likewise counteracts the destructive instincts by recathecting the preconscious verbal ideas. Since, however, these stand in no material relation to the concrete ideas, in contrast to what occurs in the compulsion neurosis, the world of the schizophrenic is fictitious. The obsessional neurotic opposes the destructive instincts in a similar way, but he cathects not merely preconscious verbal ideas but derivatives of the real, the unconscious objects. These substitute ideas are often influenced in a magical way, as in schizophrenia, with the difference, however, that in obsessional neurosis they represent real things, whereas in schizophrenia they are merely shadows of objects. An instructive example may be useful here.

The illness of the previously mentioned religious obsessional neurotic began with doubts about the existence of God. The patient was thrown into despair by his heretical thoughts. He constantly wept, castigated himself, and imposed all sorts of penances upon himself. Until his illness, he had been indifferent to his father, had not concerned himself much with him, and more or less rejected him. After the outbreak of his illness, he developed a boundless love for his father; he could not be without him for a moment, and had to accompany him everywhere. He dogged his father's footsteps, became exceedingly jealous of him, and would permit no one but his father to take care of him. We recognized in his doubt about God the unconscious hatred of his father; as further analysis disclosed, this doubt signified the unconscious destruction of his father. The suddenly awakened, excessively demanding love for the father stands in contradiction to this, for through this love Eros seems to work against the death instincts, against the loss of the object. It is true that this love grew out of ambivalence as an overcompensation for the feeling of guilt, but nevertheless its meaning is the protection of the object from destruction. Of course, even in this love the destructive drive was finally victorious, since in the end it became a torment to his father.

One may, hence, assume that in the compulsion neurosis the return of what has been repressed works against the fear of the loss of the object, similarly to the way in which the construction of a new fictitious world in schizophrenia strives to compensate for the actual loss of objects. The schizophrenic fights for the *lost object;* the compulsive neurotic against its *threatened loss;* the hysteric does not fight for the object at all, because he has not lost it, but has retained it in the unconscious. It seems that in some types of illness, as in compulsion neurosis, the failure of the repression, the re-emergence of what has been repressed, is not due simply to the intensity of the cathexis of what is repressed or to the weakness of the repressing ego, but rather the failure of the repression is furthered by the active participation of the ego in this process. The ego seeks to protect itself against the final loss of the real object by raising the instinct representatives out of the unconscious.

The compulsive neurotic, thus, in order to protect himself from instinct demands, likewise with his symptoms changes the organization of his ego and not the external world; but in this process his ego plays a more active part than that of the hysteric.

How does the neurotic behave toward reality? He evades it, *he escapes from the difficulties of life into illness,* instead of overcoming them actively. His ability to adapt himself to reality is disturbed.

We have learned that in adaptation to reality the instincts are sublimated, whereby the taking in and the ejection of stimuli from the outer world continually alternate. The external world and the functions of the ego are desexualized and freed of their magic. Thus the ego is freed of the burdensome, direct instinctual demands and is enabled to fulfill its functions.

The adaptation to reality suffers, therefore, in the first place, when the capacity to sublimate diminishes, when sexual energies break through into the higher psychic systems of the ego. Thinking and useful actions adapted to reality are then impaired. The hysteric, for instance, is disturbed in his work by libidinally colored fantasies, and the thinking of the obsessional neurotic is erotized. There are obsessional neurotics who have to give up all thinking and acting in order not to encounter sexual ideas. Every word, every idea, every external perception, and every action appear to the schizophrenic as a sexual symbol.

A patient in my office, through the window, heard birds singing in the garden and said: "Penises are singing in the garden."

In the same way, thinking and acting can become completely inhibited because of the breaking through of destructive elements with a libidinal tinge, that is, sadistic impulses. In short, in disturbances of the adaptation to reality, acting deteriorates to the employment of autoplastic measures, activity in mastering the influx of stimuli gives way to a certain passivity, thinking degenerates into magic and omnipotence, or even ceases, and in psychoses, the ego loses its ability to distinguish between the inner and the outer world; its most primitive function, that of testing perception, fails.

Although the relationship to reality is not nearly so severely disturbed in neurosis as it is in psychosis, still, it is a failure to recognize reality if a hysterical woman realizes her desire for pregnancy through nausea and vomiting, or if a phobic avoids certain objects or situations which mirror his instinct life, or if a compulsive neurotic strives to avert a calamity through some ceremonial.

However this may be in all its details, a disturbance of ego function is present in all neuroses: in hysteria, predominantly of the body ego (the organs); in compulsive neurosis, predominantly of the psychic ego (thinking and feeling); in schizophrenia, of the perceiving ego (in this illness, however, the other disturbances, the hysterical and compulsive-neurotic ones, also appear regularly in addition to the disturbance of the perceiving ego). *Symptom formation thus takes place in the ego; it is a performance of the ego and impairs its functions.* This performance is twofold, because through it the instincts of the id are gratified through the ego, on the one hand, and warded off on the other. Considered from the point of view of the id, the symptom represents an affirmation of the instinct life; from the point of view of the ego, a negation; on the whole, however, it is a *compromise*.

But it is doubtful whether this completely covers the concept of neurosis, since there are illnesses whose sole symptom is an inhibition, thus a diminished performance, and illnesses which run their course without symptoms and yet must be designated as "neuroses." In the first group, there is, for instance, a type of impotence in which there is no seminal discharge, in spite of prolonged friction. These patients suffer from the same castration anxiety as most other male neurotics, only they express this fear anally, through "withholding." The fear of the loss of the penis is, to their unconscious, identical with the fear of the loss of feces. Unconsciously they believe that they save the genital from castration by retaining their feces, that they *keep* it in this way. In intercourse the semen symbolically represents the feces, to them. Anal ideas and instinct energies take control over the ejaculation. This (the ejaculation) is then treated as if it were feces: it is retained. The inhibition is thus only an apparent one; it is, on the contrary, an increased performance, as retention of feces is in most cases. *Displacement of libido, which results in a disturbance in the functioning of the ego or of an organ, is the general sign of a symptom.* Since in our case a displacement of anal libido onto the genitals takes place, this inhibition (as an apparently lessened but actually increased performance) likewise deserves to be designated as a symptom.

There are inhibitions which are general in character, such as melancholic depression. Here the general inhibition seems to be a real one, caused by the excessive consumption of psychic energy in mastering the melancholic process of mourning, in which so much energy is used that none remains for other purposes. Therefore the course of thinking in the melancholic seems retarded, his mobility diminished, his reaction time prolonged, in short, the psychomotor inhibition of the melancholic is a phenomenon of deficiency, caused by the binding of all of the psychic energy to one sphere. Actually, melancholics do not suffer *subjectively* from their inhibitions, but from self-reproaches, self-accusations, from ideas of poverty, and so on, which predominate in the symptomatology of melancholia. An increased performance in one sphere (self-accusations and the like) corresponds to a diminished performance in the sphere in which the symptoms are formed, which first become apparent to the environment (inhibition, rejection of food, suffering, and so on). Thus it can also be understood that some forms of work inhibition (in daily tasks, in the professions, in creative work such as writing, painting, acting, in the performing arts, in laboratory work) can be helped through analysis of the symptoms or fantasies which are absorbing the psychic energy.

BISEXUALITY AND NEUROSIS

The problem of bisexuality has been discussed to some extent in a preceding section. It plays an important part in normal life as well as in neurosis. One has the impression that some patients overcompensate their homosexuality by excessive heterosexual activity or constantly oscillate between hetero- and homosexuality. Though the clinical material of the preceding pages revealed diverse manifestations of bisexuality, I should like to illustrate this topic further by a specific example concerning the behavior of a patient in the span of twenty-four hours between two psychoanalytic sessions.

The patient in question occasionally was subject to drunkenness. Whenever he had to struggle with homosexual feelings, he drank. Yet, never as an adult was he a manifest homosexual.

Now the story: One day he was drunk when he came to his psychoanalytic session. His report about the events leading to his intoxication is self-explanatory. At the end of the preceding session, he had told me that he would not attend a meeting of some young men, as he had previously planned. He felt too uneasy, he said, and too confused. Nonetheless, he did go to the meeting, but his uneasiness grew to such an extent that he had to leave early. While there, he repeatedly asked himself: "Am I resisting my love for these boys?" He went home and ate a cheese sandwich and drank a glass of milk. While eating, he wondered why he was doing this, as he never ate cheese sandwiches and never drank milk. He was particularly struck by the automatic way in which he had gone to the refrigerator and taken out the food, without even being hungry.

We may interpret this compulsive eating and drinking (cheese and milk) as a symbolic gratification at the mother's breast. The fact that he fell asleep immediately after his meal (like an infant) seems to confirm this interpretation. It was not his habit to go to bed so early—it was only eight o'clock—and he customarily went to bed at a very late hour. The fact that he was disturbed by homosexual feelings at the meeting, though they were expressed in the form of doubt, that he went home for cheese and milk, and gratified, fell asleep, justifies the assumption that he escaped in unconscious fantasy from homosexuality to heterosexuality.

After eight hours of deep sleep he awoke, angry at his wife, and vomited. Then he thought of his wife's feet. Like his father, she had crippled feet. When he became aware of this fact, he felt as if his wife were a man. She was, for him, a hermaphrodite, as were all women, for him. Then there came to his mind the times when he used to sleep in one bed with his brothers, touching their feet with his feet, their thighs or buttocks with his penis (obviously masturbating). Seized with horror, he got up and drank more than a bottle of wine, after which he fell asleep. When he woke up two hours later, he drank again, and in this drunken state, he came to me.

He would drink whenever he felt drawn to men; obviously, this was an escape and a symbolic gratification. The last such occasion had been a meeting with a man of whom he was very fond and whom he had not seen for a long time. To this meeting he reacted by getting intoxicated on beer. The very first time that he had taken alcohol, he was in the company of men whom he suspected of being homosexuals. He drank beer with them. His association to beer was urine, and an episode of his school days, when he was challenged by a group of boys to suck the penis of one of them.

This example shows with unusual clarity the fluctuations which occur within the framework of bisexuality. Tempted by thoughts about the young men, the patient escaped from homosexuality to the woman (food, milk, mother, wife). Then he vomited, disgusted with his wife; he expelled her, as it were. But afterwards, he drank alcohol and thus returned to men in a symbolic way, while at the same time fleeing from them.

NEUROSIS AND PSYCHOSIS

(Unsuccessful Adaptation to Reality)

The patient mentioned previously, who had been an Army officer, had chosen his profession out of his own inclination at the age of fourteen. In spite of being wholeheartedly a soldier and submitting to the severe discipline, he constantly opposed his superiors and provoked them. Though he came from a poor family, he lived lavishly; he contracted debts, and forged checks by signing the names of his superiors. He was soon apprehended, deprived of his rank, and imprisoned. Several years after having served his term of imprisonment, he entered analysis.

After a short time it became apparent that he had prepared his fate systematically, although unconsciously. He carried out in reality an old fantasy which had been most intense in puberty, immediately before he entered military school. This fantasy contained the idea that he was tied to a tree and beaten and cruelly tortured by a man. By his behavior in the army the patient provoked punishment in order to transform into reality this fantasy which, by the way, had been unconscious during his military service. He had no actual symptom neurosis; he did not feel ill. But his behavior was the expression of an unconscious need for punishment which had to be gratified at any cost. A man who transforms reality according to his unconscious wishes and instinctual impulses in such a manner as to harm himself, a man who transforms his fantasy into reality regardless of the consequences, is certainly not mentally healthy. His state of mind borders, perhaps, on psychosis. And yet he was not psychotic.

Another patient would hang for hours suspended by a towel from a hook in his bathroom, with the fantasy that he was St. Sebastian, into whom arrows were being shot. This fantasy was very similar to that of the other patient. But whereas the first patient retained his libidinal relations to the outside world, the second one gave them up almost completely. The world existed for him only in so far as it was capable of satisfying the wishes contained in his fantasy. The withdrawal of object libido had further consequences. The fantasy did not remain unconscious as it did with the first patient, who, through his unconscious acting out, brought about a situation corresponding to his fantasy, but was consciously surprised by the consequences of his behavior. This second patient actually believed he was a saint, whose task it was to redeem mankind. Just as he felt himself a sinner, so he believed that the world was full of sin, from which it could be freed only through his expiation. Although a Jew, he wanted to retire to a monastery. He discussed his admittance with the prior of a monastery, fell on his knees before him, and worshiped him like a god. It is impossible to relate briefly all he did and how persistently he tried to carry out in reality the idea of the redeemer.

One phenomenon, however, is already clear: his ego boundary was extended, and consequently his inner world was in part identical with his outer world. He himself became the center of the world. He felt responsible for it, for a world which was merely the reflection of his inner world, and had the firm belief that he could transform it through changes in his own self, just as he hoped to relieve his guilt-burdened ego through changes in this outer world. For him, external and internal reality were fused. Therefore outer and inner perceptions were equivalent, to him. In our first patient, there was no extension of the borders of the ego, nor was there a confusion of inner and outer reality. He changed the external reality, it is true, in accordance with his inner needs, but he was still able to distinguish between external reality and his inner life. Unconscious fantasies formed the basis of his neurotic character and directed his actions. The connection between his fantasy and his behavior was concealed from him and from others. The psychotic patient, on the other hand, was aware of his fantasy; he mistook it for external reality and sought, in his actions, to fulfill the wish contained in the fantasy. He felt narcissistically gratified through the corroboration of his omnipotence. He projected his fantasies into the outer world, while the neurotic repressed his fantasies.

The chief difference between the behavior of the neurotic and that of the psychotic is this: the neurotic does not mistake psychic reality for external reality (or, when he does, it is only within restricted limits, as for instance, in phobia or fetishism), whereas the psychotic loses this discriminatory capacity and not only mistakes inner reality for the outer, but even replaces the outer reality with the inner. *The neurotic, in his unconscious, retains relations with reality (the objects of the outer world); he represses only the instincts of the id. The psychotic loses also the objects in the unconscious, and consequently has no relationship to them; he represses reality.*

And so, perhaps, there are more "insane" people than is generally assumed, people who take the psychic reality for the external one and are able to place it at the service of their narcissism. Their first success in life may be decisive for them, in that their self-confidence is strengthened through the confirmation of their omnipotence. After their narcissism has been gratified, a part of the object libido which is still free may then flow onto the outer world. Napoleon, for instance, might have become merely an eccentric, had not his omnipotence been confirmed by his first successes, which actually were the result of his fantasies transformed into deeds.

Every mentally ill person suffers from difficulties in adapting to reality. The difficulty consists not only in the necessity to adapt oneself to external reality but also in the necessity for the ego to adapt itself to internal reality as determined by the instinct life. The manifest illness is the result of the faulty performance of these tasks. The ego may emerge victorious from this struggle of adaptation, or it may be defeated, according to the power of resistance of the object relations. In the neuroses, these are not broken off in so far as their unconscious parts are concerned; hence the object wòrld is preserved and the main functions of the ego, the functions of perception and of reality testing, are, on the whole, undisturbed. In the psychoses, on the other hand, the relationship with the external world is partially or totally suspended, and thus the main functions of the ego are disturbed.

Any psychic illness, be it neurosis or psychosis, is not merely a biological phenomenon, brought about by a more or less complete failure of instinct life, but also a social phenomenon, which is expressed in unsuccessful adaptation to the external conditions of life. For this reason, the concept of illness depends in large part on the social milieu in which it appears. Where the social and cultural organization is stricter, adaptation will be more difficult and, therefore, a person will be considered ill who, in another milieu, would perhaps be revered as a saint or a hero. On the other hand, fewer illnesses appear where the struggle for existence, thus real adaptation, is more difficult, especially where so much psychic energy is consumed in real work that there is not much left for neurotic productivity.

If we speak of adaptation to the inner life and to the outer world in relation to the genesis of the illness, we must inquire what factor is primary in psychic illness and what, secondary. Is the process of adaptation, or of symptom formation, or something else, primary?

THE PRIMARY AND THE SECONDARY PROCESS OF ILLNESS

Bleuler has differentiated between primary and secondary symptoms in schizophrenia, between those which form the nucleus of the illness and are never lacking, and those which are to be considered reactions to the primary disturbances and can, therefore, vary.

Viewing schizophrenia from the standpoint of the libido theory, we come to the same conclusions. Only, by the term "primary symptoms" we mean something else. The manifest clinical picture of the schizophrenic frequently is not accompanied by a subjective feeling of suffering. But what is felt as severe suffering is the initial phase of the illness, the feeling of the "end of the world," which we interpret as an enormous loss of libido. We consider the subsequent symptoms as an attempt at re-establishing the lost object world, reality. The actual primary process of illness, reflected in the feeling of the "end of the world," takes its course silently. The manifest symptoms are a clamorous attempt at restitution of the lost world or healing.

In the neuroses, we may likewise distinguish between a primary and a secondary process of illness. Just as, in schizophrenia, the conflict with reality leading to the withdrawal of libido represents the primary process of illness, so, in the neurosis, the unconscious neurotic conflict forms the nucleus of the entire process. The symptomatology is an attempt to solve the conflict in a way characteristic of each particular form of neurosis, thus a reaction to the primary disturbance. The symptoms are, therefore, a secondary phenomenon, which represents an attempt of the ego to do justice to the strivings of the id as well as to the demands of the superego and of reality, and to adapt itself to all of these demands in *one single act,* if possible. *This attempt at adaptation is an "attempt at self-healing."* Not even the anxiety of the phobic is the primary symptom; it is only a reaction to the instinct demand, a protection against being overwhelmed by the instinct world which is fraught with danger.

This attempt at restitution, the attempt to restore the harmonious cooperation of the psychic forces which has been disturbed, takes its course on a different level in each illness. In schizophrenia, in the effort to restore this cooperation, the preconscious verbal ideas are at first recathected by psychic energy. In the obsessional neurosis, where the conflict threatens to proceed to the point of loss of object, an attempt is made to establish a connection between unconscious and preconscious ideas. In conversion hysteria, this harmony seems to be achieved by simply keeping the disagreeable idea from consciousness, probably because the unconscious part of the object is not threatened at all. This, however, does not completely describe the pathogenic process.

The Role of the Synthetic Function of the Ego in the Development of the Neurosis

We previously have, in Chapter V, pointed out the role of the ego as a mediator in psychic conflicts. We sought to show how the ego endeavors to fulfill this particular task—the balancing of contrasts and the solving of psychic conflicts—by forming sublimations and character changes. We deferred for later consideration the problem of the extent to which the synthetic function of the ego participates in solving the conflict which leads to neurosis.

In the meantime we came to understand that the psychoneurotic symptom develops when the actual-neurotic symptom is *assimilated* by the ego. Neurasthenic symptoms and those of the anxiety neurosis as well as hypochondriacal symptoms are worked up psychically by the ego in such a way that something *new* develops; that is, the psychoneurotic symptom. Thus it seems as if the actual-neurotic symptom, felt by the ego as strange and disturbing, would spur on the ego to increased synthesis. It is, however, the neurotic conflict that forms the root of the psychoneuroses. At first, this conflict is solved in the following way: the ego takes hold of the actual neurotic sufferings and through them permits the repressed strivings to continue their psychic life, on the one hand, and, on the other, conceals their meaning from consciousness.

In the introductory, primary phase of the illness, where the ego is faced with the problem of mastering the non-ego-syntonic instinctual demands, the readiness of the ego to synthesize fails at first. The ego, *temporarily,* through the process of repression, is more or less deprived of its function as mediator between the strivings of the id and the demands of the superego and reality; it wards off the forbidden impulses and keeps them away from the motor and perceptive ego. This state of acute conflict does not, however, last long. Sometimes it is so short that it is perceived not at all or merely as a transitory state of depersonalization. In reaction to the disorganization of the harmonious cooperation of the psychic forces, the ego, here too, develops increased activity in order to restore the disturbed psychic harmony. Since the acute neurotic conflict threatens the personality with disintegration, the ego must seek to solve this conflict.

Trying to solve the neurotic conflict, the ego attempts to mediate between the opposing strivings of the personality. These attempts result in a *new* phenomenon within the psychic structure, the neurotic symptom. In Chapter V, we found that psychic creativity is linked with the synthetic function of the ego. This function, then, determines the symptom, particularly its compromise character.

But once the symptom is formed, it does not remain stationary; it grows and multiplies (phobia, obsessional neurosis) and may even invade the part of the personality that had remained intact, as it does in schizophrenia. Conversion hysteria, however, seems to be an exception in this respect. Here the pathologic process seems terminated with the establishment of the symptom; the symptom remains stationary, unchanged. For instance, when an idea is repressed, its energy may cathect a sensory organ. This organ then becomes oversensitized (its oversensitivity is identical with the symptom), and reacts to stimuli always in the same way, for instance, with pain. In the obsessional neurosis, the ego continues to participate in symptom formation, even after the symptom has been established. The ego goes on producing ever new symptoms in order to substitute them for the old ones which have meanwhile lost their original effectiveness. In phobia, the anxiety includes ever more objects and situations.

As we have learned, the symptom is a compromise between the repressed and the repressing forces of the personality; it is a substitute for both. The ego unites, in one formation, two opposing tendencies, one seeking satisfaction and the other denying it. The patient suffers, feeling the symptom simultaneously as a foreign body and as a part of himself.

Under certain conditions, the repression causes a regression of the instinct to its fixation point, followed by a regression of a part of the ego. Both instinct and ego return to a lower level of development. As long as the repression is successful, there are no striking changes of the repressed instinct, and the ego shows, at most, some inhibition. When the repression fails, however, both the repressed instinct and ego become active again and express themselves in different forms than before or during the repression. For example, the genital urge changes into a sadistic one and the repressed part of the ego loses contact with reality and acquires its old magic powers. This part of the ego no longer opposes the sadistic impulses as the total ego did before. It accepts them and carries them out, though in a form so disguised that the intact part of the ego does not understand their meaning. In collaboration with the repressed instinctual demand, the unconscious part of the ego maintains the symptom. It becomes independent of the intact portion of the ego; it is split off. *In fact, the ego is split in all neuroses.* Paradoxical as it may seem, a faculty whose task it is to integrate the personality fails when it tries to carry out this task and ends by contributing further to the disruption of the unity of the personality.

However, the ego cannot tolerate for too long such a disintegration of its unity. As long as the new formation in the ego organization, the symptom, is not assimilated, as long as it is excluded from the ego organization, it is felt as a foreign body. As such, it causes unpleasure, pain, renders the ego weak and, finally, injures its narcissism. Such a state of affairs contradicts the tendencies of the ego to mediate, to unify, to bridge gaps, to simplify, to synthesize. Thus the ego has to assimilate the symptoms, and in particular, it has to take back into its organization the repressed part of the ego. There develops a kind of symbiosis between symptom and ego in which the ego may achieve some kind of narcissistic gratification in compensation for the narcissistic injury suffered through the process of symptom formation. In this "'symbiosis," the ego turns a quantity of narcissistic libido toward the symptom and assimilates it; thus it changes its own character to a certain extent. The ego derives narcissistic gratification also from the fact that it is again able to unify its disrupted organization, to fill its gaps. The deficit in the economy of the narcissistic libido of the ego thus is balanced.

The situation may be illustrated by a short example:

A phobic patient suffered from agoraphobia. His anxiety gradually increased to such an extent that he could no longer go to his place of business and consequently was unable to work. His wife had to support him. The symptom appeared first, and his inability to work followed. But the patient became satisfied with the symptom, believing that his wife's supporting him was a proof of her love for him, that it was a sacrifice she made out of love. He accepted and assimilated his illness under the condition that it offered him narcissistic gratification.

The obsessional neurotic and also the melancholic make their illness tolerable by deriving from it the narcissistic gratification of being particularly moral. The paranoiac is proud of his intellectual achievement in the formation of his complicated delusional systems.

The narcissistic gratification of the ego through the symptom is called the *secondary* or *epinosic gain through illness,* as distinguished from the *primary* gain, which is derived from the disguised instinct gratification in the symptom. There is not invariably a secondary gain, but there is always a primary one. The secondary gain forms the fifth type of resistance mentioned previously (Chapter VIII). *It is an ego resistance,* which may cause the greatest difficulties in treatment, in proportion to the amount of narcissistic gratification it supplies. The secondary gain may strengthen the narcissism of the ego, in hysteria, through the establishment and strengthening of an object relationship; in phobia, through an excessive attachment to an object; in the obsessional neurosis, through the gratification of the superego; in schizophrenia, through the overemphasis of certain ego functions, such as thinking in paranoia; and so on. From the secondary gain through illness there thus, likewise, results a disguised instinct gratification, which, however, takes its effect in the ego.

The synthetic function of the ego is not first manifested in the secondary gain through illness, but even earlier. In conversion hysteria, it is expressed in the compromise character of the symptom itself, and even more completely in the obsessional neurosis, where the patient succeeds in combining the prohibition with the gratification and thus in bringing about the unity of the strivings of the id with the demands of the superego.

With the secondary gain through illness, the synthesis is increased as a compensatory measure. At the outbreak of the illness, the synthetic function fails at first. Soon, however, it gives impetus to the symptom formation and then dominates the course of the illness to such an extent that, in extreme cases, it helps the repressed instincts to break through (obsessional neurosis). After the formation of the symptom, however, the synthesis fails again, but it becomes active once more by the indirect route of the secondary gain through illness. Under the influence of the neurotic conflict, on the one hand, and of the threatening danger of the disintegration of the ego, on the other, the synthesis is driven to increased activity. *The tendency to synthesis is only rarely lost.* It is especially conspicuous and adopts distorted forms where Eros is most threatened, as we have seen in the example of schizophrenia. *In severe psychotic states* (confusion, catatonic stupor) *it ceases to function. In neurosis, it is merely disturbed*—disturbed in such a way that it appears where it would not appear normally. For, in the attempt to obtain gratification, every mentally ill patient comes into conflict with reality, with the superego, or with the id. He is unable to find a harmonious balance between the conflicting psychic tendencies.

SUMMARY

The neurosis, thus, is extremely complicated. A primary and a secondary process of illness may be distinguished. The primary one consists in exaggerated reactions of the ego to an instinct danger and in the neurotic conflict closely connected with this. These reactions first appear as anxiety, which, as we know, is not objectively motivated. The symptoms form the secondary process of illness, representing an attempt at a solution of the neurotic conflict; they bind the neurotic anxiety. In most illnesses, perhaps with the exception of conversion hysteria, this solution is achieved only with great difficulty. The symptom is a substitute for an inhibited instinct as well as a compromise between what has to be warded off and the warding-off force. What is warded off is the instinct. The warding-off force and the motive of the defense stem from the ego. With symptom formation, the neurotic conflict is temporarily terminated. In conversion hysteria, this termination is final; the process of illness is brought to a standstill with the formation of the symptom. In phobia and in obsessional neurosis, however, the process of illness does not come to a standstill with appearance of symptoms, for here there are always new attempts at a solution of the neurotic conflict, and therefore new symptoms continue to be formed. The schizophrenic is even more productive, and his continually expanding delusions and hallucinations completely stifle the remainder of the intact personality.

The purpose of symptom formation is, thus, to remove or to escape from the situation of danger. The symptom offers two advantages, for through it the ego evades the instinct demands, on the one hand, and gains the capacity, on the other, of removing the anxiety. The symptom serves to deceive not only the ego but also the environment. With the aid of the symptom, the ego defends itself against the dangers of the instinct strivings. Since the ego, however, is intimately connected with the id, it is able to ward off the instinct danger only by changing its own organization and forming a synthesis with the instinct. The end result of the attempts at solution of the neurotic conflict differs according to the disposition of the instincts and the ego. In any case, the symptom formation ends with a more or less extensive estrangement from reality. It leads to neurotic suffering which, in many cases, though not always, is counterbalanced by the secondary gain through illness.

Thus the id, the ego, and the superego participate in the development of the neurosis. The superego becomes intolerant toward the strivings of the id; the instinctual impulses of the id are immobilized; and the ego becomes dependent on the id, evades reality, and its synthetic function is partly disturbed.

Chapter X

CHARACTER AND NEUROSIS

We see quite a number of patients who are free of neurotic symptoms but who behave pathologically. Such patients suffer from so-called *character neuroses*. They discharge their impulses, wishes, and fantasies in the external world, while symptom neurotics usually satisfy their drives through their own person. Character neurotics perform strange actions for which they sometimes find justifications, sometimes not. However, it is usually not possible to distinguish the rational from the irrational in their behavior. Often it takes years before the irrational motivation is recognized; meanwhile they may have ruined themselves and their families. Whereas the symptom neurotic suffers from his illness and usually endures it passively, the character neurotic is hardly aware of being ill, and through his acts obtains gratification for his unconscious strivings.

Before we go further in our discussion, we must try to understand the nature of character. This is a difficult task, for character is an elusive phenomenon, not easily defined.

In evaluating a character one may perhaps rely on one's personal impressions and say: this man or that woman has a good or a bad character, a weak or a strong one. Such an opinion, however, will be wrong, at least as often as not. Or one may try to use external data as criteria of character, for instance, physical features only. Again one will soon be disappointed, for a masculine-looking woman may prove to be very feminine, a feminine-looking man, masculine, and the like.

It is therefore necessary to look for more reliable criteria. Spread throughout Freud's writings are many remarks about the nature of character. Once in a small circle, he offered a concise review of the problem, but, to my knowledge, never published it.

Character is a combination, or rather a synthesis of many traits, habits, and attitudes of the ego. Sometimes one trait prevails, sometimes, another. One may be tempted by this fact to evaluate a man's character on the basis of a single trait. Of course, this would not yield a true picture. In order to obtain a more accurate idea of an individual's character, we must consider it from several points of view—from the descriptive, genetic, structural, dynamic, economic, and libidinal angles. Consideration from each of these angles will lead to different results. The ideal picture of a character would be gained if it were possible to view all these aspects simultaneously. Then we would have a metapsychological conception of character.

It has already been mentioned that consideration from the descriptive point of view alone is not fruitful, but leads to deceptive results.

Consideration from the genetic or historical point of view offers a somewhat better insight. A brief example may perhaps afford the best introduction to our problem.

The patient was a very successful man, respected and sought after by his superiors. He, on his part, admired and loved them and was loyal to them as long as they were successful. Whenever they failed, he would leave them. His behavior in one particular instance was characteristic of him. When his father-in-law, who had guided and helped him in obtaining a rather important position, got into difficulties, he abandoned him and tried to join his enemies. Such a man could well be considered a traitor.

A few important details of his infantile history may shed some light on the development of this particular character trait. When he was three years old, a brother was born. Disappointed in his mother, he turned away from her, and became increasingly attached to his father, and inseparable from him. When he was eight years old, a sister was born. Soon she became the father's favorite. At about the same time, the father failed in business, whereupon the living standards of the family declined. The patient then turned away from his father, tried to gain favor with his wealthy uncles, and set himself the goal of becoming independent and rich.

In summation, first he turned away from his mother, next from his father, and later from men who disappointed him and could no longer be helpful. The original trauma was, obviously, the birth of his brother, to which he reacted by abandoning his mother. The birth of his sister, together with the business misfortunes of his father, seems to have been the second trauma; to this he reacted in the same way: he abandoned his father. From then on, he employed a pattern of reactions which was always repeated whenever he suffered disappointment.

One of the patterns of his behavior thus represents a repetition of his reaction to an infantile trauma. It seems that the trauma became fixated, whereby the tendency was acquired to repeat the traumatic experience and to act it out in situations reminiscent of the one in which the trauma first occurred. Our patient, abandoning his mother, withdrew his libido from her and shifted it to his father. Disappointed in his father, he again withdrew his libidinal cathexis from the object, and this reaction of withdrawing libido from a disappointing object became one of his patterns. Libido withdrawn from the object, that is, id energy, was invested in the ego to form a character trait.

It is obvious that our patient in later life re-created an infantile situation and repeated an infantile reaction. This reaction may be considered as a defense against the infantile trauma.

In other cases, the defenses may be aimed at the undoing of the effects of the trauma and appear as avoidances, inhibitions, idiosyncrasies, and the like, which thus are formed through countercathexes.

Although repetition and acting out, inhibitions, and avoidances contribute much to character formation, they do not represent the only patterns of character development. There are character traits that develop on the basis of different mechanisms and from different origins.

One of Freud's earliest discoveries in regard to character formation was the so-called "anal character." This character type is distinguished by excessive orderliness, parsimoniousness, and obstinacy.

A child who is constipated, who retains his feces, may become an overpossessive, avaricious adult, inclined to outbursts of rage. These character traits are derivatives of pregenital anal-sadistic drives. The aims of these drives, however, are inhibited, for the ego, instead of gratifying the id drives, seems to intercept and convert them into specific character traits. The inhibition of an instinctual aim and the transformation of the instinctual drive into something noninstinctual is characteristic of sublimation. Accordingly, the formation of character traits may be considered a kind of sublimation. Thus, in certain traits of character, some sexual component instincts are continued in a sublimated form.

There are, however, character traits which are not merely continuations or repetitions of aim-inhibited instinctual drives. For instance, children who are difficult to toilet-train, those who are particularly dirty and soil themselves, are often, in mature life, very clean, extremely orderly. Obviously, the ego counteracts the domination of the anal instinct of early childhood by developing excessive orderliness and cleanliness. These traits are reaction formations of the ego: the anal instinct is turned into its precise opposite.

Combined with anal character traits there are usually sadistic ones, either as continuations of infantile aggressions or as reaction formations. Anger, hate, vengefulness, temper tantrums, are repetitions of excessive infantile sadism, while overconscientiousness, extreme sense of duty and responsibility, are reaction formations against the same sadism. Thus certain character traits may be a combination of derivatives of pregenital drives in the form of both repetitions and reaction formations.

Not only anal-sadistic drives but also other component instincts are subject to transformation into character traits. Urethral disposition may lead to exaggerated ambition; oral disposition to greediness, in a physical and mental sense, to oratory as well as to opposite manifestations. Infantile sexual curiosity in combination with a certain amount of aggression may turn into a passion for scientific research (sublimation).

In latency, when the ego begins to show signs of consolidation, there develop certain traits which further enhance its integration. These new traits are: shame, disgust, and a primitive sense of guilt. The first is a reaction to exhibitionism; the second, to oral as well as anal drives, and the third, to sadism. Of course, all these traits can be either missing or they can be exaggerated, which is pathological.

The character, however, does not consist exclusively of fixated infantile traumas or of transformed instinctual drives. Its development depends to a great extent also on the interaction between id, ego, and superego.

We have just tried to understand the interaction between ego and id, using the anal-sadistic character as an example, and have come to the conclusion that certain energies of the id help in molding certain character traits of the ego. As is to be expected, however, the character is primarily determined not only by the nature of the instincts but also by the constitution of the ego with its sense organs. A deaf person, for instance, will be inclined to paranoid ideas, a cripple, to feelings of inferiority and vengefulness. A defect may, of course, also be overcompensated. Yet not all stammerers become orators like Demosthenes; not all deaf people are composers like Beethoven.

Just as the ego is dependent on the id, the internal world, so it is dependent on the external world. In other words, just as the character is molded or modified by the id, so it is influenced and changed by the environment.

The ego, influenced by the external as well as the internal world, asserts itself by mediating between the demands of the id, the superego, and reality. If this mediating function is intact, a harmonious collaboration between the internal urges and the external exigencies of life is brought about. The ego will then be adapted to reality, on the one hand, and will conform with the demands of the superego as well as with the urges of the id, on the other. Such a well-balanced personality, however, is rare. For the equilibrium of the psychic forces can easily be upset, be it in relation to reality, to the superego, or to the id. In case the demands of reality are too hard, the ego will develop character traits different from those which develop when the superego is too exacting or the urges of the id, too impelling. How the ego carries out its mediating (rather, its synthetic or integrating) function, becomes apparent, at least in part, through the example of identification.

There seems to exist an inborn tendency to identify, expressed first in relation to the nourishing person, the mother, then to other individuals. Through identification, the libidinal object is, in a sense, incorporated by the ego. As a consequence, character traits are formed after the pattern of the "incorporated" person. However, new identifications are constantly added to the primary identifications with the parents, as for instance, with the parents as they appear in later life, with teachers, friends, ideals. Thus, in the course of development, the character may undergo changes due to these sources. Yet the original identifications seem indestructible.

An individual who has successfully repressed the identification with his father and whose behavior generally has been the opposite to that of his father, may suddenly discover that in certain situations he has behaved exactly as the latter did. In other words, if the repression of an identification fails, the repressed identification becomes active and causes a change of character. It may also happen that one identification is separated from the other identifications by resistances. In this case we are confronted with a split ego, with a multiple personality. In other instances, identification takes place where normally an object relationship would be established. Then the individual does not live his own life, but lives the life of his friend, and may continue to do so even when the friend is dead.

If an individual has difficulties in forming identifications, he feels more or less lonely, a stranger in the world. He lacks understanding for others and compassion.

In the process of identification, object libido is transformed into narcissistic libido. This transformation is accompanied by the inhibition of direct sexual aims. Desexualization of libido or inhibition of direct sexual aims together with a defusion of instincts is essential for sublimation.[1] Sublimation of sensual feelings leads to the establishment of

[1] This statement may be illustrated by the following example: A young woman invariably became sexually excited when she met an interesting young man. In order to gain control of herself, she would entangle him in an intellectual conversation, in the course of which she became calm and composed and, finally, lost all sexual interest in him. Subsequently, these conversations served her often as an inspiration for writing a short story or novel.

In this case, the sexual instinct is sublimated, that is, deprived of its sexual nature whereby a certain amount of aggression is freed. Where aggression becomes socially useful, we may also speak of sublimation, but there the process is an opposite one:

tender, affectionate feelings (which, of course, also have other derivations). Such feelings in childhood are precursors of mature love, which is a blend of sensual and tender feelings. Hence those identifications which lead to tender feelings will be responsible to a great extent for future relationships with love objects and will largely determine the extent of tenderness and affection accompanying direct sexual aims. The character of a love relationship thus depends on the quality of the admixture of these feelings with the direct sexual ones. If this blending is not complete, a conflict arises between sexual and tender feelings, and the love life is disturbed.

When there is a defusion of instincts, when the instincts are separated, not fused, a conflict between these two groups of instincts sets in, manifesting itself in the ambivalence of thoughts and feelings. Identification, which is often accompanied by such a defusion, thus can be ambivalent and result in hate as well as love, either simultaneously or alternately. Frequently, hate and love are hidden behind oscillations and indecisions, not only in relation to the love object but also to the subject's own thinking processes, to work, and to other functions of daily life. All these conflicting ideas and feelings manifest themselves in the so-called *ambivalent character*.

Bisexuality is another source of oscillation and indecision. However, if the boy succeeds in identifying with his father, he strengthens his masculinity, and if the girl succeeds in identifying with her mother, her femininity will emerge victorious from the struggle between homo- and heterosexuality. There is, however, a third possibility: the man may have satisfactory heterosexual relations, may marry, and yet may prefer friendship with men and feel really happy only in their company. Homosexuality is often sublimated into friendship and social feelings.

In this connection, the castration complex should be mentioned. The fate of the boy's masculinity and the girl's femininity depends largely on the way in which this complex is mastered by the ego. The boy both fears and wishes castration by the father. If, through identification with his father, the boy loses his fear of him, he overcomes his castration complex, externalizes his aggression, and develops an active, masculine character. If, on the other hand, identification with the father encounters difficulties, for instance, due to excessive homosexuality or masochism, the

---

the aggression is mitigated by a certain *admixture* of sexuality. If, for instance, the famous Dieffenbach mentioned by Freud used to cut off dogs' tails as a boy, and later became a great surgeon, this means that his aggression was mitigated by love. He did not want to kill his patients, but to help them.

son retains his castration complex, feels inferior and passive, and acquires a feminine character. (The inferiority complex is certainly not based solely on the castration complex; it is also caused by frustration in love, by loss of love, by narcissistic injury of the ego, and by the sense of guilt.)

If the girl accepts the fact that she has no penis and substitutes the wish for a child for the wish for a penis, her aggression changes into passivity and she acquires feminine character traits. But if she persists in the illusion of having a penis, she becomes hyperactive and develops masculine character traits and masculine goals. In case she reconciles herself only half-heartedly to her lack of a penis, she may feel inferior and develop exaggerated jealousy, just as a feminine man may be excessively jealous.

Of all the various forms of identification, that which releases aggression within the ego is perhaps the most significant. In some way the aggression cathects with its energy the object representations incorporated by the ego in the process of identification. These unconscious object representations, thus cathected with energy, separate themselves from the ego and form a new and independent agency, the superego.

It is difficult to trace the first inception of the superego, but some of its elements can be traced back to the preoedipal phase. Certainly the superego is first clearly discernible in the latency period following the resolution of the oedipus complex. Its definite form, however, is established only after puberty. The superego has certain functions which determine the behavior of the individual and contribute to the final molding of the character. Conscience and self-criticism (criticism of the ego) are functions of the superego. It also forms ideals and contributes to the adaptation to reality inasmuch as it sanctions the reality-testing function of the ego.

A strong superego has control over the ego as well as over the id. If the instincts of the id are excessively strong, they invade the ego. When this happens, the superego loses control over the ego as well as over the id. The ego then is at the mercy of the instincts. It will not be able to tolerate instinctual tension nor to postpone instinct gratification. It will be compelled to fulfill, immediately, at any price, the urges of the id. Such an ego will be weak in relation to the id demands and will have traits of an *instinctual* or *impulsive* character.

It might be assumed that a weak ego, a slave of the id, an ego that escapes the control of the superego, has no feelings of guilt. This is true in some cases, but not in others. In the latter, there appear feelings of guilt which can be explained in the following way: there is an internal system of communication between the psychic agencies. Through this system the superego is informed of the changes within the id as well as within the ego. When the latter is disobedient to the demands of the superego and carries out the urges of the id, feelings of guilt arise. These feelings are equivalents of moral suffering: the "sinner" then appears to be a "hypermoral" person. He tries to atone for his "sinful" deeds by all possible means; this often ends in self-punishment. However, one gains the impression that the need for self-punishment often precedes the moral transgressions. In such instances, the ego provokes dangerous situations and seeks punishment.

The acting out of inwardly forbidden impulses is not a prerequisite to the rise of feelings of guilt. An intention, a mere wish, the inception of an idea often suffice to sensitize the conscience, if it has not been over-sensitive from the very beginning. Such a conscience is indicative of a very strict superego. And a strict, harsh, inflexible superego will force the ego to suppress the urges of the id. If the superego succeeds in sub-jugating both ego and id, an *inhibited* character results. An ego marked by this kind of character will avoid pleasure, renounce libidinal satis-faction, and be inclined to an ascetic life. Often such a severe superego demands frugality and asceticism not only of the self but also of others. This cruelty toward others probably turns excessive aggression from the subject's own person toward objects of the external world and may thus be regarded as a safety measure for the subject.

The superego creates ideals and forces the ego to live up to them. There are many ideals: religious, artistic, scientific ones, ideals of hard work, and others. That religion satisfies moral ideals is obvious. It is less obvious that the other ideals are also ruled by certain moral stand-ards, which, however, are not generally valid, but are determined by each individual for himself. If a conflict arises between ego and superego which, at first, cannot be solved, the conscience is hurt. In order to heal the wound of the conscience, the ego attempts to resolve the conflict. It tries to avoid the disfavor of the superego by restrictions in daily life. Or else, it tries to "undo" the "evil" deeds or thoughts either by hiding them, that is, by removing them from the criticism of the superego, or over-compensating them by "good" deeds, for instance, by charity, by helping others, by making sacrifices, and by hard work in the broadest meaning of the term, as if work could expiate sins. ("In the sweat of thy brow shalt thou eat thy bread.") Work of any kind, be it going to church, working in the fields or in the laboratories, writing novels or painting, acquires moral qualities. In this respect, the superego sanctions reality and gives all the activities of the ego a moral tinge. A hard worker is not only an ambitious and aggressive man but also a man driven by his bad conscience.

The superego is formed partly by reality and partly by the id. Inasmuch as it is rooted in reality it induces the ego to satisfy its social ideals. Hence an ego which is successful in harmonizing the exigencies of society with the demands of the superego will escape conflicts with the external world as well as with the superego. It will acquire character traits which are considered sociable, conciliatory, peaceful and pleasant, free from anxiety. But the superego may also help in shaping an ego with the opposite character traits; it may have ideals conflicting with the ideals of society. The same superego which, at some times, helps the ego in its adaptation to reality may, at other times, be in conflict with the external world and even feel impelled to overthrow the social order. Yet, inasmuch as the superego is rooted in the id, it is the bearer of tradition and consequently endows the ego with conservative character traits. These traits may at times be of great importance because they exercise a stabilizing influence on the entire behavior of the individual.

It is obvious that character has many facets. In order to get an approximately true picture of a certain character, one has to take into consideration all the factors discussed here, and more. Our patient mentioned in the beginning, this apparently unscrupulous and ruthless man, tried very sincerely to help those whom he had hurt. He took singularly good care of his father when the latter needed help and support. In the same manner he tried to undo the guilt he felt toward his friends. Thus, comparing the various aspects of character, it is interesting to note that our patient was immoral from the descriptive angle, but moral from the structural one. His ruthlessness could be understood from the genetic point of view; his morality from the standpoint of the superego.

Space is lacking to illustrate by examples some of the other aspects of character. At this point it seems more useful to review briefly the facts we have learned about character formation.

Each ego reacts in a specific manner to a trauma. The trauma can be repeated and acted out in a positive or a negative way. In the positive reaction, the ego tries to cope with the effects of the trauma by repetition; in the negative, by undoing the trauma with the help of various techniques. The ego may thus form character traits which determine whether the trauma is either repeated or averted. The trauma as such may have caused primarily either retardation of libido development or, if the libido had reached the genital level, its regression to one of the pregenital phases. In both instances, the ego forms character traits in reaction to urges of pregenital libido. In the first case, the character trait in question develops gradually; in the second, it changes more or less suddenly.

But character is not formed exclusively by the ego's reaction to a trauma. There are also other forces at work. In oral and anal characters, for instance, the ego's changes are not due to external stimuli, but are, rather, reactions to excessive instinctual demands. In order to cope with the instincts, the ego changes its organization as if the instincts, especially the sexual ones, represented a danger. It seems, then, as if the energy of the instincts cathected certain parts of the ego, reinforcing old character traits or producing new ones. In these character traits, the instincts seem to be sublimated. Considering character formation from the structural point of view, we find similar changes. The ego intercepts the strivings of the id or of the superego (in so far as the latter is unconscious and thus a part of the id), assimilates them, and produces something new, the particular character trait. The free-floating energy of the id is then bound in character traits of the ego (synthesis). It is interesting to note that the untamed energy of the id contributes to the formation of character traits which, in turn, help further to master the free energy of the id. Why that is the case we do not know. But we may infer from this fact that the redistribution of psychic energy within the personality plays an important part in the formation of the character.

From what has been said, the erroneous impression might be gained that character consists of individual traits independent of each other. This is not so, for all these traits combined in various proportions determine the patterns of attitudes and behavior for each individual. Accordingly, one might expect that there are groups of people who, in similar situations, react in similar ways. Each such group, then, may be supposed to represent a certain character type. Freud, however, maintained that it is a difficult, perhaps even an impossible task to define, delimit, and classify character types. Two possible reasons for this statement suggest themselves: firstly, evaluation of a character depends largely on the point of view from which it is considered; secondly, character types are seldom encountered in pure form. In one individual there may be combined characteristics of an active type with those of a passive one, of the ascetic and strict with those of the liberal and tolerant, or a combination of the characteristics of an inhibited and an impulsive type, all of which would seem mutually exclusive.

Nevertheless, Freud speaks occasionally of definite character types. In one paper he deals more extensively with psychological types as seen from the libidinal angle. He distinguishes three basic libidinal types: the *erotic,* the *compulsive,* and the *narcissistic* type.

In the *erotic* type, the libido has reached the genital level and aims at gratification through the object. The main interest of individuals belonging to this type is to love and—particularly—to be loved. They seek only pleasure, regardless of their own safety as well as that of others, since their ego and superego are not strong enough to resist the demands of the id. As they have no active sense of guilt, they have few moral inhibitions, and since they are guided only by their instinctual needs, they are unreliable and irresponsible. Dependent on objects for instinctual gratification, they fear to lose the love of their objects. As their libido is genital, they are predisposed to hysterical symptoms, such as conversion symptoms, phobias, anxieties. When aggressive, they do not suffer from pangs of conscience. From the structural point of view, we may consider this type as the above-mentioned impulsive or instinctual type.

In the *compulsive* type, the libido is anal-sadistic in nature. In contrast to the erotic type, the compulsive type has a strong superego, a very sensitive conscience, and an exaggerated sense of guilt. The instinctual life of such a person is restricted; he is inclined to asceticism, self-sacrifice, suffering. While the erotic type is dependent on objects, the compulsive type is not, but he is guided in his behavior by his conscience, subject to the approval or disapproval of his superego. Because of the dominance of the superego, he has conservative predilections and a certain degree of stability; he is reliable and faithful in love, though frequently ambivalent. In this type, as in the erotic type, libido is mixed with aggression, the latter being at times stronger than love. From the structural angle, this type may be considered as dominated by the superego.

In the *narcissistic* type, the libido is centered around the ego. The main interest, therefore, is directed toward self-love, self-glorification, and self-preservation. Since their relations with objects are loose, individuals of this type prefer loving to being loved. They strive for gratification without considering the feelings of the object. It is thus easily understood that they are not faithful in love and have no deep attachment to their love object. It is important to them only inasmuch as it contributes to the gratification of their narcissistic needs. For instance, a man of this type must have a wife who is either so beautiful or so prominent in other ways that he can be proud of her; or he may marry an ugly, insignificant woman, often of a lower social and cultural class, solely in order to be assured of his purely instinctual gratification. A woman of this type loves the man mainly as an appendage to his penis and is not much concerned with him as a human being. The narcissistic types are cool, self-possessed, conceited, and have a feeling of being irresistible. It is difficult to influence them; rather, they influence others and often are leaders. In the structural sense, this type appears to be dominated by a strong ego.

In reality, these types very seldom appear in pure form; rather, they are a theoretical construct. The mixed types are what one really sees frequently. Freud distinguished three such types: the *erotic-compulsive,* the *erotic-narcissistic,* and the *narcissistic-compulsive.* They contain contradictory elements which are integrated to a certain extent.

In the *erotic-compulsive type,* the unrestrained instinctual life of the erotic is checked by the superego of the compulsive type. The pleasure-seeking of the first is largely inhibited by the superego's demands of the second, which does not tolerate unconditional gratification of instinctual needs. The compulsive individual's dependence on the superego, on the other hand, is balanced by the dependence on current objects (wife, children, friends) characteristic of the erotic type.

The *erotic-narcissistic type* is the one most frequently met. While the erotic type seeks unrestrained sexual gratification and the narcissistic type, self-glorification as well as self-preservation, the mixed type is able to steer a middle course between dependence on objects and self-love. Through the interaction of these contradictory libidinal strivings, the extremes of the component types are mellowed. The mixed type can bring self-love into accord with object love. He can be active and aggressive inasmuch as aggression is necessary to bring the object within reach of the ego.

The *narcissistic-compulsive type* comprises the features of self-love and independence from objects of the narcissistic type together with the strong superego of the compulsive type. The character traits of the component types are mixed in various proportions and so well blended that they soften each other. The independence from external influences and the lack of concern for others peculiar to the narcissistic type are counteracted by the sensitive conscience and strict superego of the compulsive type. Such an individual does not act as impulsively as the erotic type nor is he as inhibited as the compulsive type, but he is able to gratify his instinctual demands without hurting his conscience. He may retain a well-balanced freedom in thinking and acting; he may be creative and socially valuable.

The postulation of character types is based on theoretical considerations, but these are in turn based to a great extent on clinical observations first made during the treatment of neurotics. Indeed, insight into character structure was preceded by insight into the structure of the neuroses. It was only later, after the psychology of the ego took shape, that we began to understand the character. Gradually we became aware of the fact that there exists some kind of relationship between character and neurosis, particularly when we learned that a character trait may degenerate into a neurotic symptom. Normal and useful curiosity, for example, may deteriorate into obsessional questioning. On the basis of such a relationship, one might be tempted to conclude that quick identification of the underlying character will facilitate the analysis of a neurosis. Although this may be true, it hardly ever occurs in day-to-day practice. Just as the character types are mixed, so are the neuroses. Therefore it is difficult to determine precisely what ingredient of the one mixture is contained in the other.

Usually patients do not seek treatment for the improvement of their character, but in order to be freed from their neurotic sufferings. While treating the neurosis, the analyst becomes acquainted with the patient's behavior, and only then does he as well as the patient become aware of the latter's character shortcomings. We then reconstruct the patient's character from many clinical data.

In view of the intimate relationship between character and neurosis, it is not surprising that Freud described some pathological types, in addition to the normal ones.

First he recognized three such types: *the exceptions, those wrecked by success,* and *criminals from a sense of guilt.*

The exceptions are individuals who believe that the world owes them something. They feel wronged through congenital or acquired physical shortcomings or through other forms of early narcissistic injuries, and try to heal their hurt narcissism through overcompensating their feelings of inferiority. They make excessive demands upon their environment and may take the law into their own hands. In extreme cases, they believe they are above the law. In my opinion this type may be considered a pathological variation of the narcissistic type.

Those wrecked by success are people who become ill when a long-cherished wish is fulfilled or a fantasy realized. Instead of rejoicing, they become unhappy as if disappointed by success. They cannot accept success, out of a feeling of unworthiness and guilt. In fact, they feel compelled to spend their life in misery, in never-ending longing for gratification which is never attained. Their conscience permits them only to await happiness but never to enjoy its fulfillment. Their reward is suffering. They belong to the type who derive narcissistic gratification from suffering.

To the *criminal from a sense of guilt*, the feelings of guilt are so unbearable that he is willing to commit a crime rather than to continue to suffer from guilt. It is easier for him to endure punishment than to live under the constant pressure of his bad conscience. In these cases, the guilt precedes the crime; crime and guilt seem to supplement each other.

Today we would say that the last two types just described are dominated by an unusually severe superego. Presumably, there is much aggression concentrated within the ego. In the first instance, relief and satisfaction of the superego are achieved by renouncing gratification in the external world, on the one hand, turning aggression against the self, and deriving narcissistic gratification from suffering, on the other. (Suffering takes on a moral value.) In the second instance, relief is achieved by discharging the aggression into the external world in order to be punished.

Many years later, Freud postulated some other pathological character types. One of them comprises persons with a particular *adhesiveness of libido*. They cling to others tenaciously and persevere in their ideas, attitudes, and actions. They are loyal and faithful to their love objects and friends. They can be very passionate and tend to have outbreaks of blind rage. This type calls to mind the character of a *genuine epileptic*.

In contrast to this type is the one whose *libido* is *very mobile*. Individuals of this type easily cathect objects but just as easily withdraw libido from them. They are full of ideas, plans, and enterprises, but their ideas are fleeting, and they have no endurance in carrying out their plans. Freud remarks that when dealing with such individuals one feels "as if one were writing on water." Their mood and temper is changeable but they never develop a complete mania. Such types, it seems to me, are represented by the clinical picture of *hypomania*.

Another, quite different type is the one whose *libido has lost plasticity*. Such an individual is unable to sublimate; he is inflexible, rigid, cannot change his opinion; he has lost the capacity for further development. We recognize this type in old people, but we encounter it also in younger ones (conservative types, as for instance, peasants).

Finally, there is a type characterized by *a tendency to conflicts*. People of this type are always suffering; whatever happens, good or bad, is turned into self-torment. Freud explains this in the following way: A quantity of free aggression seems to be accumulated in the ego. However, the conditions of our culture are unfavorable for its discharge onto the external world. In this particular instance, there occurs that which always happens when the discharge of an instinct is blocked; the instinct, in this case the aggression, turns toward the ego. Although these individuals succeed in avoiding external conflicts, they succumb to inner conflicts which may culminate in self-destruction.

Perhaps, with the exception of the libidinal and the obviously aggressive types, it is almost impossible to draw conclusions about the nature of the pathological types just enumerated. We do not know why one man's libido is tenacious, and why another's is fleeting and unstable; why some individuals are extremely impressionable but do not retain impressions, and why others are rigid and inflexible; why one is predisposed to conflicts and another is not.

Finally, let us compare character and neurosis. The neurotic symptom owes its origin to a failure of repression—if the ego is unable to keep the instinctual drive in a state of complete repression, the repressed striving, wish, or idea returns from the unconscious state in the id, tries to reach the ego and to become conscious. As a consequence, the old conflict between ego and id is renewed, a conflict which has once been resolved by repression. The ego tries again to solve it by renewed attempts to subdue the urges of the id, but is, this time, too weak to master them. However, it is still strong enough to form a compromise through which both the demands of the ego and the urges of the id are satisfied. This compromise constitutes the neurotic symptom which takes different shapes in the different forms of neurosis.

In certain forms of character development, repression is operative; in others, it is not. Where it is operative, it is successful, in contrast to its failure in symptom formation.

Repression is not operative in that process of character formation in which fixation has occurred in one of the pregenital phases of libido development. In such cases, the ego automatically produces very early reaction formations which then become an integral part of the character. Under these circumstances the character is a manifestation of continuous infantile reaction formations against pregenital component instincts. When repression is at work in character formation, then the successfully repressed *genital* libido makes a regression to pregenital stages, revives the component instincts, and, from the lower libidinal level, tries to reach the ego again in order to find its adequate outlet. The ego, however, has meanwhile reached a higher level of organization than it had at the time of the pregenital libido fixation. Therefore, it can neither accept pregenital urges nor act them out. Instead, the ego inhibits and transforms them into "'reaction formations" such as exaggerations, avoidances, prohibitions.

Each of these reaction formations is expressed in corresponding character traits. If the ego succeeds in assimilating and integrating these traits, character attitudes or behavior patterns are established, which is a sign of the success of the repression. If the integration fails, a single character trait becomes autonomous, the repression loses its power to resist the onrush of the id, the fixations are reinforced, and, finally, the character trait changes into a neurotic symptom. For instance, when the repression of the anal instinct begins to fail, normal habits of cleanliness degenerate into a washing compulsion.

As a rule, the neurotic symptom causes subjective suffering and is felt by the ego more or less as a foreign body, for the symptom is assimilated by the ego only to a limited extent, even when there is a symbiotic relationship between symptom and ego. Character traits or habits are much better assimilated than symptoms, and form an integral part of the ego. The assimilation is frequently so complete that the distance between character trait and ego disappears. Then the character seems to be identical with the ego, which is never true of symptom and ego. Briefly, the ego normally is not aware of its character but is aware of its neurotic symptoms. It is for this reason that a neurotic symptom is more accessible to analysis than a character trait. Indeed, a character trait may appear as resistance in analysis.

An example may illustrate the difference between character and symptom in reference to accessibility for analysis.

In a rather early phase of his treatment a compulsive patient began to understand the meaning of his compulsion. It took a very long time, however, before he began to understand why all the "good" he was doing for others (wife, stepchildren, father) called forth nothing but opposition and hatred. He himself was aware of the fact that he wished to be "good" and helpful. He was not aware of his trying to force others to accept his help and advice and to do everything that *he* considered necessary for them. He did not realize that all his altruistic efforts were reaction formations to his sadism.

Although we do not know all the factors that contribute to the development of neurotic symptoms, on the one hand, and to the formation of character, on the other, we may say that they are similar in spite of their differences. The main contributions to both character and symptom are made by frustrations and conflicts. The frustrations of the greatest consequence are internal ones which are followed by conflicts differing in nature. A conflict may occur within the ego, for instance, when a father identification is not in harmony with a mother or brother identification. If the conflict between these identifications cannot be resolved, the ego splits; this may have grave consequences. Rejection or repression of one of these identifications may have similar results. Then the character may undergo a complete change. If the content of an identification is projected into the external world, a hypersensitivity of the ego to external experiences may develop which may express itself in ideas of reference and finally degenerate into paranoia.

Secondly, conflicts may develop between ego, superego, and id. The mastering of these conflicts may lead to innumerable forms of character changes or to all the known forms of neurosis. We cannot deal here in detail with all of these transformations.

Thirdly, a conflict may arise between the ego and the external world. If the ego succeeds in mastering reality, it may become stronger as a result and more resistant to conflict; but if it escapes from reality and yields to the unconscious id, it may become weak and even psychotic. Furthermore, there are conflicts related to bisexuality. The conflict between hetero- and homosexuality may be brought to an end either through neurotic symptoms or by character changes. The same is true of conflicts between destructive and erotic instincts. In one instance this conflict may end in neurotic symptoms; in another, it may result in an ambivalent character.

In general, one may state that the difference between neurosis and character lies in the fact that the neurotic conflict is still active in the former, though frequently invisible, while it disappears in the latter, with the exception, perhaps, of the ambivalent character. Why conflict is resolved, at one time, by the formation of character traits and, at another, merely appeased by symptom formation, is still unknown.

Returning to our point of departure, the problem of the so-called character neurosis, we may conclude, on the basis of our reasoning, that the difference between symptom neurosis and character neurosis is not as significant as it seems at first glance.

As has just been stated, the ego is able to cope with the demands of the external and the internal world in an adequate way as long as the patterns of behavior and attitudes are integrated. When the integration fails, some of these patterns become autonomous and escape the control of the ego. Then the latter is split and, consequently, one part of the personality does not know the motives of the wishes and actions of the other part. Certain actions of such individuals become irrational, not coordinated with and often contradictory to the needs and strivings of the personality. Such autonomous character traits may lead to conflicts with the environment, yet seldom to the awareness of abnormality of behavior.

If such character traits or habits are exaggerated to such an extent that they come into conflict with the rest of the personality, they become symptoms causing suffering.

If for some external or internal reason the repression fails which had been successful in forming a character, the character trait or habit breaks down and degenerates into a symptom. Instead of a cluster of character traits or habits there is then a cluster of symptoms which may seem like character traits. In other words, the character neurosis is, finally, a symptom neurosis.

Chapter XI

THE CAUSATION OF NEUROSIS

We have already discussed several factors which are involved in the development of neurosis, such as frustration, fixation, the tendency to conflict, and so on. From this multiplicity of etiological factors, it is difficult to single out one as the most important cause. Apparently several factors have to coincide in order to cause a neurosis.

This has not always been the psychoanalytic view. On the basis of earlier observations, Freud at first advanced the theory that only a highly emotional experience would lead to neurotic illness. At that time one spoke of the "traumatic" causation of hysteria. By this was meant an emotionally toned experience which became fixated. According to the opinion of those days, this would then become the direct cause of the neurosis. It is true that every neurotic clings to his past and, in a sense, is ill because of it. Nevertheless it is also true that not everyone becomes ill because of "traumatic" experiences.

Later on, the concept of "trauma" was limited to a sexual experience, and a sexual trauma was considered the cause of neurosis. As analysis developed further, cases were encountered in which it was possible to relate to the illness, a sexual experience which had occurred not immediately before the onset of the illness, but in childhood. From this arose the theory that an infantile sexual trauma was the cause of neurosis. Soon, however, this theory likewise had to be abandoned, for, in the first place it was not possible to find in all patients gross sexual traumata in childhood, and in the second place, it was discovered that many children had such experiences without later becoming ill. Furthermore, it was discovered that some nongenital sexual experiences had the same traumatic effect as the genital ones. Finally, there were cases in which patients described childhood experiences of apparently traumatic significance which, on closer scrutiny, proved to be fantasies. Thus the theory of the infantile trauma likewise seemed uncertain.

The neurotic disorder, as we recall, consists of peculiar reactions of the ego to certain instinct demands. Under the influence of the superego, the ego tries in a way characteristic of the particular form of neurosis to ward off strivings which cannot be realized. We have recognized anxiety, or rather the instinct danger lurking behind it, as the driving force of defense. If the ego is *helpless* and incapable of mastering the danger, that is, the increasing tension of the instinct need, a *traumatic* situation arises in which the instinctual urge threatens the ego. *Trauma occurs when a stimulus releases a quantity of energy so great that it cannot be mastered by the ego within the usual period of time.* Through this conception of the "trauma," all contradictions about its role as the etiological factor of the neuroses are reconciled. If one cannot always uncover a strongly emotional experience at the time of the beginning of the illness, this does not mean that a trauma in our sense of the word has not occurred at all. For, the increase in quantities of inner stimuli may take place unnoticed and slowly, until it reaches a certain *maximum,* which the ego is no longer able to master, to digest (threshold of tolerance). In childhood the ego is immature, weak, and often unable to cope with the increased need tension; it is helpless in the situation in which the trauma appears. The ego's tolerance of need tensions varies with the individual. The helplessness of the traumatic situation is caused by difficulty in mastering the increase of energy produced by a stimulus. Dammed-up libido, as for instance in protracted sexual abstinence, may cause such states.

Or take another case: Let us consider the consequences of a conflict caused by frustration of a sexual demand. It is important to stress here that excitations produced by excessively increased sexual urges are pathogenic. Where such a pathogenic experience occurs, libido is dammed up, returns to earlier positions, reinforces the component instincts, and endeavors to reach the ego again; that is, it seeks motor discharge. The ego, however, which has meanwhile reached a higher level of development, defends itself and rejects libidinal strivings belonging to an earlier phase of development. Again there arises a very intensive need tension which the ego is no longer able to master within the usual time limit. The ego again becomes helpless and is unable to cope with the increased instinctual dangers stemming, this time, from the component instincts.

The predisposition to neurosis seems to rest with the weakness of the ego in relation to the sexual function "as though the biological opposition between self-preservation and the preservation of the species found psychological expression there" (Freud).

The frequent lack of an actual infantile trauma may be explained in the following way: infantile sexual development proceeds very rapidly and at an uneven pace. If the libido develops too rapidly in comparison with the ego, the latter is incapable of handling the instinct needs, that is, of distributing and binding the instinctual energy in an orderly manner. The refractory instinct then has a traumatic effect, although this effect cannot, at the beginning, be observed. Or else, a part of the instinct may be fixated and inhibited while the ego otherwise is normally developed. The ego is then compelled to ward off the retarded part of the sexual instinct; its discharge is blocked, and the need tension is increased, which again has a traumatic effect.

At this point those fantasies must be mentioned that are remembered as real experiences. Fantasies are manifestations of the actual libidinal development, substitutes, as it were, for real experiences which are yearned for when instinct needs are not gratified. Fantasies, however, are experienced as if they were real events and therefore can have a traumatic effect when they first appear, the more so, since they emerge when gratification fails to occur.

The "traumatic" theory of neuroses thus, by and large, remains unchanged. It merely has to be extended to cover the fact that while there need not always be an external trauma, there must be an inner one in the form of an instinct danger. This internal trauma, in turn, depends on a constitutional factor, namely fixation of libido, and hence is based on a disturbance in the development of the instinctual drives. Fixation and an external infantile experience form a complementary series of etiological factors which provide the disposition for neurosis. Fixation and an external experience have a reciprocal relationship: a weak fixation must be complemented by an intense experience in order to provide a climate favorable for the development of neurosis, whereas a strong fixation in itself favors the development of a neurosis even without an added external experience. At the same time, one must not overlook the fact that an intense external infantile experience may bring about a fixation and thus, in a sense, may change the constitution and predispose it to a neurosis.

There are certain infantile experiences which frequently have a traumatic effect: sexual abuse by adults, seduction, usually by older siblings, seeing or overhearing sexual play or intercourse of adults, most often the parents. The immature ego is not prepared to assimilate such experiences, it represses them either immediately or later on when their memories try to invade the ego. These experiences then form one of the preconditions of neurosis.

The instinct danger involved in the traumatic situation is, however, not sufficient to cause a neurosis. There are, indeed, persons who are able to endure great need tensions without developing a neurosis. One individual, for instance, develops an anxiety neurosis after a short period of sexual abstinence, while another does not become ill even after a long period of abstinence. Just as abstinence leads to need tensions, so do all other inhibitions of instinct discharge. If these tensions reach a certain maximum without being released, feelings of unpleasure arise. Some individuals are able to tolerate unpleasure, while others are not. Those who are not able to endure it develop a neurosis. *Hypersensitivity of the ego to unpleasure would thus be one of the direct causes of neurosis.*

Unpleasure results from a situation where certain instinctual demands which are felt as a danger cannot find gratification. The ego reacts to the instinctual danger with anxiety, a *signal of unpleasure*. Symptom formation, in turn, is initiated by the ego in order to master the danger, to bind the anxiety. The conditions under which anxiety arises are not always the same, for every level of instinct—and ego development has its appropriate precondition of anxiety. Three factors determine these preconditions—a biologic, a phylogenetic, and a psychological factor.

The biologic factor is the helplessness of the child in the first period of life. In contrast to most animals, the human being, for a long period, needs care and protection. This physical helplessness involves dangers, against which the small child is unable to protect himself. Protection is provided by the external world (mother, nurse). Since the persons who first satisfy the child's needs are ever afterward longed for by the child, the wish to be loved arises. The fulfillment of this need for love then provides the best protection against danger. If for any reason the need for love cannot be fulfilled, the danger increases and unpleasure arises, to which the undeveloped ego of the child can react only with anxiety.

The phylogenetic factor is based on the diphasic onset of sexuality, through which a pause (latency) is interpolated in the sexual development of the human being. The first (infantile) phase of this development is concluded with the onset of the latency period, at which time repression, the defense against the infantile instinct demands, occurs. Most of the demands of infantile sexuality are, indeed, felt as dangers, and the defense offers a protection against anxiety in the face of these dangers. (These repressions cause the infantile amnesias.) But with repression the warded-off impulses, at the same time, are fixated, forming a point of attraction for similar impulses in later life, and thus they acquire a tendency to repetition. There is, therefore, the possibility that the second onset of sexuality, in puberty, will be influenced by the infantile patterns.

If this happens, the infantile strivings are reinforced. Since the ego meanwhile has progressed in its development, it feels these strivings as a new danger and refuses to accept and discharge them; it again reacts to the danger with anxiety, as in childhood. *The most direct cause of neurosis would thus be increased and ungratified instinct need, overwhelming need tension* caused by the ego's inability to discharge the increased quantity of energy.

The psychological factor is based on *the inadequacy of the psychic apparatus.* The ego is situated on the boundary between the inner world (id) and the outer world (reality); its reactions, consequently, depend on both. It frequently happens that a stimulus from one side, let us say from the outer world, influences the ego in its behavior not only toward the outer world, but also toward the id. Indeed, the threats and the general attitude of the outer world often make it necessary for the ego to treat the instinctual impulses of the id like dangers from the external world and to ward them off. Against external dangers the ego can protect itself by flight, but there is no such protection against inner, instinct dangers; therefore anxiety develops at first and is followed by the neurotic symptom. The behavior of the ego becomes even more complicated when the superego is fully formed. It is then threatened not only by the external world and the id, but also by the superego. Reactions to dangers from the latter are expressed in fear of the superego (sense of guilt). When there is any disturbance in the cooperation of the psychic agencies, when there is a conflict within the personality or with the outside world, the psychic apparatus fails either totally or partially. Thus a conflict of the ego with the id as well as with the superego or with reality may give rise to a neurosis. A conflict between ego and id is a biologic one, determined by the amount of instinctual energy to be mastered by the ego. A conflict between ego and superego may be considered a social one, inasmuch as the superego is a result of social influences. Conflict with the external world is a conflict with reality. Consequently, neurosis may be precipitated partly by social or cultural factors, but such external factors must be complemented by internal factors in order to evoke a neurosis.

Normally the ego, thanks to its synthetic capacity, is able to carry out its role as mediator and to resolve conflicts. It admits certain instinctual impulses to perception and to action directed toward the outside world, while assimilating and sublimating other portions of the id. If there is a neurotic disposition, the ability to sublimate is impaired and there is an increased *tendency to conflict.* In other words, impairment of the synthetic function of the ego is another of the numerous factors responsible for the causation of neurosis. The inclination for conflict is rooted in the actual conditions under which the different forms of anxiety arise, conditions which depend upon the age level at which the moments of danger first appeared.

In those cases where the inclination for conflict has its roots in a failure of the fusion of instincts, its consequences are most serious. For the free, unmitigated aggressive instincts turn against the ego, where they take effect. Such an ego is then completely paralyzed in its synthetic function.

The particular preconditions for anxiety appropriate to the different stages of development are the following: (1) the danger of psychic helplessness corresponds to the phase of immaturity of the ego; (2) the danger of the loss of objects corresponds to the dependence of the first years of childhood; (3) the danger of castration corresponds to the phallic phase; and (4) fear of the superego corresponds to the latency period. All of these conditions of anxiety may become fixated and reappear with a later neurotic conflict. The ego then reacts with an old form of anxiety to an acute disturbance (instinct danger). It is true that all or some of these situations of danger and conditions for anxiety may persist and provide the basis for mixed forms of neurosis; this, indeed, is usually the case.

There is thus a close relationship between the situation of danger and the form of the neurosis. The danger of psychic helplessness is closely correlated with the actual neurosis, and, if the danger of object loss is combined with immaturity of the ego, a psychosis develops. The danger of the loss of love is related to hysteria; the danger of castration, to phobia; and danger threatening from the superego, to obsessional neurosis. All of these anxiety reactions represent attempts at defense against objective dangers as well as against instinct dangers. Where the anxiety reactions are excessively strong, the defense encounters difficulties. The ego is no longer able to master, within the usual period of time, the increase in the amount of energy evoked by the instinctual stimuli. Individuals who are under the constant pressure of such a defensive struggle are permanently disturbed in their psychic equilibrium and may produce manifest neurotic symptoms.

The neurotic differs from the normal person in that his reactions to dangers are intensified. The neurotic disposition is based on an increased *readiness for anxiety* on the part of the ego, which, on the one hand, clings to old, obsolete conditions for anxiety and, on the other, does not possess the ability to meet the dangers with adequate actions.

To recapitulate, we find that it is fruitless to attempt to discover a single, invariable cause of the neuroses. In general it seems that two etiologic factors have to be taken into account: one has to do with the instinct life and the other with the ego.

Disturbance of the instinct life manifests itself in the fixation of the libido. We do not know of a single factor which alone would be the unmistakable cause of fixation. Since, however, the inertia of the instincts, thus the repetition compulsion, plays a role in fixation, we may infer that where fixation of a sexual instinct is established, the conservative, the destructive component of instinct life has not been sufficiently neutralized by fusion with the sexual instincts. *The instinct disposition to neurosis would hence be based on an inadequate fusion of the two basic instincts.* Support for this assumption might be found in those illnesses where there exists an especially strong inclination to regression, for example in the obsessional neurosis or, even more, in the psychoses (schizophrenia, manic-depressive psychosis). In disorders of the ego several factors must be considered: first, when the ego is not equal to the demands of reality—that is, when it cannot master and distribute economically the stimuli reaching it from the external world—it withdraws the cathexis from perceptions of the external world and cuts itself off from it. Confused and twilight states of hysteric or psychotic type result. Second, the demands of the superego can be so excessive that they compel the ego to thwart the instinctual urges of the id; psychoneuroses then develop. Third, processes may take place in the id which either activate an old situation of danger and cause the ego to produce the anxiety signal, or, as a result of the damming up of the libido, create intense need tensions which automatically bring about anxiety reactions of the ego. In all of these cases the ego proves to be too weak to master the increased quantity of energy produced by internal or external stimuli.

The relationship between ego and id, that between sexual and aggressive instincts, as well as the bisexual factor, crystallize in the oedipus complex. The components of this very complicated formation are in a state of delicate equilibrium. The slightest disturbance of this equilibrium is reflected in the manifestations of the oedipus complex. Therefore, the oedipus complex is rightly considered the core of the neurosis.

The mother is the first love object for both boy and girl. In taking care of the child she is the first person to stimulate sensations of pleasure in him; she is his first seducer.

When the boy enters the phallic phase at the age of about two or three years, his masculinity is awakened and he begins to love and desire his mother sexually. She senses his advances and tries to suppress them. Since she is usually unsuccessful in these attempts, she finally threatens him directly or indirectly with castration. Such threats mobilize the dormant inherited castration complex which becomes manifest sooner or later. The manner in which this complex is mastered is decisive for the health or illness of the boy.

The effects of the castration complex may be manifold: (1) The sexual life of the boy may remain inhibited for the rest of his life. (2) If femininity prevails in his sexual pattern, he easily renounces his wishes for his mother and takes a passive attitude toward his father and later toward other men. (3) For a while he gives up physical masturbation but satisfies himself in fantasies which may be either masculine or feminine, according to the identifications which prevail at that time. If the identification happens to be with his mother, the boy may become homosexual. The boy's sexual development is further complicated by his attitude toward his father. He loves, fears, and hates him at the same time. He tries to avoid his father and to defy him. Such an aloof, defiant attitude toward men may last throughout life. We cannot in this context follow up all the vicissitudes of the male oedipus complex.

Instead, let us consider some vicissitudes of the female oedipus complex. Having no penis, the girl has no castration fear but is resentful of the fact that she lacks a penis; she feels *penis envy*. Disappointment over her lack of a penis induces her to give up manual masturbation much earlier than the boy does and is often responsible for her turning away from sexuality altogether. If the girl does not overcome her penis envy, she competes with boys, behaves like a boy, and often becomes a manifest homosexual.

In the boy, the castration complex puts an end to the oedipus complex, while in the girl, the disappointment, caused by the lack of a penis, and the resentment felt against the mother for having failed to equip her with a penis, contribute to the formation of the girl's oedipus complex; she loves her father and hates her mother.

Finally, identification with the father strengthens the boy's masculinity, and identification with the mother strengthens the girl's femininity.

It is easy to understand that anything which produces a disturbance in the equilibrium within the intricate structure of the oedipus complex, be it an external factor or a failure in development, may cause inner conflicts from which stem neurotic disorders.

In review, the etiology of the neuroses is not uniform. We have become acquainted with several factors, the most important being two large groups, the first of which is biologic, the second, social. The biologic series includes the instinctual disposition and the inadequate reactions of the ego to instinct dangers, namely, increased readiness for anxiety and increased sensitivity to unpleasure. The social series is the one which is dependent on external conditions, as for example, on the social milieu, on economic conditions, and the like. The oedipus complex stands between the two. On the one hand, it is a biologic product; on the other hand, a social product. No one of the etiological factors is sufficient in itself to produce a neurosis. The biologic and social factors complement each other, a fact which is the more significant since an external experience is also able to modify the instinct disposition, that is, in a broader sense, the biologic factors. It is therefore to be expected that with changes in the structure of society the form of neuroses will also change, but only to a certain degree. If one takes into consideration the part the superego plays in the formation of the neuroses, it seems not unlikely that with changed social conditions the internal causes of the neurosis likewise change, since the superego partly represents an image of the demands of society (morality) within the ego.

The external and the internal disposition are complementary and are in a reciprocal relation to each other, that is, with a stronger biologic disposition, a weaker external cause is sufficient to produce a neurosis, and, conversely, with a weaker inner disposition, a stronger external cause is necessary to produce a neurosis. It is evident that we are dealing here with quantitative relations which we cannot measure precisely with the means at our command at present. The ultimate cause of the neurosis hence would be a quantitative factor—difficulty in mastering psychically certain quantities of energy.

Chapter XII

THEORETICAL PRINCIPLES OF PSYCHOANALYTIC THERAPY

DIFFICULTIES OF TREATMENT

The theoretical aspects of the treatment of neurotic illnesses are self-evident to a certain degree on the basis of the preceding chapters. For the sake of clearer understanding, let us attempt to call to mind the essential nature of illness and briefly recapitulate what we have learned about the nature of neurosis.

The illness is in no way a simple process. We may distinguish a primary and a secondary process of illness. The *primary process*, the nucleus of the neurosis, consists of an increased instinctual drive producing pain, anxiety, and conflicts with the ego.

The *secondary process* of illness consists of ego reactions which are stimulated and initiated by the ego's need to avoid pain, unpleasure, and anxiety. These reactions are defenses, such as negation, repression, certain attitudes of the ego, and deviations of character. The entire symptomatology arises out of this defensive struggle. In other words, the final result of this struggle is inhibition and modification of the course taken by the instincts, that is, the barring of some of the unconscious material from consciousness and of the affectivity from motor discharge.

The foremost therapeutic task, therefore, is to make conscious what is unconscious and to facilitate emotional discharge. This task is not an easy one. The attempt to translate unconscious material directly into conscious material—for instance, exclusively symbolic interpretation—usually fails. Where it does succeed, it often gives rise to anxiety which had been eluded or diminished by the various defense mechanisms. There are many additional reasons why a direct approach to the unconscious material of neurotics is generally unsuccessful.

The neurotic is more or less asocial. He tries to gratify his needs not by effecting changes in the external world but by changing his organization in an autoplastic way. In other words, his adaptation to reality is impaired, to a greater or lesser extent. We know that through the mechanisms of defense a part of the neurotic's ego has been split off from his total ego and clings to infantile gratifications and reactions. This part of the ego evaluates as dangerous, stimuli which, in reality, no longer exist. Thus any attempt to influence directly these split-off parts of the ego has little chance of success. Moreover, as a consequence of the split, only a part of the original ego remains active and in contact with reality. Such an ego is a weakened ego which has difficulty in cooperating with the analyst.

The unconscious material which represents the strivings of the id always has the tendency to press forward, to reach the ego through the system Cs, and to abreact in emotions and motility. The defense mechanisms block this pathway and erect various barriers against the intrusion of the id strivings into consciousness. Because of their continuous nature, the instincts cannot be excluded permanently from consciousness by a defense set up only once. In order to maintain such a defense permanently, the ego must expend its energy continuously. We call this continuous expenditure of energy *resistance*. We may thus state that resistances serve as *protector of repression*.

If the nature of resistance is understood, it is clear that the ego, which has expended so much energy for protection against instinct dangers and has organized itself to reject at least a part of the instinctual life, will not abandon its defensive position without a struggle. Some of the resistances may become utterly inaccessible to external influence, while others may yield. One cannot determine in advance how tenacious a resistance is going to be. One might assume that those resistances which are formed latest in the course of illness, such as the *secondary gain through illness*, are the ones which can be most easily broken down through direct influence. But this is not always the case. The traumatic neurosis is a classic example. This neurosis appears comparatively late in life, and yet it is very difficult to cure it. As a matter of fact, the same kind of resistance may be accessible to direct attack at one time, while at another time it can be approached only by first being undermined from the depths. Thus, resistance due to the sense of guilt may in some cases be easily routed, while in other cases it is indestructible.

Direct access to the *repression resistance* is often likewise extremely difficult. This resistance is at work at the very beginning of the process of illness, initiates the defense, as mentioned above, and is usually the real cause of all later resistance, whose task it is to strengthen and to insure the success of the original repression.

The *transference resistance* presents no less difficulty. The treatment meets with a resistance arising from the direct relationship with the analyst; or, the instinct which is under the pressure of the defense becomes reactivated in analysis and is directed toward the person of the analyst. As in the transference, old relations are *repeated compulsively*, the patient has the tendency to act them out in the treatment rather than to recollect. Since the transference resistances also serve to gratify repressed instinctual drives, they will strive to assert themselves under all circumstances.

The *repetition compulsion* appears not only in the transference situation but also independently, outside of the transference situation. It stems from the unconscious id and fixates the patterns of instinctual expressions. These patterns are resistant to change; they cannot be influenced directly. If, in the course of treatment, resistances arising from the compulsion to repeat are transformed into ego resistances, they become accessible to direct influence; this may lead to a changed attitude of the ego toward the demands of the id. Such changes, however, do not always take place, and the analyst may be powerless in all his attempts to help the patient to escape his perhaps tragic fate.

It seems that many of the resistances form a narcissistic protection of the ego against the dangers threatened by the excessive demands of the id. Apparently the onrush of the instinctual drives mobilizes the libido of the ego to form countercharges (countercathexes). The narcissistic libido of the ego is then increased at the expense of object libido. Thus a patient with an overnarcissistic ego will have difficulty in establishing a firm transference. In other words, the degree of influence the psychoanalyst can exercise upon the patient depends upon the amount of free object libido. It is difficult, though not impossible, to establish contact with extremely narcissistic patients, among whom we may count the psychotics; hence it is difficult, though not impossible, to influence them. Moreover, very narcissistic patients are excessively disturbed in their relation to reality, which adds to the difficulties of treatment.

Aside from narcissism, there are other factors that limit the application and results of psychoanalytic therapy. Outstanding among them is the relation of ego strength to the strength of the instincts. It is difficult to define the concept of a "strong" ego or a "strong" instinct, for we cannot measure either the energy of the ego or the energy of the instincts. We can only estimate their *relative* strength or weakness. The stronger the instincts, the stronger the ego will have to be in order to *master* or to *subjugate* them. If this relation is disturbed, the ego breaks down. If the energies of the instincts overflow the ego, the latter becomes, to a greater or lesser extent, confused in its relation to reality; it distorts or even severs its relations with the external world. Recovery thus depends on the ability of the ego to re-establish an optimal relationship between its own strength and the strength of the id strivings.

Here again we are confronted with the problem of relative quantities. Thus the concept of psychic health again seems to depend on the relative strength of the energies of the id and those of the ego.

The harmony between the three agencies of the personality—id, ego, and superego—depends on the reliability of the synthetic function of the ego, that is, on its ability to mediate intrapsychically as well as to mediate between the demands of reality and those of the internal world (psychic derivatives of the instincts as well as the superego). Frequently there exists a latent conflict between the agencies of the personality— a conflict which remains silent so long as it is mitigated by the mediation of the ego. It may, however, become manifest if the synthetic function of the ego is weakened.

As we know, psychic conflicts may arise between various elements— between ego and external world, and between ego and id or superego. The conflict between ego and superego results in the state of mind called feeling of guilt. Here, again, the intensity of this feeling determines the pace of recovery. Sometimes it is so overwhelming and the need for punishment so imperative that all attempts of the analyst to help the patient are futile.

As we are confronted with a variety of conflicts whose origin and localization in the psychic structure differ from each other, it is easily understood that analysis cannot solve all of them at once and that always, even after a successful analysis, there remains a residue of conflicts which may flare up on some later occasion.

Besides, we frequently meet with an *inclination to conflict* and suffering which is derived from masochistic tendencies of the individual and is, therefore, very difficult to overcome. This inclination seems to express itself also in the castration complex of the male and the penis envy of the female. Their derivatives are often so complex and tenacious that they resist all endeavors of the analyst to diminish their power over the patient.

Another factor to be considered in psychoanalytic treatment is the ego's ability to endure pain and tension. Lack of this ability, or rather the inability to learn how to endure frustration, sets a limit to all treatment.

Constitution, for instance homosexuality, or the state of fusion or defusion of instincts on the part of the id, and the capacity for sublimation on the part of the ego have also to be taken into consideration as limiting or favoring factors in psychoanalytic treatment. The same applies to certain traits of character. Persons with certain character deviations often do not know that their behavior is neurotic. They have no insight into the motives of many of their convictions, predilections, and actions, which are frequently harmful to themselves or to others. They always find superficial rationalizations for actions that they carry out impulsively. The discrepancy between their conscious intentions and their achievement is the result of a split ego; one part of the ego does not know what the other part wants or does. It is very difficult to influence such an ego because the communication between the "realistic" ego and the repressed one is blocked.

We have certainly not enumerated all of the limitations of psychoanalytic treatment, but for our purposes it may suffice to have mentioned the most important ones.

Since the core of the neurosis consists essentially of the conflict between the strivings of the id and those of the ego, it seems that besides converting unconscious material into conscious material the therapeutic task involves establishing peace between the opposing parts of the personality. How is this to be done when, as we know, it is impossible to gain direct access to the id? We can influence the ego to give up certain resistances and thus to facilitate the conversion of repressed unconscious material of the id into preconscious material of the ego. When the material of the id enters the orbit of the ego, the unconscious conflict between these two agencies of the personality can be solved in one way or another. Thus it is obvious that psychoanalytic therapy, by directly influencing the ego, at the same time influences the id indirectly.

However, the fact that the neurotic employs so many defenses as a protection against the intrusion of the repressed material into the ego, makes one wonder why the patient seeks help through psychoanalytic treatment at all. From a priest, a hypnotist, or another kind of psychotherapist he could receive reassurance, comfort, and the like. Treatment by such a person would temporarily enforce the repressions and thus appease the conflicts. The psychoanalyst, on the contrary, first of all calls the patient's attention to his inner conflicts, the sources of which are not known to either of them, and asks him to be helpful in discovering the unknown, the repressed. Thus, from the very beginning, the aims of the analyst are opposed to those of the patient, to the wishes of his repressing ego. How then is psychoanalytic treatment introduced—and a cure accomplished—in spite of these seemingly insurmountable obstacles?

PREREQUISITES OF TREATMENT

Certain recuperative tendencies are at work in neuroses as they are in organic diseases. They express themselves even in the symptom formation as such. The analyst, like any other physician, takes advantage of these tendencies, provided that certain basic preconditions for successful treatment are fulfilled. The most important one among them is the possibility of establishing rapport between patient and analyst. This can be accomplished only if at least a part of the patient's ego is intact, that is, if he has retained the ability to comprehend and to express his thoughts, feelings, and emotions, even if only in a distorted and primitive way. It is true that the ego of every neurotic is split and thus limited in its relations with reality. Nevertheless, it is also true that a part of the neurotic's —and to a lesser extent, a part of the psychotic's—ego remains intact and capable of rapport with the environment. Such an ego, however limited its function may be, has enough free libido for object cathexis so that transference can develop. It is this part of the ego with which the analyst can start his work.

If such an ego is aware of the illness, if the patient suffers and feels that his symptoms, peculiarities, and character traits interfere with his life, he is ready for treatment. If such awareness is missing, it must be provoked, even at the risk of a temporary psychic breakdown.

In character neuroses such awareness is very rare. The ego of this kind of patient always has a ready stock of rationalizations for the unconscious motivations of his ideas, convictions, emotions, and actions. The analysis of this group of patients is very difficult. Many candidates for psychoanalysis in didactic treatment may be counted among those who are not aware of their peculiarities of character. Lack of suffering and of insight frequently causes the inordinate duration of didactic analyses. Often, however, the lack of suffering and insight is overcome by scientific curiosity and the wish to learn to be a psychoanalyst, though more often by a psychic breakdown. Suffering can speed the analysis of character neuroses and, in symptom neuroses, stimulate the wish for recovery. It is very difficult to analyze an individual who is not aware of his illness or who has no real wish for recovery.

THE WISH FOR RECOVERY

When a person who is physically ill seeks help from a physician, he follows the latter's advice and collaborates with him toward their common goal, which is an active one on the part of the physician and a passive one on the part of the patient: to cure and to be cured. There is no disagreement between them as to the meaning of cure. When a neurotic turns to an analyst for help, he generally expects from the treatment something other than what the analyst can offer him. Thus, a patient who is a professional but unsuccessful writer expects that the analyst will make him a prominent writer. The analyst, however, can promise him only that, after a successful analysis, he will be as good a writer as, according to his talent, he would have become under normal circumstances. This type of initial misunderstanding on the part of the patient often forms the core of conflicts between patient and analyst which, however, can for the most part be directed into useful channels.

In introducing the treatment, the analyst demands of his patient absolute sincerity in confiding to him all of his most intimate ideas, memories, fantasies, and experiences, even at the expense of temporary discomfort or suffering. In exchange, the analyst promises him help in regaining health, that is, in becoming able to enjoy life and to cope with the exigencies of reality. A pact is made between patient and analyst. This pact is based on the need of human nature for help, security, and protection. Every ill person, be he physically or psychically ill, is helpless, like a little child. In his helplessness he is passive and ready to accept help from anybody who promises relief. He craves reassurance and comfort from his therapist (no matter who he may be), like a child who actually needs for his survival protection by father or mother.

In general, the patient expects from the analyst liberation from all his inhibitions, anxieties, and symptoms, as well as the license to fulfill all his instinctual desires. Although sooner or later he becomes disappointed in his analyst's omnipotence, the treatment can be carried on, in the beginning, if the conscious wish for recovery is matched by the unconscious infantile need for help, as well as by the unconscious wish to satisfy the repressed strivings. These factors together stimulate the transference which finally takes over the wish for recovery and thus becomes one of the main driving forces of the treatment. When the positive transference sets in, the real collaboration with the analyst can begin. Thus, in spite of the inner forces working against analysis, the patient starts his treatment when the aims of his "realistic" ego are enforced by those of the split-off ego as well as by the repressed instinctual demands; in other words, when the conscious wish for recovery is supported by the unconscious id.

Gratification derived from the realization of the motives contained in the wish for recovery thus forms the premium which induces the patient to begin his analysis in a conscientious way. In fact, sometimes the material flows in such a full stream that the analyst can easily guess the patient's basic conflict; of course, he does not communicate his insight to the patient at this point, as it would be useless or even harmful.

However, the pact with the analyst is seldom kept to the letter; the psychoanalytic rule of *free associations* is soon broken in one way or another. But the patient still talks. If he stops talking, the analysis stops unless the analyst can guess the meaning of the silence. Talking without communicating much of the secret ideas which at the time may be unknown to the patient can have many meanings. Usually the patient is afraid of silence; then talking is a reaction formation and protection against anxiety. But talking may also be used directly as a means of resistance, for hiding unwelcome ideas or memories. In this case, the patient derives narcissistic pleasure from the belief that he has the power to mislead his analyst. Talk, which in analysis is almost the exclusive and the best means of communication, may thus become one of the most important tools of resistance. When the analyst tries to detect the meaning of this resistance, he discovers that there are many ways of talking in analysis and that they indicate certain character traits of the patient.

One brief example out of many: a patient who associated conscientiously, reporting in a meticulous way, produced endless chains of associations. When I interrupted him and gave an interpretation, he would seemingly accept it, yet would have to explain further and further, in more detail, what had already been interpreted, and then give the interpretation in his own formulation. By talking in this way, he revealed the essence of his relationship to his father and later to his superiors. He displayed his compulsion to make ever-renewed attempts to triumph over his father, and likewise over his analyst, in order to show his own superiority. In his apparent obedience to the basic psychoanalytic rule, the patient is able to spite the analyst with his talk, just as he may have done in childhood in relation to his father or mother. Spite contains an element of narcissistic gratification.

The analysis cannot proceed if the patient does not develop a positive transference. In other words, he cannot collaborate with the analyst if he does not love him, nor can the analysis proceed if the patient does not feel loved by the analyst. One cannot be intimate with another person if he feels that this person does not care for him. The fact that the analyst pays attention, listens to the patient, and works on his problems with him, is often sufficient evidence for him that the analyst loves him. When a patient has the impression that his analyst does not listen or does not pay attention to him, he feels hurt and often becomes angry. The gratification that the patient derives from his relation with the analyst is not only one of object relations but also a narcissistic one. His ego feels uplifted, stronger. Further narcissistic gratification is offered by the legitimate occupation with himself. It is not only not forbidden to pay attention to one's own thoughts, fantasies, and wishes, but it is even required by the analyst. On similar lines, if in a more sublimated way, narcissistic gratification is gained from the intellectual performance, when the patient starts to understand himself and to see the motivations of the main trends of his life. This is particularly true of those who began their analysis out of interest in the unconscious working of the mind, such as psychiatrists, psychologists, educators.

All such gratifications are agreeable to the patient and, in the beginning, they further the treatment. But very often they contain the seeds for future resistances. At any rate, the introductory stage of analysis is only a transitory one which varies in duration and is only a preparation for the actual analysis. Certainly not all analyses begin in the way described above. They may, from the start, present difficulties which have to be considered as resistances and dealt with accordingly.

Frequently patients discuss topics at the beginning of the analysis which are disagreeable and painful to the conscious ego—and yet this provides temporary relief. The following considerations may offer a partial explanation of this phenomenon.

Every process which starts in the unconscious has a progressive tendency. It endeavors to reach the system of consciousness and perception, that is, to become conscious and to find affective and motor discharge. In neurosis, where direct instinctual expression is inhibited, the pressure from the unconscious id is stronger than in health, and therefore the *need for discharge is greater* than where instinct energy is not dammed up. Hence the neurotic has the tendency involuntarily to *unmask his repressed unconscious.* One may say that there exists in every neurotic a compulsion to unmask himself. If the patient, in addition, suffers from a strong feeling of guilt, this compulsion takes on the character of a *compulsion to confess* (Reik). The patient suffers and humiliates himself as if the confession were a self-punishment. It fulfills a need to share the knowledge of one's sin and brings relief analogous to that of confession in the Catholic church. In fact, for many patients, analysis is at the begining of treatment a confession in which they unburden themselves of their feeling of guilt and are prepared to take the punishment. This "confessing," however, can also serve as an enormous resistance, since the patient may make use of it to speak endlessly of his real or supposed sins. Often it seems as if feelings of guilt and need for punishment were considered meritorious, something to be proud of, thus satisfying narcissism.

The introductory phase of the treatment fulfills an important task. It deepens the transference. Then the patient entrusts himself to the guidance of the analyst, and as a result, transference replaces the wish for recovery.

THE ANALYST AS PROTECTOR AGAINST ANXIETY

Contact between patient and analyst is established through the transference, which is facilitated by the fact that every human being feels the need for a companion. The majority of neurotics, perhaps all of them, are, in spite of their disturbed social relations, anxious for contact with another person; in some instances, as in the initial phases of schizophrenia, there exists even a hunger for objects. But the tendency to make contact with another person meets with resistances.

We know that the symptom formation removes the necessity for the patient to develop anxiety. How, then, is it possible that he does not immediately react with anxiety when forced by his analyst to reveal the repressed material which had originally caused anxiety? Frequently the anxiety is not perceived in its original connection but, instead, the analyst is felt as an object of anxiety. Briefly, it seems as if every patient were afraid of his analyst. This, naturally, often makes the treatment difficult. However, when the patient suffers intensely enough and his need for help becomes very urgent, he overcomes his initial anxiety and submits to the influence of the analyst. Then the analyst changes, in the patient's mind, from an object of anxiety into a protector against anxiety.

Trying to understand this change in the patient's attitude, we must not forget that there are various kinds of anxiety. Expressed in general terms, anxiety is a reaction to the threats of the superego and the excessive demands of the id. In the course of analysis, the patient partly identifies with the analyst, which results in the latter's introjection, incorporation in the patient's ego. The analyst becomes a part of the patient's ego, as it were, and strengthens it. The patient feels in alliance with the analyst, united with him, and protected by him against the dangers of superego and id. Therefore he temporarily gives up the anxiety reaction as superfluous under the circumstances. This may explain why most severe states of anxiety disappear at the beginning of the treatment and flare up again only later. Indeed, the patient's superego is mitigated through contact with the analyst. Moreover, his need for object relation as well as for protection is satisfied; he is no longer alone.

However, the objection that not every patient is afraid of his analyst cannot be ignored. It is a matter of fact that there are many patients who freely express their love, hate, or defiance toward the analyst, even at the beginning of the analysis. Nevertheless, close observation will always reveal some sign of anxiety. If we remember how timidly the majority of patients begin their analysis, how they must be encouraged to give free expression to their thoughts, feelings, and ideas, we cannot overlook the concealed anxiety. Many patients declare openly that they would like to say everything but are prevented from doing so by their anxiety. Others talk at the beginning with such speed and urgency that they seem to be running away from their anxiety. If there is an excessive feeling of guilt, the patients talk only of their "sins" in the beginning and attach themselves to the analyst in a masochistic way. This attachment seems to protect them from anxiety.

To recapitulate: the patient sets up the analyst as his ideal, finds protection in him and, finally, transfers onto him the id strivings—love and hate. With this preparation, the influencing from within can be effected and the slow dissolution of the repression resistance can be undertaken.

Topography and Dynamics of Treatment

We have learned that it is the aim of all the various resistances to secure the success of the original repression. We also know that the defense mechanisms prevent the unconscious material first from becoming preconscious and then from entering the system Cs of the ego. The defenses can be considered successful when they have brought about amnesias in hysteria, displacement in phobia, disruption of connections between certain psychic elements in compulsive neurosis, projection in paranoia, and so on. In order to maintain the defenses, however, the ego undergoes changes of its organization which result in certain reaction formations, in deviations of character traits, in the split of the ego, and so on. As analysis aims at the lifting of repressions or the weakening of defenses and the reproduction of precisely those old infantile memories whose repression stimulated the ego changes, the task of analysis can be accomplished only if the attitude of the ego toward the warded-off material of the id is changed. The ego, once it is protected by the analyst, relaxes its defenses or resistances, thus enabling the patient to face the hitherto warded-off material without fear or with only slight fear. Then he can recollect what was forgotten and reproduce and relive old infantile experiences which in the past caused. anxiety. Thus he gains courage to look into himself and to see connections between fantasies, memories, and experiences of the past which had been interrupted by the process of defense or which never existed on a conscious level. He is freed not only of the fear of remembering, but also of the fear of seeing connections between separate elements of his complex psychic life. Freed of this anxiety, he is now able to recognize his conflicts and, consequently, the unconscious meaning of his neurosis.

At the beginning of the psychoanalytic era, the recollection and abreaction of the traumatic events was considered the active agent of the cure. Although the technique of analytic treatment as well as the conception of psychic trauma underwent certain changes, nevertheless the basic ideas of both trauma and treatment in principle have remained the same. Through the most precise possible recollecting, the original "traumatic" situation, experiences, or a whole such chain, is reproduced, and the more accurate this reproduction, the better the therapeutic result. Since the infantile trauma is no longer an actual one, it can be reproduced without fear and subject to reality testing. (When the trauma occurred, the patient was a child, but now he is grown up.) Since, in addition, the patient is forced to relive unpleasure in remembering painful experiences, he learns to endure unpleasure or pain. (Hypersensitivity to pain, inability to tolerate need tensions, and readiness for anxiety are indeed characteristic of the neurotic.)

Not all traumatic experiences are real experiences; those which are found to be imaginary belong to one or another of the typical fantasies of mankind. One might be inclined to assume that their reproduction is of no therapeutic value. Yet, strange as it may seem, it brings at least temporary relief. More important, however, is the fact that the recapture of these fantasies is of great help for further psychoanalytic procedure.

The processes which lead to the recapture of infantile, repressed unconscious material and to its conversion into conscious thoughts, ideas, wishes, strivings, and so on, are called "working through." They are of various categories and can be considered from different points of view— the topographic, the economic, and the dynamic. Freud has named "metapsychology" the consideration of a psychic process in terms of topography, economy, and dynamics. Since he used this term before the formulation of ego psychology, I should like the *structural* aspect to be included in the concept of metapsychology. Though topographically the system Ucs coincides with the id, structurally parts of the ego are unconscious, as is the case with the sense of guilt or the need for punishment.

The unconscious material of the id can be perceived by the ego as a chain of associations which contain preconscious thoughts, ideas, recollections, fantasies, and so on. Examining the material thus gained in the course of psychoanalytic treatment from the standpoint of mental topography, one can see how this material progresses from the system Ucs through the system Pcs into the system Cs. One can also observe that, through passage from one psychic system to another, the rebellious strivings of the id are integrated and mastered by the ego, whereby the ego itself undergoes certain changes.

Considering the same material from the economic or energic point of view, one can observe how, by the undoing of the repression or the lifting of the repressed unconscious material into consciousness, unpleasure is spared. Simultaneously the approximate amount of psychic energy expended for the maintenance of the defenses can be estimated.

In addition, the process of becoming conscious is accompanied by a reshuffling of certain cathexes and countercathexes, that is, a redisplacement of psychic energy from one psychic system to another. As long as the pathogenic material is unconscious, the patient cannot, of course, perceive it; as soon as it becomes preconscious, it is within the reach of the system Cs of the ego. Repression consumes much psychic energy. The lifting of repression makes the spending of excessive psychic energy unnecessary, and through the redistribution of this energy within the psychic systems an equilibrium is achieved.

Studying the analytic material from the dynamic point of view, the analyst can recognize that the symptoms emerge from psychic conflicts and that they are the result of these conflicts. He can also see that analysis frees psychic forces that hitherto were employed in maintaining the burden of defense. Following the further vicissitudes of these freed forces, one can often observe that they are used in the formation of sublimations.

The neurotic symptom appeases the neurotic conflict. The symptom is formed by an interplay of forces of the id and the ego. Through analysis, the psychic representations of the id are uncovered and the opposing demands of the ego exposed. The analytic work bares the layers of the psychic conflicts and, opening to inspection one layer after another, demonstrates how the symptoms developed.

As long as the ego is in control of the repression, the psychic conflict remains dormant, but when the ego is weakened or the pressure of the instincts increased, the repressions fail and the conflict is reactivated. In order to render it inactive again, the ego employs various new means of defense and succeeds in this way in keeping the conflict under control again. These means consist in new cathexes and countercathexes which, in fact, enforce the original repression. The result of this psychic struggle is usually a neurotic symptom which forms a compromise. Both the ego as the repressing agent, on the one hand, and the repressed instinctual drives, on the other hand, find their satisfaction in the symptom. In this respect, as in many others, the symptom is similar to the dream. The latter, too, forms a compromise in which wishes of id and ego are fulfilled.

The actual ego is preconscious and ruled by the secondary process; the id is unconscious and ruled by the primary process. If it is correct that the neurotic symptom is a compromise between ego and id, then it may be assumed that both the primary and the secondary process participate in the symptom formation. As a creation of the ego, the symptom is subject to the laws of the secondary process; as a creation of the id, to the laws of the primary process. In so far as it is a creation of the ego, it may thus appear quite reasonable, while in so far as it is a creation of the id, it appears nonsensical. In fact it is a mixture of both in which, at the end, the nonsense prevails. In the course of treatment both these ways of working of the psychic apparatus are laid open and subject to the interpretation of the analyst.

Let us stop here and try to see how our theories look in practice. For this purpose I am going to examine an example from the analyst's daily work. This example represents a small fragment of the analysis of a patient suffering from attacks of obsessional questioning. He would ask himself questions and try to answer them. When the answers did not satisfy him, he became very excited and was overwhelmed by severe attacks of anxiety.

His first attack occurred when he was about sixteen years old. At this time he was studying the Renaissance period at school. One day on his way home from school he asked himself for the first time, when, precisely, the Renaissance started and when it ended. He could, of course, find no satisfactory answer. Then he reformulated the question, until finally he became confused, dizzy, and panicky.

His question about the beginning and end of the Renaissance was a legitimate and reasonable one. Scholars before him had tried to answer this question and failed. What was unreasonable were his forced and passionate attempts to answer increasingly difficult questions which seemed *a priori* doomed to remain unanswered.

In his analysis, after a long time, his associations brought to the surface a recollection from his eleventh or twelfth year: One day his sister, four years his senior, came down to the kitchen carrying a bundle. He asked her what it contained but she became very embarrassed, ran out of the kitchen, and threw her bundle in the ash can outside. He ran after her, got hold of the package, unwrapped it, and found bloody cloth in it. This discovery upset him enormously; he did not understand what all this meant, but did not dare to ask any questions.

At such a point, the analyst feels compelled to do something with the material, to make an interpretation.

I told the patient that he had wanted to ask his sister questions about menstruation, but did not dare to do so at that time and forgot the whole incident. Much later, however, a legitimate question emerged which, though apparently having nothing to do with sexuality, yet had some hidden connection with it.

Obviously, what he wanted to know at the onset of his illness was not the meaning of a historical period but that of the menstrual period. Each of these two questions belonged to a different psychic system. The first was conscious, the second unconscious. The word "period" used in the context of history was acceptable to the ego, it was ego-syntonic; the same word in a sexual connection was rejected by the ego; it was ego-dystonic.

Up to puberty, his sexuality was kept more or less under the control of the ego, through athletics and an idealized friendship with a boy. When the sexual demands increased in puberty, his ego was not strong enough to keep them under control but was strong enough to prevent them—at least in part—from entering consciousness. This was accomplished by shifting the psychic accent from questions about menstrual periods to those about historical periods. Through this kind of displacement of psychic energy—called countercathexis—the original repression was enforced. For this process Freud used the term "actual" repression or afterexpulsion of the originally repressed material. The word "period" was very suitable for this purpose because, with its double meaning, it formed a sort of bridge between the conscious and the unconscious, and thus expressed the attitude of the ego as well as that of the repressed id. The word comprised two contrasting ideas and was the representative of a compromise which, put in question form, resulted in a symptom. That it was just this word and not another one was accidental, brought about by the fact that the boy happened to be learning about historical periods in school, at a time when he was being torn by conflicts. Under different circumstances, another word might have been amalgamated with the dynamic repressed sexual ideas and formed another, yet essentially not different, symptom.

The associative material produced by the patient in the course of an analysis is mostly chaotic, since it is a derivative of the unconscious id. The analyst tries to bring order out of this chaos. He achieves this by interpreting. To make an interpretation means to supplement or guess an idea which was alluded to in the associative material, to reduce a distorted idea to its simpler components; briefly, to make the material intelligible, to read sense into it.

There are two kinds of interpretation—ego and id interpretation. This means that at one time we approach the problem from the point of view of the ego and at another time from the standpoint of the id. In the first case, we demonstrate to the patient the reactions of his ego in relation to his problems; in the second case, the strivings of the id. In the initial stages of treatment we usually try to discover the resistances of the ego. Later on, such sharp delineation between ego and id interpretations occurs less frequently; they become even more interrelated. After all, we must not forget that the ego originally is one with the id and only in the course of development becomes differentiated from it.

I gave my patient the interpretation that he had at an early time instantaneously repressed the impulse to ask his sister questions about the menstrual period, and then much later had tried in an unconscious way to get an answer to this question from a quite different angle. This interpretation did not impress him at the moment. He denied any knowledge about menstruation at the age of eleven. Yet, apparently the interpretation made some dent in his resistances because he produced more and more material which subsequently confirmed the interpretation. Slowly, at long intervals, bits of material came up which finally culminated in recollections of the events immediately preceding the appearance of his first manifest symptoms.

When he was fifteen years old, his family moved from a house in the country to a city apartment. Here he had the opportunity to peep into neighbors' windows. Among many exciting scenes, he saw a couple having sexual intercourse. More exciting than this, however, was the sight of the nude man's genitals. His erect penis seemed enormous to him and stimulated a number of questions. How is sexual intercourse performed? How can a man penetrate a woman? How is the penetration performed? Does the man rip open the woman with his penis? Does blood flow then, and how much? He became so restless that he left the apartment, ran out into the streets, to movies, to burlesque shows, hoping to find somewhere the answers to his painful questions. But he could not recover his peace of mind and continued to torture himself with questions which climaxed in the one simple question: "How can a man do that to a woman?"

At this point in his report I felt compelled to help him by adding another question which, it seemed to me, the patient was avoiding to repeat. It was: "Does my father do that to my mother?" This question, which implied an interpretation, produced a storm in the patient. He exclaimed that that was just what he thought but never dared to think about; that he had always pushed away faster than it appeared any mental picture of father and mother in connection with these questions.

The following night he dreamed that he was in bed with his wife making love to her but felt as if his son were watching him. When he turned his head toward his son's bed in order to verify his uneasy sensation, he saw the child lying quietly in the crib, but he was not sure whether the boy was actually asleep or only pretending to sleep. This dream reproduced unmistakably the primal scene. However, the patient could not believe in the correctness of the interpretation, although he felt it plausible. First he could not remember anything. Yet the attitude of his son in the dream, pretending to sleep, seemed familiar to him. He remembered that he himself often pretended to sleep when he was supposed to be asleep. Then slowly he remembered his crib, the parents' bedroom, the noises coming from their bed which awoke him at night. One could sense the excitement and the unformulated questions of the little child, questions which the mature man tried to answer in his neurosis. Such experiences occurred repeatedly between the patient's first and third year, certainly not later than when he was three and a half years old.

Here we must stop because a further study of all the ramifications of this case could fill a volume. However, this example demonstrates to a sufficient degree the psychic forces forming a symptom, their ramifications, and stratification.

This example throws light also on the question of ego and id interpretation; we do not interpret at will, but we interpret as and when the material warrants interpretation. In a sense, the patient has the lead in analysis; *he* gives the clue in his free associations, and we follow after him with our interpretations, although the analyst often understands the situation before the time indicated for interpretation by the patient's associations. When I gave my patient the interpretation about his sexual curiosity, I showed him also the reactions of his ego to his sexual problems. The interpretation was an id interpretation in so far as it concerned his repressed sexual life, an ego interpretation in so far as it involved his defensive attitude toward it. On the surface, this total (ego and id) interpretation seemed unsuccessful. The patient denied any early knowledge about menstruation as well as the existence in his mind of a connection between menstrual period and periods in history. But he confirmed that he had always shied away from all sexual problems, that he was still so bashful and timid that he did not undress even in the presence of his own wife, and so on.

Thus he confirmed the ego interpretation directly, the id interpretation indirectly, by reporting further sexual material which was disconnected. Only when the id interpretation succeeded in establishing a connection between his sadomasochistic ideas about sexual intercourse in relation to the oedipus complex and his despairing questioning about sex problems did the memory of the primal scene emerge in the form of a dream. This dream contained the traumatic experience of observing parental intercourse, material which probably never had been conscious in the true sense.

In the first stages of analysis, ego interpretations prevail, of course. However, there is always an interaction between ego and id interpretation. An ego interpretation often leads to the emergence of id material and reconstruction of instinctual development, while an id interpretation often sheds light on certain character traits or certain habits and permits the reconstruction of their meaning.

In addition, this example shows the part that language plays in the act of repression as well as in the act of restitution or of the undoing of repression.

Our patient's first manifest symptom appeared when he tried to find an answer to his question about the Renaissance period of history. The stress was laid upon the word "period"; the patient wanted to know how long this period lasted, exactly when it started and when it ended. When he first reported the symptom, he did not in the least suspect that this question had any connection with sexual problems. He used a word with a double meaning, a sexual and a nonsexual one; its deeper meaning was unknown to him. Obviously, the sexual meaning was repressed, its nonsexual counterpart was not repressed. But the choice of the word serving the symptom was influenced by the repressed. This word was suited to representing both the repressed and the repressing force.

In analysis we often see that not only the choice of words but also the way in which they are used are in the service of further resistances. (A patient's speech, for instance, may become unintelligible at times.) In our example we see clearly that—as we have learned before —with repression the verbal ideas are separated from the concrete ideas to which they belong. Thus the respective train of thoughts becomes unconscious. What remains conscious and is perceived by consciousness are words. These verbal ideas are remnants of an entity of optic, acoustic, tactile, visceral, coenesthetic perceptions, which genetically precede them. Indeed, our consciousness is a sense organ for the perception not only of external but also of internal processes.

In the course of analysis, our patient recovered his unconscious, repressed ideas which he then could unite with the verbal ideas (period) previously disconnected from them. Consequently, his conscious idea (the question about the historical period) disclosed a quite different meaning.

If repression is brought about by the separation of verbal from concrete ideas, it follows that the lifting of repression occurs with the reestablishment of the connection between these ideas, a process through which the excessive expenditure of psychic energy used in maintaining the repression becomes superfluous.

No doubt, finding verbal expression for unconscious ideas is a creative act. The poet feels relieved when he finds words to express his stirring thoughts and feelings; sometimes he invents new words, as does the schizophrenic. There is, however, the difference that the schizophrenic operates only with the preconscious verbal ideas whereas in the poet's mind they are connected with the unconscious concrete ideas. In the course of the cure the neurotic, too, learns to connect again unconscious and preconscious ideas.

We know how relieved we feel when we can finally formulate an idea which had been stirring in us without taking clear shape. It is striking how happy children are when they become able to name things and to give verbal expression to thoughts and emotions hitherto not fully conscious. Indeed, the child begins to become conscious with the development of speech.

RECOLLECTING

Memories are elicited in many ways. First, in a direct way, when the analyst asks the patient in an authoritative manner to associate freely, the patient involuntarily produces memories as if in a hypnotic trance. The material obtained in this stage of quasi-hypnotic submission is then interpreted. Interpretation of the psychoanalytic material and gradual reconstruction of the psychological background in turn facilitate the emergence of new memories of repressed unconscious ideas, wishes, fantasies. It is true that our "suggestions," interpretations, and constructions help to weaken the resistances against the unconscious memories, thus preparing the ground for the entering into consciousnes of the repressed material. But is this sufficient to cause the material actually to become conscious?

Clinical observation shows that, in spite of all resistances, the majority of patients wish to remember the events of their life. Even those who have forgotten their most important experiences produce at least substitutes for them. What is the real cause of this? Is it an automatic process or are there other factors at work which propel the repressed material into the preconscious ego and then change it into conscious memories?

First of all, the material of the system Ucs seems to have a "progressive" tendency, that is, a tendency to propel itself upward, to enter the system Cs of the ego. This tendency seems to be the result of strong pressure within the id caused by the defenses; it manifests itself in various ways— in the patient's restlessness, in his behavior, symptoms, and many other expressions. If the repressive power of the ego is weakened through the analysis or through other reasons, the dammed-up energy of the id can, without difficulties or with only slight ones, reach the system Cs of the ego and be discharged not only in affectivity but also in the act of recollecting. This seems to be accompanied by a feeling of relief.

While this kind of recollecting apparently decreases the intrapsychic tension and thus produces pleasure, there is another kind of recollecting which is not accompanied by pleasure. This latter kind is promoted by the repetition compulsion. According to the principle of the repetition compulsion, previous experiences are relived automatically and often contrary to the needs of the ego. While the progressive tendency of the strivings of the id is governed by the pleasure-unpleasure principle and thus ruled by an economic factor, the tendency to repeat is beyond any pleasure principle. It represents a principle which seems constantly at work, without regard to the happiness or unhappiness of the individual. It drives the individual to repeat or act out wishes, fantasies, ideas, of the id, rather than to remember them. Nevertheless, in the course of treatment, the tendency to repeat is brought more or less under the control of the ego, which can then increase its capacity to recollect and decrease repetition in acting out.

There is still another factor that stimulates remembering, a factor which is possibly a variation of the repetition compulsion. Memories revived under the influence of this factor are felt as if they were actual, present experiences. They are called forth by a tendency to re-establish in a hallucinatory way what once was experienced in reality. It seems that this tendency is normally counteracted by another factor, the reality-testing faculty of the ego. When this latter factor is weakened, the tendency to hallucinate—which may also be considered as a tendency to establish "identity of perception"—gains the upper hand.

This phenomenon can be observed in dreams of normal persons, in hallucinations of psychotics, and in illusions or hallucinations of neurotics in an analytic session. When dreaming, the ego has abandoned its reality-testing and its logical thinking. As a result, the thinking process makes a regression to perception of internal stimuli. A similar, though not identical process seems to occur in hallucinatory psychoses, and not infrequently, in analytic sessions. In the latter, we ask the patient to give up his judgment, his testing of reality. It then often happens that the patient sees mental pictures which seem to him actual experiences. Soon, however, he tries to devaluate the reality of these pictures, but further analysis usually proves that they do contain a grain of truth. Old experiences are not only revived in analysis but perceived with the vividness of recent events. To the dreamer, the inhibitory and selective function of reality testing is restored after awakening; to the psychotic, in the remission; and to the neurotic after the session, and largely during the session.

In analysis, the repressed unconscious material is thus brought to the attention of the actual ego with the help of the progressive tendency of the id strivings, of the repetition compulsion, and of the tendency of the ego to "identity of perceptions." The conversion of a repressed experience into a conscious memory may then, in one instance, follow the pleasure-unpleasure principle and ease the intrapsychic tension; at another time, it may follow the repetition compulsion and be a substitute for action and, in still another case, it may follow the tendency to "identity of perceptions" and revive the core of a real event, which it is sometimes difficult to differentiate from fantasy. Thus the analyst may see that a recovered memory is at the same time pleasurable and unpleasurable, substituting for an action, and containing the core of a historical truth or historical reality. The historical reality may then be represented by one of the typical fantasies. After all, the fantasy of seduction by an adult or about witnessing parental intercourse or other such fantasies may contain a grain of truth. It is obvious that the main task of analysis—to make conscious what is unconscious—is achieved through the revival of old repressed memories. The patient usually sees then that the memory is not an actual experience, but a trace of a past experience. Having compared the past experience with the present, actual one, he can recognize it as unreal, and reject it. With the memory, a feeling or emotion belonging to this memory is activated. The emotion, however, is felt not as belonging to the past but as something present and actual. In this sense, emotions are always formed anew and are actual experiences. The defense mechanisms had made them latent, inhibited in their full development and blocked in their discharge. For this reason they are charged with a relatively great amount of psychic energy. When, in the course of treatment, the pressure of the defenses is lifted, the affective states that were inhibited and therefore could not express themselves as such can proceed to the system Cs and discharge their energy in the complex of sensations and innervations called emotions.

The emotions as a phenomenon of discharge naturally bring relief to the psychic system. But why should the reproduction of memory traces also bring relief? The answer might be that it is not the revived memory that brings relief but the activated emotion or motility which accompanies the memory. The fact, however, that relief is felt only once, at the moment of remembering an experience for the first time, and that its effect is lost when the remembering of the experience is repeated, justifies the assumption that the act of converting repressed ideas from unconscious into conscious ones is also a kind of discharge of psychic energy.

Freud explains this in the following way: The system Ucs and Pcs store memory traces of excitations; the system Cs cannot do so and therefore has no contents. It can only register psychic phenomena, no matter whether they are released by external or internal stimuli. These phenomena become conscious as perceptions of either the external or the internal world. The latter are thoughts, ideas, fantasies, of the preconscious ego, as well as drives, wishes, sensations, feelings, originating in the deep unconscious id. Experience shows that the unconscious material—with a few exceptions such as symbols—has no direct access to the system Cs. An unconscious wish, impulse, or idea can enter consciousness only when it has first become preconscious. The conversion of an unconscious idea or impulse into a conscious one can be accomplished when the receptive apparatus of the system Cs is alerted, in other words, when the ego sends out its own cathexes and thus attracts the preconscious ideas or impulses which, through analysis, have become ready for expression. Parenthetically, this is the problem of attention. The act of consciousness is a momentary, fleeting act. It can be repeated at will, but it cannot be fixated as a memory. Each act of consciousness is a new act of perception. In this act, which is equivalent to recollecting, psychic energy stored in the repressed material is released and discharged. As Freud formulated it, the psychic energy set free through the conversion of a *repressed* idea into a conscious memory "explodes" in the moment when this idea is perceived by the perceptive apparatus of the ego. The act of recollecting *repressed* ideas or experiences can thus be considered also as abreaction, like discharge in emotions and actions. This may perhaps explain why patients feel relief when they have brought to light their repressed memories, even if these are subsequently forgotten again. To stress it once more: only the recollection of *repressed* ideas brings relief through "abreaction."

It is interesting to note that someone who wants to recollect something and is unable to do so feels inferior, as if he had lost an important faculty. If he succeeds in remembering what he had forgotten, he feels elated. This elation is probably caused not only by the feeling of having regained mastery over one's faculties (and of having regained the infantile omnipotence) but also by the freeing of energy which had been used for the fact of repression, as in wit.

Thus the old theory of abreaction seems still valid to a certain extent; this comprises discharge in recollections in addition to discharge in affects. In practice, of course, this distinction cannot be drawn as precisely as in theory, for only rarely does an idea become conscious without the accompanying affect. In analysis, a small measure of abreaction occurs repeatedly with the emergence of repressed ideas or with the revival of inhibited emotions. Very small quantities of energy are used for these abreactions. Indeed, neurophysiologists assume that infinitesimal quantities of energy are used for the activities of the central nervous system.

ACTIVITY AND PASSIVITY IN ANALYSIS

Abreaction, though providing temporary relief, does not always remove symptoms. Therefore we must consider other factors which might be at work in completing the cure.

The process of associating freely, which finally leads to the emergence of repressed material, never takes a smooth course. It is almost a rule that with the deepening of the analysis, the resistances increase. Thus we can observe again and again that at certain points in the train of associations, uneasiness appears, varying in intensity in different individuals. A *feeling of discomfort* arises, almost anxiety, which may paralyze the patient's analytic work. It looks then as if the patient had given himself up. This inertia, this passivity, or whatever the state of mind might be called, can be overcome only with the help of the analyst, although the *active cooperation* of the patient is still absolutely necessary. We have already called attention to the fact that the patient in analysis turns his active interest to his inner processes—compounded of experiences and memories—not only out of love for the analyst but also because he feels *protected by the analyst.* This protection enables him to overcome his fear of remembering and to give free play to his memories and the affects holding them together. Out of love for the analyst and in the security of his protection, the ego then forces itself to work actively at further recovering repressed material.

The illness absorbs much psychic energy. Relatively little energy is left at the free disposal of the ego. Thus, in situations which demand action, the patient behaves passively. He does not try to change reality in any way to make it meet his wishes; on the contrary, he changes himself and eventually withdraws from reality. It is clear that the longer the illness lasts, the greater is the loss of contact with reality. This predominantly passive attitude to the real demands of life is also reflected in the transference situation.

For some time, complete accord may prevail between patient and analyst, with the patient relying completely on the analyst and his interpretations; if it were possible, he would even depend on the analyst for memories. But there soon comes a moment when this harmony is disturbed. The resistances become stronger as the analysis goes deeper, and even more so, the nearer one approaches the original pathogenic situation. Moreover, in addition to these difficulties, there is a moment of frustration which must at some time or other appear in the transference, when the patient's personal demands upon the analyst cannot be satisfied. Most patients react to the frustration with spite, stubbornness, neglect of the analytic work, and acting out; that is, they behave just as they behaved in earlier analogous situations.

One might say that a certain activity is displayed on the part of the patient; it is clearly not one which could change the reality. On the contrary, the patients evade reality, thus behaving in a fundamentally passive manner toward it. The repetition compulsion, which previously helped to bring about fixations, thus also governs the psychic expressions of what has been repressed in the transference situation. The patient now leaves it to the analyst to work for him in the analysis—to guess what he wants to express but cannot put into words. This passivity is connected in some way with the need to be loved. The patient's own omnipotence of expression (which may be wordless) and the supposed omnipotence of the physician (his magic) are put to the most severe test. In part, the analyst succeeds in unmasking these resistances; in part, conjecture is impossible. The conflict, which is no longer an inner one but one between the patient and the analyst, is now brought to a climax. There is a threat that the analysis will break down; that is, the patient has the choice of losing the analyst and his love or of participating actively again in his analysis. If the transference is strong enough, that is, if at least a minimum of object libido has already been freed from fixations, the patient becomes anxious over this prospective loss and starts again to work actively.

There is much more to be said about the problem of passivity, but I prefer to stop here and to call attention to a phenomenon which, at times, occurs when the patient becomes afraid of losing his analyst's love. When it happens that the analyst has given up hope for a favorable outcome of the analysis and has lost interest in the case, an abundance of material may suddenly appear, promising a rapid conclusion of the analysis. This behavior is analogous to that of many patients who bring interesting material only at the end of the session in the hope of prolonging it; in other words, in an effort to lengthen the period of being with the analyst. I can explain this only in this way: the patient notices the analyst's loss of interest and, as a result, anxiety develops as if over the loss of love.

Those cases in which one is forced, for some reason, to set a definite time for the termination of the analysis also fit into this conception. Many patients react to this termination with anxiety which they attempt to overcome through increased activity in remembering. (Incidentally, it can in no way be said that analysis can be concluded merely by setting a time limit.) In order to avoid anxiety, the patient may endure the pain which comes from the frustration and the reproduction of the pathogenic traumatic situation. He may submit to active cooperation in the analytic work and bring from his unconscious the last repressed memories. *The passivity of his behavior or the inertia of the instinct life is now overcome through the activity of the ego and of mobilized object libido.* The motivation for the transformation of the passivity of instinct life (in the form of the repetition compulsion) into the activity of the ego is fear of the loss of love, thus mobilized object libido, freed through the treatment. And this object libido induces the patient to accept the result of the analytic work, a behavior analogous to the carrying out of a posthypnotic suggestion. The patient has not only to understand his conflicts but also to accept the insight gained through analysis.

The activity of the ego now serves not only to loosen the last fixations of the instincts and to create the most favorable conditions for abreaction, but also to improve the function of reality testing. This improvement has been prepared by the analysis itself, since, with the conscious recollection of infantile strivings, these are repeatedly proved to be psychic formations of the past which no longer find a response in the present reality. The transference likewise provides continual opportunity to learn to distinguish between psychic and external reality.

That the more exact testing of reality attained through analysis must lead to the giving up of omnipotence and magic, or at least to minimizing them, is almost as self-evident as the fact that the regained activity can bring about real changes in the outer world, thus procuring more favorable conditions for the real gratification of instinct needs which have been freed from repression.

If that were all that analysis could accomplish, its result, at best, would be an individual who abreacts his erotic and destructive strivings on suitable objects. But this is not so in reality, nor would it be feasible in a civilized society. Actually, we see that the individual after analysis is not only freer in his instinct life, but also better able to endure pain, to control himself, to tolerate instinct tensions, to sublimate, to adapt himself to reality, and to avoid becoming ill because of neurotic conflicts. Even the best analysis, of course, cannot save anyone from actual conflicts or new neurotic setbacks when new conflicts arise which cannot be solved in a way satisfactory to both ego and id.

CONSCIOUSNESS AND THE ROLE OF SYNTHESIS IN THE HEALING PROCESS

The neurotic process disorganizes the ego. Through repression or other defense mechanisms, not only a portion of the instinctual life is cut off from the control of the ego, but also a part of the ego itself is eliminated from its organization. This part becomes unconscious, leads an independent existence, and is governed by the primary process; that is, it acquires characteristics of the unconscious. The orderly secondary process of the preconscious ego has been degraded by the repression and symptom formation to the primary process. This split-off part of the ego satisfies its demands independently of and contrary to the needs of the unaffected part of the ego. Let us take as a paradigm the case of a fetishist.

One of my patients becomes sexually excited when he sees a woman in black stockings and shoes with high heels. Consciously, he knows that the fetish is not a sexual organ; and yet, he is constantly on the lookout for such a woman, and when he finds one satisfying his specific qualifications, he cannot resist the temptation to masturbate. There are obviously two egos in him; what one rejects, the other carries out. He does not know that the black stockings and high heels are a symbolic substitute for mother's pubic hair with a penis sticking out, and yet he behaves as if he knew.

The ego tries to avoid splits and contradictions of behavior. It has a specific faculty which tries to prevent a split or to heal it if it has occurred. This faculty is called the synthetic function of the ego. It endeavors to mediate between id, superego, and reality, and to reconcile contradictions.

In a normal state of mind the psychic systems are interconnected so that the synthetic function of the ego can exercise its influence. With repression and symptom formation, the intersystemic communication is interrupted, and thus the synthetic function fails. Through repression, certain ideas are separated from the affect belonging to them. The idea becomes unconscious and the affect inhibited or attached to another idea. The personality becomes disorganized, logic is neglected, reality misinterpreted; thinking is inhibited, which causes gaps in knowledge. When the repression is lifted by the psychoanalytic work, the repressed idea is reconnected with its affect, order is re-established where chaos ruled, the secondary process again replaces the primary process.

Just as the ego cannot tolerate contradictions, it cannot tolerate gaps in thinking. Both factors cause feelings of doubt and uncertainty. In order to avoid these feelings, people ask questions and expect answers. These questions concern the origin of things. Briefly, there exists a *need for causality,* a need which the primitive as well as the highly civilized man wishes to satisfy. Every patient, be he physically or psychically ill, looks for a cause of his illness. Therefore, when the patient understands that analysis tries to find the unconscious cause of his illness, he is, in the beginning, very cooperative. Then it often happens that the patient very soon believes that he has already found the cause of his illness and thus understands it and that he is satisfied for the moment. This is in most cases what we call a rationalization. Thus the need for causality can be a stimulus not only for cooperation but also for rationalization, and it may increase the already existing resistances. The need for causality is gratified throughout the analysis from the very beginning (where it may at times serve the purposes of resistance) to the last moment. It stimulates recollections which are the most important aid in uncovering what has been repressed. Stimulated by the need for causality, which is one of the determining factors of the individual's tendency to introspective investigation, the patient discovers intimate relationships between individual experiences, thoughts, and fantasies, which he at first connects with each other and then with the actual ego. He finds relationships which previously had been unknown to him. He reunites with the ego the part which had been estranged and detached from it by the process of defense, and thus permits the synthetic function of the ego to operate again. Thereby the gaps in thinking are also filled in, *order* is brought to the psychic processes, the patient understands himself better than before. In short, the continuity and unity of the personality is restored. (There is a need for the feeling of continuity of the personality.)

As has been stressed, a connection between the systems Ucs and Pcs, that is, a connection between concrete and verbal ideas, is in itself not sufficient to bring about the act of becoming conscious. As long as the system Cs is not receptive to the preconscious material, the process remains beneath the threshold of consciousness. It is easy to observe that, as the removal of the repression progresses during treatment, the perceptive ego, responding better than before to the preconscious derivatives of the unconscious, perceives and assimilates them. All of this leads to self-understanding. Thus the need for causality finds its satisfaction. Psychologically, understanding means to find and assimilate the inner cause in relation to its effect. Analysis enriches the ego; self-knowledge leads to a better understanding of others.

The act of becoming conscious, the "exploding" of psychic energy occurs under the influence of the synthetic function of the ego. I should like to stress the fact that consciousness is a fleeting act, while "understanding" becomes a permanent possession of the preconscious ego.

I wish to emphasize once more that the entire process described above is the opposite to that of repression, the prerequisite for which is, indeed, a temporary insufficiency of the synthetic function of the ego. The process of healing ultimately becomes a process of assimilating the psychic strivings which had been estranged from the ego through the measures of defense; in this way it seems to insure the *continuity and unity of the personality.*

In the psychoanalytic treatment of neuroses something takes place that is somewhat similar to the attempts at spontaneous recovery of the various forms of schizophrenia. In schizophrenia, the most heterogeneous elements are connected with each other and frequently fused with impressions of the external world, thus creating new formations, as, for instance, delusional ideas. It is true that in psychoses the synthesis is applied to material which is different from that of the neuroses. In the neurosis, the act of becoming conscious is preceded by a connecting of the preconscious verbal and the unconscious concrete ideas. In schizophrenia, this connection is missing and the preconscious verbal ideas are subject to the primary process which otherwise governs the unconscious. These preconscious verbal ideas are then hypercathected with psychic energy and united with the ego. Then the ego treats them as if they were real things. And yet, this phase of the illness represents an attempt to regain the lost world, thus an attempt at recovery. In fact, the reconstruction of this world, although carried out merely in fantasy, corresponds to a spontaneous cure. This "cure" is effected not merely by the craving of the direct libidinal strivings of the id for the lost objects but also by the tendency of the ego to mediate, unite, and integrate, which we call its synthetic function. In the psychoanalytic cure of the neuroses we have likewise seen synthesis at work. What takes place spontaneously but in a bizarre fashion in the schizophrenic, is effected in analysis through cooperation with the analyst.

However this may be in its details, in any case, in the final phase of the process of healing of the neuroses, there is manifested the power of Eros, whose derivatives play their mediating and uniting role even in the desexualized libido of the ego.

The other psychotherapeutic methods, including the not strictly "psychoanalytic" ones, probably utilize this. Whereas we try to attack the neurosis at its foundations and to help the patient to unite with his ego what is present within himself, the other methods start from the surface and try to impose something upon him from the outside. The essential difference between all of these methods and our own consists in that *in other methods, the patients have to assimilate something imposed upon them from the outside, whereas with our method, through painful self-mastery, they have to take into their ego and unite with it, something that is their own.*

It may be due to this fact that some patients get well even though they did not recover the entire unconscious material in their analysis, if they accept and assimilate the repressed material which had been *reconstructed by means of psychoanalysis, but not remembered.*

The synthetic function of the ego does not cease to operate, except in the most severe cases of psychosis; it merely takes wrong paths. Analysis corrects the derailments by enabling the ego, on the one hand, to bring the strivings of the id into accord with the demands of the superego; on the other, to bring the strivings of the id into accord with reality (the objects of the external world). In other words, at the end of the treatment the ego-syntonic drives are admitted to action and consciousness, whereas the non-ego-syntonic drives are curbed by the ego, worked through, no longer used for neurotic production but shifted to mental productivity, that is, sublimated. At the end of the properly conducted treatment, restoration of the synthetic function of the ego takes place automatically, without the analyst's consciously pursuing this aim. Thereby the patient should be enabled either to gratify his instinct needs directly or to sublimate them without coming into particularly acute conflicts with reality or with himself.

CHANGES BROUGHT ABOUT THROUGH ANALYSIS

A successful analysis calls forth many changes in the personality of the patient. These changes take place gradually. First of all, what was hitherto unconscious becomes conscious. This implies that the various resistances have been gradually recognized and abandoned as being unsuitable ways for the ego to operate. The representatives of the instincts may enter consciousness more easily after analysis and may discharge their energy in affects and actions; consequently the id is under less tension than before the cure. The ego becomes stronger since it does not have to expend its energy for defenses; it controls the instincts and acquires the ability to *master* and *tame* them. "Fantastic" thinking, subject to the primary process, is now replaced by realistic thinking, subject to the secondary process. The ego is enriched through the assimilation of the repressed material. The severity of the superego is mitigated; it tolerates the repressed instinctual strivings better. The chaotic, disorderly neurotic ego, so full of contradictions, is replaced by an orderly, unifying, and mediating ego. In other words, the ego regains its synthetic function, its capacity to mediate between superego and id, as well as between id and external world.

The ego whose energy is no longer absorbed by the defensive struggle becomes more and more adequate to its most important work, *the task of reality testing*. It learns better to distinguish between objective and psychic danger, between external and internal stimulus. It learns to master such instinctual demands as entail external danger and to direct them to other goals (sublimation), or else it learns to keep instinctual demands in suspension until a moment arrives propitious for their fulfillment. With this mastery of instincts, the analyzed person learns also to endure pain. He has become able to procure gratification for ego-syntonic instincts through suitable changes in the external world. He is now more concerned with the objects of the outer world and becomes more social.

The "natural" powers of healing, of which the psychoanalytic method makes use, are partly in the ego and partly in the id. Analysis offers help to the ego in its struggle against the instincts, but at the same time releases the instincts from their fixations. In short, the changes which are achieved through treatment in the *ideal case* involve the entire personality and are as follows: the energies of the id become more mobile, the superego becomes more tolerant, the ego is freer from anxiety and its synthetic function is restored.

BIBLIOGRAPHY

ABRAHAM, K. (1927), *Selected Papers on Psycho-Analysis.* London: Hogarth Press.
AICHHORN, A. (1936), *Wayward Youth.* New York: Knopf.
ALEXANDER, F. (1923), The Castration Complex in the Formation of Character. *Int. J. Psa.,* VI.
—— (1930a), *Psychoanalysis of the Total Personality.* New York: Nervous and Mental Disease Publishing Co.
—— (1930b), The Neurotic Character. *Int. J. Psa.,* XI.
ARLOW, J. A. (1949), Anal Sensations and Feelings of Persecution. *Psa. Quart.,* XXVIII.
—— (1953), Masturbation and Symptom Formation. *J. Am. Psa. Assn.,* I.
BAK, R. (1939), Regression of Ego-Orientation and Libido in Schizophrenia. *Int. J. Psa.,* XX.
—— (1953), Fetishism. *J. Am. Psa. Assn.,* I.
—— (1954), The Schizophrenic Defense against Aggression. *Int. J. Psa.,* XXXV.
BALINT, M. (1952), *Primary Love and Psycho-Analytic Technique.* London: Hogarth Press.
BERLINER, B. (1940), Libido and Reality in Masochism. *Psa. Quart.,* X.
BERNFELD, S. (1921), Bemerkungen über Sublimierung. *Imago,* VII.
—— (1923), Ueber eine typische Form der männlichen Pubertät. *Imago,* IX.
—— (1929), *Psychology of the Infant.* London: Kegan Paul.
—— (1938), Types of Adolescence. *Psa. Quart.,* VII.
BIBRING, E. (1928), Klinische Beiträge zur Paranoiafrage, I: Zur Psychologie der Todesideen bei paranoider Schizophrenie. *Int. Ztsch. Psa.,* XIV.
—— (1929), Klinische Beiträge zur Paranoiafrage, II: Ein Fall von Organprojektion. *Int. Ztsch. Psa.,* XV.
—— (1941), The Development and Problems of the Theory of the Instincts. *Int. J. Psa.,* XXI.
—— (1943), The Conception of the Repetition Compulsion. *Psa. Quart.,* XII.
—— (1947), The So-called English School of Psychoanalysis. *Psa. Quart.,* XVI.
—— (1953), The Mechanism of Depression. In: *Affective Disorders,* ed. P. Greenacre. New York: International Universities Press.
—— (1954), Psychoanalysis and the Dynamic Psychotherapies. *J. Am. Psa. Assn.,* II.
BIBRING, G. L. (1933), Ueber die phallische Phase und ihre Störungen beim Mädchen. *Ztsch. Psa. Päd.,* VII.
—— (1940), Ueber eine orale Komponente bei männlicher Inversion. *Int. Ztsch. Psa.,* XXV.
—— (1953), On the "Passing of the Oedipus Complex" in a Matriarchal Family Setting. In: *Drives, Affects, Behavior,* ed. R. M. Loewenstein. New York: International Universities Press.
BLEULER, E. (1912), *Dementia Praecox or the Group of Schizophrenias.* New York: International Universities Press, 1950.
—— (1916), *Textbook of Psychiatry.* New York: Dover, 1952.

361

BOEHM, F. (1920, 1922), Beiträge zur Psychologie der Homosexualität. *Int. Ztsch. Psa.*, VI, VIII.

BONAPARTE, M. (1947), *Myths of War*. London: Imago Publishing Co.

—— (1953), *Female Sexuality*. New York: International Universities Press.

BORNSTEIN, B. (1930), Zur Psychogenese der Pseudodebilität. *Int. Ztsch. Psa.*, XVI.

—— (1934), Phobia in a Two-and-a-half-year-old Child. *Psa. Quart.*, IV.

—— (1936), Leugnung durch die Phantasie. *Ztsch. psa. Päd.*, X.

—— (1945), Clinical Notes on Child Analysis. *The Psychoanalytic Study of the Child,* I. New York: International Universities Press.

—— (1946), Hysterical Twilight States in an Eight-year-old Child. *Ibid.*, II.

—— (1948), Emotional Barriers in the Understanding and Treatment of Children. *Am. J. Orthopsychiat.*, XVIII.

—— (1949), The Analysis of a Phobic Child. *The Psychoanalytic Study of the Child,* III/IV.

—— (1951), On Latency. *Ibid.*, VI.

—— (1953), Fragment of an Analysis of an Obsessional Child. *Ibid.*, VIII.

BRIERLEY, M. (1937), Affects in Theory and Practice. *Int. J. Psa.*, XVIII.

—— (1951), *Trends in Psycho-Analysis*. London: Hogarth Press.

BRILL, A. A. (1912), Anal Eroticism and Character. *J. Abn. Psychol.*, VII.

—— (1921), *Fundamental Conceptions of Psychoanalysis*. New York: Harcourt, Brace.

—— (1939), The Concept of Psychic Suicide. *Int. J. Psa.*, XX.

BRUN, R. (1946), *General Theory of Neuroses*. New York: International Universities Press, 1951.

BURLINGHAM, D. (1952), *Twins*. New York: International Universities Press.

BUXBAUM, E. (1949), *Your Child Makes Sense*. New York: International Universities Press.

BYCHOWSKI, G. (1952), *Psychotherapy of Psychosis*. New York: Grune & Stratton.

—— (1954), The Structure of Homosexual Acting Out. *Psa. Quart.*, XXIII.

CLARK, L. P. (1919), Practical Remarks upon the Use of Modified Psychoanalysis in the Borderline Neuroses and Psychoses. *Psa. Rev.*, VI.

—— (1922), A Study of Unconscious Motivations in Suicides. *N. Y. Med. J.*

—— (1933), The Question of Prognosis in Narcissistic Neuroses and Psychoses. *Int. J. Psa.*, XIV.

COHN, F. (1928), Analyse eines Falles von Strassenangst. *Int. Ztsch. Psa.*, XIV.

—— (1940), Practical Approach to the Problem of Narcissistic Neuroses. *Psa. Quart.*, IX.

CORIAT, I. H. (1924), The Character Traits of Urethral Eroticism. *Psa. Rev.*, XI.

—— (1928), *Stammering*. New York: Nervous and Mental Disease Publ.

DALY, C. D. (1938), Der Menstruationskomplex. *Imago*, XXIV.

—— (1950), The Psychobiological Origins of Circumcision. *Int. J. Psa.*, XXXI.

DERI, F. (1939), On Sublimation. *Psa. Quart.*, VIII.

—— (1942), On Neurotic Disturbances of Sleep. *Int. J. Psa.*, XXIII.

DE SAUSSURE, R. (1939), Identification and Substitution. *Int. J. Psa.*, XX.

—— (1950), Reflections on Psychodynamics. *Samiksa*, IV.

DEUTSCH, F. (1922), Psychoanalyse und Organkrankheiten. *Int. Ztsch. Psa.*, VIII.

—— (1924), Zur Bildung des Konversionssymptoms. *Ibid.*, X.

—— (1926), Der gesunde und der kranke Körper in psychoanalytischer Betrachtung. *Ibid.*, XII.

—— (1939), *The Production of Somatic Disease by Emotional Disturbance*. Baltimore: William & Wilkins.

DEUTSCH, H. (1929), The Genesis of Agoraphobia. *Int. J. Psa.*, X.

—— (1930), The Significance of Masochism in the Mental Life of Women. *Int. J. Psa.*, XI.

—— (1933), *Psycho-Analysis of the Neuroses*. London: Hogarth Press.

—— (1944), *The Psychology of Women*, 2 Vols. New York: Grune & Stratton.

EISSLER, K. R. (1950), The Chicago Institute of Psychoanalysis and the Sixth Period of the Development of Psychoanalytic Technique. *J. General Psychol.*, XLII.

—— (1953a), The Effect of the Structure of the Ego on Psychoanalytic Technique. *J. Am. Psa. Assoc.*, I.

—— (1953b), Notes upon the Emotionality of a Schizophrenic Patient and Its Relation to Problems of Technique. *The Psychoanalytic Study of the Child*, VIII. New York: International Universities Press.

FEDERN, P. (1913, 1914), Beiträge zur Analyse des Sadismus und Masochismus. *Int. Ztsch. Psa.*, I, II.

—— (1928), Narcissism in the Structure of the Ego. *Int. J. Psa.*, IX.

—— (1952), *Ego Psychology and the Psychoses.* Introduction by E. Weiss. New York: Basic Books.

FENICHEL, O. (1945), *The Psychoanalytic Theory of Neurosis.* New York: Norton.

—— (1953, 1954), *The Collected Papers of Otto Fenichel*, 2 Vols. New York: Norton.

FERENCZI, S. (1926), *Further Contributions to the Theory and Technique of Psycho-Analysis.* London: Hogarth Press.

—— (1938), *Thalassa.* New York: Psychoanalytic Quarterly Inc.

—— (1950), *Sex in Psychoanalysis.* New York: Basic Books.

FLUGEL, J. C. (1925), A Note on the Phallic Significance of the Tongue and of Speech. *Int. J. Psa.*, IV.

—— (1938), Stage Fright and Anal Erotism. *Brit. J. Med. Psychol.*, XVII.

FREUD, A. (1923a), The Relations of Beating Fantasies to a Daydream. *Int. J. Psa.*, IV.

—— (1923b), Ein hysterisches Symptom bei einem 2½jährigen Kinde. *Imago*, IX.

—— (1928), Zur Theorie der Kinderanalyse. *Int. Ztsch. Psa.*, XIV.

—— (1929), *Introduction to the Technique of Child Analysis.* New York: Nervous and Mental Disease Publishing Co.

—— (1935), *Introduction to Psychoanalysis for Teachers and Parents.* New York: Emerson Books.

—— (1936), *The Ego and the Mechanisms of Defense.* New York: International Universities Press, 1946.

—— (1945), Indications for Child Analysis. *The Psychoanalytic Study of the Child*, I. New York: International Universities Press.

—— (1946), The Psychoanalytic Study of Infantile Feeding Disturbances. *Ibid.*, II.

—— (1949a), Aggression in Relation to Emotional Development: Normal and Patho logical. *Ibid.*, III/IV.

—— (1949b), Certain Types and Stages of Social Maladjustment. In: *Searchlights on Delinquency*, ed. K. R. Eissler. New York: International Universities Press.

—— (1949c), Notes on Aggression. *The Yearbook of Psychoanalysis*, VI. New York: International Universities Press, 1950.

—— (1950a), The Significance of the Evolution of Psychoanalytic Child Psychology. *Congrès International de Psychiatrie, Paris, 1950.*

—— (1950b), Clinical Observations on the Treatment of Manifest Male Homosexuality. Lecture at the New York Psychoanalytic Society.

—— (1951a), Observations on Child Development. *The Psychoanalytic Study of the Child*, VI.

—— (1951b), An Experiment in Group Upbringing. *Ibid.*, VI.

—— (1951c), The Contribution of Psychoanalysis to Genetic Psychology. *The Yearbook of Psychoanalysis*, VIII. New York: International Universities Press, 1952.

—— (1951d), Negativism and Emotional Surrender. Read at the International Psychoanalytic Congress, Amsterdam.

—— (1952a), The Mutual Influences in the Development of Ego and Id. *The Psychoanalytic Study of the Child*, VII.

—— (1952b), The Role of Bodily Illnesses in the Mental Life of Children. *Ibid.*, VII.

—— (1953a), Some Remarks on Infant Observation. *Ibid.*, VIII.

—— (1953b), The Bearing of the Psychoanalytic Theory of Instinctual Drives on Certain Aspects of Human Behavior. In: *Drives, Affects, Behavior*, ed. R. M. Loewenstein. New York: International Universities Press.

—— (1954a), Psychoanalysis and Education. *The Psychoanalytic Study of the Child*, IX.

—— (1954b), Discussion: Problems of Infantile Neurosis. *Ibid.*, IX.

—— (1954c), The Widening Scope of Indications for Psychoanalysis. *J. Am. Psa. Assn.*, II.

—— (1954d), Problems of Technique in Adult Analysis. *Bull. Philadelphia Assn. Psa.*, IV.

—— and BURLINGHAM, D. T. (1943), *War and Children*. New York: International Universities Press.

—— —— (1944), *Infants Without Families*. New York: International Universities Press.

FREUD, S. (1892-1939), *Gesammelte Werke*, Vols. I-XVII. London: Imago Publishing Co.

    This book is based on all of Freud's writings. Therefore, no specific papers or books will be cited. For the English editions of Freud's works, see the *Standard Edition: The Complete Psychological Works of Sigmund Freud*, current Vols. (Hogarth Press); *Collected Papers*, 5 Vols. (Hogarth Press); the translations of individual books and articles (London, Psycho-analytical Library, Hogarth Press; New York: Norton, Macmillan, etc.); and *The Basic Writings of Sigmund Freud* (Modern Library); among others.

FRIEDLANDER, K. (1947), *The Psychoanalytical Treatment of Juvenile Delinquency*. New York: International Universities Press.

FROSCH, J. et al., eds. (1950), *The Annual Survey of Psychoanalysis*, I. New York: International Universities Press. (See also subsequent Volumes.)

GERO, G. (1936), The Construction of Depression. *Int. J. Psa.*, XVII.

—— (1951), The Concept of Defense. *Psa. Quart.*, XX.

GILLESPIE, W. H. (1940), A Contribution to the Study of Fetishism. *Int. J. Psa.*, XXI.

—— (1952), Notes on the Analysis of Sexual Perversions. *Int. J. Psa.*, XXXIII.

GITELSON, M. (1952), Re-evaluation of the Role of the Oedipus Complex. *Int. J. Psa.*, XXXIII.

GLOVER, E. (1925), Notes on Oral Character Formation. *Int. J. Psa.*, VI.

—— (1926), The Neurotic Character. *Int. J. Psa.*, VII.

—— (1928), The Etiology of Alcoholism. *Proc. Roy. Soc. Med.*, XXI.

—— (1929), The Screening Function of Traumatic Memories. *Int. J. Psa.*, X.

—— (1931), Sublimation, Substitution and Social Anxiety. *Int. J. Psa.*, XII.

—— (1932), On the Aetiology of Drug Addiction. *Int. J. Psa.*, XIII.

—— (1933), The Relation of Perversion Formation to the Development of the Reality Sense. *Int. J. Psa.*, XIV.

—— (1935), A Developmental Study of the Obsessional Neurosis. *Int. J. Psa.*, XVI.

—— (1938), A Note on Idealization. *Int. J. Psa.*, XIX.

—— (1939a), *Psychoanalysis*. London: John Bale Medical Publ.

—— (1939b), The Psychoanalysis of Affects. *Int. J. Psa.*, XX.

—— (1945), Examination of the Klein System of Child Psychology. *The Psychoanalytic Study of the Child*, I. New York: International Universities Press.

—— (1950), *Freud and Jung*. New York: Norton.

—— (1955), *The Technique of Psychoanalysis*. New York: International Universities Press.

GLOVER, J. (1926), The Conception of the Ego. *Int. J. Psa.*, VII.

GREENACRE, P. (1952), *Trauma, Growth and Personality*. New York: Norton.

GREENSON, R. R. (1950), The Mother Tongue and the Mother. *Int. J. Psa.*, XXXI.

GRODDECK, G. (1923), *The Book of the It*. New York: Funk & Wagnalls, 1950.

GROSS, A. (1951), The Secret. *Bull. Menninger Clin.*, XV.

HARTMANN, H. (1927), *Die Grundlagen der Psychoanalyse.* Leipzig: Thieme.

―― (1939a), Ich-Psychologie und Anpassungsproblem. *Int. Ztsch. Psa.*, XXIV.

―― (1939b), Psychoanalysis and the Concept of Health. *Int. J. Psa.*, XX.

―― (1948), Comments on the Psychoanalytic Theory of Instinctual Drives. *Psa. Quart.*, XVII.

―― (1949), On Rational and Irrational Action. *Psychoanalysis and the Social Sciences*, I. New York: International Universities Press.

―― (1950), Comments on the Psychoanalytic Theory of the Ego. *The Psychoanalytic Study of the Child*, V. New York: International Universities Press.

―― and KRIS, E. (1945), A Genetic Approach in Psychoanalysis. *The Psychoanalytic Study of the Child*, I. New York: International Universities Press.

―― ―― and LOEWENSTEIN, R. M. (1946), Comments on the Formation of Psychic Structure. *Ibid.*, II.

―― ―― ―― (1949), Notes on the Theory of Aggression. *Ibid.*, III/IV.

HENDRICK, I. (1939), *Facts and Theories of Psychoanalysis.* New York: Knopf.

HITSCHMANN, E. (1913), *Freud's Theories of the Neuroses.* London: Kegan, Paul.

―― (1952), Freud's Conception of Love. *Int. J. Psa.*, XXXIII.

HOFFER, W. (1926), Ueber die männliche Latenz und ihre spezifische Erkrankung. *Int. Ztsch. Psa.*, XII.

―― (1950a), Oral Aggressiveness and Ego Development. *Int. J. Psa.*, XXXI.

―― (1950b), Three Psychological Criteria for the Termination of Treatment. *Int. J. Psa.*, XXXI.

HORNEY, K. (1924), On the Genesis of the Castration Complex in Women. *Int. J. Psa.*, V.

―― (1926), The Flight from Womenhood. *Int. J. Psa.*, VII.

ISAKOWER, O. (1938), A Contribution to the Pathopsychology of Phenomena Associated with Falling Asleep. *Int. J. Psa.*, XIX.

―― (1939), On the Exceptional Position of the Auditive Sphere. *Int. J. Psa.*, XX.

―― (1954), Spoken Words in Dreams. *Psa. Quart.*, XXIII.

JACOBSON, E. (1937), Wege der weiblichen Ueber-Ich-Bildung. *Int. Ztsch. Psa.*, XXIII.

―― (1943), Depression, the Oedipus Complex in the Development of Depressive Mechanisms. *Psa. Quart.*, XII.

―― (1953), Contribution to the Metapsychology of Cyclothymic Depression. In: *Affective Disorders*, ed. P. Greenacre. New York: International Universities Press.

―― (1954), On Psychotic Identifications. *Int. J. Psa.*, XXXV.

JEKELS, L. (1952), *Selected Papers.* New York: International Universities Press.

JONES, E. (1913), *Papers on Psychoanalysis.* New York: Wood. (See also subsequent volumes and editions.)

―― (1920), *The Treatment of the Neuroses.* New York: Wood.

―― (1923), *Essays in Applied Psycho-Analysis.* London: Hogarth Press.

―― (1931), *The Nightmare.* London: Hogarth Press.

―― (1948), *What Is Psychoanalysis?* New York: International Universities Press.

―― (1953), *The Life and Work of Sigmund Freud*, I. New York: Basic Books.

JUNG, C. G. (1908), *Der Inhalt der Psychose.* Leipzig: Deuticke.

―― (1909a), *The Psychology of Dementia Praecox.* New York: Nervous and Mental Disease Publishing Co.

―― (1909b), Die Bedeutung des Vaters für das Schicksal des Einzelnen. *Jb. psa. & psychopathol. Forsch.*, I.

KANZER, M. (1953), Past and Present in the Transference. *J. Am. Psa. Assoc.*, I.

KATAN, A. ANGEL (1951), The Role of "Displacement" in Agoraphobia. *Int. J. Psa.*, XXXII.

KATAN, M. (1939), The Understanding of Schizophrenic Speech. *Int. J. Psa.*, XX.

—— (1940), Die Rolle des Wortes in der Schizophrenie und Manie. *Int. Ztsch. Psa.*, XXV.

—— (1950), Schreber's Hallucinations about the "Little Men." *Int. J. Psa.*, XXXI.

—— (1952), Further Remarks about Schreber's Hallucinations. *Int. J. Psa.*, XXXIII.

—— (1953), Schreber's Prepsychotic Phase. *Int. J. Psa.*, XXXIV.

—— (1954), The Importance of the Non-psychotic Part of the Personality in Schizophrenia. *Int. J. Psa.*, XXXV.

KLEIN, M. (1932), *The Psycho-Analysis of Children*. London: Hogarth Press.

KNIGHT, R. P. (1940a), Introjection, Projection and Identification. *Psa. Quart.*, IX.

—— (1940b), The Relationship of Homosexuality to the Mechanism of Paranoid Delusions. *Bull. Menninger Clin.*, IV.

—— et al. (1954), *Psychoanalytic Psychiatry and Psychology*, I. New York: International Universities Press.

KRIS, E. (1950), The Significance of Freud's Earliest Discoveries. *Int. J. Psa.*, XXXI.

—— (1951), Some Comments and Observations on Early Autoerotic Activities. *The Psychoanalytic Study of the Child*, VI. New York: International Universities Press.

—— (1952), *Psychoanalytic Explorations in Art*. New York: International Universities Press.

KRONENGOLD, E. and STERBA, R. (1936), Two Cases of Fetishism. *Psa. Quart.*, V.

KUBIE, L. S. (1941), The Repetitive Core of Neurosis. *Psa. Quart.*, X.

—— (1950), *Practical and Theoretical Aspects of Psychoanalysis*. New York: International Universities Press.

LAGACHE, D. (1950), Homosexuality and Jealousy. *Int. J. Psa.*, XXXI.

—— (1951), Quelques aspects du transfert. *Rev. Franç. Psa.*, XV.

LAMPL-DE GROOT, J. (1928), The Evolution of the Oedipus Complex in Women. *Int. J. Psa.*, IX.

—— (1933), Problems of Femininity. *Psa. Quart.*, II.

LAMPL, H. (1927), A Case of Borrowed Sense of Guilt. *Int. J. Psa.*, VIII.

LANTOS, B. (1929), Analyse einer Konversionshysterie im Klimakterium. *Int. Ztsch. Psa.*, XV.

—— (1952), Metapsychological Considerations on the Concept of Work. *Int. J. Psa.*, XXXIII.

—— (1955), On the Motivation of Human Relationships. *Int. J. Psa.*, XXXVI.

LEWIN, B. D. (1932), Anal Eroticism and the Mechanism of Undoing. *Psa. Quart.*, I.

—— (1933), The Body as Phallus. *Psa. Quart.*, II.

—— (1948), The Nature of Reality, the Meaning of Nothing, with an Addendum on Concentration. *Psa. Quart.*, XVII.

—— (1950), *The Psychoanalysis of Elation*. New York: Norton.

—— (1952), Phobic Symptoms and Dream Interpretation. *Psa. Quart.*, XXI.

—— (1953), The Forgetting of Dreams. In: *Drives, Affects, Behavior*, ed. R. M. Loewenstein. New York: International Universities Press.

—— (1955), Dream Psychology and the Analytic Situation. *Psa. Quart.*, XXIV.

LOEWENSTEIN, R. M. (1935), Phallic Passivity in Men. *Int. J. Psa.*, XVI.

—— (1945), A Special Form of Self-Punishment. *Psa. Quart.*, XXIV.

—— (1949), A Posttraumatic Dream. *Psa. Quart.*, XVIII.

MACK-BRUNSWICK, R. (1928), A Supplement to Freud's "History of an Infantile Neurosis." *Int. J. Psa.*, IX.

—— (1940), The Pre-oedipal Phase of the Libido Development. *Psa. Quart.*, IX.

MAHLER, M. S. (1949), Psychoanalytic Evaluation of Tics. *The Psychoanalytic Study of the Child*, IIII/IV. New York: International Universities Press.

—— (1952), On Child Psychosis and Schizophrenia: Autistic and Symbiotic Infantile Psychoses. *Ibid.*, VII.

MENNINGER, K. A. (1937), *The Human Mind*. New York: Knopf.

—— (1938), *Man against Himself*. New York: Harcourt, Brace.

NACHT, S. (1948), Clinical Manifestations of Aggression and Their Role in Psychoanalytic Treatment. *Int. J. Psa.*, XXIX.

—— (1951), Les nouvelles théories psychanalytiques sur le moi et leur répercussions sur l'orientation méthodologique. *Rev. franç. psa.*, XV.

NIEDERLAND, W. G. (1951), Three Notes on the Schreber Case. *Psa. Quart.*, XX.

NUNBERG, H. (1948), *Practice and Theory of Psychoanalysis*. New York: International Universities Press, 1955.

—— (1949), *Problems of Bisexuality as Reflected in Circumcision*. London: Imago Publishing Co.

—— (1950), A Commentary on Freud's *An Outline of Psychoanalysis*. *Psa. Quart.*, XIX.

—— (1951), Transference and Reality. *Int. J. Psa.*, XXXII.

—— (1952), Discussion of M. Katan's Paper on Schreber's Hallucination. *Int. J. Psa.*, XXXIII.

—— (1954), Evaluation of the Results of Psychoanalytic Treatment. *Int. J. Psa.*, XXXV.

OLDEN, C. (1941), About the Fascinating Effect of the Narcissistic Personality. *Am. Imago*, II.

—— (1942), On Neurotic Disturbances of Sleep. *Int. J. Psa.*, XXIII.

—— (1943), The Psychology of Obstinacy. *Psa. Quart.*, XII.

OPHUIJSEN, J. H. W. (1920), On the Origin of the Feeling of Persecution. *Int. J. Psa.*, I.

—— (1924), Contributions to the Masculinity Complex in Women. *Int. J. Psa.*, V.

—— (1929), The Sexual Aim of Sadism as Manifested in Acts of Violence. *Int. J. Psa.*, X.

PAYNE, S. (1939), Some Observations on the Ego Development of the Fetishist. *Int. J. Psa.*, XX.

PFISTER, O. (1910), *Die Frömmigkeit des Grafen von Zinzendorf*. Vienna: Deuticke.

PIOUS, W. (1950), Obsessive-Compulsive Symptoms in an Incipient Schizophrenic. *Psa. Quart.*, XIX.

RADO, S. (1926), The Psychic Effects of Intoxicants. *Int. J. Psa.*, IX.

—— (1928), The Problem of Melancholia. *Int. J. Psa.*, IX.

—— (1933), The Psychoanalysis of Pharmacothymia. *Psa. Quart.*, II.

RANK, O. (1912), Völkerpsychologische Parallelen zu den infantilen Sexualtheorien. *Centralbl. f. Psa.*, II.

—— (1923), Perversion and Neurosis. *Int. J. Psa.*, IV.

—— (1925), Genese der Genitalität. *Int. Ztsch. Psa.*, XI.

—— (1929), *The Trauma of Birth*. New York: Harcourt, Brace.

RAPAPORT, D. (1942), *Emotions and Memory*. New York: International Universities Press, 1950.

—— (1951), *Organization and Pathology of Thought*. New York: Columbia University Press.

—— (1953), On the Psychoanalytic Theory of Affects. *Int. J. Psa.*, XXXIV.

REICH, A. (1940), A Contribution to the Psychoanalysis of Extreme Submissiveness in Women. *Psa. Quart.*, IX.

—— (1953), Narcissistic Object Choice in Women. *J. Am. Psa. Assn.*, I.

REICH, W. (1925), *Der triebhafte Charakter*. Vienna: Internationaler Psychoanalytischer Verlag.

—— (1926a), Ueber die chronische hypochondrische Neurasthenie mit genitaler Asthenie. *Int. Ztsch. Psa.*, XII.

—— (1926b), Ueber die Quellen neurotischer Angst. *Int. Ztsch. Psa.*, XII.

—— (1927a) Zur Technik der Deutung der Widerstandsanalyse. *Int. Ztsch. Psa.*, XIII.

—— (1927b), *Funktion des Orgasmus*. Vienna: Internationaler Psychoanalytischer Verlag.

—— (1928), Ueber Charakteranalyse. *Int. Ztsch. Psa.*, XIV.

—— (1929), Der genitale und der neurotische Charakter. *Int. Ztsch. Psa.*, XV.

REIDER, N. (1953), Reconstruction and Screen Function. *J. Am. Psa. Assoc.*, I.

REIK, T. (1915), Die Pubertätsriten der Wilden. *Imago*, IV.

—— (1924), *Dogma and Compulsion*. New York: International Universities Press, 1951.

—— (1925), *Geständniszwang und Strafbedürfnis*. Vienna: Internationaler Psychoanalytischer Verlag.

—— (1929), Neurosenpsychologie und Religion. *Int. Ztsch. Psa.*, XV.

RIVIERE, J. (1936), On the Genesis of Psychical Conflict in Earliest Infancy. *Int. J. Psa.*, XVII.

RÓHEIM, G. (1923), Heiliges Geld in Melanesien. *Int. Ztsch. Psa.*, IX.

—— (1950), *Psychoanalysis and Anthropology*. New York: International Universities Press.

—— (1953), *The Gates of the Dream*. New York: International Universities Press.

—— (1955), *Magic and Schizophrenia*. New York: International Universities Press.

ROSENFELD, H. (1952), Notes on the Psycho-analysis of the Super-ego Conflict of an Acute Schizophrenic Patient. *Int. J. Psa.*, XXXIII.

—— (1954), The Psycho-analytic Approach to Acute and Chronic Schizophrenia. *Int. J. Psa.*, XXXV.

SACHS, H. (1923), Zur Genese der Perversion. *Int. Ztsch. Psa.*, IX.

SADGER, J. (1911a), Haut-, Schleimhaut- und Muskelerotik, *Jb. f. psa. Forschungen*, III.

—— (1911b), Ist das Asthma bronchiale eine Sexualneurose? *Centralbl. f. Psa.*, I.

—— (1913), Ueber Gesässerotik. *Int. Ztsch. Psa.*, I.

—— (1926), A Contribution to the Understanding of Sado-Masochism. *Int. J. Psa.*, VII.

SCHILDER, P. (1923), *Medical Psychology*. New York: International Universities Press, 1953.

—— (1925), *Introduction to a Psycho-analytic Psychiatry*. New York: International Universities Press, 1951.

—— (1934), *The Image and Appearance of the Human Body*. New York: International Universities Press, 1951.

SCHUR, M. (1953), The Ego in Anxiety. In *Drives, Affects, Behavior*, ed. R. M. Loewenstein. New York: International Universities Press.

SCOTT, W. C. M. (1954), Libidinal and Aggressive Instincts. *Int. J. Psa.*, XXXV.

SECHEHAYE, M. (1951a), *Symbolic Realization*. New York: International Universities Press.

—— (1951b), *Autobiography of a Schizophrenic Girl*. New York: Grune & Stratton.

SHARPE, E. F. (1930), Certain Aspects of Sublimation and Delusion. *Int. J. Psa.*, XI.

—— (1949), *Dream Analysis*. London: Hogarth Press.

—— (1950), *Collected Papers on Psycho-Analysis*. London: Hogarth Press.

SIMMEL, E. (1925), A Screen Memory in Statu Nascendi. *Int. J. Psa.*, VI.

—— (1926), The Doctor Game, Illness and the Profession of Medicine. *Int. J. Psa.*, VII.

—— (1944), Self-Preservation and the Death Instinct. *Psa. Quart.*, XIII.

SPERBER, H. (1914), Ueber den Einfluss sexueller Momente auf Entstehung und Entwicklung der Sprache. *Imago*, I.

SPITZ, R. A. (1937), Wiederholung, Rhythmus, Langeweile. *Imago*, XXIII.

—— (1945), Hospitalism. *The Psycho-analytic Study of the Child*, I. New York: International Universities Press.

—— (1946), Anaclitic Depression. *Ibid.*, II.

—— (1951), The Psychogenic Diseases in Infancy. *Ibid.*, VI.

—— (1953), Aggression: Its Role in the Establishment of Object Relations. In *Drives, Affects, Behavior*, ed. R. M. Loewenstein. New York: International Universities Press.

—— and Wolf, K. M. (1946), The Smiling Response. *Gen. Psychol. Mon.*, XXXIV.

STAERCKE, A. (1920), The Reversal of the Libido Sign in Delusions of Persecution. *Int. J. Psa.*, I.

—— (1921a), The Castration Complex. *Int. J. Psa.*, II.

—— (1921b), Psychoanalysis and Psychiatry. *Int. J. Psa.,* II.
—— (1929), Conscience and the Role of Repetition. *Int. J. Psa.,* X.
STERBA, R. (1928), An Examination Dream. *Int. J. Psa.,* IX.
—— (1934), The Fate of the Ego in Analytic Therapy. *Int. J. Psa.,* XV.
—— (1940), The Dynamics of the Dissolution of the Transference Resistance. *Psa. Quart.,* IX.
—— (1942), *Introduction to the Psychoanalytic Theory of the Libido.* New York: Nervous and Mental Disease Publ.
—— (1951), Character and Resistance. *Psa. Quart.,* XX.
STERN, M. M. (1951a), Anxiety, Trauma and Shock. *Psa. Quart.,* XX.
—— (1951b), Pavor Nocturnus. *Int. J. Psa.,* XXXII.
STONE, L. (1954), On the Principal Obscene Word of the English Language. *Int. J. Psa.,* XXXV.
STRACHEY, J. (1931), The Function of the Precipitating Factor in the Etiology of the Neuroses. *Int. J. Psa.,* XII.
TARACHOW, S. (1951), Circuses and Clowns. *Psychoanalysis and the Social Sciences,* III. New York: International Universities Press.
TAUSK, V. (1924), Compensation as a Means of Discounting the Motive of Repression. *Int. J. Psa.,* V.
—— (1933), On the Origin of the Influencing Machine in Schizophrenia. *Psa. Quart.,* II.
WAELDER, R. (1926), Schizophrenic and Creative Thinking. *Int. J. Psa.,* VII.
—— (1936), The Principle of Multiple Function. *Psa. Quart.,* V.
—— (1937), The Problem of the Genesis of Psychical Conflict. *Int. J. Psa.,* XVIII.
—— (1951), The Structure of Paranoid Ideas. *Int. J. Psa.,* XXXII.
WAELDER-HALL, J. (1935), Analyse eines Falles von Pavor Nocturnus. *Ztsch. psa. Päd.,* IX.
WEISS, E. (1925), Ueber eine noch nicht beschriebene Phase der Entwicklung zur heterosexuellen Liebe. *Int. Ztsch. Psa.,* XI.
—— (1932), Regression and Projection in the Superego. *Int. J. Psa.,* XIII.
—— (1935), Agoraphobia and Its Relation to Hysterical Attacks and to Traumas. *Int. J. Psa.,* XVI.
WINDHOLZ, E. (1942), On Neurotic Disturbances of Sleep. *Int. J. Psa.,* XXIII.
WINNICOTT, D. W. (1953), Transitional Objects and Transitional Phenomena. *Int. J. Psa.,* XXXIV.
—— (1955), Metapsychological and Clinical Aspects of Regression within the Psychoanalytic Set-up. *Int. J. Psa.,* XXXVI.
WITTELS, F. (1933), The Superego in Our Judgment of Sex. *Int. J. Psa.,* XIV.
—— (1937), The Mystery of Masochism. *Psa. Rev.,* XXIV.
—— (1940), Psychology and Treatment of Depersonalization. *Psa. Rev.,* XXVII.
ZILBOORG, G. (1941), Ambulatory Schizophrenias. *Psychiatry,* IV.
—— and HENRY, G. W. (1941), *A History of Medical Psychology.* New York: Norton.

INDEX

Abraham, Karl, 87, 89, 93, 162
Abreaction, 155, 341, 351-352, 354
Acting out, 247, 305, 310-311, 349, *see also* Cases
Activity (passivity), 59, 67-69, 88, 98-99, 174-176, 199, 221-225, 228, *see also* Cases, Femininity, Masculinity, Changing into the opposite
Actual neuroses, 178-187, 205, 297, 326
Adaptation, *see* Ego, Reality
Adolescence, *see* Puberty
Affect
 and anxiety, 189-191
 and discharge of psychic energy, 350-352
 and unconscious, 35-36, 39
 fixated, 190-191
 in dream, 25-26, 35, *see also* Cases
 partially repressed, 239-240
 psychogenesis of, 190
Affectivity, 31, 49, 244, 267-268, 330
Afterexpulsion, 235, 270, 344
Aggression
 against first object, 166
 and anal organization, 66
 and character, 303-320
 and feelings of guilt, 158-173, 235-236
 and identification, 307-309
 and resistance, 248-249
 and superego, 138-149, 236, 279-280
 and urination, 277
 as reaction to external stimuli, 85-86
 in neurosis, 251-302
 turned against the self, 138-139, 143, 147, 159, 166, 202-204, 221-225, 236, 280, *see also* Guilt, Superego, Sadism
 see also, Ambivalence, Destructive instincts, Instincts, Obsessional-compulsive Neurosis
Agoraphobia, 284, 299
Alexander, Franz, 141
Ambivalence, 88-89, 91, 93-101, 132-134, 141-144, 166, 219, 277
 and identification, 91, 132-134, 141, 146, 166
 and oedipus complex, 69, 94-101, 142
 and restriction of aggression, 166
 increase in latency, 77

Amnesia, 4-5, 240-242, 272, 324, 340, *see also* Recollection, Repression
Amphimixis, 67
Anal-sadistic phase (zone), 66-67, 80-81, 88, 91-93, 158-159, 229
 and becoming active, 88
 and obsessional neurosis, 103-105, 145, 241, 275, 278
 regression to, 98, 103, 107, 144, 177, 237-239, 275
 see also Sadism, Masochism, Feces, Defecation, Character
Anesthesia, 42
Animals, *see* Phobia
Animism, 9, 41, 93, 124, 130-131, 240-241
Anlage, bisexual, 68
Anxiety
 and affects, 189-191
 and birth, 195-200
 and danger, 188-189, 198-199, 206-207
 and destructive instincts, 202-204, 207
 and pain, 200-202, 324
 and self-observation, 193-195
 and trauma, 191-193, 198, 205
 conditions for, 206-210, 326-329
 development of, 195-212, 326-329
 dreams, 12, 189, 191, 205
 in neuroses, 271-273, *see also* Phobia
 neurotic, 196, 204-206, 209-210
 objective, 189, 196
 readiness for, 209, 326-327
 role of in treatment, 339-340, 354
 signal, 118, 193-195, 205, 226
 social, 159-160, 171
 theories of, 188, 206
 see also Affect, Cases, Castration, Guilt, Hysteria, Phobia
Anxiety hysteria, 205
 compared to conversion hysteria, 271-273
Anxiety neurosis, 179-180, 185-188, 191
Assimilation, *see* Synthetic Function
Asceticism, 79, 144, 147, 165, 236, 239, 276
Attention and preconscious cathexis, 351
Autoerotism, and narcissism, 63, *see also* Masturbation

Basedow's disease, 186

Beethoven, 306
Bernfeld, Siegfried, 207
Bible, 182
Bibring, Edward, 39, 93
Biology, 54
Birth
fantasies about, 74-75, 81, 161-162, 207-209
symbolic representation in dream, 11-17, 31
see also Anxiety, Trauma, Womb, Childbirth
Bisexuality, 69, 94, 292-293, 308, 319, see also Cases
Bleuler, Eugen, 242, 296
Body
and anxiety, 189, 192, 200-202, 208, 283
ego, 117-119, 140, 279, 281, 285, 290
image (scheme), 117
see also Organ, Conversion hysteria, Hypochondria
Bornstein, Berta, 77
Boy, sexual development of, 67-73, 92, 94-97, 308-309, 327-328
Breast, 65, 66, 71, 90-91, 93

Cannibalistic phase (fantasies), 65, 81, 87, 155-156, 214, see also Oral phase
Cases, illustrating
acting out, 247
affect in dream, 35
bisexuality in neurosis, 292-293
"Bodily speech," 119-120
castration anxiety and anal persecution, 106-108
character development, 304-305, 317
compulsive-obsessional symptoms, 5-6, 168-169, 237, 256, 274-279, 318, 343-346
delusional idea, 50, 221-222
depersonalization, 264-267
development of normality, 168-169, 318
development of phobia, 202-203, 271
displacement of pregenital libido, 83
distortion of reality, 45, 293-294
dream analysis, 11-30, 111, 161-162, 346
enuresis, 276-278
failure of repression, 154, 251-252, 269
fetishism, 355
guilt and need for punishment, 161-169, 275
hypochondria, 183-184
hysterical identification, 215-216
hysterical symptom, 267-273
identification, 40-41
id resistance, 248
meaning of symptom, 3, 33-34, 37
mechanism of displacement, 39-40
moral masochism, 112
obsessional displacement, 220

Cases (cont'd)
obsessional questioning, 343-348
paranoid jealousy, 108-109
primal scene, 256-257
regression from genital to anal activity, 237
relation of character trait and symptom, 318
relation of fantasy and neurosis, 254-257, 264-267
relation of neurosis and perversion, 61-62, 256-263
relation of neurosis and psychosis, 293-294
schizophrenic regression, 110
schizophrenic's masochistic relation to objects, 132-133
schizophrenic's relation to object, 132-133, 288-290
screen memories, 5-6
sources of anxiety, 205-206
split of ego in neurosis, 149, 286, 355-356
sublimation, 154, 251-252, 307-308
symptom formation, 251-252, 263-292
synthetic function in symptom formation, 299
talking as a means of resistance, 337
transformation of activity into passivity, 221-225
transformation of sadism into masochism, 111, 221-225, 318
types of interpretation, 343-348
Castration complex (anxiety), 71-73, 202, 206-208, 230, 235-236
and anal persecution, 106-107
and identification, 308-309
and masochism, 169, 333
and object relations, 94-100, 230
and primal anxiety, 198-199
and sadism, 169, 202
and superego, 146, 167-170, 176
effect of, 326-329, 333
in men and women, 94-100, 156-157, 235-236, 291, 308-309, 327-328, see also Boy, Girl
see also Cases
Catatonic attack (stupor), 36, 50, 84-85, 110, 119, 126, 129, 163, 212-213, 224, 232-233, 300
Causality, need for, 151-152, 356-357
Chaldeans, 8
Changing into the opposite, 221-225
Character
ambivalent, 308
anal, 80, 92, 305-306, 312, 313
compulsive, 313
development, see Cases
erotic, 313
impulsive, 309

Character *(cont'd)*
  inhibited, 310
  mixed type, 314
  narcissistic, 313, 315
  neurosis, 303-320
  neurotic types, 315-317
  oral, 306, 312
  phallic, 306
  treatment of, 334, 335
  types, 312-317
  urethral, 306
Child
  anxiety in, 195-200, 207-208
  defenses of, 211-212, 219-220
  development of object relations, 90-102, 153, 171, 327-329
  fears in, 197
  helplessness of, 65, 90, 99, 199, 207, 324, 336
  play of, 199
  reporting of dream, 9
  sexual development of, 60-84, *see also* Infantile sexuality
  speech in, 348
  thought processes in, 16, 41, 121, 123-124, 127, 129, 138, *see also* Fantasy
  wish for, 11-17, 31, 92, 119-120, 164, 309
  without parent, 172
Childbirth, relieving guilt, 164
Cleanliness, 241, 276
Clitoris, 68, 97-98, 157, 225
Cloacal theory, 80, 86
Coitus
  anal concept of, 83, 86
  interruptus, 184, 185
  violent concept of, 80, 203, *see also* Cloacal theory
Component instincts, 60-61, 78-79
  and character traits, 305-320
  see also Libido, Sadism, Masochism, Pregenitality, Oral, Anal *and* Phallic Phases
Compulsion
  neurosis, *see* Obsessional-compulsive neurosis, Cases
  to confess, 338-339
  washing, 50-51, 188, 276-278
Condensation, 21-25, 31, 39-41, 288
Conflict
  and psychic systems, 318-320, 327-329
  neurotic, 270-273, 334, *see also* Symptom formation
  tendency to, 316, 325-326, 333
Conscience, *see* Superego
Conscious(ness), 30-33, 114-116, 233
  and perception, 29, 44-46, 116, 350
  properties of, 44-48, 351, 357
  through projection, 137, *see also* Self-observation

  see also Memory, Recollection, Repression
Constitution, 68, 187, 323
Conversion hysteria
  autoplastic measures in, 282-283
  compared to hypochondria, 82, 184-187
  condensation in, 40-41
  countercathexis in, 281
  destructive instincts in, 282
  guilt in, 163
  libido in, 282, 284, 285
  sexual fantasies in, 81-82, 267-268
  verbal ideas in, 38, 287, 297
  see also Hysteria, Anxiety hysteria
Coprolalia, 83
Coprophagia, 156
Countercathexis, 243-244, 246, 281-282, 332
Creativity, 52, 151-154, 292
Criminal, from sense of guilt, 165, 315-316
Curiosity, 74-75

Darwin, C., 190
Daydream, 10, 51, 79, 125
Day residue, 13, 36
Deafness, 306
Death, fear of, 207
Death instincts, 54, 57-58
  and thought processes, 122-136
  concept of, 84-113
  see also Aggression, Destructive instincts, Sadism
Defecation
  and guilt, 162-163, 277
  equals childbirth, 164
  see also Feces, Anal phase
Defense (mechanisms), 194-195, 206, 211-250
  against aggression, 213, 222, 280-281, 288
  against stimuli, *see* Protective barrier
  and ambivalence, 89
  and narcissism, 226-229, 253
  and neurotic conflict, 271
  and psychoanalytic therapy, 330-335, 340-348, *see also* Resistance
  and repetition compulsion, 213, 226-229
  and resistance, 229-230
  and thought processes, 286-288
  see also Obsessional-compulsive neurosis, Hysteria, Restitution, Cases
Delirium, 50
Delusion, 9, 43, 45, 50, 103, 117, 137-140, 153
  of being watched, 137
  of end of world, 131-135, 232, 287, 296
  of grandeur, 122-125
  of persecution, 92, 106-110, 132, 140, 147, 164, 171, 175, 217-222
Demosthenes, 306
Denial, 139, 275

Fantasy *(cont'd)*
  of being beaten, 80, 112
  of flying, 120
  of pregnancy, 287
  of prostitution, 202
  oral, 81
  primal, *see* Primal scene, 74-76
  rescue, 86
  see also Cases, Neurosis, Seduction,
    Womb
Feces, 66-67, 71, 91-92, 110, 157, 162-163,
  291
Federn, Paul, 180, 186, 239
Fellatio, 256, 262
Femininity, 95, 98-99, 169-170, 308-309, 328
Ferenczi, Sandor, 67, 120, 124-125, 128, 133,
  145, 201, 283
Fetishism, 59, 263, 294, 355
Fixation
  and character formation, 317-320
  and defense, 226-229
  and regression, 102-113, 261, 298
  and repetition compulsion, 353-354
  instinctual, 80-84, 208
  see also Cases, Hysteria, Obsessional-
    compulsive neurosis
Flexibilitas cerea, 212
Folie de doute, 278
Folklore, 14
Food
  and libidinal gratification, 158
  aversion to, 262
  refusal of, 81, 109
Forepleasure, 59, 61
Forgetting, 3, 23-25, *see also* Amnesia, Recollection, Repression
Free association, 9-10, 26-27, 337, 352
Freud, Anna, 79
Freud, Sigmund, 4 *et passim*
  on affect, 190
  on anxiety, 188, 206
  on character types, 312-317
  on death instinct, 58, 85, 87
  on dream, 8-11, 26
  on ego ideal, 146
  on fusion of instincts, 94
  on guilt, 161
  on judgment, 128-129
  on lifting of repression, 351
  on love, 182
  on neuroses, 179-180, 183
  on predisposition to neurosis, 322
  on protective barrier, 46
  on psychic processes, 193
  on psychic systems, 30
  on shame, 155-156
  on sublimation, 308
  on superego, 173

  on unconscious part of ego, 115, 116
Frigidity, 100

Genital, 60, 67-73, 83, 95, 104
  as magic instrument, 123
  body identified with, 184
  excitability in oral phase, 67
  fear of loss of, *see* Castration
  phase, *see* Phallic phase
Genitalization, *see* Erotization
Girl, sexual development of, 67-73, 92, 97-
  99, 309, 327-328, *see also* Penis envy
Globus hystericus, 155, 282-283
Gorki, M., 122
Gratification, 55-58, 99, 130
  and defense, 275-276
  extragenital, 97
  in neurotic symptoms, 282
  libidinal, in food intake, 158
  masochistic, 279, 282
  of aggression, 282
  of ego-syntonic drives, 359
  postponement of, 56
Guilt feelings
  and dream, 12
  and neurosis, 279-292
  and repression, 235-236
  borrowed, 170
  development of, 157-173, 306-307, 333
  see also Cases; Hysteria; Masochism,
    moral; Obsessional-compulsive neuro-
    sis; Punishment, need for; Schizophre-
    nia; Superego

Hallucination, 41, 117-119, 129, 175, 198,
  227, 283, 285, 349
  and dream, 9, 37
  auditory, 15, 139-140, 147
  magic, 124-125
  negative, 130-131
  see also Delusion, Wish fulfillment
Hartmann, Heinz, 135
Healing process, *see* Recovery
Health, psychic, 49, 101, 117, 120-121, 127,
  137-138, 234, 282-283, 333
Hebrews, 8, 182
Helpfulness, exaggerated, 157
Homosexuality, 59, 69, 106-109, 132, 253,
  260, 269, 292-293, 308, 319
  and identification, 91, 216
Hypnosis, 10, 148, 151, 212, 334
Hypochondria, 82, 132, 136, 171, 182-185,
  193-194, 288, 297
Hypomania, 316
Hysteria, 42, 47, 51
  affectivity in, 267-268
  amnesia in, 5, 231, 240-242, 272
  and identification, 215-216

Schizophrenia *(cont'd)*
  thought processes in, 36-39, 41-42, 51, 81, 122-123, 126-136, 151-153, 220, 287-290, 296, 349-350, 357
  see also Cases, Psychosis
Scoptophilia, 60, 138, 221-225
Scotoma, 233, 243
Screen memory, 4
Secondary elaboration, 50, 151
Secondary gain, *see* Epinosic gain
Secondary process, 26, 32, 39, 50-51, 118-119, 254, 343
Seduction (fantasy of), 75-76, 323, 350
Self-mutilation, 84-85
Self-observation, 135-137, 139, 193-195
Self-preservation, 118
Self-punishment, *see* Guilt, Punishment, need for
Separation (anxiety), 24-25, 71, 197-201, 206-207
Sex differences, 71-74, *see also* Boy, Girl
Sexual instincts
  aim-inhibited, 97
  aim of, 58-59
  and neurosis, 60-62
  and perversion, 59-62
  concept of, 53-59
  developmental disturbances of, 79-84
  object of, 58-59
  see also Component instincts, Infantile sexuality, Instincts, Lidibo, Sexuality
Sexuality
  and extragenital excitement, 83
  and regression, 236-238
  and repression, 230-236, 240-243, 249, 275, *see also* Hysteria
  concept of, 53-54
  diphasic onset of, 78, 324
  see also Fantasy, Infantile sexuality, Oedipus complex, Schizophrenia
Sexualization, *see* Erotization
Shakespeare, 195
Shame, 156-157, 306
Sibling rivalry, 4-5
Sleep, 10-12, 78, 90, 212, 254
Sleeping ritual, 5-6
Social milieu
  and concept of illness, 295
  and etiology of neurosis, 328-329
Somatic symptoms and unconscious, 37, *see also* Body, Conversion hysteria, Organ
Speech, 38, 91, 119, 121-122, 125, 174-175, 341-348, *see also* Language, Schizophrenia
Sperber, H., 121
Sphincter morality, 145
Steinach, A., 54, 186
Sterility, 119-120

St. Ignatius Loyola, 144
Stimuli
  and aggression, 85-87
  and anxiety, 195-208
  and perception, 44-45, 117-120
  barrier against, *see* protective barrier
  energy of, 47, 322
  excessive, 191, 322, *see also* Trauma
  reaction to inner, 45, 211, 217, 234, 322
Stuttering, 83, 306
Sublimation, 52, 76, 81, 97, 102, 141, 153-154, 251, 268-269, 280, 290, 334, 342, 359
  and character traits, 305-308
  and identification, 307-308
  see also Cases, Desexualization, Synthetic function
Sucking, 64, 66, 90-91, *see also* Fellatio
Suicide, 84, 109, 111, 143, 168-169, 176
Superego, 27-29, 76, 119, 137-149, 154, 302, 329
  and character, 306-317, 319
  and guilt, 159-173, 236
  and identification, 91, 95, 138-150, 161, 214-215, 309
  and preconscious, 48
  and reaction formations, 239-240, 280
  anxiety, 199, 202, 205-209, 326, 339-340
  formation of, 96-97, 141-149, 151, 153, 166-168, 280, 309-311
  negative, 149
  resistance of, 248-250
  see also Cases, Ego, Hysteria, Obsessional neurosis, Schizophrenia
Superstition, 8-9, 14, 122, 138, 240
Symbolism, 14-15, 42, 290
  of fingers, 86-87
  see also Primary process, Symbols
Symbols, 31
  in dreams, 13-15
  typical, 14
Symptom
  and affect, 39, 188
  and anxiety, 188-190, 205-206
  and castration complex, 73
  and character trait, 317-320
  and dream, 8, 343
  and experience, 3-6, 190, 241, 267
  and fantasies, 76, 81, 254-257
  and repetition compulsion, 55-56
  and sexual conflict, 60
  countercathexis, and formation of, 281-282
  formation of, 263-292
  meaning of, 6, 33-34, 42, 126
  primary and secondary, 296-297
  see also Cases, Neurosis, Hysteria, Obsessional neurosis, Phobia
Symptomatic action, *see* Parapraxes